Lin Mease

Wright's Ferry Mansion

THE HOUSE

Wright's Ferry Mansion

THE HOUSE

Elizabeth Meg Schaefer

THE von HESS FOUNDATION
Columbia, Pennsylvania

in association with
ANTIQUE COLLECTORS' CLUB LTD.

Principal support for this publication was made possible by The von Hess Foundation and the Richard C. von Hess Foundation. Additional support has been provided by the Wright-Cook Foundation.

Copyright © 2005 The von Hess Foundation
All rights reserved. No part of this publication may be reproduced, stored in a retrieval system, or transmitted in any form or by any means, electronic or mechanical, including photocopying, recording, or otherwise, without prior permission in writing from the publisher.

ISBN 0-9744202-4-7

Distributed in the USA and Canada by
Antique Collectors' Club, Ltd.
116 Pleasant St., Suite B060
Easthampton, MA 01027
www.antiquecc.com

Endpapers: Whitework apron, England, 1700–1725
Frontispiece: Wright's Ferry Mansion built in 1738 for Susanna Wright
Page 6: Detail, needlework picture, England, circa 1700
Page 10: East façade of Wright's Ferry Mansion
Page 12: Detail, whitework picture, England, dated 1727
Page 18: Wright's Ferry Mansion, kitchen end with bake oven
Page 24: Detail, needlework picture of Queen Anne, England, circa 1700
Page 138: Detail, crewelwork picture, England, circa 1730
Page 188: Bust of Homer, poplar ?, possibly America, 1750–1790
Page 228: Detail, vellum portfolio with signature of Susanna Wright, England, circa 1710
Page 260: Walnut desk in parlor, Philadelphia, 1710–1740
Page 268: Six engravings by John Kip, London, circa 1710
Page 274: Dresdenwork picture dated 1728 by Sarah Hil, England
Page 280: Silk yardage, England, 1740–1770
Page 284: John Parkinson, frontispiece to *The Theatre of Plantes*, London, 1640
Page 292: Detail, celestial globe, by W. and J. Blaeu and Jacob de la Feuille, Amsterdam, 1701

Photo Credits
Paul Rocheleau: pp. 2, 10, 18, 40–41, 72, 76–77, 82–83, 86, 87, 88, 93, 94–95, 96, 97, 98, 100–101, 105, 108, 110–111, 112, 114–115, 116, 120, 122, 126–127, 128, 130, 137, 260, 268
Carl K. Shuman: pp. 1, 6, 12, 24, 36, 38, 52, 56, 57, 71, 85, 90 (top), 104, 117, 118, 119, 121, 125, 138, 188, 266, 274, 280, 284
Frank Errigo: pp. 26, 27, 34, 39, 42, 44, 54, 55, 62, 80, 89, 90 (bottom), 92, 103, 106, 124, 228, 291, 292
Stenton, Jim Greipp: pp. 32, 84
The Library Company of Philadelphia: p. 61

Content Editor: Gerald W. R. Ward
Copyeditor: Melissa W. Duffes
Designed by Susan E. Kelly and Andrea Thomas
Proofread by Courtney Randall and Carrie Wicks
Typeset in Bell MT and Caslon Italic Swashes
Color separations by iocolor, Seattle
Produced by Marquand Books, Inc., Seattle
  www.marquand.com
Printed and bound in China by C&C Offset Printing Co., Ltd.

CONTENTS

8	Acknowledgments
11	Foreword *Thomas Hills Cook*
13	Prologue *Richard C. von Hess*
16	Preface *Elizabeth Meg Schaefer*

19	WRIGHT'S FERRY MANSION: AN HISTORICAL OVERVIEW
25	SUSANNA WRIGHT AND HER FAMILY
73	THE MANSION'S INTERIOR: THE ROOMS AND THEIR FURNISHINGS
137	APPENDIX
	139 Selected Letters
	189 Poetry
	229 Wills and Inventories
	261 The Library of Susanna Wright
	269 Miscellaneous Documents
	275 Description of Susanna Wright by Deborah Norris Logan
	279 Genealogical Chart
	281 Susanna Wright's Treatise on the Raising of Silkworms
	285 James Wright's Treatise on Hops and Hemp Growing
293	Selected Bibliography
295	Index

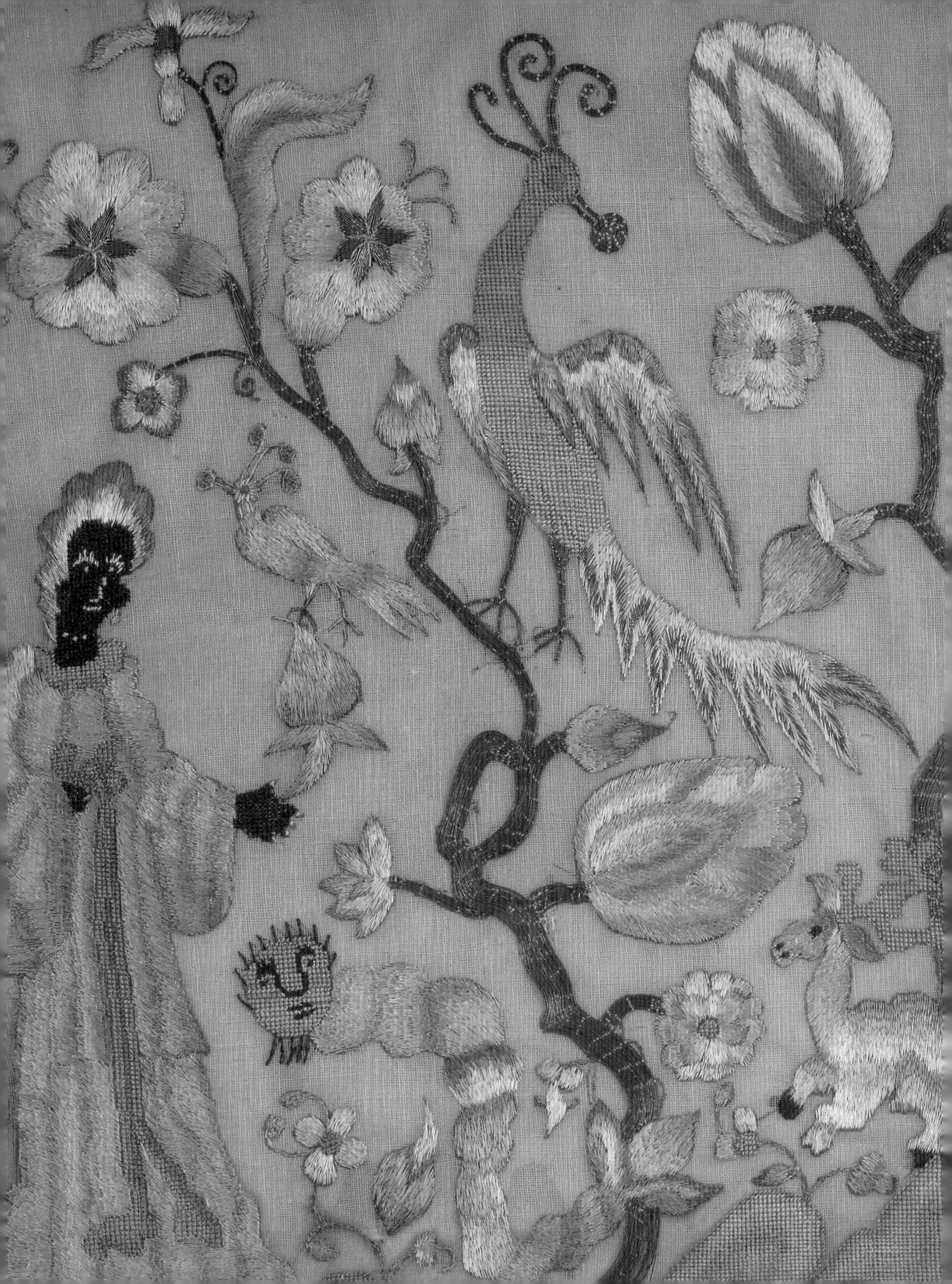

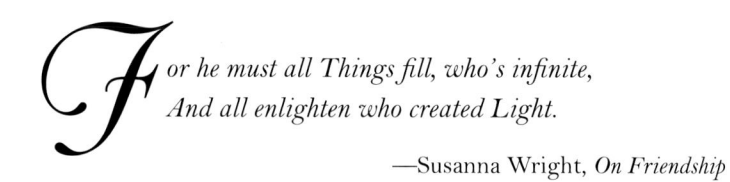

*For he must all Things fill, who's infinite,
And all enlighten who created Light.*

—Susanna Wright, *On Friendship*

ACKNOWLEDGMENTS

I would like to thank Thomas Hills Cook for making *Wright's Ferry Mansion: The House*, and its companion volume, *Wright's Ferry Mansion: The Collection*, a reality. It is through his perseverance and unwavering support that this project has been made possible. Thomas Hills Cook, Joe K. Kindig III, John Brace Latham, Bruni Mayor, and William H. Pope have provided great encouragement, support, and assistance for these publications.

I am extremely grateful for the scholarly reviewing and editorial work on this text by Dr. Gerald W. R. Ward and to Melissa W. Duffes for the final editing of the work. For entering and checking the many changes and corrections to this text, I would like to thank Tammy L. Roberts, Jan Langmuir, Shirley Wissing, and Cindy A. Weaver. I also thank the photographers Frank Errigo, Carl K. Shuman, and Paul Rocheleau, who have worked many years to capture the beauty of Wright's Ferry Mansion and the collection. I greatly appreciate the work of Ed Marquand and the staff of Marquand Books for producing these volumes so beautifully.

For the primary funding of this publication, my gratitude to The von Hess Foundation and to the Richard C. von Hess Foundation, and for additional funding, the Wright-Cook Foundation. The latter was established by Susanna Wright Cook, who has been a great source of encouragement. Because of her interest and generosity, Wright's Ferry Mansion has been able to contain objects owned by Susanna Wright, like the silver cann, books, letters, and poetry. I am also grateful to many other Wright descendants for their help and generosity, especially Mr. and Mrs. Andrew J. Kauffman, Mary Elizabeth Stark, John Wright Mifflin, Peter Alsop, and Francis J. Dallett.

For locating seventeenth-century wills and inventories pertaining to the Wrights in England and for outlining the Wright genealogy from that material, I thank Thomas

Woodcock, Somerset Herald of the Royal College of Arms. I greatly appreciate the help of Dr. Timothy C. Miller for his insights into the literary influences in Susanna Wright's poetry and his generous assistance in textual clarification.

I also appreciate the help and interest through the years of H. Richard Dietrich, Jr., Deborah Rebuck, Allaire du Pont, Dr. Donald Shelley, Barry Stover, Eric de Jonge, William K. du Pont, Dudley Godfrey, Willman Spawn, Edwin Wolf 2nd, Dick Whitson, Deborah Kraak, Susan Swan, John C. Dann, the staff of Winterthur Museum, Stenton, the Library Company of Philadelphia, Haverford College Library, and the American Philosophical Society.

My appreciation to Richard von Hess is inestimable. The freedom he has given me to explore, develop, and discover has been my joy and great privilege.

Elizabeth Meg Schaefer
Curator

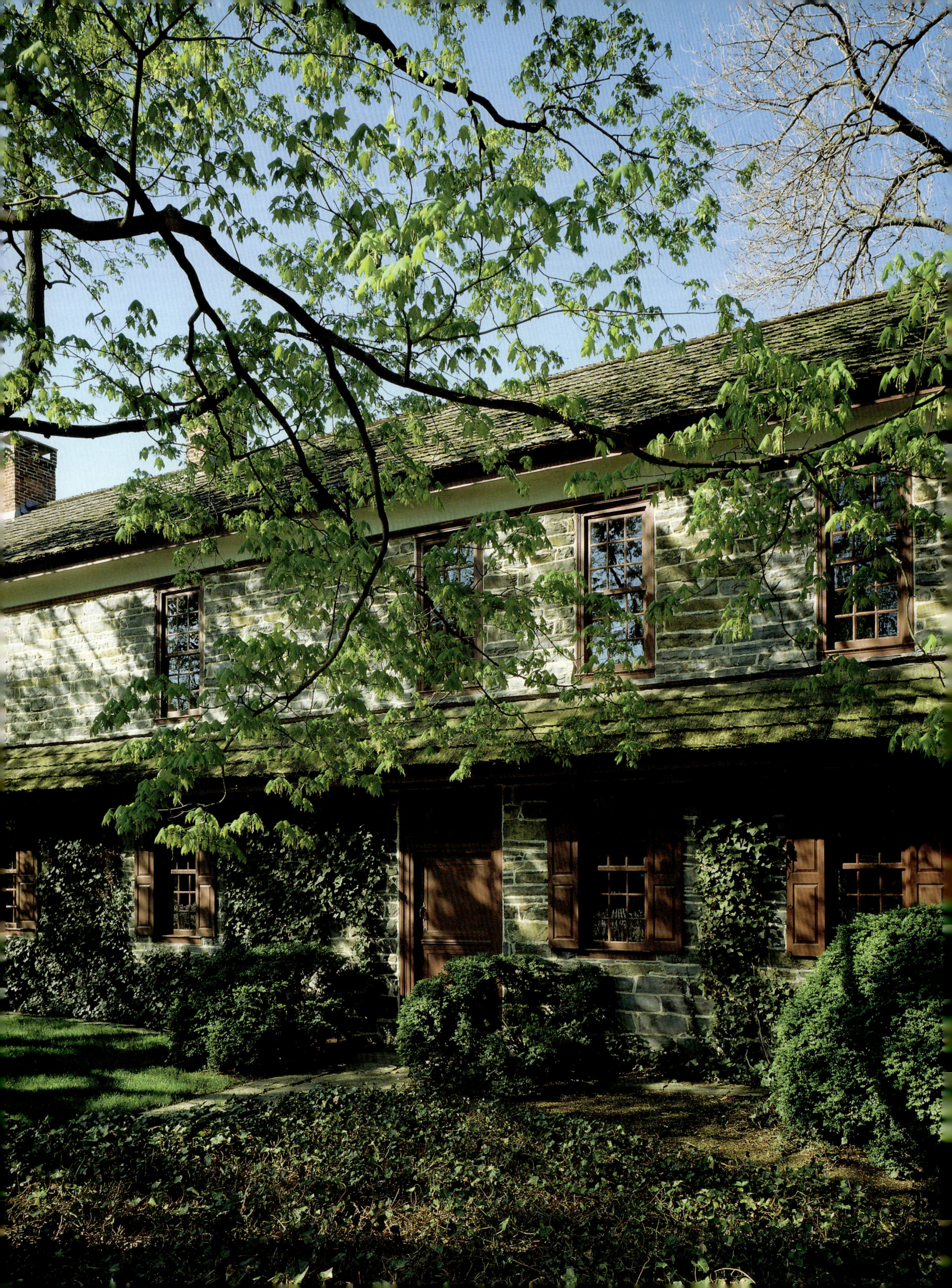

FOREWORD

*L*ocated in Pennsylvania along the Susquehanna River, Wright's Ferry Mansion has existed for more than 250 years. Built in 1738 for Susanna Wright, the house reflects her English Quaker heritage and her ties to Philadelphia. In 1973 Louise and Richard von Hess purchased the property and began a long project of restoration to preserve this unique example of architecture. They formed The von Hess Foundation to protect and preserve the house and to develop a collection for scholars, collectors, and visitors.

Richard von Hess had the vision to create a splendid museum, a project which he refined over nearly twenty-five years. This house and collection were his true passion. He looked forward to the creation of a book on the history of the house and its supporting collection and, before his death, wrote down his own recollection of the project as a prologue for the book. It is a great pleasure to dedicate this publication, *Wright's Ferry Mansion: The House* and its companion volume *Wright's Ferry Mansion: The Collection*, to his memory and to introduce the creative spirit of Wright's Ferry Mansion in his own words.

I am indebted to Meg Schaefer, curator of Wright's Ferry Mansion, for her authorship and guidance of this project, and to Joe Kindig for his description of the philosophy behind the collection, and I am grateful to all the contributors to this publication. I hope that readers and visitors will continue to be inspired by the connoisseurship of Richard von Hess at Wright's Ferry Mansion.

Thomas Hills Cook
Director
The von Hess Foundation

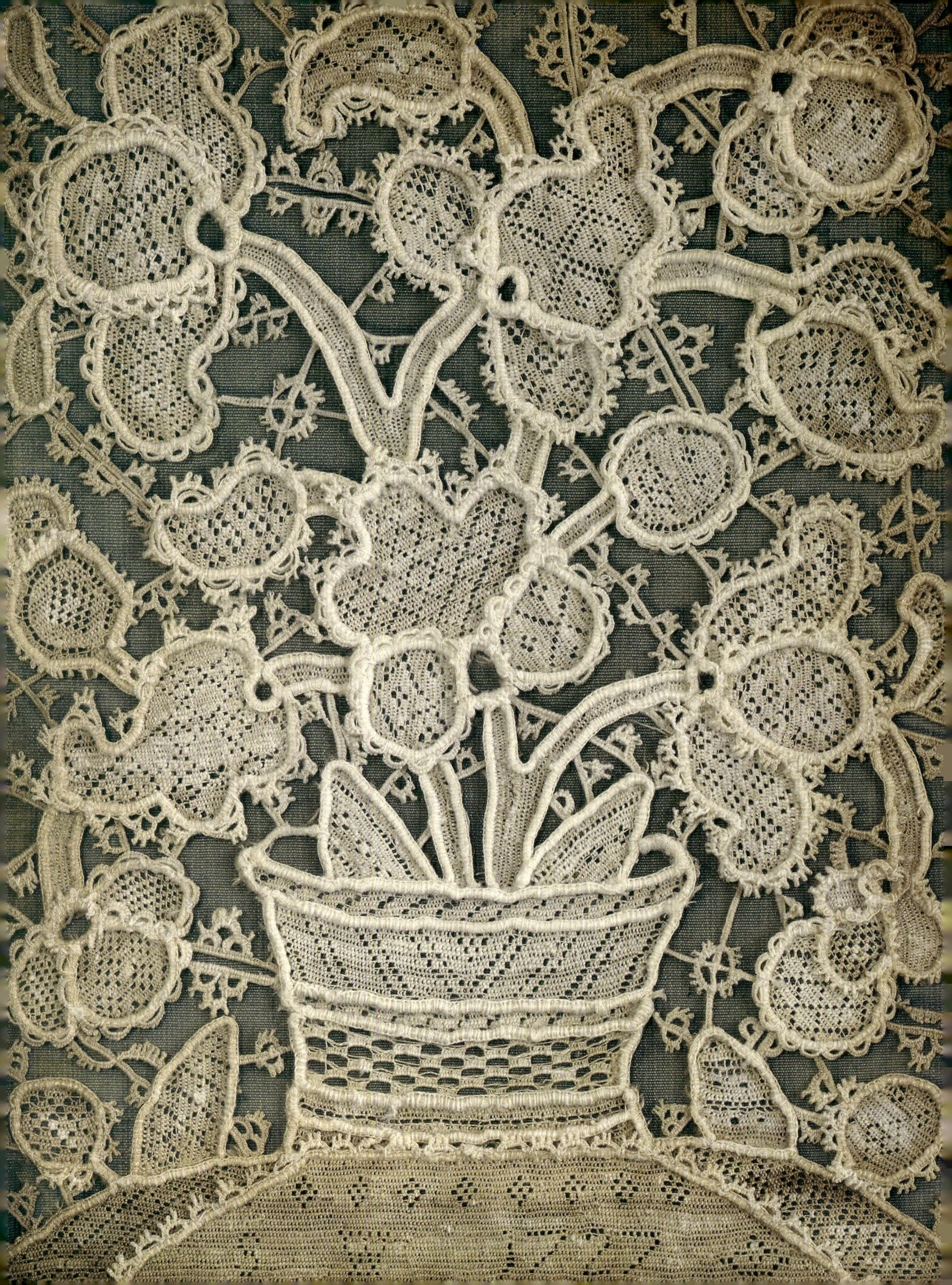

PROLOGUE

My first recollection of the house at Wright's Ferry was in the early evening in autumn. I had been taken there to visit the owner, Emmett Rasbridge, and to see his wonderful house. As we walked through those venerable rooms, Emmett told me the story of the house and how it came to be his.

Emmett's mother bought the house from the Wright descendants in 1922, saving it from impending demolition. It had been slated to become a coal yard. Having limited funds, the Rasbridges made only simple changes to the house. The interior was painted in colors inspired by one of the best examples of the time, Mount Vernon.

Emmett was a Dickensian character with white hair and rosy cheeks, who possessed a certain panache. He had wit, charm, and a true sense of hospitality. As we toured the house, Emmett shared some of its history and I was struck by the warmth and style of the house. Despite the spare interiors, it had a certain elegance. Emmett even had his own special names for certain rooms, like the "Petit Salon," a room upstairs where he entertained friends, and the "Wedgwood Room," his mother's, which was painted blue. Subsequently, Emmett and I became lifelong friends. My wife and I enjoyed frequent hospitality at his house.

In the early seventies, my wife and I were traveling in Asia. During the trip, we discussed the idea of purchasing Emmett's house and giving up our country place at Havre de Grace. We both were interested in architecture, interiors, and gardens and felt that this was the perfect opportunity to take on a project that would fulfill our needs and that could be shared with others, too. This plan delighted Emmett, who had been finding upkeep of the property too difficult in his later years. Thus the course was set and the house acquired new owners and a new future.

There were two streams of thought that needed to be united in regard to the use of the house. We both wanted to restore the house to its original state. I persuaded my wife that since we only lived ten miles away in a perfectly wonderful house which included a ballroom, two drawing rooms, and extensive gardens, we hardly needed a second house for entertaining. I always knew that this house had a more profound purpose. Louise agreed.

The next big question was, "Who is going to restore the house?" I grew up in Gwynedd, Pennsylvania, and, in my youth, I knew Edwin Brumbaugh, one of the foremost restoration architects. He seemed ancient then and I wasn't sure if he were still alive. Louise told me to telephone him: he answered the phone! I told him briefly about our plans and he said he would be there the next day. We toured the house and he was impressed with its untouched condition. Due to the Rasbridges' limited means, the house had survived with minimal changes. We recognized the great opportunity not only to restore a virtually untouched house of this early period, but also to furnish it exclusively to its time. This we knew would fulfill a great need in the field of American decorative arts: to show an early Pennsylvania house furnished exclusively to the first half of the eighteenth century.

All the pieces were in place. Restoration began and a board was formed. Knowing that furniture is the backbone of a collection, we contacted Joe Kindig III, one of the foremost authorities on seventeenth- and eighteenth-century Pennsylvania furniture, and invited him to become a founding member of our board. Joe accepted with great enthusiasm.

We then tackled the problem of what the house originally might have contained. Discussions ensued, focused on the fascinating history of the house and its intriguing owner, Susanna Wright. An English Quaker, Susanna Wright was a cultivated woman who maintained associations with some of the most brilliant minds in the colonies. Philadelphia and London were her cultural centers. Our task was now before us: to capture the spirit of her soul in the house and its contents.

In order to do this, we had to tread a strict scholarly path, yet still take advantage of unexpected opportunities as they arose. Great joy has come not only with acquisitions, but also with associations with dealers, with amazing coincidences, and with interesting adventures. One of the first acquisitions was a Philadelphia highboy with Spanish feet and heart piercing by Isaac Moss. By a lovely coincidence, a televised tour of the house was seen by Mrs. Richard C. du Pont, who had just inherited a Spanish-footed dressing table with heart piercing. She called us immediately and offered to give it to our collection. These two pieces became the nucleus of our best bedchamber. In the same room is a small piece of needlework which we found in London and later discovered contained the initials "S W."

Not only did the house occupy our attention, we also had to consider the gardens. Susanna Wright's land was originally a one-hundred-acre tract that had dwindled to a little over one acre. Louise viewed everything on a grand scale. She understood proportion and wanted to create a feeling of seclusion within the confines of a town. To achieve this, she brought in enormous specimens of trees and bushes to screen out the intrusion of the present. One afternoon, we drove to the house to inspect the progress and, on the way, passed a convoy of flatbed trucks loaded with a forest. I exclaimed, "Who in the world would move trees that size?" Then I realized they were ours.

From the very beginning Louise and I both felt that if we were going to do this, we should do it the best way we knew how.

Richard C. von Hess

PREFACE

*R*are it is to have an early eighteenth-century Pennsylvania house imbued with exceptional architectural merit, a wonderful collection, and a fascinating history. This publication presents each of these aspects of Wright's Ferry Mansion, threading them together with rich and evocative documents of the period which have been drawn together for the first time. As the project of restoring and furnishing Wright's Ferry Mansion unfolded and research progressed, the importance of this early house became more evident. In the beginning of the project, very little was known about the history of the house and the Wrights. The limited published information was often contradictory or unsupported by early sources. It has been for me both a great adventure and challenge to track down early documents pertinent to the Wrights in order to piece together the history of this remarkable house and its original owner. The rewards have been great—the early documents reveal an exciting vision of the Wrights' contribution to early America. The information has formed the basis of interpreting the house and the collection.

Wright's Ferry Mansion: The House is arranged in three sections. The first gives a history of Susanna Wright and her family, emphasizing the buildings and objects associated with the Wrights from the late seventeenth through the mid-eighteenth century. The second part consists of a description of the architectural fabric and restoration of the house and a summary of the use and evolution of each room. The third section contains seventeenth- and eighteenth-century documents pertinent to the house, its furnishings, and its original owner, Susanna Wright.

The documents are not only rich and colorful in the depth that they bring to the house and collection but are also extremely important in their own right. Here, published for the first time, is a wonderful contribution to voyage literature: Susanna Wright's letter of 1714, recounting her voyage to America written when she was only sixteen. When she was eighteen, she was corresponding with one of the most learned men in the colonies, James Logan. Eventually, other luminaries like Benjamin Franklin, Benjamin Rush, Anthony Benezet, and Charles Thomson became her friends and correspondents. Her letters provide a vivid glimpse into this time. Since the house and collection reflect her taste and interests, the writings allow us into her intimate world of thought and help to evoke not only her personality but also the social, cultural, and intellectual life of early eighteenth-century America. Her poetry was regarded by contemporaries as some of the finest produced in early Pennsylvania. The full significance of her poetry is only now being appreciated and today she is esteemed as one of the outstanding poets in colonial America. Since poetry, as John Milton writes, is a "distillation of the spirit," it, too, is important in understanding the house, sharing its beauty, clarity, and elegance. And Susanna Wright's poetry is no less than revolutionary, as she takes the Quaker belief that all people are equal in the eyes of God and applies it to men and women, saying "No right has man his equal to control."

In addition to her literary pursuits, Susanna Wright and her family were deeply involved in domestic manufactures. Because textiles figured largely in the history of the Wrights even in the seventeenth century and have been emphasized in the collection of furnishings assembled for the house, I have included a detailed section describing sericulture in eighteenth-century Pennsylvania. One of the first people in Pennsylvania to raise silkworms, Susanna Wright wrote a treatise on the subject, which is also published here. In addition, there are inventories, wills, and other documents that help to illuminate the world in which Susanna Wright lived. Just as Richard von Hess tells of his aim "to capture the spirit of her soul in the house and its contents," so is the aim of incorporating the very words of the Wrights and their friends throughout this volume and its companion, *Wright's Ferry Mansion: The Collection*, a catalogue of the objects in Wright's Ferry Mansion, one of the finest collections of its kind in a house of this period in the country.

Elizabeth Meg Schaefer
Curator

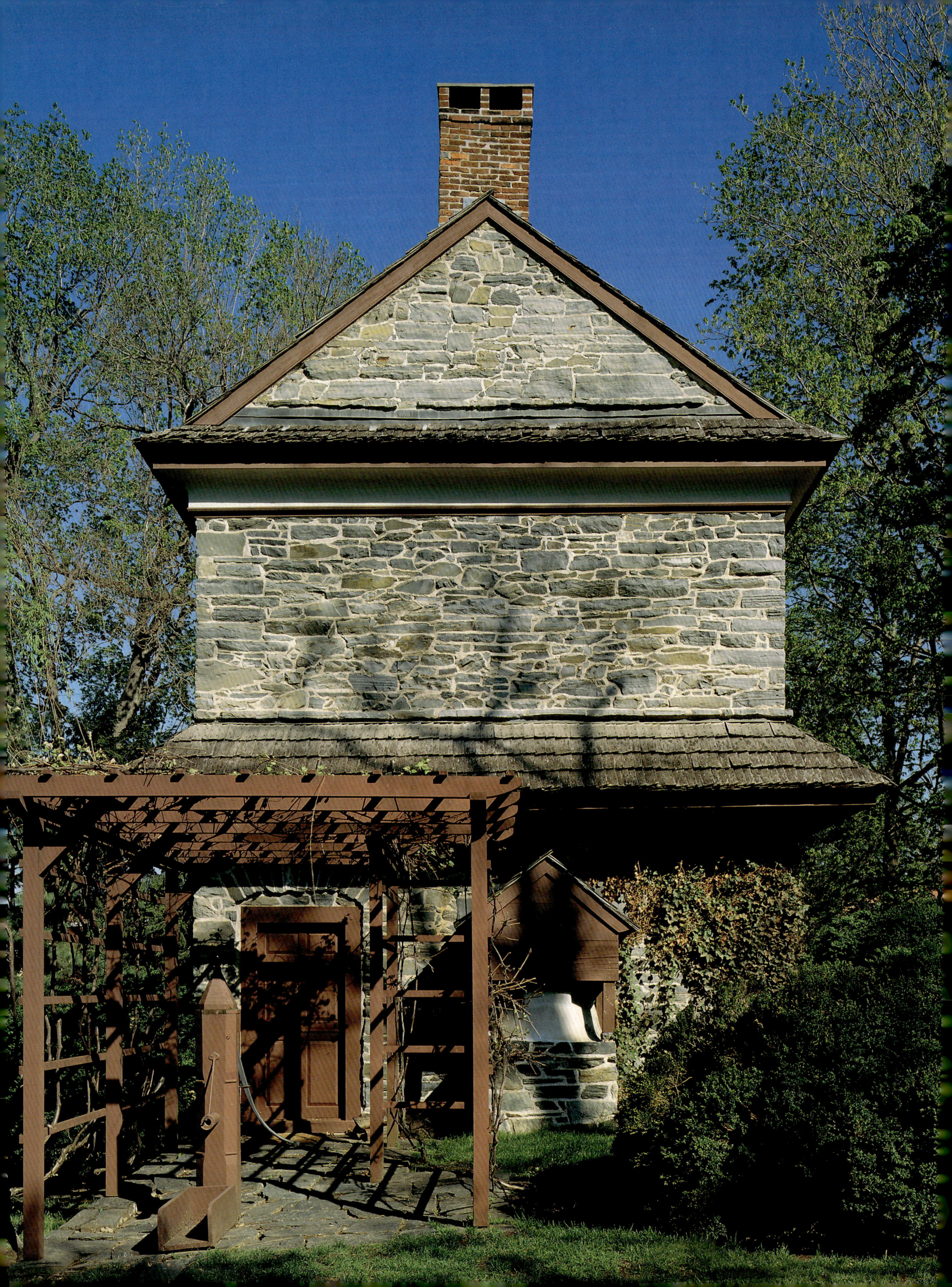

WRIGHT'S FERRY MANSION:
AN HISTORICAL OVERVIEW

This Town is a mere Oven. How happily situated are our Friends at Hempfield! I languish for the Country, for Air and Shade and Leisure; but Fate has doom'd me to be stifled and roasted and teaz'd to death in a City. You would not regret the Want of City Conversation if you considered that 9/10ths of it is Impertinence.

—Benjamin Franklin to Susanna Wright, July 11, 1752[1]

The location of Wright's Ferry Mansion is pivotal in understanding the house. It is situated in Pennsylvania near the Susquehanna River, which for centuries had been important for trade. Although too shallow for ships, small boats and canoes could navigate the river, which travels hundreds of miles from New York to the Chesapeake Bay. For millennia, both shores of the river near Wright's Ferry Mansion were important Native American habitation sites. In the early eighteenth century, a few English, Scots-Irish, and German settlers were moving into the region, which contained exceptionally rich soils for agriculture. An Indian trading post important for furs was located nearby at Conestoga. Negotiations were underway with the Indians at that time for the Provincial government of Pennsylvania to obtain vast lands west of the Susquehanna River, which marked Pennsylvania's frontier.

The house was built in 1738, a time when the boundaries of the province of Pennsylvania were still being defined: Maryland was claiming land that reached miles up from the southern border, and the northern boundaries still had not been fixed nor would they be until the very end of the eighteenth century. France claimed vast lands from the south and west that stretched right up to the banks of the Susquehanna River. Moreover, Indian holdings in the province were still extensive.

When the Wrights came to the area along the Susquehanna River, it was called Shawanah town on Susquehanna, but quickly became known as Wright's Ferry when they established the ferry. The Wrights, the Barbers, and the Blunstons, affluent English Quakers who had been living in the Philadelphia area, moved there together in 1726, continuing to maintain close ties with Philadelphia. Wright's Ferry Mansion reflects the cultural mingling that was taking place in Pennsylvania, manifesting itself in architecture and the decorative arts in forms distinctive to Pennsylvania, differing from other colonies, as well as from England and Europe.

Along with reflecting these broad cultural influences, the house also reflects the particular qualities of its original owner Susanna Wright. To obtain a fuller understanding of the house, its furnishings, the uses of its rooms, and its significance, research into seventeenth- and eighteenth-century sources of the Wrights was essential. The enormity of the project quickly became evident. There was a wealth of unpublished material that needed to be located, transcribed, organized, and analyzed. From hundreds of diverse, scattered, and often abstruse sources, I have tried with scholarly care to piece together a clear and comprehensive image of the Wrights and Wright's Ferry Mansion and to convey the intellectual, spiritual, and scientific milieu of which they were a part.

Although Susanna Wright lived in the country, she was infinitely urbane in her sensibilities. Steeped in the tenets of her Quaker beliefs, she also possessed a radical open-mindedness, like Benjamin Franklin. She was exceptional in her versatile intellect and in the breadth of her knowledge and interests. She was one of the first people in Pennsylvania to raise silkworms and, with her brother, grew flax for linen, hemp for rope and coarse cloth, hops for beer and ale, and had a notable orchard. Respected for her knowledge and judgment, Susanna Wright was relied upon by some of the most brilliant minds in the colonies—Benjamin Franklin and James Logan, among others. Her highly informed memory and imagination were permeated by the best in literature. She was recognized in the eighteenth century as one of the finest poets in Pennsylvania, an estimation that has grown even greater today. She and her friends were prolific writers and the location of Wright's Ferry, nearly seventy miles from her Philadelphia friends, resulted in a rich exchange of letters.

Along with drawing together the documents, I have also been attempting to reconstruct Susanna Wright's library. Gleaning titles from letters, receipts, and other sources, I compiled a list of books that Susanna Wright owned in order to purchase appropriate volumes for Wright's Ferry Mansion. This work has had an unexpected and marvelous result. For example, Susanna Wright's namesake, Susanna Wright Cook, visited Wright's Ferry Mansion with her son, a bibliophile, who was intrigued with the project. When he returned home, he went into the attic where he discovered a box of books that had originally belonged to Susanna Wright with her signature on the title page. The discovery saved those volumes, as a leak in the attic had damaged some of the books, which were beginning to deteriorate. Treated by a conservator, the books are now part of the collection at Wright's Ferry Mansion.

Not only providing the basis for interpreting the house and collection, the research into early source materials has actually been a catalyst to preserve Wright manuscripts and objects that otherwise would have been lost or dispersed and has helped renew appreciation of Susanna Wright's significance to the development of eighteenth-century America. It has also provided a wonderful vehicle to present both the architecture and the collection, tying them not only into the Wrights' history but also the intellectual and cultural history of early eighteenth-century Philadelphia.

The architectural work to preserve the house, accomplished from 1974 to 1978, was done by G. Edwin Brumbaugh, a pioneer in the field. He had worked on hundreds of important buildings in Pennsylvania, like the State House in Philadelphia and buildings in Valley Forge National Park, as well as in neighboring states, and was recognized for his work by the National Trust for Historic Preservation. Wright's Ferry Mansion was one of his last restorations. He was in his eighties then and said Wright's Ferry Mansion was his favorite because he could do it "as precisely as possible in every detail," and also because it was "a wonderful 'document' house." It had survived largely intact with relatively few changes, and thus provides important architectural information for other early structures.

Predominantly English in style, the building is one room deep for almost its full length. It has a central, asymmetrically placed entry or hall, with external doors directly opposite each other and a staircase to the second floor in the corner. The rooms are placed hierarchically, from the most formal room, the parlor, at one end, to the kitchen at the other. The second floor is arranged in the same way with the best bedchamber above the parlor, and the opposite end containing servants quarters above the kitchen.

In the principal rooms, the wall opposite the door is paneled, creating a rich focal point that anchors the room visually. There are fireplaces in the paneled wall of each room, allowing for closet space at either side of them.

The overall style of the house is early Georgian, but there are some late seventeenth-century stylistic elements also. These are especially evident in the entry with its massive sheathed doors, oak door frames, and staircase with elegant turned banisters, the most complex form extant in a Pennsylvania house of this period. Although the house is typically English in style, there are a few Germanic details, like the oak side-lapped shingles on the roof. The pattern of nailing in the rafters and one of the original red oak shingles, which survived in a crevice in the attic, indicated the type of shingles the house had in the eighteenth century.

The house survived in outstanding condition. All the window frames are original, as are some of the sashes and glass. The windows are double-hung sashes with weights and pulleys in the frames, a window type developed in England in the late seventeenth century. All the exterior doors but one (to the kitchen) are original. Most of the paneling is original, as are most of the pine floors.

Since the original structure had had few alterations, it was decided during the restoration of the building to remove any later additions, like the small porches that had been added to the main doors. Other architectural elements, like the pent roof, had disappeared, leaving clear evidence of their original presence, and were restored accordingly.

Once the restoration was underway, the quality of the house became even more evident. Knowing that there was a need in the field of American decorative arts to show a Pennsylvania house furnished exclusively to the first half of the eighteenth century, the von Hesses decided to pursue that path for the house. They began furnishing the house in 1974, while the building restoration was still underway, engaging one of the foremost authorities in the field of American decorative arts, Joe K. Kindig III, as consultant. It was fortunate that all the key pieces of furniture were assembled in the early years of the project, just before the American furniture market changed and such items became much more difficult to obtain.

The collection shows how a household would be composed of a mixture of older furnishings, which the Wrights would have brought with them from their previous house in Chester, when they moved out to the back country. The older pieces would then have been supplemented with the Queen Anne style, current when the house was built in 1738. In a similar way, the building itself reflects a combination of late seventeenth- and early eighteenth-century elements.

Susanna Wright maintained close ties with Philadelphia throughout her life. She had an early acquaintance with some of the important houses there, like those of the Norrises, the Logans, and the Pembertons. The Wrights owned a good deal of silver, bringing some with them from England. Once established in Pennsylvania, the Wrights went to the Philadelphia silversmith Joseph Richardson, Sr., who also supplied silver to Samuel Blunston, their neighbor at Wright's Ferry. Susanna Wright knew Philadelphia cabinetmakers, like Stephen Armitt, whose daughter corresponded with her and who married the son of James Logan, Susanna Wright's mentor.

Shards, receipts, and other early documentation were used to determine what the collection should contain. Moreover, Susanna Wright's particular interests needed to be reflected in the collection. Although public records indicate that an inventory was made at the time of her death in 1784, it has been lost. However, if found, it would be difficult to use as a source for what had been in the house in the 1738–1755 period, since it was made nearly thirty years after Susanna Wright had left Wright's Ferry Mansion.

Richard von Hess insisted on using only natural light in the rooms, except in the cellar, where artificial light was a necessity. He wanted the special quality of daylight suffusing the rooms with the luminosity seen in seventeenth- and early eighteenth-century paintings of interiors. Windows and floors have been kept bare, as was typical at the time; the floors are not varnished or stained but are simply scrubbed pine. Where reproduction fabrics were sometimes needed for upholstery and cushions, a wool damask was used. An authority on color, Richard von Hess selected fabric with great care to evoke the sophisticated and complex use of color in the eighteenth century.

Great care went into selecting not only the remarkable pieces of furniture in the collection but also the small, personal items that bring life and a greater sense of personality to a room. Such items are often scarce, because they were common or utilitarian, like brushes, and were not kept when worn out. Richard von Hess sought out these objects and placed them in the rooms to make them look as if they were being used as part of a living household. To imbue the rooms with life, there are always fresh flowers and fruits and vegetables. The use of flowers in houses in Pennsylvania in the mid-eighteenth century was documented by the Swedish naturalist Peter Kalm in his *Travels into North America;* when he was visiting the Bartrams near Philadelphia in 1748, Kalm wrote that the "English ladies" put:

> *fine flowers which they had gathered both in the gardens and in the fields, and placed them as an ornament in the rooms. The English ladies in general are much inclined to have fine flowers all the summer long, in or upon the chimneys, sometimes upon a table, or before the windows, either on account of their fine appearance, or for the sake of their sweet scent.*[2]

Wright's Ferry Mansion's grounds have been planted with native trees, shrubs, and English boxwood to create a feeling of seclusion, since a town now surrounds the house rather than the fields, orchards, and woodland that were there before. Nestled among the trees toward the river, a building was constructed to serve as the headquarters for The von Hess Foundation, the private, nonprofit foundation entirely responsible for the restoration and furnishing of Wright's Ferry Mansion. Containing staff offices, Wright's Ferry Cottage was designed by Edwin Brumbaugh in keeping with the style of Wright's Ferry Mansion.

NOTES

1. Leonard Woods Labaree, et al., eds., *The Papers of Benjamin Franklin* (New Haven, CT: Yale University Press, 1975), vol. 4, pp. 335–36 (hereafter cited as *Papers*). Hempfield was the name of the township in which the Wrights lived.
2. Peter Kalm, *Travels into North America*, trans. John Reinhold Forster (Barre, MA: The Imprint Society, 1972), pp. 72–73.

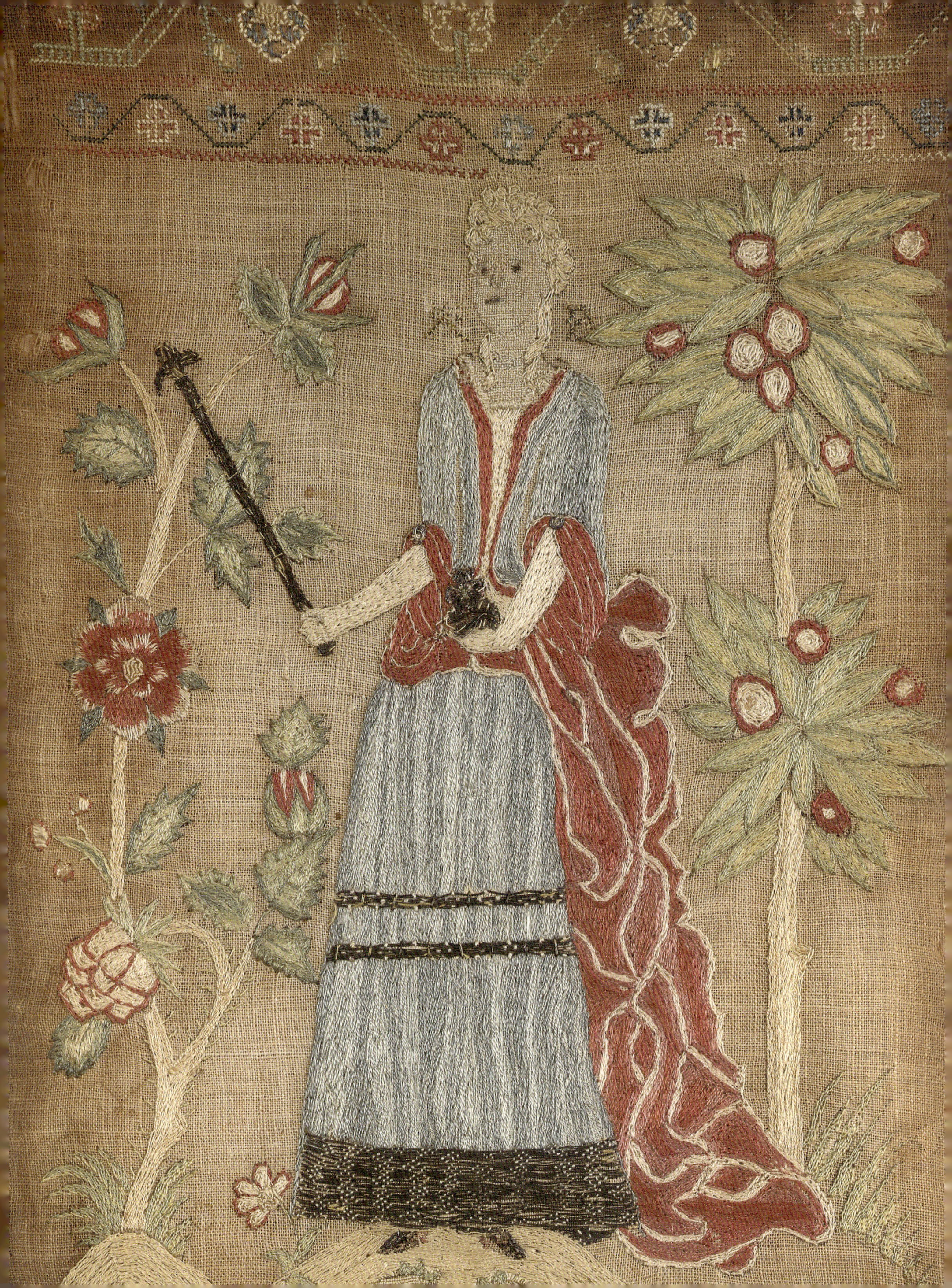

SUSANNA WRIGHT
AND HER FAMILY

... when I shal find leasure and proper encouragement to write Our History I (as Burnet Says) will not fail to mention you with a great regard, and some very extraordinary notes on the Winter 28—To propagate civility, good Sence, Reason, & Good maners, to propagate Moral Justice, & Erect a Church, In a Land 'till then Barbarous is a Revolution of some Importance & may make some future Age Inquisitive into ye truest motives of such Change, ... a Citty Sett upon a hill whose light cannot be hidd.

—Isaac Norris to Susanna Wright, April 18, 1728[1]

It was a spring day when the Wrights embarked on their journey to America—April 15, 1714, John Wright's birthday, in the last year of the reign of Queen Anne. He was forty-seven and his wife, Patience, at forty, was about to give birth to another child. The child would be named James, after John Wright's father and great-grandfather who had lived in Cadishead, a hamlet in the parish of Eccles in Lancashire, England, and was the only one of John Wright's children to be born in America. He and his sister Susanna would eventually be the first inhabitants of Wright's Ferry Mansion.

John Wright and his family made the journey from Liverpool, where two of his aunts lived, Ann Owen, widow of Abel Owen, a tobacconist, and Jane Robinson, widow of Peter Robinson, a prosperous mercer, a dealer in textiles. They were among the few remaining relatives of John Wright. He was the eldest child of James Wright and Susannah Croudson, and the only one of the six children to survive to adulthood. In 1688, when he was twenty-one, John Wright lost both his parents. He named his first child Susanna, after his mother. The child was born on August 4, 1697.

John Wright had brought with him to America the great Bible that his father had owned and in it he carefully recorded his son's birth:

All my aforesd. Children were born in the town of Manchester in the Kingdome of great Brittain. I removed thence to the Province of Pensilvania the 15th of ye 2 mo. 1714.

James Wright was born on the 19th of the 9 month the middle of the day it being the 6th day of the week in the year 1714. He was born at my house called Chadeshead in County of Chester, Pensilvania.[2]

Silver cann, made by William Keatt, London, 1698–1699, inscribed *S*W*. This cann was owned by Susanna Wright and descended through the line of her brother James.

Detail with Wright coat of arms, which includes the distinctive element of a camel's head above the helmet.

In the same volume, and with similar attention, he had entered the day, the hour of the birth, and sometimes the death, of each of his children. Of those that survived, he had three girls, Susanna, Patience, and Elizabeth, and two boys, John and James. In addition to the Bible, he brought his grandfather's pocket watch and a silver cann, or mug, engraved with the Wright coat of arms (above).

Although John Wright's parents were from Warrington in Lancashire, England, his grandfather James had lived nearby at Cadishead, on the road between Warrington and Manchester, as did John Wright's uncle William, who had a small farm there. After William's death in 1686, his wife Dorothy continued to live there until her death in 1708. At that time, she had "Four Cowes, Three heifers, One Weaning Calfe," one swine, "Corne [here denoting "wheat"] uncut," in the field, and bees. Her house was modestly but well furnished with several chests, a table, a cupboard, two beds, thirty pounds of pewter, and a fair quantity of linen—twelve pairs of sheets, a table cloth, a dozen napkins, new cloth and linen yarn, and a "parcel of Tow."[3] Lancashire was renowned for its textile trade.

In her will dated 1696/7, Dorothy Wright described her nephew John Wright as a "linen draper" in Manchester. In 1703, his uncle Peter Robinson of Liverpool described John as a "yeoman" and made him an executor of his will.[4] First a silk weaver, Peter Robinson became a very prosperous mercer. Perhaps the young Susanna had early memories

26   *Wright's Ferry Mansion*

Detail of terrestrial globe (one of a pair), made by Willem Jansz. Blaeu, Johannes Blaeu, and Jacob de la Feuille, Amsterdam, circa 1701. This portion shows the Azore Islands (*Asores Insulas*) at the upper left, which the Wrights passed en route to America in 1714.

of her great uncle and his shop filled with bolts of beautiful fabrics, plushes and crapes, sarge and shalloons, tamarines, kersey and cantaloons, sagothys, camlett and calamanco, solids and stripes, flowered or spotted. Her uncle also sold trimmings, such as ribbons, galloon, gold and silver lace, buttons, hats, and stockings.

Peter Robinson's house, which was near the shop on Liverpool Common, was also well stocked. It contained, among other things, "a Clock & Case"; fifty-six pounds of pewter; twelve chairs and six cushions; three beds, two sumptuously dressed with curtains and valances; a looking glass and chest of drawers; a small desk and eight candlesticks; a "possitt Cup" and punch bowl; and a brewing pan and spit jack.

Liverpool was the Wrights' last view of England. They sailed from there to Cork and on to the Azores, the young Susanna recounting the wondrous journey for her cousin William Croudson in Warrington. Acutely interested in every detail, she told how many leagues they were off course between Liverpool and Cork and gave the latitudes of the places they passed. In the Azores, she described the towering rock Pico, "Pico Latitude 38. I saw pico several times, tis so high it lookt higher then the Clouds." She told of fish that were caught, dolphins of "the finest Coulers as tis posable anything Can bee," of flying fish and tortoises, and of storms they encountered, including a "Sea Spout" which "was Like a great black twisted Cloud reached betwixt the Skie & Sea." In one storm:

Susanna Wright and Her Family

> *the Ship rould the End of her main yard in the water & broke her foreyard & losoned the main mast & broke the main top gallant mast. I was asitting in the great Cabin & See came in Just on mee & wet mee almost all over. We have had the cabin swim with water Several times & our Close cabbin broke down. The ship would rowl & tumble us all to one End of the cabbin & tumble us out of bed; but all the hardShip we Endured I hope will be maid up with the pleasanties of this Land.*

Finally, after nearly two months at sea, on the 17th of June:

> *we sounded & had 16 fathom & the next day Saw Land. We smelt the sweet pines before we saw them . . .*

> *Tis Certainly the pleasantest Country as Can be—always Clear wether & a wholesome air. . . . Abundance of sweet Shrubs & Charming trees with abundance of birds Singing. . . . Indeed the country & City answers what we have heard of it. . . . It is indeed a charming Country & City—more frds then other people in it & 2 great meeting houses . . .*

Nonetheless, the move was a painful, and decisive, separation:

> *I often think of all my relations & frd Left in England but cant think of Seing England any more. The pleasantnes of this Country & the toyle of the Sea Journey will hinder mee. I must once more bid the farewell but hopes not forever. Thy truly Loveing Cousin, tho at this distance—thee in one quarter of the world & I in one.*[5]

She maintained vivid memories of her life in Lancashire, recounting, when in her seventies, the house of her grandfather where "my father was Born, 105 years agoe, and where his Parents lived and Died," and where, "I had past many of the happyest days of my life . . . days, unclouded by care or Sorrow, which are quickly over, and can never Return."[6]

She sent the letter about the voyage to her cousin just after their arrival in Philadelphia. Her father, meanwhile, was "a few miles off on some business." Perhaps he was settling details on the house in which they were to live in nearby Chester. Chester was an older Pennsylvania settlement, established by Swedes in the seventeenth century, before Penn's arrival.

John Wright had purchased a little over 221 acres from the Hendricks family in January 1714. The land ran along the Delaware River; was bordered by a run and by lands owned by Jeremiah Carter, Thomas Bright, and Jacob Rowan; and it included a house, "where the said James Hendricks lately dwelt." A carpenter, James Hendricks, and his brother Albert, owned the land, as did their father, Albert Hendricks, Sr., who had bought it from William

Penn in 1702 as part of a 570-acre tract. In all likelihood, this was the house which John Wright called "Chadeshead," where his son James was born in November 1714.

John Wright brought a letter of introduction written by his neighbor Daniel Moore in Warrington, England, addressed to John Sharples, Moore's cousin in Chester: "John Wright, has been my neighbor, a vary honest man & has been very Serviceable amoungst us & will be sore mised out of our little meeting: if it so fall out yt he should Settel neer any of you I hope you will be assisters & Encouragers of him."[7]

John Wright also brought a certificate of membership from the Lancashire Monthly Meeting at Hartshaw, addressing the Pennsylvania meeting in which they would be new members: "The Church here will greatly miss them on diverse accounts, he having proved himself in some eminent services and engagements on Truth's behalf a workman that need not be ashamed."[8]

The Wrights were accepted quickly into the small community of Chester. Not only was John Wright respected for his work in the Society of Friends, but so was the family of his wife, Patience.

Although Patience had been born in London, her parents, like her husband's, were from Lancashire. Her father William Gibson (1629–1684), first a Puritan soldier, became a zealous convert to the Society of Friends. *A History of the People Called Quakers* by John Gough tells of this eminent minister, "in whose conversion there was something peculiarly remarkable":

> *He was born at Caton in Lancashire about the year 1629, and during the civil war inlisted as a soldier. Being in garrison in Carlisle and hearing that a Quaker preacher had appointed a meeting in that city, he, in concert with three of his comrades, made an agreement to go to the meeting, with a design to insult and abuse the preacher; but William Gibson coming thither before his confederates, and the friend, who was Thomas Holmes, being in the course of his ministry, it was attended with such demonstration of power, as almost immediately wrought an effectual change in William's disposition, for he was so affected therewith, that instead of executing his intended purpose, he stepped up near to the friend to protect him from insult or abuse, if offered by any other. From that time he frequented the meetings of this society, and soon after quitted his military engagements, and employed himself in the occupation of a shoemaker; waiting upon God in silence, under the refining operation of his saving grace for about the space of three years. He afterwards received a dispensation of the gospel to preach to others. In the year 1662 he married, and settled in the precincts of Sankey meeting, near Warrington.*[9]

Preaching throughout England for twenty-nine years, William Gibson suffered beatings, fines, and imprisonment for his beliefs.[10] He became so respected and loved that at his death in 1684, over a thousand people attended his burial in London.

William Gibson had visited William Penn at Rickmansworth in 1672 and in London and was one of Penn's First Purchasers of land in Pennsylvania.[11] He bought five hundred acres, which were not laid out until later.[12] In 1683, Penn had directed the Surveyor General Thomas Holme to survey a lot for William Gibson in Philadelphia, proportional to Gibson's purchase of five hundred acres.[13] In addition, on March 15, 1682/3, William Gibson was one of the Duke of York's grantees of East Jersey.[14] William Gibson died in 1684, probably before he could see his lands in the colonies.[15]

Despite the vicissitudes he suffered for his beliefs, William Gibson had been a prosperous haberdasher in London, as is shown by his will.[16] There he mentions the lands he owned in East Jersey and Pennsylvania. Among his various bequests, he left his two sons, as well as his daughter Patience, two hundred pounds each. Patience was to receive this either when she would turn twenty-one, or when she would marry. In 1692, at twenty, Patience married John Wright at Penketh in Lancashire.

After her father's death in 1684, Patience continued to live in London with her mother Elizabeth, who died there four years later, at the age of fifty-eight.[17] Since Patience was only fifteen at the time, perhaps she moved to Warrington in Lancashire to be with her apparently childless aunt and uncle, John Gibson and his wife Elizabeth, also Quakers.[18] It was probably there that Patience met John Wright, perhaps through mutual friends or relatives, like the Barnes family, who were close to both the Gibsons and the Wrights. At William Gibson's death, Jane Barnes was appointed to help administer the estate, while his children John, William, and Patience were still minors.[19] The wedding of John Wright's parents in 1666 took place at William Barnes's house in Great Sankey, near Warrington.

Like their parents, John and Patience Wright were active members of the Society of Friends, John Wright eventually becoming a Quaker minister. He was also active in civic affairs and quickly rose to positions of importance. In 1718, after only four years in Pennsylvania, John Wright became a justice of the peace for Chester County, a position he was to hold again in 1726.[20] He was also elected to the Provincial Assembly in 1718 and in 1725.[21] During these early years in Chester, the Wrights became close friends with James Logan, William Penn's secretary, and one of the most influential public figures in colonial Pennsylvania—a brilliant scholar, bibliophile, fur merchant, and astute politician.

Susanna Wright's intellectual brilliance caught James Logan's attention early, for by 1718 he was encouraging her studies by sending her books, a grammar, a dictionary, and "a small french piece, that, if thou couldst read freely, would I believe yield thee some pleasure. I doubt not but capacity and the application thou threatens will afford it to thee."[22]

The Wrights forged close relationships with other families who shared their love of learning and books, like the Norrises, whose friendship continued for over forty years through several generations. Many years later Susanna Wright commented: "the first Intimacys I contracted, and the happyest hours I ever enjoyed Since I left my native land, were in thy Grandfather Norris's house, the Strongest friendship I formd there, was only dissolvd by death which must sooner or later break every human tye."[23]

"Grandfather Norris" was Isaac Norris I, who, in 1716, built a gracious country house called Fairhill, which was on the road to Germantown. Surmounted by a cupola with an imported weathercock, the house had imported window sashes, unusual when casement windows predominated, and marble hearths. Norris's Fairhill, which was based on the design of Dolobran, the ancestral seat of Thomas Lloyd, father of Isaac's wife, in Wales, was surrounded by formal parterres, gravel walks, and outbuildings, including one that housed the library of Isaac Norris.[24] Like the Norrises and Logans, many of the Wrights' friends were of the affluent Quaker elite.

About 1726, when James Logan was building his own imposing house, Stenton, in Germantown, the Wrights were about to leave the house they owned in Chester to venture into the back country about seventy miles away along the Susquehanna River. The Wrights, Norrises, and Logans knew the strategic importance of the region. James Logan owned land in the vicinity and was involved with the large Indian trading post at Conestoga.[25]

Isaac Norris had come to the area in 1701, where having "well traversed the wilderness" he had "lived nobly at the King's palace in Conestogoe."[26] Three years later, the Indians at Conestoga were visited by the Quaker minister Thomas Chalkley, who came with twelve or thirteen others and an interpreter. In their fascinating encounter he describes an ancient Indian empress, a kind of female Solomon in their midst:

> *They were kindly received by the Indians, and upon their application, for the opportunity of a religious meeting. They called a council, which they conducted with great gravity, and in their deliberation expressed their sentiments coolly one after another. Some of their women being present, T. Chalkley, who was admitted to the council, enquired of the interpreter, Why they introduced women into their councils?* to which he replied, some women are wiser than some men. *Observing an antient grave woman who spoke frequently, it excited his curiosity to make particular enquiry concerning her. The interpreter informed him that she was an empress, and a woman of such authority among them, that they undertook nothing of consequence without consulting her. That she then said, she looked upon this visit to be of an extraordinary nature as the persons were not come to buy or sell or get gain, but in love and regard to them, from a desire of their well doing both here and hereafter, and that a meeting among them might be beneficial to their young people. There were two tribes of them, the Seneca's and Shawanese. They had first a meeting with the Seneca's, who were much affected with what they heard and understood, and calling the other tribe they interpreted what they had heard to them. These friends had also another meeting with the Shawanese Indians. Their visit was gratefully accepted, and the Indians expressed their desire of more opportunities of the like kind, which it is hoped divine providence will afford them.*[27]

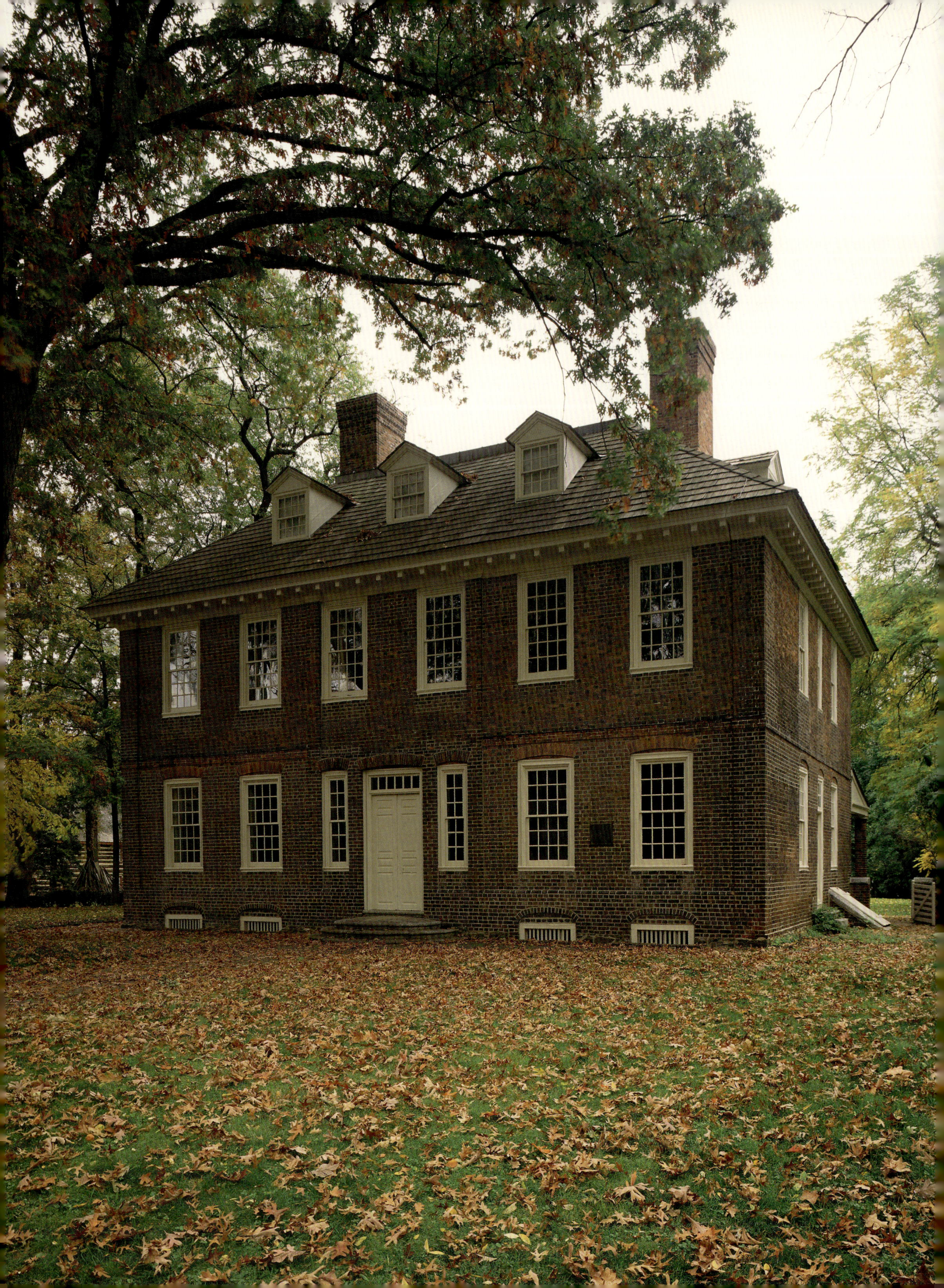

The opportunity was afforded them. In the year 1722, John Wright went to the remote site of Conestoga to preach to the Indians. In that year his wife Patience died, leaving John Wright and his eldest child Susanna to manage the household and raise the children, the youngest, James, only eight. Despite these demands, Susanna Wright was able to continue her studies and writing, sending samples of her poetry to James Logan. She and her father probably discussed Conestoga with him, since he had visited there often and had also traveled there that year.

The vision that William Penn had had for a city established along the Susquehanna River certainly must have threaded through those conversations. In 1690, Penn had published the broadside, "Some Proposals for a Second Settlement." There he described a plan in which tracts of land of five thousand acres would be offered to purchasers who would then receive lots in the new city.[28] He began with the success of Philadelphia, which advanced from "a Wood, to a good forwardness of Building (there being above One Thousand Houses finisht in it)" within nine years. He continued:

> *It is now my purpose to make another Settlement, upon the River of Susquehannagh, that runs into the Bay of Chesapeake, and bears about fifty Miles West from the River Delaware, as appears by the Common Maps of the English Dominion in America. There I design to lay out a Plat for the building of another City.*

The qualities that recommended this land were:

> *the known Goodness of the Soyle, and Scituation of the Land, which is high & not Mountainous; also the Pleasantness, and Largness of the River, being clear and not rapid; and broader then the Thames at London-bridge, many Miles above the place designed for this Settlement; and runs (as we are told by the Indians) quite through the Province, into which many fair Rivers empty themselves. The sorts of Timber that grow there are chiefly Oake, Ash, Chestnut, Walnut, Cedar, and Poplar. The native Fruits are Pawpaws, Grapes, Mulberys, Chesnuts, and several sorts of Walnuts. There are likewise great quantities of Deer, and especially Elks, which are much bigger than our Red Deer, and use that River in Herds. And Fish there is of divers sorts, and very large and good, and in great plenty.*

> *But that which recommends this Settlement in perticular, and the Province in general, is a late Pattent obtained by divers Eminent Lords and Gentlemen for that Land that lies North of Pennsylvania up to the 46th Degree and an half, because their Traffick and Intercourse will be chiefly through Pennsylvania, which lies between that Province and the Sea. We have also the comfort of being the Center of all the English Colonies upon the Continent of America, as they lie from*

Stenton (1727–1730), built in Germantown by James Logan (1674–1751), William Penn's secretary and Susanna Wright's mentor. Courtesy of Stenton.

Map of Pennsylvania, made by Sayer and Bennett, London (after William Scull), 1775. This map shows Chester on the Delaware River (on the lower right-hand side), where the Wrights first settled, and Wright's Ferry, which spanned the east and west banks of the Susquehanna River (at far left).

34   *Wright's Ferry Mansion*

the North-East parts of New-England to the most Southerly parts of Carolina, being above 1000 Miles upon the Coast.[29]

In 1700 William Penn had come to the Indian trading post of Conestoga near the Susquehanna River, where he made a treaty with the Indians for the lands that "formerly were the Right of the People or Nations called the Susquehannagh Indians."[30] This was land he had purchased from the governor of New York in 1694 that had been claimed by the Iroquois. The Indian settlement consisted primarily of Susquehannocks, Senecas, and Shawnees who lived in long, narrow cabin-like houses of frame construction and who farmed corn and other crops, trapped, and hunted.[31] European traders also lived in the area and in 1717 a manor for the Proprietors of Pennsylvania was laid out nearby. Shawanah town on Susquehanna, another Indian settlement, was about ten miles away, beside the Susquehanna River and the Shawnee Run, where the town of Columbia now stands.

It was to this site that the Wrights, along with a handful of other English Quakers who had been living in Chester and Darby, Pennsylvania, were drawn. On August 31, 1726, Susanna Wright purchased one hundred acres here. Two weeks later, her father bought the neighboring one hundred and fifty acres. This land was part of three thousand acres that originally had been sold by William Penn to George Beale of Surrey, England, and was then purchased by Jeremiah Langhorne on October 17/18, 1718. Five hundred acres of this land had been located and laid out for him the previous year, however, by land commissioners Richard Hill, Isaac Norris, and James Logan. In 1726, the five hundred acres were sold to Robert Barber of Chester, who then sold acreage to both Susanna Wright and her father. The neighboring three hundred acres owned by James Logan were sold to Samuel Blunston of Darby, Pennsylvania.

James Logan realized the strategic significance of this particular location and undoubtedly encouraged the Wrights, Blunstons, and Barbers to form a settlement here. In addition to the qualities Penn had identified to recommend the lands, other factors had arisen to make this particular location of crucial importance for a strong settlement. For example, the boundary between Pennsylvania and Maryland was under dispute, Lord Calvert of Maryland claiming that the boundary extended into Pennsylvania above this point. To further this claim, Pennsylvania settlers were being threatened, often violently, by Marylanders. A subtler threat that surfaced through the complexities of Indian relations was that of France. Louis XV claimed vast North American territories stretching through the southern colonies into Pennsylvania, right up to the banks of the Susquehanna River. Aware that the balance of power in the Anglo-French struggle for the continent was determined largely by Indian diplomacy, the French were actively cultivating relations with the Shawnee.[32] Another problem in this area along the Susquehanna River was the influx of European settlers who were beginning to encroach on lands west of the river, which were still owned by the Indians. It was important to control that problem until negotiations

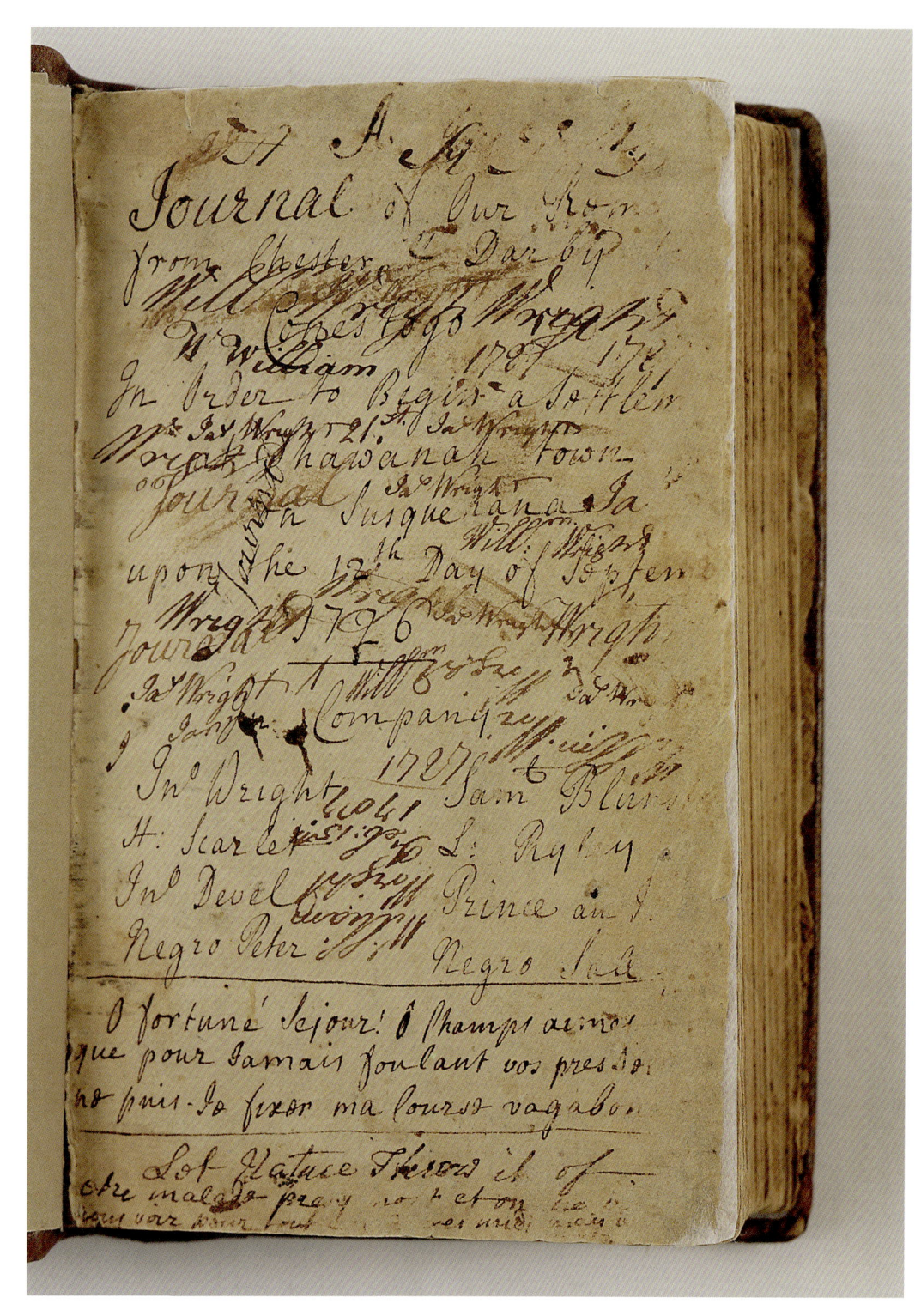

Manuscript book, bound by William Davies in 1726. It contains the title page (shown here), passages from a French grammar, and an English-Indian vocabulary list, in the hand of Susanna Wright, as well as numerous entries in other hands recording business transactions for the settlement at Wright's Ferry. Years later, in the 1780s, children of Susanna's brother James used the pages to practice writing, as can be seen here.

Wright's Ferry Mansion

for these lands were finalized.[33] In addition, as settlement was pushing westward and as Chester County was growing—this area was part of Chester County at that time—it was increasingly evident that the area was too large for the courts at Chester to administer, and it was necessary to divide the area into another county. The Wrights, Blunstons, and Barbers had the experience and training that would be needed to establish a new county.

In anticipation of their momentous move, Susanna Wright had obtained a small journal bound in leather, simply tooled, by Quaker bookbinder William Davies, who lived in Chester. In her neat hand, she wrote a formal title page to the book (see opposite):

A Journal of Our Removal from Chester & Darby to Conestogo In
Order to Begin a Settlement at Shawanah town on Susquehana
upon the 12th Day of September 1726
    In Company

Jnº Wright	*Samˡ Blunston*
H: Scarlet	*L: Ryley*
Jnº Devel	*Prince an Indian*
Negro Peter	*Negro Sall*

Despite the title, the book was used not as a written journal but primarily as an account book by various people for the new settlement.[34] Until they could construct a house at Shawanah town on Susquehanna, the Wrights undoubtedly made various trips between the house they still owned in Chester, which they did not sell until 1733, and their newly acquired land.

The serious intent in venturing to this area is evident in the rapid train of accomplishments. One of the first endeavors the small community achieved was to establish the new county. John Wright was instrumental in separating and setting up the new county of Lancaster, which was named after the Wrights' native Lancashire, England. John Wright was named first justice of the peace for the county, their neighbor Robert Barber became the first sheriff, and Samuel Blunston helped direct the building of the courthouse. The settlers here probably had hoped that their new settlement at Shawanah town would become the seat of government of Lancaster County, but the small settlement of Lancaster was selected instead.

Other developments quickly ensued. In order to control the influx of settlers, James Logan appointed Samuel Blunston, a surveyor, to issue temporary land licenses for Indian-owned land across the river until negotiations with the Indians for those lands could be complete. These licenses would then be confirmed when the land was finally purchased from the Six Nations.

In 1730 John Wright obtained a patent for a ferry at Shawanah town that would enable easier access to the lands west of the Susquehanna. With Pennsylvania settlers established

L

Looking glass	wawpuma-wih
Laugh	I,yoalih
Lead	Olloowih
Log	nocautokih

M

Mony	Cshathuh
milk	millenapuh
man	Lonnih
won	Lonowah
mouth	toonih
to morrow	wopockih

N

noodle	Sapunegah
Hickry nut	pocaunnah
nose	koshaavih
no	mattah

O — P

Powder	Muckattak
pipe	gwaguh
pin	pocattapoaugah
punk	attoowah

Silk purse, eighteenth century. Embroidered with the Ark and Dove of Noah, the ladder to Heaven, and the Eye of God, with the words GOD IS OUR GUIDE. The reverse is embroidered with the word HOPE and its personification as a lady with an anchor. Wright provenance.

OPPOSITE TOP: English-Indian vocabulary list in the hand of Susanna Wright, in manuscript book bound by William Davies in 1726.

OPPOSITE BOTTOM: White quartz arrowhead found on site at Wright's Ferry Mansion.

OVERLEAF: Wright's Ferry Mansion. Façade facing the Susquehanna River, the front prospect of the house in the eighteenth century. Today one approaches the house from what would have been the back.

on both sides of the Susquehanna at that point, the land would be strengthened against Maryland's claims and encroachments. The ferry was established on Susanna Wright's hundred acres and the site soon became known as "Wright's Ferry."[35]

Although protecting the border, controlling settlement, and establishing a new county played a part in the making of the settlement, the heart of the Wrights' motivation in coming to this remote site is reflected in a letter to Susanna Wright from Isaac Norris, who was composing a history of Pennsylvania:

> *when I shal find leasure and proper encouragement to write Our History I (as Burnet Says) will not fail to mention you with a great regard, and some very extraordinary notes on the Winter 28—To propagate civility, good Sence, Reason, & Good maners, to propagate Moral Justice, & Erect a Church, In a Land 'till then Barbarous is a Revolution of some Importance & may make some future Age Inquisitive into ye truest motives of such Change.*[36]

Susanna Wright and Her Family

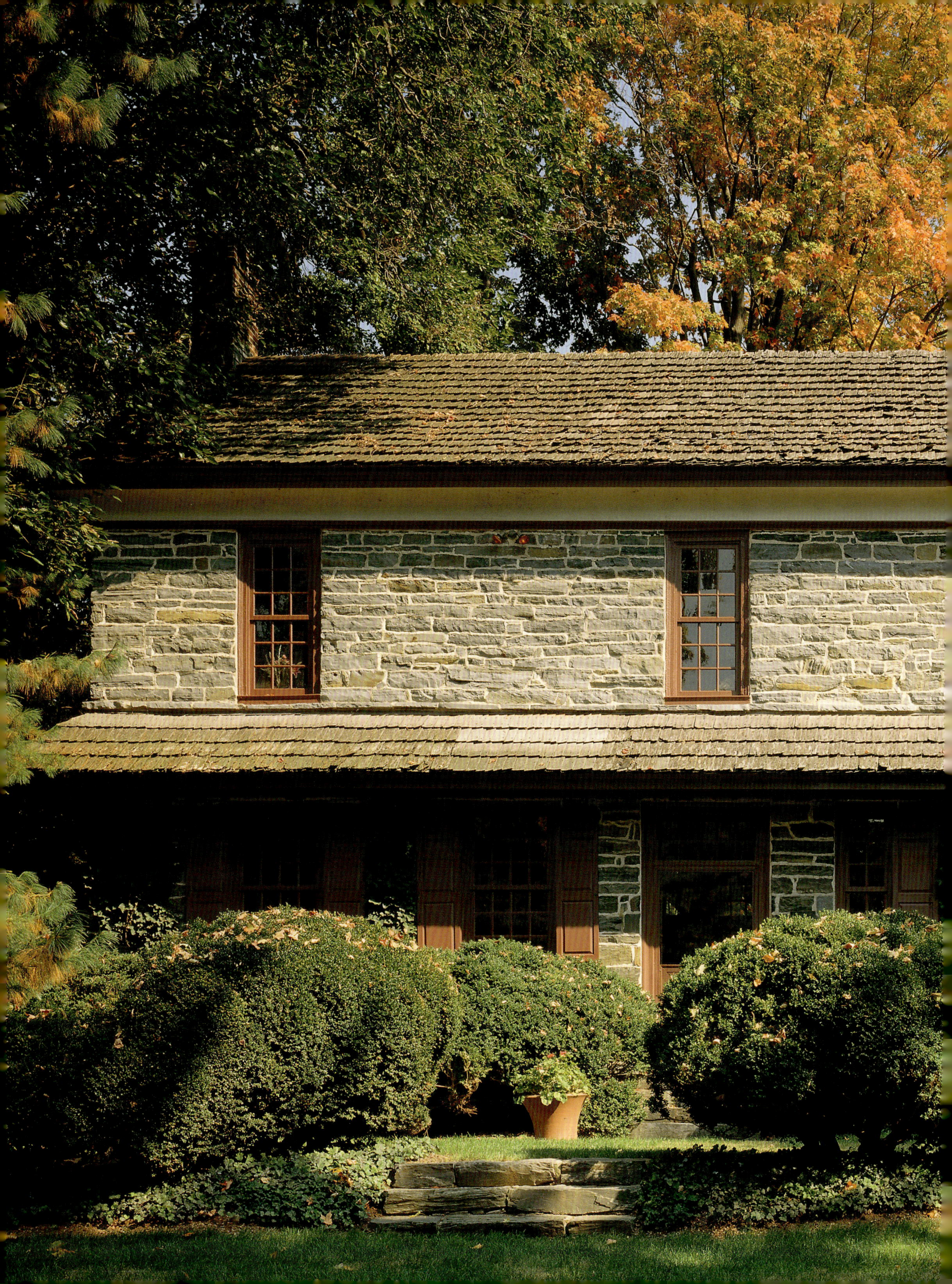

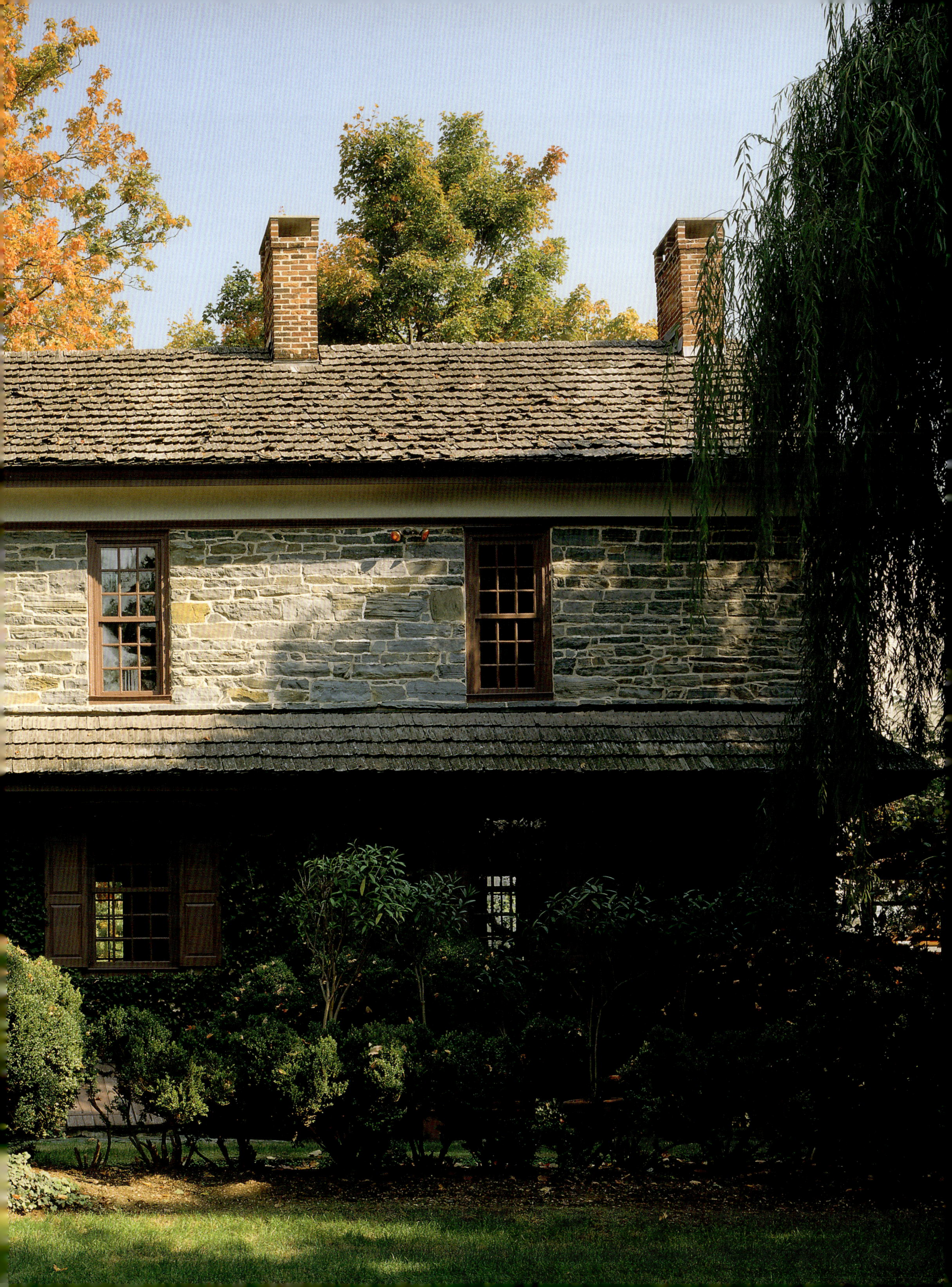

Gable end of Wright's Ferry Mansion, with coved plaster cornice and pent roof, which encircle the building. Oak side-lapped shingles about three feet long, tapered on both sides and very thin, were specially made for the roof, following evidence in the building for the original shingling.

Like their forebears for several generations, Susanna Wright and her father were pursuing the spiritual ideals of the Society of Friends. Because a Quaker meetinghouse was not built at the settlement until the middle of the eighteenth century, the houses of John and Susanna Wright were used for meetings.

John Wright's house was built first, shortly after the settlers' arrival in 1726. It was a log structure begun in February, and notes for its construction were the first entries after Susanna Wright's 1726 title page in the account book, along with those for Samuel Blunston's house. The number and dimensions of rafters, joists, laths, collar beams, and scantling were given. The building must have neared completion by September 12, 1727, when "Thomas ye plaisterer Came." When this building was demolished in 1874, a description was given of it:

> *The building as it appeared when torn down was nothing like the original one. The first story of the south end was the original building and measured about thirty feet front by twenty feet deep, and was built with oak, walnut and hickory logs, cut from the woods surrounding the spot upon which the house was erected.*

> *Several years later an addition was attached to the north end, built of logs. After the death of Judge Wright and the erection of saw mills in the neighborhood, a second story was built upon the logs, and the entire building was weatherboarded. A few years ago the late John Wright remodeled and greatly improved the outside appearance of the building, and erected a kitchen to the southwest corner. The first story was but seven feet high.*[37]

Another description from the same year differs by saying that the second story was part of the original structure:

> *[John Wright] built his dwelling upon a level spot of ground fronting the river. This dwelling was torn down in 1874 to give place to a more stately brick mansion of modern times. The logs used in its construction were hickory, white and Spanish oak, and a number of black walnut. The dwelling, as first constructed, seems to have contained but one room upon the first story and one upon the second.*[38]

An inventory taken of the house in 1749 does not resolve whether the original building consisted of one floor or two, since it does not refer to floors or to specific rooms, other than the kitchen.[39] It does, however, suggest a modest structure, which, among other furnishings, included the luxuries of a silver pint cann, a folio Bible and other books, "Two Beds & Furniture" valued at ten pounds, a clock and a table together valued at five pounds, and a writing desk valued at one pound ten shillings. The next to highest valuation came to twenty pounds for John Wright's wearing apparel and riding horse. The highest valuation (twenty-six pounds) was for his eight cows, six yearlings, and six calves. "Kitchen furniture," the only room reference here, has a modest two pound estimate.

It was in this dwelling that Susanna Wright and her brother James, who was only twelve, probably lived when they first moved to Shawanah town on Susquehanna, since their father's log house was one of the first buildings to be constructed, along with the houses of Samuel Blunston and Robert Barber.[40] Her two sisters, Patience and Elizabeth, who married and set up households of their own in spring of 1728, would have been there only a short while, if indeed at all, since the Wrights still owned their house in Chester.

Apparently, a log or frame house with no cellar had been built on Susanna Wright's property prior to the construction of Wright's Ferry Mansion, although we do not know when it was built or by whom.

John Wright's tract was largely uncleared and was covered with forest until well after Susanna Wright's death, as the tax lists show. The rich forests and fertile soil of this area along the Susquehanna River were long lauded by inhabitants and visitors alike. Reminiscing about the settlement in the years of her youth, Sarah Barber (1766–1841) wrote: "Large Buttonwood and other trees grew at the waters edge. Many of these were torn away by the ice; the largest trees would go down with the weight & force of the ice, seemingly as

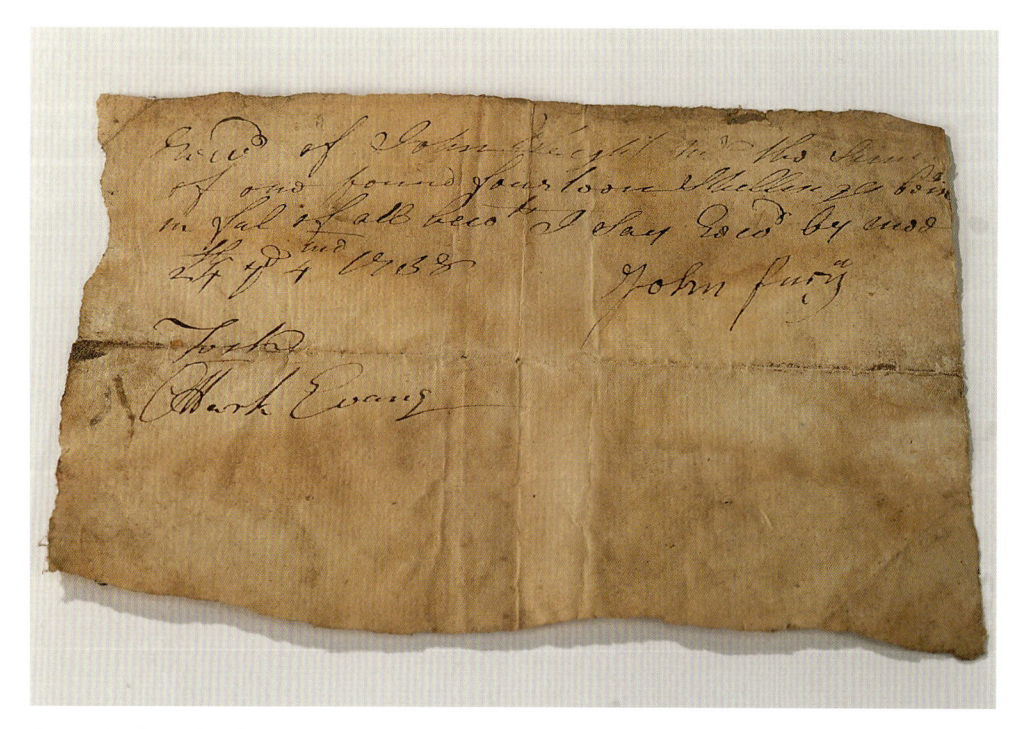

Receipt dated 1738, found in a wall at Wright's Ferry Mansion during restoration.

easy as a child would break off a twig."[41] In describing the area, William Penn had listed "Oake, Ash, Chestnut, Walnut, Cedar, and Poplar," as the predominant trees.[42]

This forest provided the material for John Wright's log house and other structures in the vicinity, including the two-story stone house that Susanna Wright eventually built. Oaks, roughly hewn and so retaining a tree-like form, lie whitewashed beneath the pine floors of Wright's Ferry Mansion, providing sturdy support. Oak also frames the doors and is used even for the lath that supports the plaster. Wide boards of poplar richly panel the primary wall of four rooms. Lustrous black cherry, a singular use of that wood in the house, is seen in the banisters of the staircase, the most elaborate architectural element in the house.

It was perhaps in admiration of this staircase that the Wrights' close friend Charles Norris asked James Wright to send him scantling, asking:

> *Have you any wild Cherry tree Scantling Remg on hand, does the wood take long seasoning, is the Diffr of Good or Bad Grain to be known while the Tree is standing, or is there any other Question to be asked by an Ignoramus to make fully acquainted with all its Qualitys. thy Answer will Oblige.*[43]

The Norris staircase was later noted for the beauty of the cherry that was compared in richness to mahogany.[44]

In addition to forest, part of the land was devoted to pasture for John Wright's cows and their offspring and another part, to his "26 hoggs," which would have fed on the mast from the oak trees and perhaps also on peaches, since the site had formerly been an Indian settlement. In 1683, Penn wrote:

> *The Fruits that I find in the Woods are the White and Black Mulberry, Chestnut, Wallnut, Plumbs, Strawberries, Cranberries, Hurtleberries and Grapes of divers sorts. . . . Here are also Peaches and very good and in great quantities, not an Indian Plantation without them; but whether naturally here at first I know not, however one may have them by Bushels for little; they make a pleasant Drink.*[45]

Peter Kalm in his travels through the colonies in 1748 mentions that there was such an abundance of fruit that it could be fed to the animals:

> *Every countryman, even a common peasant, has commonly an orchard near his house, in which all sorts of fruits, such as peaches, apples, pears, cherries, and others, are in plenty. The peaches were now almost ripe. . . . They are rare in Europe, particularly in Sweden; for in that country hardly any people beside the rich taste them. But here every countryman had an orchard full of peach trees, which were covered with such quantities of fruit that we could scarcely walk in the orchard without treading upon those peaches which had fallen off; many of which were usually left on the ground, and only part of them sold in town, and the rest was consumed by the family and strangers. Nay, this fine fruit was frequently given to the swine. . . . The orchards have seldom other fruit than apples and peaches. Pear trees are scarce in this province. They have cherry trees in the orchards, but commonly on the sides of them towards the house, or along the enclosures.*[46]

Thomas Paschall mentions this as early as 1683: "Here are peaches in abundance, of three sorts. I have seen them rott on the ground and the Hogs eate them."[47]

Although at first thought to be native, peaches were probably introduced from Spain. Europeans also introduced pears, apricots, quince, and edible species of apple and cherry. Samuel Blunston had cherry scions imported from London for his plantation. On March 5, 1736/7, Edward Shippen wrote to him: "I shall be sure to furnish you with all the curious Scions of apples pears and Cherrys that are within my reach indeed I have sent to London for some & if they come well you may expect a sortment."[48]

Beside her father's tract was Susanna Wright's hundred acres. Here there were orchards that extended to the back of her house. Along with cherries, she raised apples. A "Stire apple" is recorded in the account book bound by William Davies, and spitzenbergs and pippins are mentioned in a letter to Deborah Franklin:

Dear friend:

I ought long ago to have acknowledged your last obliging letter, but if you knew how sick, and how hurried and how everything we have been, you would excuse me. I now do it very sincerely.

Sister Rhoda beggs your acceptance of a few of our apples, spitzbergen & pippins and a little pickled salmon (that is what we call salmon). She could not get as much of it as she wished and was forced to fill up the kegg with perch. When you have taken it out, you will please to let a serv. return the Kegg to the waggoner, as it is a borrowed one and the people insist on having it again. This is ill manners, but with you our good friend, we can be quite free. We rejoiced to see Mr. Franklin here for a quarter of an hour, and to hear of you and Sally. My brother, Jemmy will return Mr. Franklin's book and I have desired him, and now I desire you to return for me a thousand thanks. Everybodys kind and affectionate regards are to you all, in great haste

Your truly obliged Servant
S. Wright[49]

A lane of cherry trees eventually led to the ferry. Visitors came to the area not only for the ferry but also for the cherry trees. Having been planted early on in the settlement, the cherry trees abundantly flourished and eventually, probably not until the late eighteenth century, became a source of great festivity. In the early nineteenth century, Philadelphia merchant Thomas P. Cope describes them:

Before the Town of Columbia was laid out, a number of large cherry trees, some of which are still standing, used once a year to attract great collections of people to celebrate a festival which by common consent was called Cherry fair. Four and five hundred and even a thousand people have some seasons assembled on that occasion, to eat cherries and to make merry over the bottle, to sweat at a "hoop-si-saw," and riot on the green. This practice has lately been abolished by the townsmen and very wisely, as the morals of the people were greatly injured at those scenes of frolic.[50]

The Ferry

The ferry was run by Susanna Wright's two brothers, James on the east shore, on Susanna's tract, and John on the opposite shore on a tract which he owned. In 1750, James leased the ferry on the east shore to Robert Barber for one year and the document that was drawn up gives details about the property and its operation:

for one year rental of the ferry . . . along with: 1) his house where Thomas Ives lately dwelt, the field behind it to the middle fence, the stabling and the Clover field in which it stands, except such as James Wright shal fence off betwixt his house & the River for a Garden, the Wood pasture (except about 3 or 4 Acres which was Cleared this Spring) with priviledge to Clear Six acres within it for his own use, and Liberty to cut fire wood in such places as the said James Wright shal direct. The said James Wright Lets to the said Robert Barber the keeping of the profits of the ferry from the East to the west side of the River, and two boats, He also Lets him have Sundry Household Goods. Conditions: that he shall give due attendance at the ferry & shal not make any person pay more than the usual fare nor Demand of any travelers who pass or repass the River pay for their Lodging, Nor demand pay for Carrying over preachers of any Comunity. He shal as the Custom is Bring Back at the Return of his Boat what Loading he can John Wright doing the same for him And shal when his Boats go on other Ocasions carry back & forwards baggs or people who come to the said James Wrights mill without demanding pay for them, the said Robert Barber shal fetch or Carry over Saml Tayler and whatever Belongs to him whenever he desires it ferriage free as likewise James Wright Susanna Wright or any of their familys and Shal let John Wright have the use of the Big Boat as often as he wants it til his own shal be built the above-named James & Susa. Wright shal have free use of the pump. It is further agreed . . . that the Buildings & Boats shal be delivered by James Wright in good repair. . . . Rent—£ 100 paid every third.[51]

The house "where Thomas Ives lately dwelt" is probably the "House Builded for a Smith to live in," which Susanna Wright mentions in her will in regard to the ferry. The "stabling" is perhaps the "log Stable 28 × 18 On the corner of Locust Street" in the 1798 Direct Tax lists of Columbia for William Wright. William Wright and his brothers Samuel, John, and James had inherited the ferry from their aunt and guardian, Susanna Wright, in 1784. At that time the ferry was rented by Joseph Jeffrys, a Quaker from Chester County. In 1788, the town of Columbia was laid out on adjoining properties, the ferry property being kept intact. In 1795, however, the ferry property was divided up and sold.[52]

The high rent paid by Robert Barber in 1750 is indicative of how prosperous the ferry proved to be. There were no bridges across the Susquehanna River at this point until the early nineteenth century and, although there were other ferries in the vicinity, Wright's Ferry was a major one, so much so that eventually it was referred to as "the gateway to the West."[53] Although Robert Barber rented the ferry, James Wright continued ownership, paying one pound fifteen shillings for seven years rent to the Proprietor of Pennsylvania Thomas Penn for the ferry in 1754.

About four miles north of Wright's Ferry was Anderson's Ferry. A traveler's account from 1780 contrasts the two and describes the experience of using the ferry:

In the sixth hour we reached Anderson's Ferry, where the Susquehannah is 1¼ miles wide. On the side from which we approached there is a high sandy bank, and the wheels of Conrad's wagon sank to the axle in the sand, and were freed only after one and a half hours of work with levers and extra horses. On the other side is a high stony ridge. We were so fortunate as to get our two wagons and three riding horses across within two hours, by means of two Flats, which are too small for a river of such considerable size; but frequently travellers are detained here for an entire day. Each crossing takes only ten minutes, and they race with each other. But they had to cross over and back three times, and the loading and unloading takes as much time as the crossing. Here they charge $56.00 for taking over a six-horse wagon, and $8.00 for a horse and rider; at Wright's Ferry, where the Susquehannah is two miles wide, the charge is $90.00 for a six horse wagon, and $12.00 for a horse and rider. Some two miles from the Susquehannah, on a creek called Susquehannah Creek, we made our first outdoor night-camp, in a pretty open space surrounded by tall trees.[54]

At Wright's Ferry, the ferry house faced south and the road leading to Lancaster ran in front of it.[55] The tavern there was described in the late nineteenth century:

It was built of logs, two stories high, with a large room at either end, with a passage-way between. John Wright, Jr., was the first person who kept this tavern. He remained there until he married, in 1734, when he removed to the western side of the ferry, where he built a hotel.[56]

A brother of Susanna's, John Wright (1710–1759) was married in 1734 to Eleanor Barber (1718–1767), the eldest daughter of Robert Barber who had arrived in 1726, and sister of the Robert Barber who rented the ferry from James Wright. A description of John Wright's ferry on the west side of the river (where Wrightsville is today) appeared in the *Pennsylvania Gazette*, July 31, 1793:

To be rented, and may be entered on the 9th of October next, that ancient and well accustomed Ferry, on the west side of Susquehanna, in York County, known by the name of Wright's Ferry; the lot on which the improvements stand contains nearly seven acres, there are three suitable Boats, and the Tavern (which is commodious) if properly managed, will produce considerable profit; the premises are so generally known, that a particular description is unnecessary. None need apply but such as are capable, and will engage to do strict justice to both Tavern and Ferry.

James Ewing.

A description of the countryside immediately around the ferry on Susanna Wright's property was written by Sarah Barber, daughter of Robert Barber who ran the ferry in 1750 and who, about 1762, built the brick house, where his father's house had previously stood.[57] His father had been the first sheriff of Lancaster County and near the house stood a log prison, "I remember it well—a strong-looking log building—was pulled down not many years since," recalls Sarah Barber in her description of the area, written in 1830, by which time a bridge spanned the Susquehanna River. She and her sister lived in the brick house that her father had built. She writes:

> *The ferry across the Susquehanna at this place appears to have been early set up. At first it was necessarily very imperfect. Two large canoes lashed together were used to take over a wagon which first had to be unloaded. In 1750 it rented for £100. per annum, with the ground allotted to it. The ferry course was a little below the bridge; there was a tolerable road from the old ferry house to the landing—above that it was wild and unfrequented—the "point-rock" first then the well known "Chicques rock" rising in solitary grandeur. There was scarcely a foot path between the rock and the river, and a hunter or fisher might be seen climbing his way along the side of the hill. Strangers used to visit this rock as a great natural curiosity, but they generally went over the hill, as the path at the shore was nearly impossible. Pine and Spruce bushes grew in the crevices of the rock and on the hill. It was a great place for fox hunting. The old ferry house, now occupied by Peter Epley, in Locust Street, was built in the early settlement of the place; the large room at the upper end was built long after the other part of the house, by J. Lowdon, who kept the ferry for many years. There was a stone kitchen at the lower end which was pulled away a few years ago to make room for the brick buildings now there. The barn was across the road where Haldeman's store is. It was burned by lightning the last day of 8th month 1769 or 70.*[58]

The John Lowdon mentioned was the son of Susanna's sister Patience. After fighting in the Revolutionary War, he moved to Buffalo Valley, Pennsylvania. The log barn that was destroyed by lightning was perhaps replaced by the "Log Barn 70 × 27 Adj. John Wright," listed in the 1798 Direct Tax for Samuel Wright, in association with the tax on Wright's Ferry Mansion. Samuel Blunston had a road from his house to his landing near the ferry, which is mentioned in his will of 1745 and which is probably the "tolerable road" from the old ferry house to the landing.

Chickies Rock, a short distance north of the ferry, near the Chicaselungo creek, rises to a height of 305 feet, as measured by Benjamin Franklin. He commented on it in a letter to Susanna Wright, thanking her for the "Hospitality of Hempfield," and added: "In the Magazine of August, I find that the magnificent King of Portugal has rais'd his Marble

Aqueduct near 100 Foot higher than your Chicaselungo. It must be a most stupendous Work. I send you the Prospect of it."[59]

His visit must have been a particularly welcome one for Susanna Wright, since the previous several years had been filled with great loss for her: all three of the founding patriarchs of Wright's Ferry had died—Robert Barber, Samuel Blunston, and her father John Wright—and she had just lost her mentor, James Logan, the previous month. Regarding her father and Robert Barber, she wrote to Isaac Norris:

Nov. 14th 1749

Much Esteemd Friend.

Tho it is out of time to acknowledge the Receipt of thy Kind Letter, it is not so to Congratulate you on the safe Return of your Brother, which I rejoice I have an Opportunity to do. As whenever we part with our friends we know not but it may be forever, How happy an Event it is to meet them again? But those we See Laid in the dust we are Sure to see no more—at least in this World.

My Father Judged Rightly when thou took leave of him that it would be the last; He Continued in the Same Happy Disposition of Mind thou left him, to his last hour his understanding perfectly Clear, & Every way Easy. I ask^d. him a few minnets Before he dyed, if he was in any pain, he said he was not, but was Cold & almost gone, ask^d. what time it was, and Dyed as if he had gone to Sleep, with his Eyes Closed as he lay upon his Side.

I well knew whenever it pleased God to Call him it would very Sencibly Affect me, But I thought if I could see him taken away without much pain, It would be the Greatest Satisfaction I could Ever feel, and what I should to the last day of my life Remember With thankfullness, for Setting Aside all Apprehensions of futurity Dying is a Dreadful & Shocking Circumstance, as I had seen but a few weeks Before in my poor Neighbour Barber, who Certainly Suffered more than the tortures of an Execution, and tho we dare not Expostulate, Yet to be Called into Being without any wil or act of our own, and taken out of it again, in the manner the Greater part of mankind are, to humane Reason has an Appearance of Severity—But there we must leave it, and as wel as we can Rest Satisfied in Concluding that all that is, is Right, tho we Yet know not in what manner it is So—

I hope thy pretty Girls & all thy Good family are wel and I desire to be Kindly Remembered to them.

I am very Sincerely thy Obliged Frd.
S. Wright[60]

Susanna Wright had been the mainstay of both her family and the settlement, caring for her younger siblings after her mother's death in 1722, and, once in the new settlement, caring not only for her relatives but also friends and neighbors at Wright's Ferry, when they were sick. As Deborah Norris Logan, daughter-in-law of James Logan, says of her:

> *She never married; but after the death of her father became the head of her own family, who looked up to her for advice and direction as to a parent; for her heart was replete with every kind affection, and with all the social virtues. . . . She was often resorted to as a physician by her neighbourhood. The care and management of a large family, and of a profitable establishment, frequently devolved entirely upon her.*[61]

In caring for the sick, she had guidance from three of Philadelphia's renowned physicians, all of whom were grandsons of Thomas Lloyd, Drs. Samuel Preston Moore, Charles Moore (1724–1801), and Lloyd Zachary (1701–1756).

In 1744 Dr. Lloyd Zachary sent Susanna Wright instructions for the care of her neighbors Samuel Blunston and his wife Sarah, who were extremely ill, dying within the same year.[62] In 1761, Dr. Charles Moore sent Susanna Wright medicines "for thy Sister Nelly," describing how the medicines should be taken and the possible turns the case might take. He also tells of inoculating members of his own family against small pox: "we are now preparing my Brother Mordecais eldest Daughter & second son for it . . . if they are as much favoured as Dickey I shall probably arm myself with Contagion for your little charge."[63]

James Logan, who also had his children inoculated, wrote to Samuel Blunston: "Perhaps it may please Susy Wr. to hear that my Hannah & Jemmy having been inoculated for the Small pox, the pock was well turned yesterday, & we think they are past all danger."[64]

The Management of Silkworms

Like James Logan, Charles Moore was seriously interested in the development of a silk industry in Pennsylvania, which had been pursued as early as 1642. At that time, John Printz was commissioned governor for the Swedish government and was instructed to cultivate tobacco, cattle, and silkworms.[65] After a hiatus in interest, the idea of raising silkworms in Pennsylvania was taken up again seriously in the early eighteenth century and received its greatest impetus when the American Philosophical Society, one of America's first learned societies of international standing, established a public filature where silk would be processed at a house in Philadelphia between Arch and High Streets in 1770.[66] Charles Moore was on the board of a special society for the promotion of silk culture established under the auspices of the American Philosophical Society.

Writing to the Penn family in 1725, James Logan tells of the promise of silk and writes the following year of silk sent to England, saying he is glad "it proves so good" and "doubts not, in time, the country may raise large quantities."[67] That year, James Logan began a serious study of silk so that he could publish an article, "to be made up of Greek

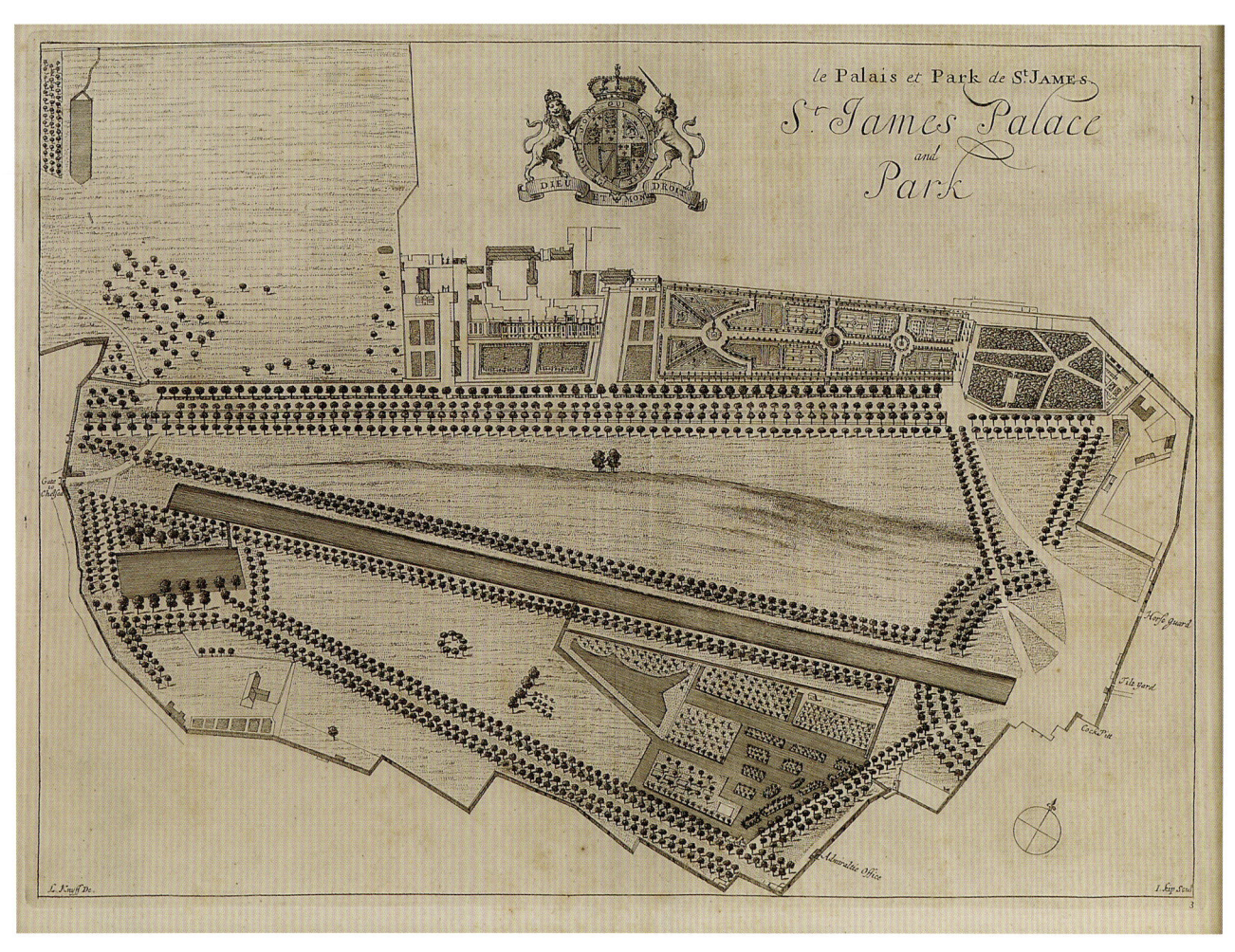

Engraving, by John Kip and Leonard Knyff, London, 1706. In the seventeenth century, a section of St. James Park in London was devoted to the raising of silkworms.

and Latin Quotations with some Hebrew perhaps," to encourage public interest.[68] By 1734 Governor Gordon states that "some among us have shown its practicability by making some small quantities."[69]

Susanna Wright was winning premiums for her silk when she was in her seventies, and producing silk that was sent to England to be presented as a gift to the Queen. The first pair of silk stockings made entirely in Pennsylvania were of Susanna's creation and are described in a letter from Charles Norris to Susanna Wright, on April 19, 1759:

> *I cannot omit mentioning that when Genl Amherst was in Town, the Day his Brothr was drinking Tea with us when as a Curiosity thy Silk Stockings was produced & my Brother taking notice that he seemed much pleased with them propos'd presenting them to the Genl as the 1st pr made here, the Eggs hatched Balls wound Silk twisted & Stockings wove in the Province of Pensilva. and on*

the reception he Express'd Surprise at the perfection of the first and declared he would not put them on till he had the pleasure of waiting on his majesty on his Return (if please God he shod live to see that day) when he did Protest he would display them to the full, and shd write Mist Amherst he was already fixed with Stockings for that occasion such as was not in her power to procure & drank the Ladys health who made them—So I am to take Isaacs pr when done to honour my marriage with, if I shall live to that day.[70]

In a 1769 letter to Benjamin Franklin, Cadwalader Evans, one of the managers of the public filature in Philadelphia, suggests that a small premium be given by the legislature for every pound of cocoons produced, the expense of the premium being "defray'd by a Tax upon dogs, whose great number is become a nusance."[71] That same year, Franklin sent Evans a French treatise on the raising of silkworms, along with the Act of the Society of Arts in England, which offered a bounty for silk production in the colonies. Since this was for silk "wound from the Cocoons, and sent over in Skeins," he recommended that either a public filature should be set up or else "every Family should learn to wind their own." He continued, "In Italy they are all brought to Market, from the neighboring Country, and bought up by those that keep the Filatures. In Sicily each Family winds its own Silk, for the sake of having the Remains to card and spin for Family use."[72] The managers of the society for the promotion of silk culture in Philadelphia petitioned the legislature on October 3, 1771, asking that premiums be offered to encourage silk production. As a result, the following premiums were established:[73] for fifty thousand cocoons raised in Pennsylvania of saleable quality, fifty pounds; for forty thousand, ten pounds; for thirty thousand, six pounds; and for each of six raisers with no less than twenty thousand, three pounds. The first prize was won by Susanna Wright.[74]

Susanna Wright even wrote a treatise on the raising of silkworms in which she described every step of the process:

Lay the sheets of eggs in folds of dry ironed linen, in a drawer, in a room where but little fire is kept. As soon as the mulberry-buds begin to open into leaves in the spring, we should bring the sheets of eggs into a warm room, and lay them in a south window, where the sun may shine through the glass upon them . . .

Once the eggs have hatched, the silkworms would begin immediately to eat the mulberry leaves laid out for them and were then transferred to clean sheets of paper. When the silkworms were ready to spin their cocoons, their skins would "shine" and they would begin to "ramble in search of convenient places." Paper cones could be prepared for them, or "old trunks or boxes" filled with "small bushes, stript of their leaves." The cocoons were then either steamed over kettles of boiling water or placed in ovens "after the bread [was] taken out."[75]

Flowered silk damask cut as a bodice, circa 1770, a fragment of brown silk damask, and a carved wooden spindle wound with silk filament that were, by family tradition, of silk raised by Susanna Wright.

When the historian Robert Proud visited her in 1772, she had fifteen hundred silkworms under her care and told him she could have a million if properly encouraged. To promote the industry, the American Philosophical Society raised money by private subscription to set up a filature, hire a supervisor, and set prices for cocoons. In London, Benjamin Franklin conferred with some of the outstanding silk merchants to determine the best means of establishing the industry and wrote to Cadwalader Evans:

> *I have not now before me your Letter which came with the Sample of Silk, having put it into the Hands of Mr. Walpole with the Sample, who has promised me full and particular Answers to all your Queries, after the Silk has been thoroughly examined. In the mean time he tells me, the best Sort appears to him to be worth in itself 27 or 28 s. a pound; and will fetch that Price when some Imperfections*

54 *Wright's Ferry Mansion*

Brass smoothing iron with burl elm handle, probably England, 1750-1790. Hot iron slugs inserted into the hollow base provided the heat.

> *in the Reeling it are remedied. He tells me farther, that the best Eggs are to be had from Valentia in Spain, whence he will procure some for you against the next Year; the Worms from those Eggs being the strongest, healthiest, and producing the finest Silk of any others: And he thinks you should get some Reelers from Italy, which he would likewise undertake to do for you if desired. He is one of the most opulent and noble spirited Merchants of this Kingdom.*[76]

The shipment of eggs from Valencia duly followed but, unfortunately, spoiled en route. Evans wrote to Franklin requesting another supply and suggested a different method for packing them:

> *If Mr. Walpole, coud, without much trouble, procure us one or two pounds of Valencia eggs, I think they had better be put into wide mouth'd bottles, and several grooves cut in the sides of the corks, so as to admit a free communication with the outer air. Jarrs cover'd with Leather, and peirced with a large needle, or awl, might do as well. Another circumstance is worth attention; we think, a much*

Susanna Wright and Her Family 55

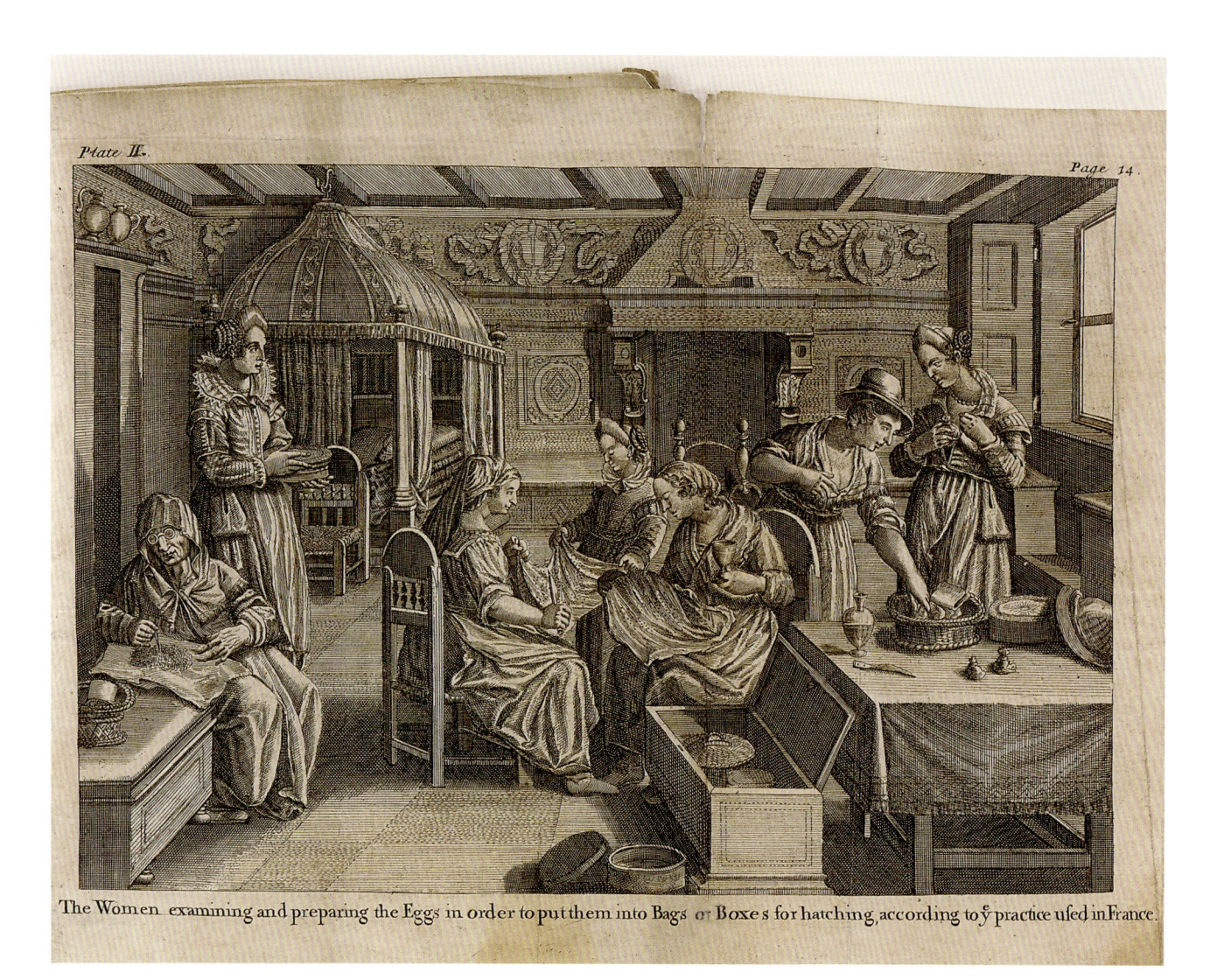

The Women examining and preparing the Eggs in order to put them into Bags or Boxes for hatching, according to ye practice used in France.

Copperplate engraving from *A Compendious Account of the Whole Art of Breeding, Nursing and The Right Ordering of the Silk-Worm*, London, 1733. A technique for speedier hatching was to keep the eggs constantly warm in a bodice (as shown on the right), or in a pocket (as seen on left), and at night, between warm pillows or under a bolster or bed. Susanna Wright's method was to put them on a sunny windowsill facing south.

lower degree of heat, will hatch the eggs in the Spring than the fall; if so, it will be best to send them in the forepart of winter, hung to some of the battens in the cabbin, rather than put in a chest, without the weather shoud be extream cold. We have hired a Languedocian to superintend the Filature next season, who says he was born and bred in the middle of a silk country; was always employed in the culture and manufacture of it, and having been in the East Indies, has some knowledge of their method and management of it also.[77]

By November of 1771, the filature in Philadelphia had produced 155 pounds of raw silk for exportation to London.[78] In the shipment, which was sent to Benjamin Franklin,

56 *Wright's Ferry Mansion*

Another illustration from *A Compendious Account*, which was published to promote the raising of silkworms in the "dominions of Britain," especially by the "new inhabitants of Georgia."

were gifts, including six pounds of silk for the Queen and four pounds each for Lady Juliana Penn, wife of Thomas Penn; Hannah Lardner Penn, widow of Richard Penn; and Ann Allen Penn, second wife of John Penn. On July 29, 1772, Franklin wrote back, reporting that the silk:

> *was presented to her Majesty, representing it as the first Fruits of a new Produce in Pennsylvania, humbly offered as a Mark of the affectionate Respect of her Subjects there; and that if she vouchsafed to do them the Honour of accepting and wearing it, they might be the more encouraged to proceed in producing a Commodity, very beneficial to her British Subjects. Her Majesty was pleased to accept*

it very graciously, and to say, that she would have it woven, and wear it on some public Occasion. I since hear that she proposes it for the King's Birth-day.[79]

While the silk had been at his house in London, Franklin had a number of people in the trade examine it and give their opinions and suggestions. "They all agreed, that the Staple was as good as any in the World, and that some of it was well reeled."[80] Their suggestion was to change the water often when reeling to clean the silk more thoroughly. This would also make it glossier. The previous year, Franklin had sent Cadwalader Evans "a Skain of what is called the best Italian Silk imported here, and [Mr. Patterson, an English silk manufacturer] advised me to send over as a Pattern, for our People to endeavour to imitate, with regard to its Evenness, Cleanness from Nibs and Lustre." He continued, "I observe that the Italian Silk had a sweet smell as if perfumed. He thinks it is the natural smell of the Silk when prepared in perfection."[81]

Within two weeks, Franklin followed with another letter, regarding the "Specimen of Italian Silk" for the colonists to imitate. "But they must not be discouraged if they should not come up to the Lustre of it, that being the very finest, and from a particular District in Italy, none other being equal to it from any other District or any other Country."[82]

Franklin tells how the silk from Europe, as well as that from India, is all yellow, whereas silk from China is white. Referring to John Ogilby's translation of Johan Nieuhof's *An Embassy from the East India Company of the United Provinces, to the Grand Tartar Chan, Emperour of China*, published in London in 1669, Franklin points out that in the province of Chekiang "they prune their Mulberry Trees once a year as we do our Vines in Europe, and suffer them not to grow up to high Trees," for "the greater Facility of gathering the Leaves." There, they also have cocoons from two spinnings: the first in March, which are superior, since the small, young leaves make the best silk, and the second in June, which make a coarser silk. He was not sure whether two crops would be feasible in Pennsylvania, since "it is not practis'd in Italy, tho' it might be try'd."[83]

The silk not sent as gifts to the Queen and to the Penns was sold at auction. Franklin was advised that by sending it to auction to be sold with silk from other countries, as well as from Carolina and Georgia, its true value could be discovered. The Pennsylvania silk sold for only four pence a pound less than the Carolina and Georgia silk. The Chinese, Indian, and Italian silks were only slightly higher.

I am farther told, what I did not know before and should not have imagined, that there is a vast Difference in the Waste of different Silks when they come to be dyed, viz from 5 to 30 per Cent. and that 'tis therefore a Wonder our Silk, the Waste of which is yet unknown, the Trade having had no Experience of it, would sell so well.[84]

Other details were recounted by Franklin. The Austrian Ambassador in London who was an Italian, Count Ludovico Barbiano di Belgioioso, had told him that in Italy "they have lately found the Reeds or Stalks of Indian Corn to make the best Grates, whereon to feed the Silk-worms."

Franklin pointed out that one "very knotty" bundle "sold extreamly low." Silk of that sort he said should not be sent to London but that it would be better "to work it up into stockings at home." He was heartened to hear that "besides what was sent here, fifty-four pounds [of silk] had been reeled at the filature of private persons, who are getting it manufactured into mitts, stockings, and stuffs."[85] Humphrey Marshall had also written to Franklin about local production: "there is Numbers of people that raises Silk reels it them Selves and mixes it With Worsted Which makes Good Sort of Crape Which Some of our people have made themselves Cloathes of already."[86]

Pennsylvania silk was also sent by individuals to England to be woven. Benjamin Franklin had learned from one silk broker that several Americans had sent:

> *small Parcels of 4, 5, or 6 lb. to be manufactered for them here to particular Patterns, which he said was very injudicious, as it was not worth while to set a Loom for a few Yards, and besides most kinds of Manufacture required Silk of different Sorts for the Warp and for the Woof, so that what the People expected was impracticable but at a greater than common Expence, and the Silk after all not entirely of their own Produce. This should be made known, that our People may rather work up their small Parcels at home.*[87]

Franklin was prevailed upon by the Rhode Island silk agent to supply Pennsylvania silk for one small commission that was lacking ten ounces for fabric to use for a gown. The silk was to be woven for the wife of Ezra Stiles, a proponent of American sericulture, "who had made many Experiments to improve the Knowledge in raising the Worms." The agent "knew Mrs. Stiles would not like her Silk mix'd with any not American."[88] Franklin provided the needed silk.

Franklin had witnessed directly the expense of these small commissions when his young neighbor in Philadelphia, Rebecca Haydock Garrigues, entrusted to him silk she had raised, asking that it be woven to a special pattern with specific colors. He wrote to his wife Deborah:

> *I receiv'd your young Neighbour Haddock's Silk and carried it my self to her Relations, who live very well, keeping a Linnen Drapers Shop in Bishop's Gate Street. They have a Relation in Spitalfields that is a Manufacturer who I believe will do it well. I shall honour much every young Lady that I find on my Return dress'd in Silk of their own raising.*[89]

When the young lady learned that the weaver could not do the specific pattern, she asked that the colors could be used that she had requested. The woven silk was ready to send the following February and the bill amounted to eight pounds six shillings for weaving forty-one and a half yards, which her father, a plumber, glazier, and house-painter, paid to Mrs. Franklin.[90]

The managers of the Philadelphia Silk Filature had sent a gift of four pounds of raw silk to Benjamin Franklin in appreciation for his assistance. He wrote to Deborah:

> *I have had it work'd up with some Addition of the same Silk into a French Grey Ducape, which is a fashionable Colour either for an old or young Woman. I therefore send it as a Present to you and Sally, understanding there is enough to make each of you a Negligée. If you should rather incline to sell it, it is valued here at 6 s. 6 d. per Yard; but I hope you will wear it.*[91]

Accordingly, Deborah Franklin and her daughter Sally had the heavy corded silk made into negligées, or loose gowns. Sally wrote, "I give you many thanks for the very elegant Silk, I never knew what it was to be proud of a new Garment before. This I shall wear with pride and pleasure."[92]

John Fanning Watson reports, "As early as 1770, Susanna Wright made a piece of mantua of sixty yards length, from her own cocoons, of which I have preserved some specimens in my MS. Annals in the City Library, page 165 and 170. She also made much sewing silk."[93] Heavier than taffeta, mantua was a silk of plain weave, named for the city renowned for its superb production of this fabric, which the English found "more Difficulty in imitating than any other."[94] The mantua of Susanna Wright's production was fashioned into a court dress for Queen Charlotte in 1770.[95]

Brother Jemmy

Susanna Wright's brother James also worked with her in raising silkworms. Because of his interest in natural history and colonial manufactures, he was elected to both the American Society and the American Philosophical Society of Philadelphia in 1768.[96] He had supplied John Bartram with information on an important find of mastodon fossils in the Ohio River Valley and had published a treatise on hemp and hop growing in Pennsylvania, having had firsthand experience with both those crops on the lands that he farmed.[97] He had inherited his father's land and farmed Susanna's, as well. He also had a still and, with neighbor Samuel Blunston, he owned and operated a grist mill on Shawnee Creek and provided much needed flour for General Braddock's troops during the French and Indian War.[98]

In 1745, 1746, and each year from 1749 through 1767, James Wright was elected to the Pennsylvania Assembly.[99] In 1753, he was one of the representatives for the Pennsylvania Assembly at the Treaty of Carlisle. It was perhaps because he remained in the Assembly

Page from John Fanning Watson's *Manuscript Annals of Philadelphia*, 1823, with a sample of silk raised by Susanna Wright at lower left. Courtesy of The Library Company of Philadelphia.

Susanna Wright and Her Family 61

Mezzotint, by John Smith (after a painting by Sir Godfrey Kneller), London, 1717. The image is of Queen Charlotte, who received sixty yards of silk raised by Susanna Wright.

throughout the French and Indian War that he was excluded from the Quaker meeting, since he "was responsible for collecting and shipping flour and other supplies to the army; he counseled and helped draft laws to quarter troops, house refugees, and tax the people 'for the King's use.'"[100]

James Wright worked with Samuel Blunston in public service, as well as on the lands at Wright's Ferry. The families had been close from first coming to the site in 1726. Susanna and James' sisters, Patience and Elizabeth, had been married on the same day in 1728 at the Blunstons' elegant new house; and their father John had worked closely with Samuel Blunston for many years.

Samuel Blunston and his wife had no children. He had married Sarah Bilton, a widow, on May 15, 1718. Samuel's brother John had two daughters, Hannah, who married Thomas Pearson in 1732, and Sarah, who married Samuel Bethel in 1729/30. In 1730, Samuel and

Sarah Bethel owned a tavern in Lancaster, eventually called Cross Keys Tavern, at 12–14 West King Street, near the courthouse. The tavern catered to Quakers and was a meeting place for the county commissioners. Samuel Bethel also had a brickyard and he furnished brick and other materials for the new courthouse, a project in which both Samuel Blunston and John Wright were involved. Samuel and Sarah Bethel had two children, Samuel and Mary.

In 1740, Samuel Bethel died and Samuel Blunston was made guardian of the two children in 1743/44.[101] In October 1744, however, both Sarah and Samuel Blunston became extremely ill. Although they had one of the finest doctors advising treatment, Dr. Lloyd Zachary of Philadelphia, Sarah was unable to recover and died on December 13, 1744. Samuel died the following September. New guardians appointed for the children were Thomas Cookson, Peter Worral (who had married their mother Sarah in 1741), and James Wright. It was James's niece Susannah Taylor (whose mother Elizabeth had been married in the Blunston house in 1728) that the young Samuel Bethel would eventually marry.[102]

One of the first buildings in the settlement at Wright's Ferry, Samuel Blunston's house was also one of the finest. Rather than being built of log, it was of stone and brick. Its entrance hall had elaborately turned staircase banisters and was virtually the same design that was used in Wright's Ferry Mansion. A looking glass was hung in the stair hall. The family had china bowls and plates, and "7 Chocolate Cups." The silver was valued at 143 pounds, some of it made for them by Philadelphia silversmith Joseph Richardson, Sr. The "River Chamber," with two looking glasses, six leather chairs, a bedstead dressed with white linen curtains, a calico quilt and a cotton coverlet, even included a "Swinging Bed & Fly Curtains." All of the chambers with bedsteads had luxurious feather beds, bolsters and pillows and were dressed with calico, silk, and cotton. The inventory, which was made in 1745, mentions old pieces, too, undoubtedly brought from their former house in Darby, outside of Philadelphia, including a chest, a tea table, and five leather chairs. One of the most sumptuous pieces was the "Scrutoire," or writing desk.[103] These furnished rooms Samuel Blunston left to Susanna Wright for use during her lifetime.

Samuel Blunston was generous to all of his friends in his will, which included Susanna Wright's brothers, James and John, and sister Patience; Robert Barber; the Norrises; Samuel Armitt, son of cabinetmaker Stephen Armitt; and his nieces Sarah Worral, mother of Samuel Bethel, and Hannah Pearson; as well as the young Samuel and Mary Bethel, when they would come of age. He also provided for his servants, insuring that those who were slaves would be freed at a specific time. "Negroe Sal," who was listed among the initial settlers who came in September 1726, was to be freed after one year and was to be paid five pounds annually. One of his paid servants was Rhoda Patterson, who was left thirty pounds "over and above any Wages that may be due to her." Eventually she was to marry James Wright.

To Susanna Wright, Samuel Blunston left "my Scrutoire; the Use and occupation of such other Household Goods as she may have occasion for to furnish her rooms during her Naturall Life and also two Milch Cows." In addition, she was given "all my Books & Vessells of Plate called Silver I also give her full Power & Liberty to Live on this Plantation and take and receive the Benefitt Use and Profitts of such part of the Buildings Land & Plantation as she shall think fitt during her Natural Life."[104] It was to this house that Susanna and James and his family moved between 1750 and 1755.

In 1753, James had married Rhoda Patterson. Their first child, Samuel, was perhaps born in Wright's Ferry Mansion, before they moved to the Blunston house. At about that time, Samuel Bethel had married their niece Susannah Taylor. Wright's Ferry Mansion was to be the new home of Samuel and Susannah Bethel. The first inventory of the house which was rented to them was made during their occupancy. This occurred in 1777, after the death of Samuel Bethel in 1775. The Bethels had had a large family—six girls and a boy—who continued to live there until 1785. Then they moved to the Blunston house, which the young Samuel Bethel eventually owned.

James Wright also died in 1775, leaving a large family, three girls and four boys. Susanna Wright became one of the guardians of his children, whom she raised with love and care, just as she had done when her mother had died and she was the eldest. By 1775, none of her other siblings were alive and she was the last of the group who had purchased land in the early settlement.

"A bubble on the water's shining face"

Musing on the ephemeral quality of life, Susanna Wright composed this line on the occasion of her birthday in 1761.[105] Writing—both poetry and letters—was central to her life and she was highly esteemed for her work. By the 1770s her associations with Philadelphia grew stronger and she corresponded often with the Norrises, Charles Thomson, the Franklins, and the Pembertons. Through her lifetime, she had corresponded with several different generations, which, by this time, included aspiring young poets who were the children of friends. Fortunately it was the ongoing exchange of letters and poetry that has provided such a clear image of this period and has helped preserve these writings.

Philadelphia friends would always make a point of coming to visit her. On April 7, 1784, Dr. Benjamin Rush, returning from the first meeting of the trustees of Dickinson College with John Dickinson, recorded in his diary:

> *Dined at Col. Hartley's and rode after dinner to Wright's Ferry. Mr. Dickinson introduced me to Mr. Wright's family, where I saw the famous Suzey Wright, a lady who has been celebrated above half a century for her wit, good sense and valuable improvement of mind. She has been for many years the friend and correspondent of Dr. Franklin. She is now in her 88th year and has declined a good deal in strength and in her mental faculties. She told me that she had lived 62 years at this place and that when she first came here there were no inhabitants in*

York County and none on this side of Lancaster 10 miles from the ferry. She told me further that her appetite was good, that she still retained her relish for books "that she could not live without them"—and that, to use her own words, "the pleasure of reading was to her a most tremendous blessing." She said she could remember the events of childhood better than she did in the middle of her life.[106]

On December 1 of that year, Susanna Wright died. The notice of her death in the *Pennsylvania Gazette* read:

On the first instant departed this life, at Hempfield, in Lancaster County, Mrs. Susanna Wright, in the 88th year of her age. She was born in Lancashire, in England, and removed with her father's family, in the autumn of 1726, to the banks of the Susquehanna, at that time nearly a wilderness. Possessed of an elevated understanding, improved by acquired knowledge to an eminent degree, she was distinguished by her superior benevolence, evinced by a multitude of pious and charitable offices done in the course of her long life, towards those within her beneficent sphere.[107]

This remarkable woman carefully provided for the children of her brother James. To the eldest, Samuel, she bequeathed most of her estate, with the stipulation that:

his Mother Rhoda Wright shall have Absolute Right and Privilege to Occupy with her Children the Dwelling house on the said Land Now Occupy'd By Susanna Bethel with the Garden and other Conveniences appertaining to the said house

which would be a "home for all the Children as long as they or any of them are destitute of other Convenient home." She added: "I need not Inforce their Brothers Kindness to them his Afectionate Regard for every Part of his family and his Rectitude of heart will Secure to his Mother & Brothers & Sisters every good Office in his Power."[108]

For advice and assistance, Samuel was to rely upon "the able and never failing friend of our whole family the Benevolent John Dickinson." Samuel was to hold in equal shares with his three brothers John, James, and William, the ferry property, which was then "in the tenure of Joseph Jeffrys." It consisted of the ferry house and surrounding land and "Also the House Builded for a Smith to live in with the Garden."

Samuel was also to receive Susanna Wright's "escrutoire" and her silver coffeepot, while the rest of the silver was to be divided equally among the children of her brother James, as were other "tryfles." At that time there were seven children, the two youngest being eleven and fourteen: Samuel (1754–1811), John (1760–1806), Elizabeth (1758–1785), Susanna (1764–1821), James (1766–1838), William (1770–1846), and Patience (1773–1821).

To Susanna ("Sukey"), she left the "Silver tweezer which was given me by my Father." She instructed that "the Old Watch which was my Grandfathers & has Continued to go more than 100 years, I desire may not be Suffered to goe out of the family." The disposal of her books was left to the discretion of her executor, Samuel Wright, "after what shall be taken out for the use of the Family."

After Susanna Wright's death, in keeping with her wishes, Wright's Ferry Mansion became a home for her eldest nephew Samuel, who was still unmarried, his mother Rhoda, and his siblings Susanna, James, William, and Patience. Two of his siblings had married: John in 1782 to Amelia Davies and Elizabeth in 1784 to Colonel Thomas Boude. In 1788 his brother James married Elizabeth Barber.

The year 1788 marked another important event. Samuel Wright had divided a portion of the land he had inherited into a series of lots laid out in a gridiron pattern, like the city of Philadelphia (see p. 71). He numbered them and auctioned them off in a lottery, a common method used to encourage the settlement of a town. He named the town Columbia, which was proposed as a site for the capital of the new nation in 1788, losing by a narrow margin to Washington, DC.

When the land was divided, a large portion was kept surrounding the house, which was designed with an open expanse toward the river, the original front prospect of the house (see pp. 40–41, 71). The orchards, which were to the back of the house, remained there at least as late as 1840.[109] About 1800 a brick meetinghouse was built a short distance away, on Cherry Street near Third Street, on land that Samuel Wright had given to the Society of Friends.

In 1795 Samuel Wright married Susan Loudon and probably made changes to the house at that time, since alterations from that period were present in the house at the time of its restoration in 1974. At the end of the eighteenth century, Samuel's remaining siblings married.

Samuel and Susan Wright had three children but only one survived to adulthood, John Loudon Wright (1797–1856). His mother died three years after he was born. At his father's death in 1811, he inherited the house. He was married twice, first in 1820, to Elizabeth Strickler, who died two years after their marriage, and then to Ann Evans (1806–1894) in 1828. They had ten children. The eldest, named Samuel after his grandfather, took great interest in the family history and published his research on the history of Columbia.[110] He and his brother William fought in the Civil War. Columbia played a significant role in the war, when the bridge across the Susquehanna was burned to prevent the advance of Confederate troops. The Wright family was also active in the Underground Railroad.

John's children who had inherited the house as tenants in common were the last generation of Wrights to own the house. In 1922 it was sold to Carrie W. Rasbridge, whose son Emmett lived in the house until it was purchased by The von Hess Foundation in 1973. By the time of the Rasbridges' occupancy, the house had lost its pent eaves and two small porches had been added, as well as a frame extension on the kitchen end. When the extension had been added, the squirrel tail oven had been removed, although the foundation of it remained. Overall, however, the house survived remarkably intact.

NOTES

1. Norris Papers, Family Letters, vol. 2, p. 42, Historical Society of Pennsylvania; see Appendix in this volume.
2. Bible Records II, Ph. 42 A:8, Genealogical Society of Pennsylvania. According to the method of dating used here, the first month was March, so the second month would be April and the ninth month would have been November.
3. Dorothy Wright of Cadishead, inventory dated 1708; WCW Dorothy Wright 1708, Lancashire Record Office; see Appendix in this volume.
4. Peter Robinson of Liverpool, will dated 1703; WCW Peter Robinson 1703, Lancashire Record Office; see Appendix in this volume.
5. Susanna Wright to William Croudson, Jr., July 1, 1714, Library of the Religious Society of Friends, Friends House, London; see Appendix in this volume. This letter and other correspondence disproves the statement made by some twentieth-century writers that Susanna Wright did not come to America with her family, but stayed in England to complete her education. No eighteenth-century source supports that idea. Perhaps that assumption was made because of the arrival of only three Wright children and their parents. The fourth child, James, was born several months later.
6. Susanna Wright to Mary Norris, September 22, 1772, Wright's Ferry Mansion, 83.18.104 (hereafter cited as WFM); see Appendix in this volume.
7. Gilbert Cope, *Genealogy of the Sharpless Family* (Westchester, PA: Dando-Printing Co., 1887), p. 41 (hereafter cited as *Genealogy*).
8. Ibid.
9. John Gough, *History of the People Called Quakers*, vol. 3 (Dublin: Robert Jackson, 1789), pp. 154–55 (hereafter cited as *History*).
10. Walter Lee Sheppard, "John Wright, Lancaster County, Pennsylvania," *American Genealogist* 40, no. 1 (January 1964): 40 (hereafter cited as *John Wright*). Joseph Besse, *A Collection of the Sufferings of the People called Quakers*, vol. 1 (1753), pp. 102, 255, 309, 437–38, 443, 469. These are also recorded in Friends Records of London and Middlesex and the Lancashire Quarterly Meeting.
11. F.J. Dallett, "Certain Pennsylvania Settlers," *American Genealogist* 41, no. 4 (October 1965): 219 (hereafter cited as *Settlers*). In 1682 in a letter to Jasper Yeates, Penn mentions "dear . . . Willm Gibson."
12. W.L. Sheppard, *John Wright*, p. 41–42. Pennsylvania Archives, 1st Series, vol. 1, p. 45, has five thousand in error. The five hundred acres were laid out in 1701 in Bucks County for his son, William Gibson. William's brother John had inherited the land; see F.J. Dallett, *Settlers*, p. 219.
13. W.L. Sheppard, *John Wright*, p. 42. This was lot 35 Delaware Back between Front Street and Delaware Avenue, where Cherry Street eventually cut through. See Warrants and Surveys, vol. 1, Philadelphia Municipal Archives, p. 387.
14. F.J. Dallett, *Settlers*, p. 218; New Jersey Archives, 1st Series, vol. XXI: p. 56.
15. F.J. Dallett, *Settlers*, p. 219; because of the dating of documents, he was present in London to sign during this period.
16. Ibid. His son John was also a haberdasher and his son William, a mercer.
17. W.L. Sheppard, *John Wright*, p. 40.
18. Ibid., p. 41.
19. F.J. Dallett, *Settlers*, p. 219; William Gibson, Will dated 1685, folio 5, PCC Register, London.
20. H. Frank Eshleman, "The Public Career of John Wright, Esq.," *Journal of the Lancaster County Historical Society* XIV, no. 9 (1910): 251 (hereafter cited as *Public Career*).
21. Ibid.
22. James Logan to Susanna Wright, December 27, 1718. *Publications of the Pennsylvania Society of Colonial Dames of America* no. 2 (1906): 9.
23. Susanna Wright to Hannah Griffitts, April 5, 1762, WFM 83.18.11; see Appendix in this volume.

24. This description is taken from Frederick B. Tolles, *Meeting House and Counting House: The Quaker Merchants of Colonial Philadelphia 1682–1763* (1948; reprint, New York: W. W. Norton, 1963), p. 133 (hereafter cited as *Meeting House*).
25. James Logan came to the site in 1705, 1720, 1721, and 1722. See Barry C. Kent, *Susquehanna's Indians* (Harrisburg, PA: Pennsylvania Historical Society and Museum Commission, 1989) p. 61 (hereafter cited as *Susquehanna's Indians*); citing Hanna 1911, II: 40, 151, 153, 164, 208; III: 347.
26. John Fanning Watson, *Annals of Philadelphia and Pennsylvania*, vol. 2 (Philadelphia: E. S. Stuart, 1884), p. 167 (hereafter cited as *Annals*).
27. J. Gough, *History*, vol. 4, pp. 153–54. The quotation in the sixth line set off as in Gough.
28. Edwin B. Bronner and David Fraser, *The Papers of William Penn*, vol. 5, *William Penn's Published Writings 1660–1726* (Philadelphia: University of Pennsylvania Press, 1986), pp. 367–69 (hereafter cited as *William Penn*). The five thousand acres has been changed to three in two copies of this document.
29. Ibid., p. 369.
30. Pennsylvania Archives, 1st Series, vol. I, 133.
31. B. C. Kent, *Susquehanna's Indians*, p. 60, 382–83. Excavations revealed houses fifteen feet by fifty feet, fifteen feet by thirty-five feet, and twenty feet by at least forty feet.
32. Frederick B. Tolles, *James Logan and the Culture of Provincial America* (Westport, CT: Greenwood Press, 1957).
33. Ibid.
34. The text and a commentary on this complex and fascinating manuscript are currently being prepared for publication.
35. Since the ferry crossed the river, both landings were sometimes referred to as Wright's Ferry.
36. Isaac Norris to Susanna Wright, April 18, 1728; Norris Papers, Family Letters, vol. 2, p. 42, Historical Society of Pennsylvania; see Appendix in this volume.
37. Unidentified newspaper clipping among Wright family papers.
38. Franklin Ellis and Samuel Evans, *History of Lancaster County, Pennsylvania* (Philadelphia: Evarts and Peck, 1883), p. 583 (hereafter cited as *Lancaster County*). This source contains many inaccuracies regarding Wright history, but it is cited here because of the dearth of information regarding John Wright's house. When the house was demolished, Samuel Evans and James Wright had walking sticks made of the wood from John Wright's log house. James Wright's has a silver head engraved, "James Wright, July 8th 1874, From Timber of House built by John Wright Sen. at Columbia, Pa. in 1726." The other stick has an ivory head and two ferrules, a plain one of brass and one of silver, which is engraved, "John Wright/Samuel Evans 1874."
39. Inventory of John Wright, October 31, 1749, Lancaster County Historical Society, Court House Records.
40. See Appendix in this volume for inventories of these houses.
41. Sarah Barber, *Extracts of Columbia's History* (1830), p. 4, WFM 83.18.125 (hereafter cited as *Extracts*).
42. E. B. Bronner and D. Fraser, *William Penn*, pp. 367–69.
43. Charles Norris to James Wright, February 15, 1753; Norris Papers, misc. vol., p. 15, Historical Society of Pennsylvania.
44. Charles A. Poulson in J. Thomas Scharf and Thompson Westcott, *History of Philadelphia*, vol. 2 (Philadelphia, 1884), p. 870 (hereafter cited as *History of Philadelphia*).
45. Stevenson Whitcomb Fletcher, *Pennsylvania Agriculture and Country Life* (Harrisburg, PA: Pennsylvania Historical and Museum Commission, 1950–1955), pp. 206–208 (hereafter cited as *Pennsylvania Agriculture*).
46. Peter Kalm, *Travels in North America*, trans. by John Reinhold Forster (Barre, ME: Imprint Society, 1972), pp. 44–45.
47. 1683 "Letter" of Thomas Paschall, cited in S. W. Fletcher, *Pennsylvania Agriculture*, p. 207.
48. Edward Shippen to Samuel Blunston, March 5, 1736/7, WFM 83.18.50.
49. Undated letter from Susanna Wright to Deborah Franklin, published in George L. Heiges, "Benjamin Franklin in Lancaster County," *Journal of the Lancaster County Historical Society* 61, no. 1 (January 1957): 5.
50. Eliza Cope Harrison, ed., *Philadelphia Merchant: The Diary of Thomas P. Cope 1800–1851* (South Bend, IN: Gateway Editions, 1978), p. 14.

51. Son of the Robert Barber who established the settlement in 1726, Robert Barber (1722–1782) was married to Sarah Taylor, Susanna Wright's niece, daughter of Samuel and Elizabeth Wright Taylor; Articles of Agreement with Robert Barber, March 30, 1750, WFM 83.18.173.
52. Samuel Wright, "Hempfield: The Beginning of Columbia," *Journal of the Lancaster County Historical Society* 17, no. 8 (1913): 225.
53. There were a number of ferries on the Susquehanna River in the eighteenth century. The two closest to Wright's Ferry were Anderson's Ferry and Thomas Cresap's. F. Ellis and S. Evans, *Lancaster County*, p. 540, says that in 1730 Thomas Cresap received a patent from Lord Baltimore for a ferry at "Blue Rock," four miles below Wright's Ferry.
54. "Travel Diary of Bishop and Mrs. Reichel and their Company from Lititz to Salem in the Wachau (Wachovia) from May 22 to June 15, 1780," in *Travels in the American Colonies*, ed. Newton D. Mereness (New York: Antiquarian Press, Ltd., 1961), pp. 586–87.
55. John Wright had petitioned for a road between Lancaster and Wright's Ferry in 1734.
56. F. Ellis and S. Evans, *Lancaster County*, p. 547.
57. The house still stands today. Edwin Atlee Barber, *Genealogy of the Barber Family* (Philadelphia: William F. Fell & Co., 1890), pp. 36–37. The elder Robert Barber's house had previously been owned by his other sons, Thomas and then by Nathaniel Barber, ibid., p. 91.
58. Ibid., p. 147.
59. In his journal entry for August 30, 1787, Samuel Vaughan says that he "went from the ferry to NE point where is Chickies Rock. 305 feet high as measured by Dr. Franklin;" see Diary of Samuel Vaughan. Benjamin Franklin to Susanna Wright, November 21, 1751; see L. W. Labaree, et al., eds., *Papers*, vol. 4, pp. 210–11; see Appendix in this volume.
60. Susanna Wright to Isaac Norris, November 14, 1749, Family Letters, vol. 2, p. 46, Norris Papers, Historical Society of Pennsylvania.
61. Deborah Norris Logan, "Notice of Susanna Wright," *Analectic Magazine* V (Philadelphia, 1815): 250–52 (hereafter cited as *Susanna Wright*); see Appendix in this volume.
62. See pp. 148, 149, 272 in Appendix in this volume.
63. Dr. Charles Moore to Susanna Wright, May 15, 1761; copy (partial text), private collection; Dr. Charles Moore to Susanna Wright, March 20, (n.d.); copy (partial text), private collection.
64. James Logan to Samuel Blunston, February 25, (n.d.), WFM 83.18.162.
65. J. F. Watson, *Annals*, vol. 3, p. 21.
66. Brooke Hindle, *The Pursuit of Science in Revolutionary America 1735–1789* (Chapel Hill, NC: University of North Carolina Press, 1956), pp. 139–45 (American Philosophical Society); and pp. 107–108, 140, 199–204, 355 (silk); for the public filature, see J. F. Watson, *Annals*, vol. 2, p. 437.
67. J. F. Watson, vol. 2, p. 436.
68. Edwin Wolf 2nd, *The Library of James Logan of Philadelphia, 1674–1751* (Philadelphia: The Library Company of Philadelphia, 1974), p. xxv.
69. J. F. Watson, *Annals*, vol. 2, p. 437.
70. Norris Papers, misc. vol., p. 24, Historical Society of Pennsylvania.
71. L. W. Labaree, et al, eds., *Papers*, vol. 16, p. 179.
72. Benjamin Franklin to Cadwalader Evans, September 7, 1769; ibid., vol. 16, pp. 200–201.
73. Albert K. Hostetter, "The Early Silk Industry of Lancaster County," *Proceedings of the Lancaster County Historical Society* XXIII, no. 2 (1919): 30 (hereafter cited as *Early Silk*). The premiums were published in the *Pennsylvania Gazette*, July 29, 1772.
74. Ibid. See also Scharf and Westcott's *History of Philadelphia*, vol. 3, p. 2312.
75. Susanna Wright, "Directions for the Management of Silk-Worms," *Philadelphia Medical and Physical Journal* I, no. XXVIII (1804): 103–107; see Appendix in this volume.
76. Benjamin Franklin to Cadwalader Evans, February 10, 1771; L. W. Labaree, et al., eds., *Papers*, vol. 18, pp. 31–32.
77. Cadwalader Evans to Benjamin Franklin, May 4, 1771; ibid., vol. 18, p. 97.
78. The Managers of the Philadelphia Silk Filature to Benjamin Franklin and John Fothergill, November 8, 1771; ibid., vol. 18, p. 245.
79. Benjamin Franklin to the Managers of the Philadelphia Silk Filature [May 10, 1772]; ibid., vol. 19, p. 135.
80. Ibid.

81. Benjamin Franklin to Cadwalader Evans, July 4, 1771; ibid., vol. 18, pp. 159–60.
82. Benjamin Franklin to Cadwalader Evans, July 18, 1771; ibid., vol. 18, p. 188.
83. Ibid.
84. Ibid., vol. 19, p. 138. On December 27, 1775, Benjamin Franklin wrote to an Italian, Philip Mazzei, that the Pennsylvania silk for the three years in which it had been sent to London sold at auction for about nineteen shillings and six pence, for "the small pound [i.e. sixteen ounces; the great or Italian pound was twenty-four ounces], which was not much below the Silk from Italy" (pp. 308–309).
85. Benjamin Franklin to Cadwalader Evans, May 5, 1772; L. W. Labaree, et al., eds., *Papers*, vol. 19, pp. 129, 136. See also J. F. Watson, *Annals*, vol. 2, pp. 436–38; and *The Pennsylvania Magazine of History and Biography* xxxiii (1914): 123–24.
86. Humphrey Marshall to Benjamin Franklin, November 27, 1771; L. W. Labaree, et al., eds., *Papers*, vol. 18, p. 254.
87. Benjamin Franklin to the Managers of the Philadelphia Silk Filature, May 10, 1772; ibid., vol. 19, p. 137.
88. Ibid., vol. 19, p. 137.
89. Benjamin Franklin to Deborah Franklin, January 28, 1772; ibid., vol. 19, p. 43. See also pp. 64–65, 212, 231, 365.
90. Benjamin Franklin to Rebecca Haydock Garrigues, February 14, 1773; ibid., vol. 20, p. 68. The original bill had come to £11.1.4, which mistakenly included a charge for the silk itself. Franklin had caught the error and had the receipt corrected.
91. Benjamin Franklin to Deborah Franklin, July 15, 1773; ibid., vol. 20, p. 318.
92. Sarah Bache to Benjamin Franklin, October 30, 1773; ibid., vol. 20, pp. 449, 452.
93. J. F. Watson, *Annals*, vol. 2, p. 437.
94. Florence M. Montgomery, *Textiles in America 1650–1870* (New York: W. W. Norton, 1984), p. 289.
95. A. K. Hostetter, *Early Silk*, p. 30, says that as a result of this, the Pennsylvania Assembly voted the society £10,000.
96. Whitfield J. Bell, Jr., *Patriot Improvers: Biographical Sketches of Members of the American Philosophical Society* (Philadelphia: American Philosophical Society, 1997), vol. II, pp. 114–18 (hereafter cited as *Patriot Improvers*). Those two societies merged that same year. James Wright sent to the society "seeds of the cucumber tree 'resembling Cucumbers for Pickling.'"
97. James Wright, "Hemp and Hop Growing in Lancaster County in 1775," *Journal of the Lancaster County Historical Society* 9, no. 9 (1905): 285–93, 301–302; see Appendix in this volume.
98. Michael Gross to James Wright, October 30, 1755; see Appendix in this volume. Accounts for distilling grain are given in the account book bound by William Davies.
99. 2 *Pennsylvania Archives*, vol. XI, pp. 772, 773, 776–78.
100. W. J. Bell, Jr., *Patriot Improvers*, vol. II, p. 115.
101. Lancaster County Miscellaneous Book: 1742–1760, February 1743/44, Lancaster County Orphans Court.
102. Sadsbury Meeting Monthly Minutes. "Account of Recd. and paid by James Wright one of the Guardians of Samuel Bethel"; WFM Vellum Portfolio, p. 9.
103. Inventory of Samuel Blunston, 1745, Pearson Family Papers, Historical Society of Pennsylvania; see Appendix.
104. Will of Samuel Blunston, September 22, 1745; see Appendix in this volume.
105. "My Own Birth day August 4th, 1761"; see p. 219 in Appendix in this volume.
106. George L. Heiges, "Benjamin Franklin in Lancaster County," *Journal of the Lancaster County Historical Society* 61, no. 1 (January 1957): 6.
107. *Pennsylvania Gazette*, December 22, 1784, no. 2846.
108. Will of Susanna Wright, January 28, 1782; see Appendix in this volume.
109. F. Ellis and S. Evans, *Lancaster County*, p. 550, records that in that year a salute was fired in the orchard of John L. Wright, between Second and Third Streets and alleys J and K.
110. Samuel Wright, "Hempfield: The Beginning of Columbia," *Journal of the Lancaster County Historical Society* 17, no. 8 (1913): 215–16.

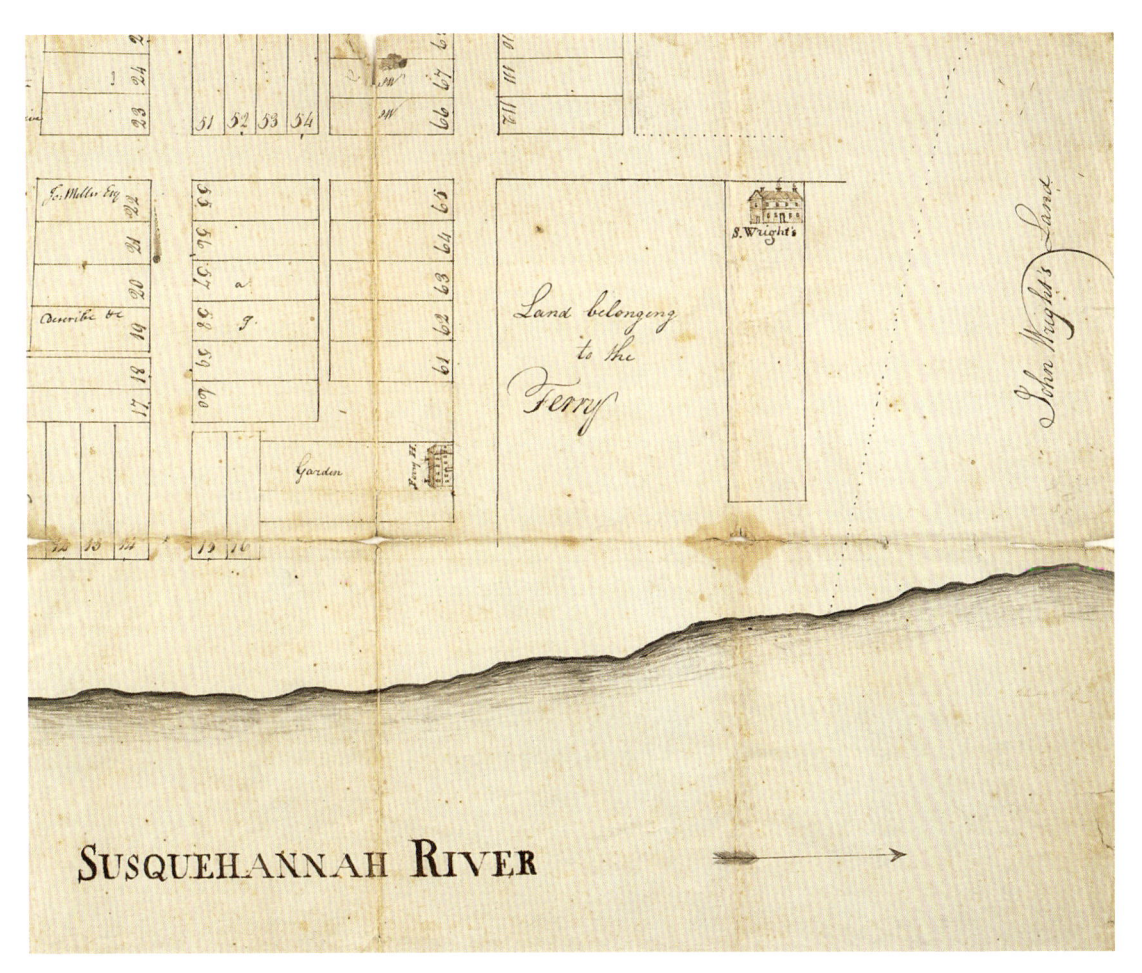

Drawing of lots laid out in 1788 by Samuel Wright for the newly established town of Columbia. He inherited Wright's Ferry Mansion, which is shown as "S. Wright's," and kept the land behind it as orchards. His brother John's land is shown at the right. The land belonging to the ferry and the Ferry House and Garden were also kept intact. Although other buildings were on these properties, like their grandfather's log house, they are not shown.

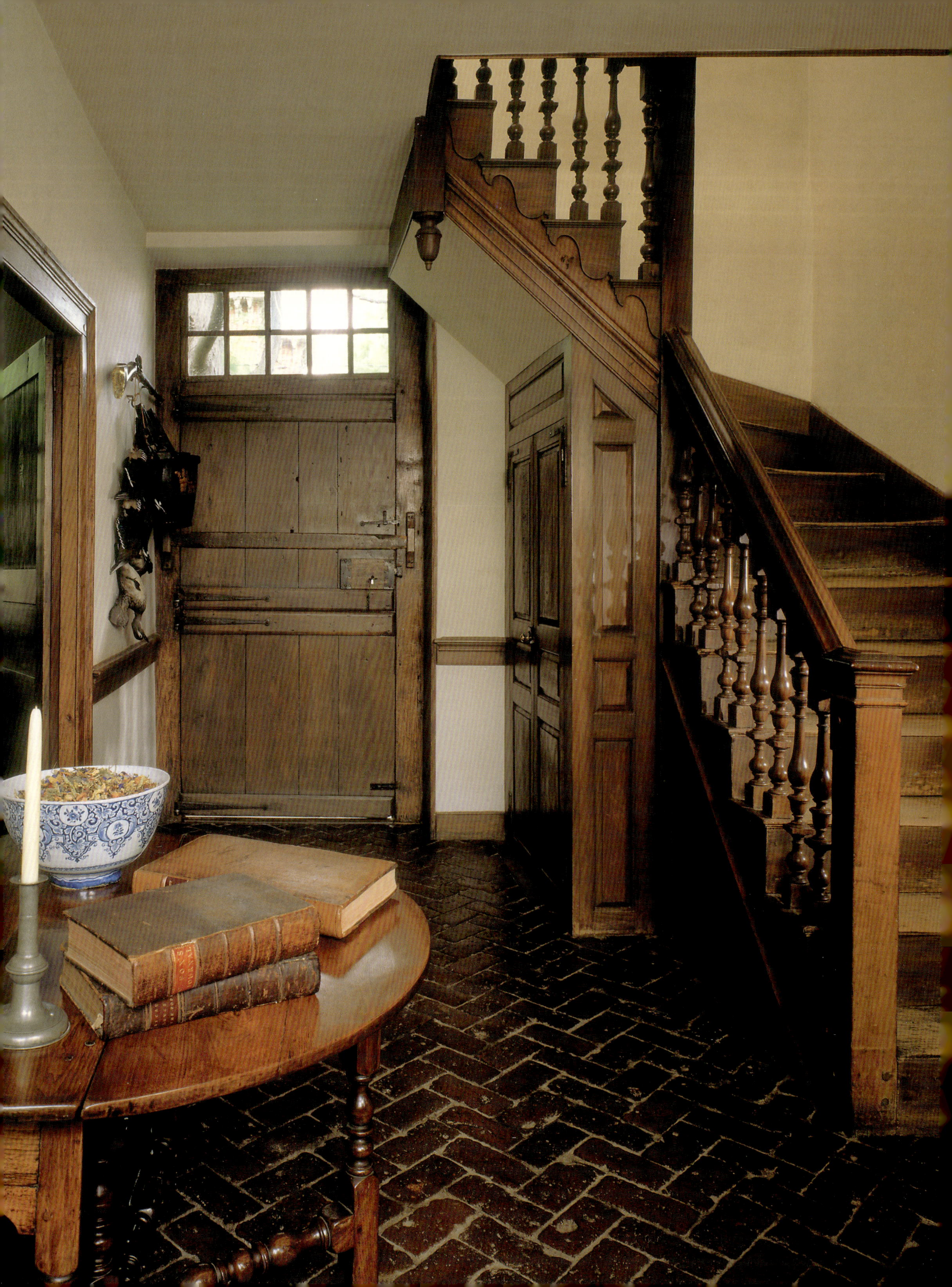

THE MANSION'S INTERIOR:
THE ROOMS AND THEIR FURNISHINGS

*F*ollowing an English architectural form, Wright's Ferry Mansion is one-room deep almost its full length, with rooms laid out in a linear, or "processional," plan, moving hierarchically from the most formal room at one end of the building to the least at the opposite end (see p. 74). The entry, or hall, with stairs to the upper chambers, is placed off-center with the parlor to one side and the dining room and kitchen to the other. There are exterior doors on each gable end of the house, one to the parlor, the other to the kitchen. There are no windows on the gable ends. The plan has an elegant simplicity accentuated by long windows on both sides of the rooms, high ceilings, and paneling on the fireplace wall of each of the four formal rooms. The clarity and practicality of the design reflect careful thought in planning.

The Entry

The entry, or "passage," eighteenth-century terms for what we would now call a hall, is axial to the house, giving access to the outside, both front and back, to the adjacent rooms, and to the upstairs and downstairs. It contains two massive pine-sheathed doors, opposite each other, one leading originally (as the front door) onto an open expanse traveling down to the Susquehanna River, the other giving access to the back of the house onto orchards, fields, and woodland. Double transoms provide illumination above each exterior door and are augmented by a long narrow window, just two panes wide, beside the front door facing west toward the river. Dominating this room is the marvelous staircase with its boldly turned banisters of black cherry (*Prunus serotina*). Beneath the staircase is a door leading to cellar steps. This room shows the transitional style of the house since

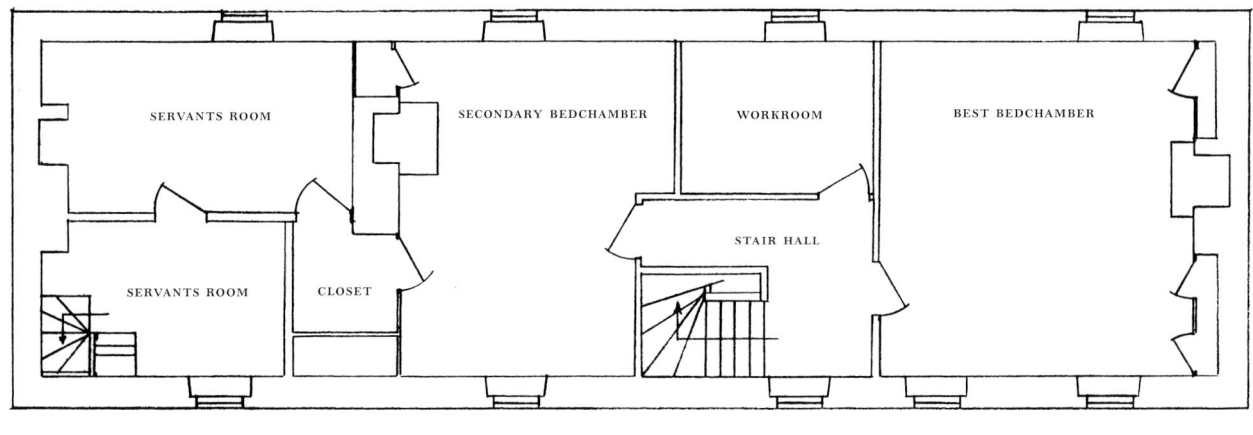

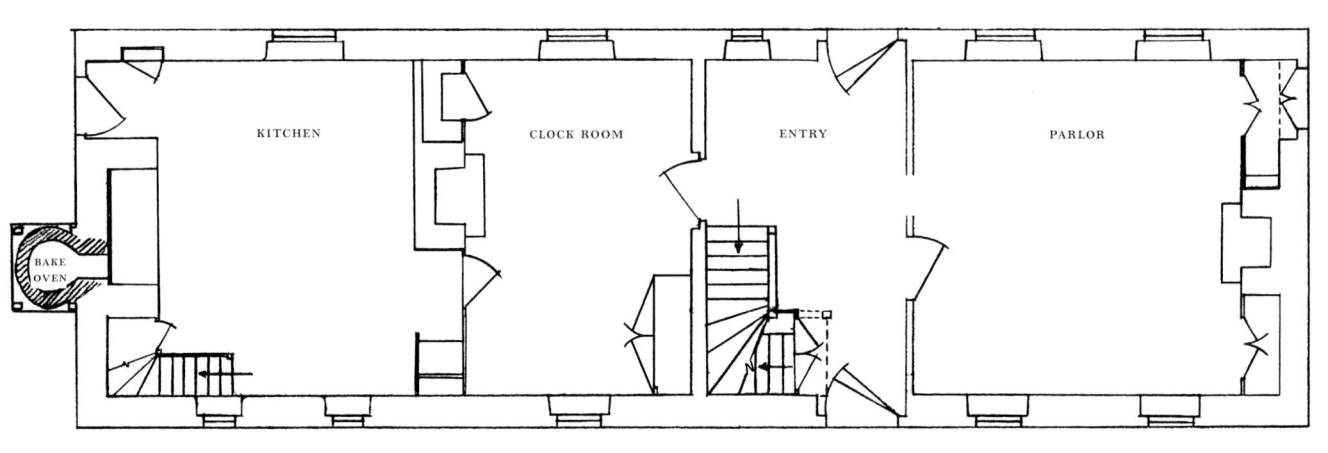

Floor plan of Wright's Ferry Mansion — SECOND FLOOR / FIRST FLOOR — SCALE: ¼" = 1'0"

it contains William and Mary features while revealing early Georgian elements in the neighboring rooms.

The late seventeenth-century architectural elements in the entry would have had a welcome familiarity, particularly appropriate to a room that is the main entrance to the house. The use of these seventeenth-century elements for an entry echoes Susanna Wright's own reminiscences of beloved houses from the past—that of her grandfather in Lancashire, England, of which she remembered "every part & Cranny of it" and that of one of her close friends in Pennsylvania, Isaac Norris I.[1] The older architectural elements present in this entry include the doorways strongly framed in oak, with frames and moldings all of one piece rather than applied separately; the squarish shape of the room; the use of a brick floor rather than wood; the fine line incised in the plaster surrounding the window; the massive, sheathed doors, divided horizontally, commonly known as a "Dutch door," although it was a style used in England and in Europe; the cyma curve of the upper face of the chair rail; and the stairway with its vigorously turned banisters, so typical of the William and Mary period and outstanding in their vitality and refinement of detail. Although the interior walls in the rest of the house are made of plaster and lath, the interior walls of this room are made of brick that was plastered and whitewashed. This is a seventeenth-century feature that stems from building codes instituted in England as a result of the fire of London in 1666, the brick acting as a masonry core in the center of the building to protect against fire.

Prototypes for architectural elements in this entry are evident in the houses of two of Susanna Wright's friends, James Logan and Samuel Blunston, both of whom were building houses in 1726, when the Wrights moved to this site. Logan's house, Stenton, located near Philadelphia, at Germantown, has a brick floor in the entry, a staircase with a similar molded handrail, a long, narrow window two panes wide beside the door, and a transom above the door. Stenton also has arched doors with a central keystone, as does Wright's Ferry Mansion in the adjacent parlor.

The most striking similarity with another house of the period, however, is seen in the close resemblance of the entry of Wright's Ferry Mansion and that of the neighboring house that was built by Samuel Blunston. Although Blunston's house was greatly altered in later years, portions of the original house remained. Photographs taken of the entry before the house was demolished in the 1930s reveal a striking similarity with Wright's Ferry Mansion. The similarities include the placement of the staircase with a Dutch door beside it leading to the outside, the door with the same sheathed construction and bearing similar hinges; a paneled door with HL hinges beneath the staircase; and the same molded handrail on the staircase. The closest connection, however, is the marvelous form of the turnings in the staircase banisters, which are identical to those in Wright's Ferry Mansion, a form which is complex and distinctive with an urn-shaped element.[2]

A turner who could produce work of the sophistication shown in these banisters would be rare to find at this time in the remote country along the Susquehanna River. Samuel Blunston began building his elegant house soon after his move to the site in 1726, and it is likely that the banisters were made in the Philadelphia area. The quality of the turnings certainly supports this, since it reflects the same quality present in the turnings of furniture that was made in Philadelphia. In addition, banisters of the same elegance and complexity, with the distinctive urn-shaped element found at Wright's Ferry Mansion, were present in a house near Chester and Darby called the Glebe House, which was built in 1698, on the lower Schuylkill River.[3] The structure of the house also shares similarities with Wright's Ferry Mansion.[4]

In addition, that the staircase at Wright's Ferry Mansion was made elsewhere and then installed here is supported by evidence in the staircase itself. Edwin Brumbaugh notes two mistakes made in the original installation of the staircase, at odds with the quality of the banisters, posts, and trim. At the first newel post, the peg is in the wrong position (see p. 76) and, in the second floor hall, where the railing turns, instead of using a post, there is a clumsy doubling of banisters.[5]

OVERLEAF: Entrance hall, or entry, with furniture made in Philadelphia of walnut: the oval-leaf table (1710–1740); the side table (1710–1740); and the armchair (1690–1720). The bowl (1720–1735) and urn with flowers (1725–1735) are English delftware.

The Mansion's Interior: The Rooms and Their Furnishings 75

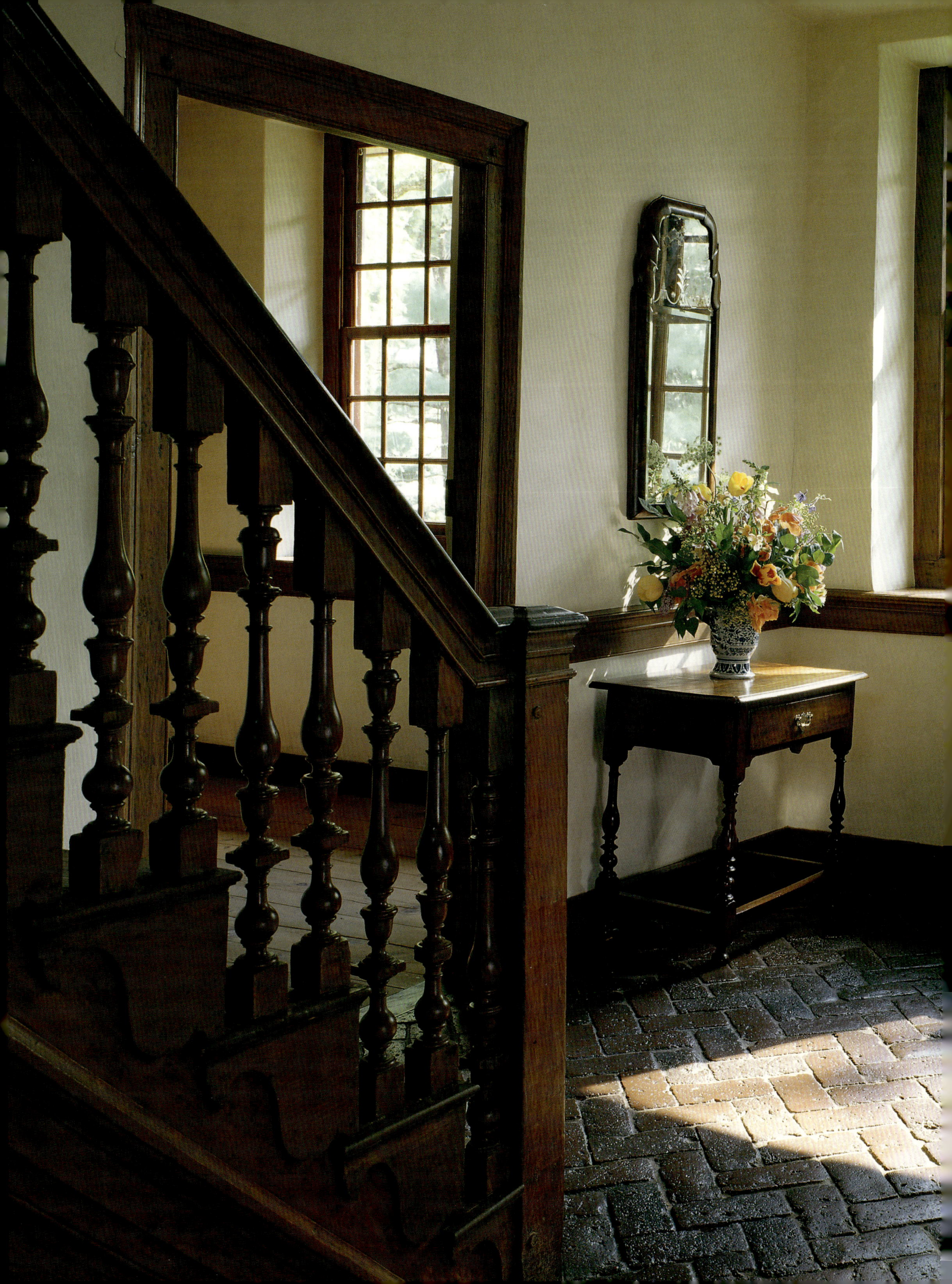

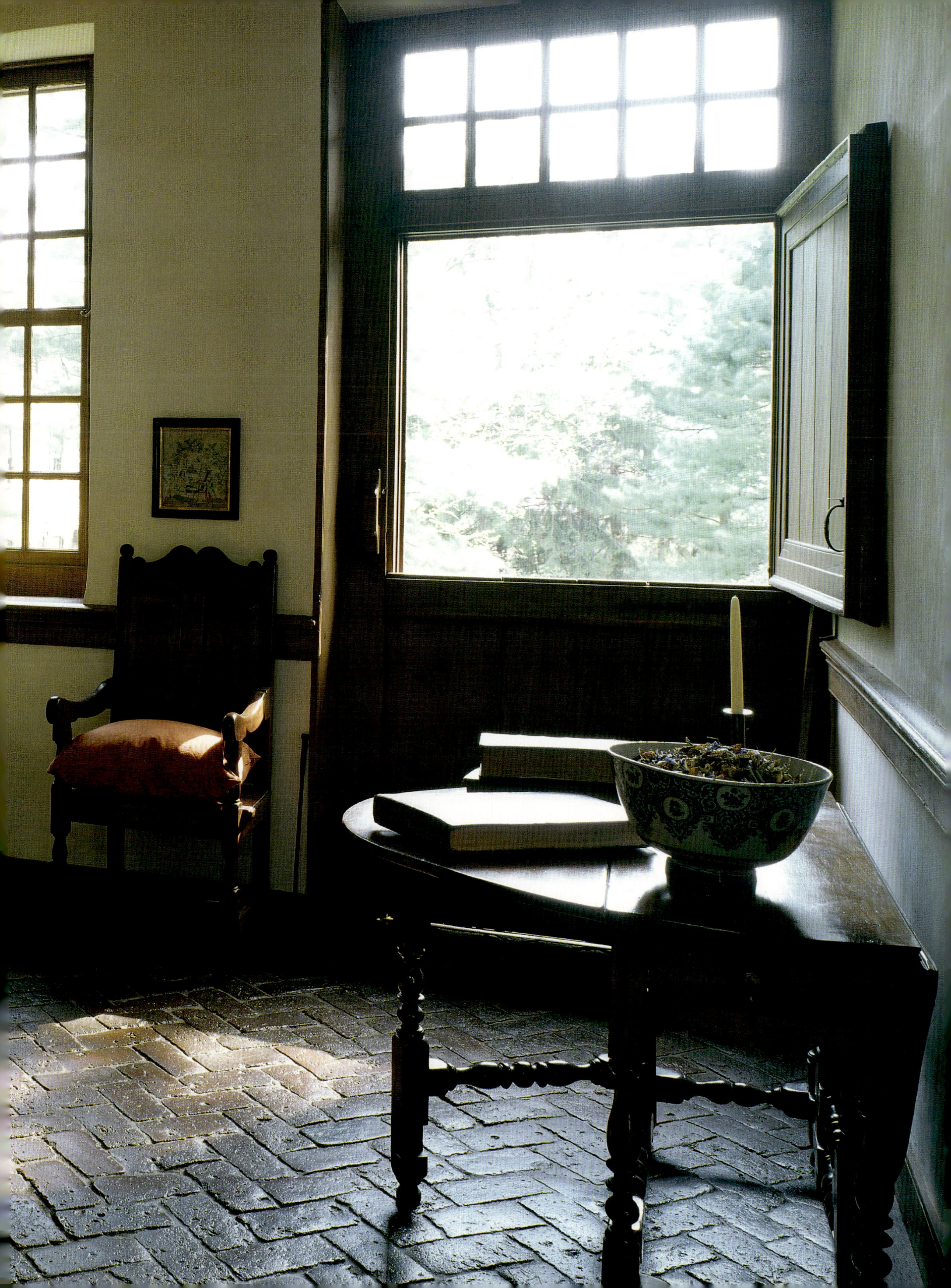

The Wrights had associations with various carpenters and joiners in Chester, Philadelphia, and Lancaster but none that can with certainty be identified with the building of Wright's Ferry Mansion.[6] The account book bound by William Davies lists workers involved in the building of Samuel Blunston's house but does not include information for Wright's Ferry Mansion. One carpenter known to both Samuel Blunston and the Wrights was Cornelius Verhulst. His name appears in Samuel Blunston's accounts for 1730 in the book bound by William Davies, although it is unclear what the payment was for. It perhaps could be for interior paneling for Samuel Blunston's house but this is purely speculative.[7] Cornelius Verhulst was involved with the building of the courthouse in Lancaster, as was Samuel Blunston; and Susanna's father John Wright, who presided regularly as judge at the court in Lancaster until 1741, would have been familiar with him because of Verhulst's work there.[8] It is tantalizing to draw a connection but the evidence is inconclusive that he was involved in the building of Wright's Ferry Mansion.

The furnishings that have been placed in this room echo the baroque quality of the architecture. The side table, the gate-leg table, and the two panel-back chairs, made in Philadelphia in the first quarter of the eighteenth century, reflect the boldness of the staircase banisters in their turned legs and stretchers and contain stylistic elements typical of the late seventeenth century and early eighteenth century.

Relatively few architectural changes had been made to this room over time. During the Federal period, the brick floor was changed to a wooden floor; the evidence for a brick floor in this room was revealed in the cellar directly beneath. The original oak beams supporting the floor showed early masonry stains and were set seven to eight inches lower than the joists in the adjoining cellar chambers. The deeper space between the cellar beams and the floor above allowed for a bed of large flat stones to support a brick floor. Lack of nailing evidence also indicated the original use of a masonry floor here.[9]

The woodwork in this room is almost entirely original, except for the narrow side panel that projects from beneath the stairs for the doors to the cellar. Although at a later time the doors had been made flush with the staircase, marks in the original plaster showed the doors had projected out.[10] The handrail, posts, and balusters are all of black cherry and originally had a natural waxed finish, with the jigged ornament, moldings, and paneled spandrel all of poplar stained to match the black cherry.[11] The treads to the stairs were unfinished, but intact, as was the turned pendant drop above the staircase. The banisters were heavily varnished but had never been painted. The original beauty of the black cherry used in the banisters of this staircase might have prompted Charles Norris to write to James Wright, requesting the "wild Cherry tree Scantling" for the staircase he was planning to build in his own house in Philadelphia. The entry and staircase in Charles Norris's house (which had been located in Chestnut Street, between 4th and 5th Streets in Philadelphia) was later described in Westcott's *History of Philadelphia:*

> *It was a spacious and very commodious dwelling, and in its palmy days was said to be esteemed one of great elegance and splendor. The main house was sixty feet front, and its ground-floor consisted of four rooms, which were intersected by a wide hall running through its center to a cross entry at the foot of the spacious staircase, with doors opening into the piazzas on the east and west sides. The stairway, which entirely occupied the middle section of the building, was a fine-grained, highly-polished wild cherry wood, so dark and well-kept as to be taken for mahogany.*

During the Federal period a brass box lock had been put on the door. When the house was restored, this was removed and a rubbing made of the area beneath determined that a wooden box lock was originally there.

Other than those changes, the woodwork and even most of the plaster were intact, including the original hooks from which fire buckets hang. With no running water in the house and no metal fire screens in use during this period, fire was a great threat, and buckets like these were kept close at hand. Chimney fires were common; in one of Susanna Wright's letters, her calm script is suddenly broken with agitation, and she says: "our Kitchen chimny has been on fire within this half hour, and put me into such a tremor that my hand Shakes yet,—can I write So as to be Read."[12]

The Parlor

A glimpse of the parlor clearly reveals this as the most formal room in the house. Confronting one's gaze from the doorway is an elegant paneled wall set with two tall arched doors on either side of a fireplace. The arched doors with their central, molded key blocks certainly could be viewed as a nod to James Logan's Stenton. The door on the left leads to a small vestibule with an outside entrance. The arched door to the right of the fireplace contains a shallow closet. The practicality of this closet was impeded, however, by the design of the beautiful key block that extends below the arch. Because of this extension, the doors cannot open out into the room but only into the closet space itself. The original paneling survived with only a few alterations. In the nineteenth century, a marble mantel and iron grate had been installed in the fireplace, and the closet had been converted to a display cupboard by adding shelves and cutting off the base of the key block to allow the doors to open outward. When Edwin Brumbaugh examined this later change, he found the early nail holes and paint and trim marks that proved that the doors originally did not open into the room but into the closet space. He restored the end of the key block as well as the hearth and the molding around the fireplace. The other arched door, the small vestibule, and the exterior doors were entirely original and required no restoration work.[13] Evidence showed that originally there was a red wax stain finish on the poplar paneling and this was accordingly restored.[14]

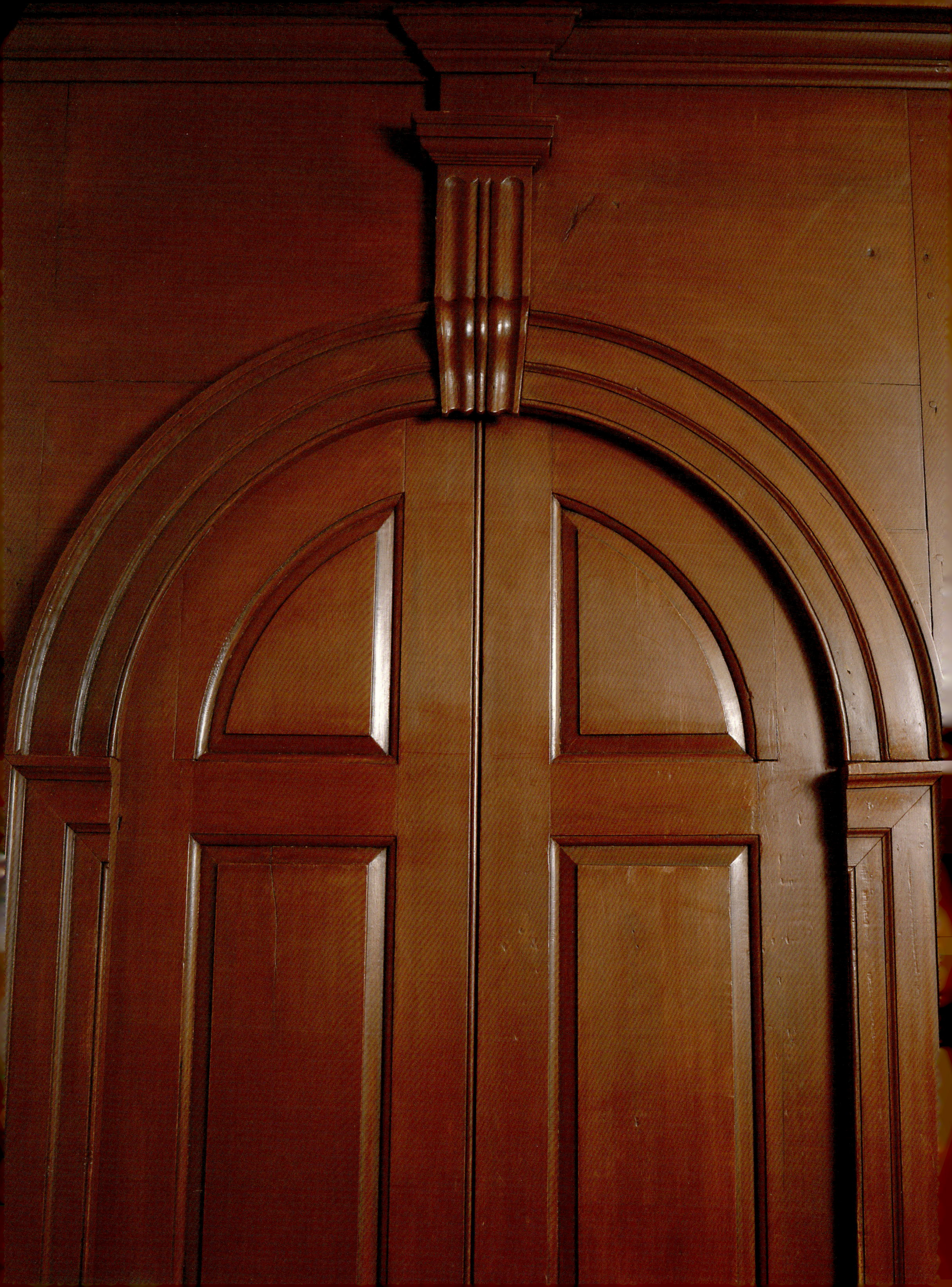

That the river was intended as the primary view from this room is emphasized by the presence of broader windows (four panes wide instead of three) on the side of the house facing the river, with narrower windows facing the back toward the orchards and fields. The one-room depth of the house enabled the windows to provide cross ventilation as well as illumination. All of the window frames in the house are original, as well as many of the double-hung sashes.[15] This type of window, composed of a sliding sash with a counterbalancing system of weights and cords running over pulleys, was developed by the 1670s and was in widespread use in England and Holland by 1700.[16] The Wrights' friend Isaac Norris I ordered window sashes from England when he was building Fairhill in 1716.[17] In 1747/8, his son, Charles Norris, ordered for the Wrights "a Box of London window Sash Glass 8 × 10," the size used in Wright's Ferry Mansion.[18] Architectural evidence at these windows indicated that there had never been support for curtains. The windows were left bare, which was typical in the colonies at this time.[19]

Bare floors were also typical in the colonies in the seventeenth and eighteenth centuries, with the use of carpets on floors rare, even among the wealthy.[20] The original soft pine floors in this house were neither varnished, stained, nor waxed. Polished floors were rare in the seventeenth and eighteenth centuries, varnished and stained floors being used primarily in grand houses in urban centers, like Philadelphia and Boston. There were various methods for maintaining these unfinished floors. They could be scrubbed with soap (as little as possible), small beer, or vinegar, or "dry scrubbed" with fuller's earth and fine sand or with the herbs tansy, mint, and balm, which gave a mahogany color to the boards and a sweet scent to the room.[21]

Sand was used not just for cleaning the floors but also for decorating them, as John Fanning Watson describes in his *Annals of Philadelphia*, where he also tells of the early use of carpets:

> *A lady, giving me the reminiscences of her early life, thus speaks of things as they were before the war of Independence. Marble mantels and folding doors were not then known, and well enough we enjoyed ourselves without sofas, carpets, or girandoles. A white floor sprinkled with clean white sand, large tables and heavy high back chairs of walnut or mahogany, decorated a parlour genteelly enough for any body. Sometimes a carpet, not, however, covering the whole floor, was seen upon the dining room.*
>
> *The silver sand on the floor was drawn into a variety of fanciful figures and twirls with the sweeping brush, and much skill and pride was displayed therein in the devices and arrangement.*
>
> *The rarity of carpets, now deemed so indispensable to comfort, may be judged of by the fact, that T. Matlack, Esq., when aged 95, told me he had a distinct recollection of meeting with the first carpet he had ever seen, about the year 1750, at the house of Owen Jones, at the corner of Spruce and Second streets. Mrs. S. Shoemaker, an aged Friend of the same age, told me she had received as a*

OPPOSITE: Parlor doors with molded key block above, which prevents the doors from opening outward.

OVERLEAF: Parlor: Maple daybed, eastern Pennsylvania, 1730–1750; walnut easy chair, Philadelphia, 1740–1750; overmantel looking glass, probably England, circa 1740; andirons, Philadelphia, 1740–1750.

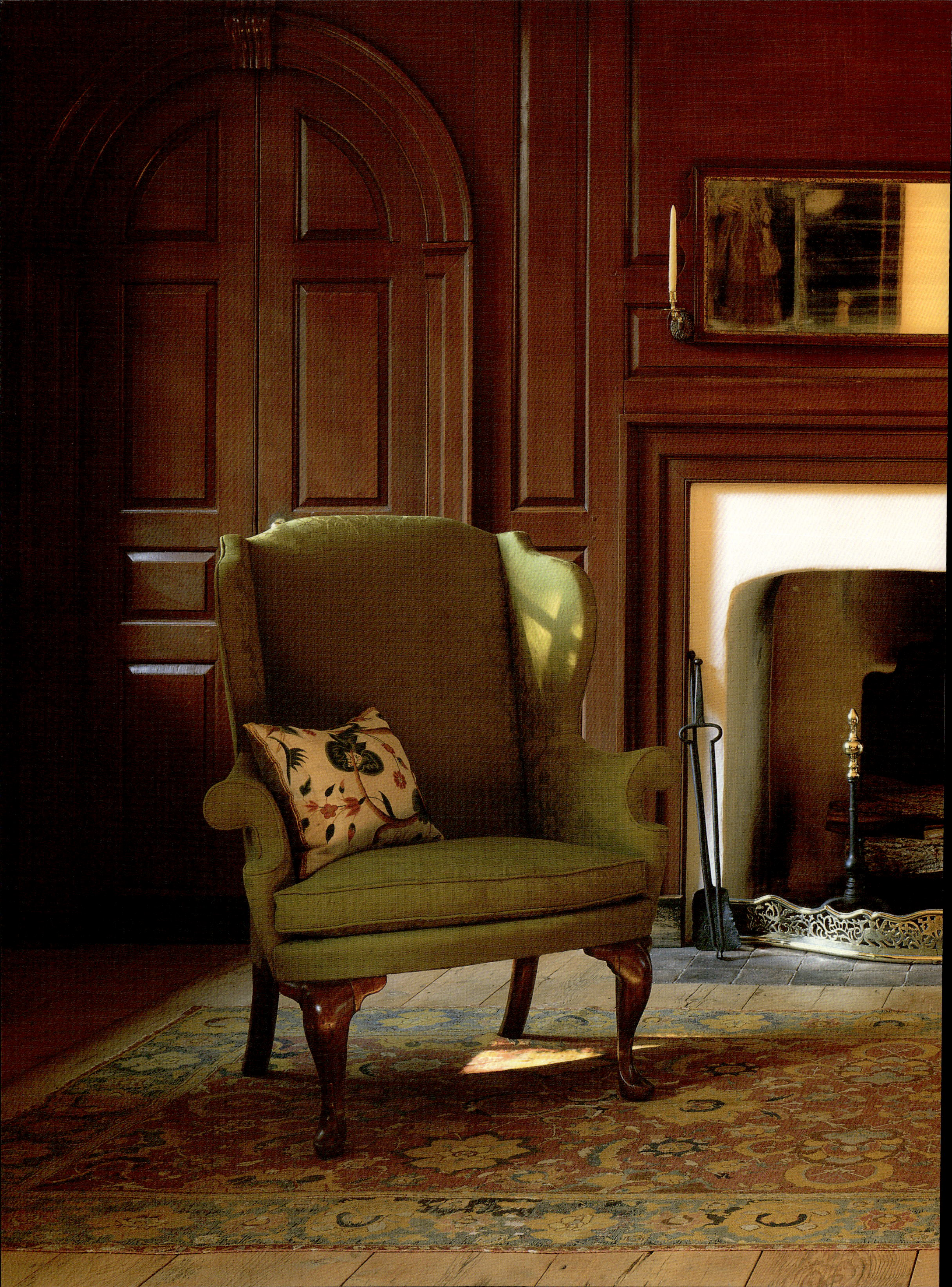

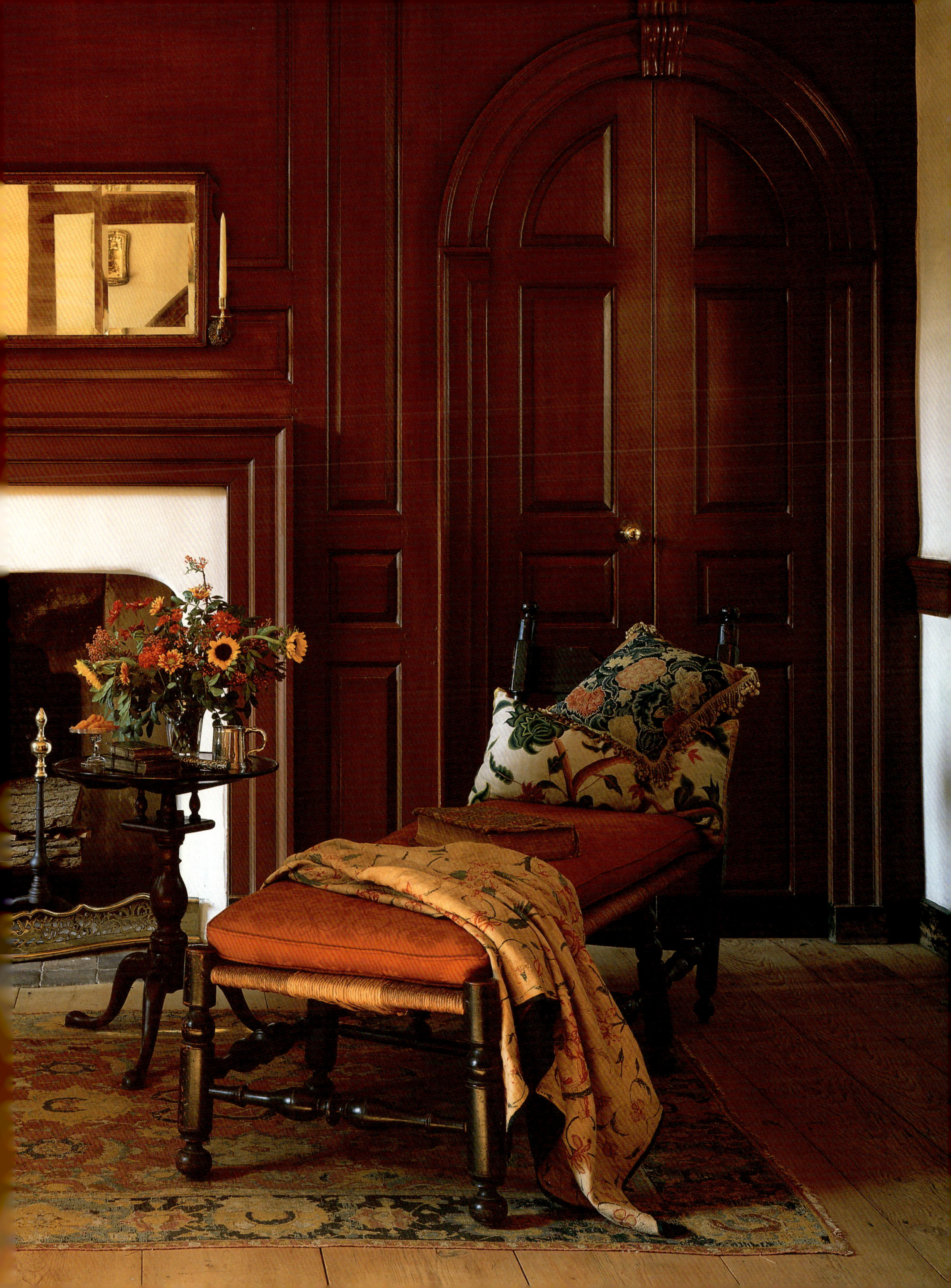

rare present from England a Scotch carpet; it was but twelve feet square, and was deemed quite a novelty then, say seventy years ago. When carpets afterwards came into general use they only covered the floor in front of the chairs and tables.[22]

A variety of activities filled this room—entertaining, conducting business, writing, and studying. The room was a center of vibrant intellectual exchange: a virtual *salon* in the wilderness. Susanna Wright's visitors included many luminaries of early Philadelphia—James Logan, Benjamin Franklin, Anthony Benezet, Benjamin Rush, John Dickinson, and Charles Thomson. In July 1752, Benjamin Franklin wrote to Susanna Wright:

Paneled door in James Logan's Stenton.
Courtesy of Stenton.

We have had excessive hot Weather now near two Weeks. My Thermometer has been almost every Day at 94, and 95, once at 97, which is but 3 Degrees short of the hot Sunday June 18, 1749. This Town is a mere Oven. How happily situated are our Friends at Hempfield! I languish for the Country, for Air and Shade and Leisure; but Fate has doom'd me to be stifled and roasted and teaz'd to death in a City. You would not regret the Want of City Conversation if you considered that 9/10ths of it is Impertinence.[23]

City conversation was exceptional in Philadelphia, not only because of its intellectual vitality but also because of the purity of the English spoken there, which is described in the journal of an English officer who traveled in America and the West Indies in 1764 and 1765: "the propriety of Language here surprized me much, the English tongue being spoken by all ranks, in a degree of purity and perfection, surpassing any, but the polite part of London."[24]

Susanna Wright's father was known for the great eloquence of his speeches to the court and Assembly. Susanna's own conversational abilities were so renowned that they were recalled over thirty years after her death in a description of her by Deborah Norris Logan (1761–1839), the daughter of Susanna's close friends Charles and Mary Norris,

84   *Wright's Ferry Mansion*

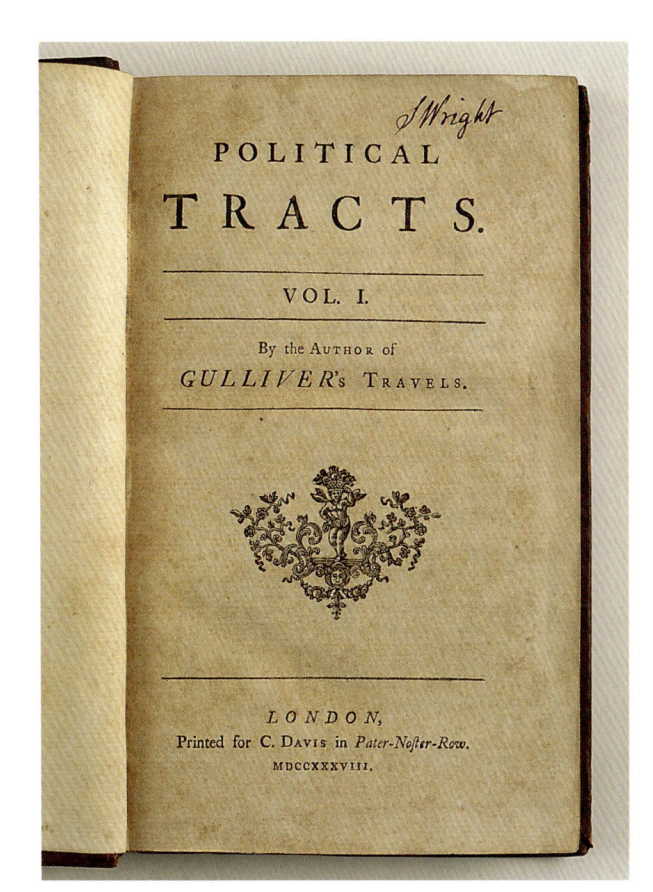

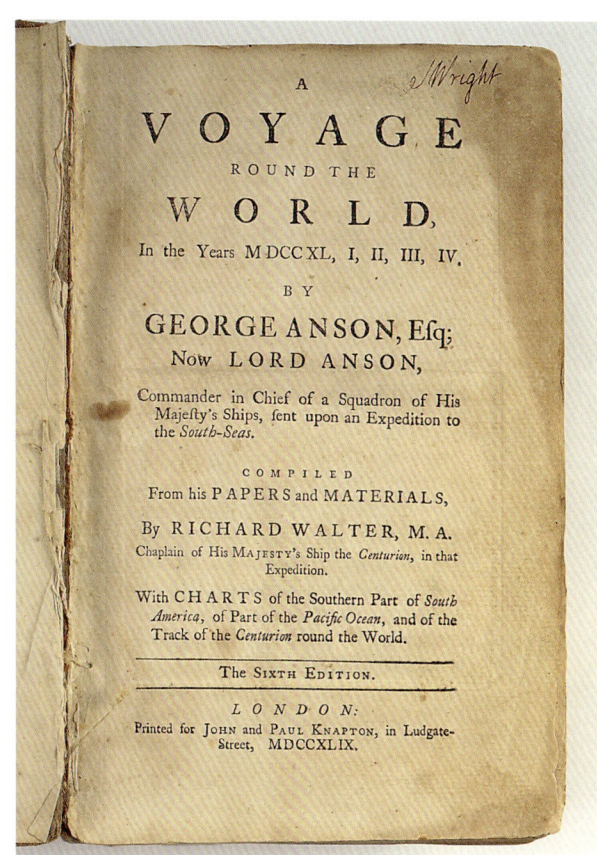

Books from Susanna Wright's library, which reflects the range of her interests—politics, exotic travels, biography, natural history, literature, and religion.

and wife of James Logan's grandson: "I had the pleasure, when very young, of seeing her, and can remember something of the vivacity and spirit of her conversation, which I have since heard some of the best judges of such merit affirm they had seldom known to be equalled."[25]

The spectrum of her talents, which would have shone in this room, are delineated further by Deborah Norris Logan:

> *after the death of her father [she] became the head of her own family, who looked up to her for advice and direction as to a parent; for her heart was replete with every kind affection, and with all the social virtues. She was well acquainted with books, had an excellent memory, as well as a most clear and comprehensive judgment; she spoke and wrote the French language with great ease and fluency; she had also a knowledge of Latin, and of Italian, and had made considerable attainments in many of the sciences. Her letters written to her friends, were deservedly esteemed for their ingenuity. She corresponded with James Logan, Isaac Norris, and many other celebrated characters of that period; and so great was the esteem*

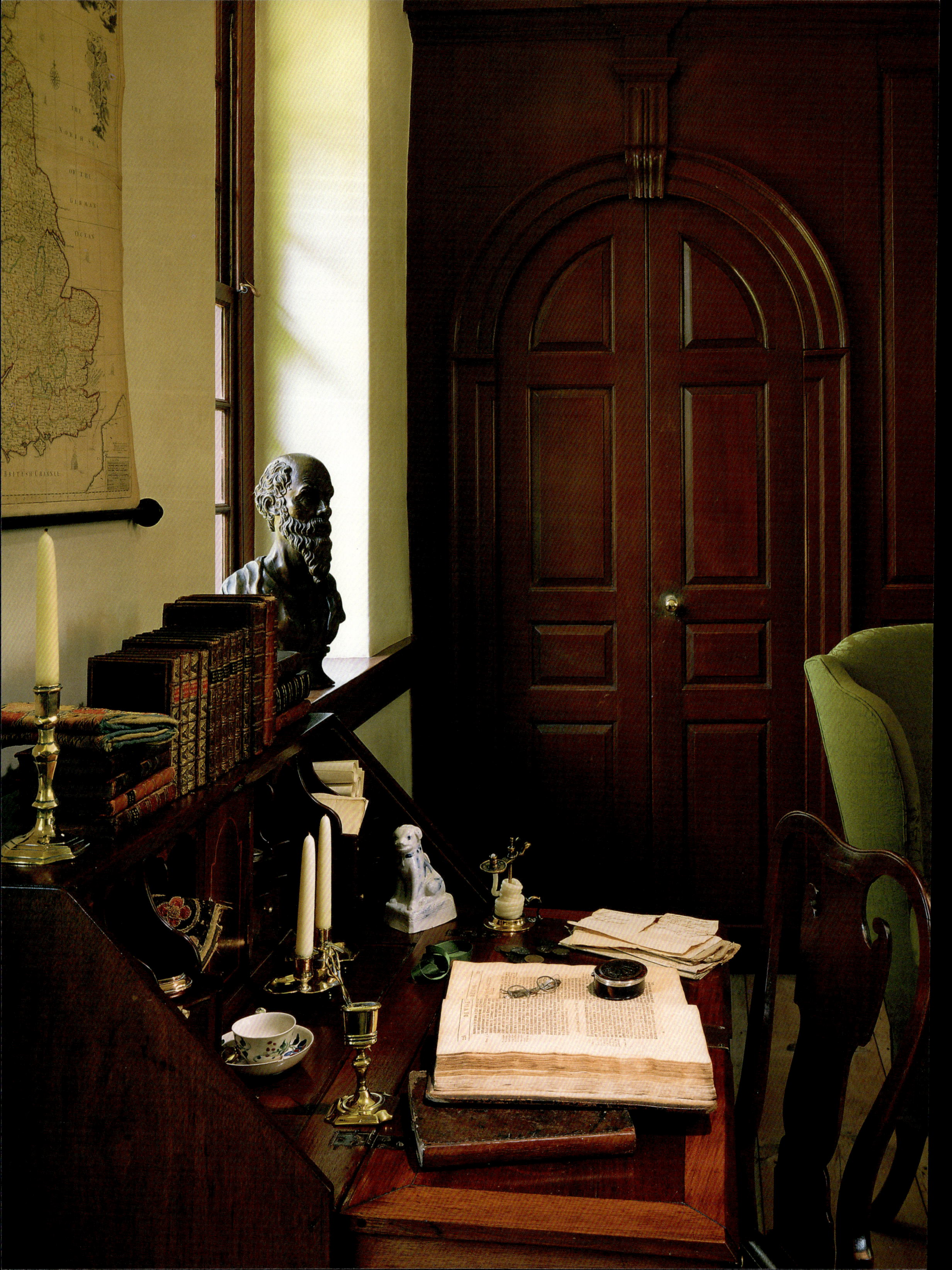

Parlor with walnut armchair and pair of side chairs, Philadelphia, 1740-1755; and mahogany tea table, Philadelphia, 1745–1765.

> *in which she was held by her neighbours, for integrity and judgment, that disputes of considerable interest were frequently left to her sole arbitration by the parties concerned. Her advice was often desired on occasions of importance respecting the settlement of estates, and she was often resorted to as a physician by her neighbourhood. The care and management of a large family, and of a profitable establishment, frequently devolved entirely upon her; and she appeared to be so constantly occupied with the employments usual to her sex and station, that it was surprising how she found time for that acquaintance with polite literature which her conversation displayed, when she met with persons capable of appreciating it.*[26]

Even Benjamin Franklin relied upon Susanna Wright's advice and conferred with her about the best means to obtain support in the area for General Braddock's troops during the French and Indian War.[27]

Franklin's influence would have been visible in this room in the books, pamphlets, and almanacs he sent; later he even sent a thermometer from London. Books, maps, and

Desk in parlor and door leading to an outside entrance. Map of England, by John Senex, London, circa 1720.

Tea table in Parlor, set with English plain and polychromed salt-glazed wares, 1745-1755; and, at left, an English delftware plate dated 1729 and tea caddy.

engravings ordered by James and Susanna through the Norrises from the London bookseller Elias Bland would also have been in this room. A desk was essential for the various activities that took place here. Storage space for documents as well as for special linens necessary for entertaining could also have been provided in this room. John Fanning Watson comments on the use of chests of drawers in a parlor in the early eighteenth century:

> *Every householder in that day deemed it essential to his convenience and comfort to have an ample chest of drawers in his parlour or sitting room, in which the linen and clothes of the family were always of ready access. It was no sin to rummage them before company! These drawers were sometimes nearly as high as the ceiling. At other times they had a writing desk about the centre with a falling lid to write upon when let down.*[28]

The Clock Room

The name of this room is indicated by the earliest inventory for Wright's Ferry Mansion, which is not Susanna Wright's, but rather Samuel Bethel's, made in 1777.[29] When Susanna Wright and her brother James's family moved to the house that had been owned by Samuel Blunston about 1750–1755, she rented Wright's Ferry Mansion to Samuel Bethel and his

Shards found at Wright's Ferry Mansion. Upper left: English salt-glazed "scratch-blue"; upper right: English polychrome and embossed salt-glazed wares; below: Chinese export porcelain.

The Mansion's Interior: The Rooms and Their Furnishings 89

TOP: Rare English salt-glazed strainer, circa 1745.
BOTTOM: English salt-glazed charger with embossed border, 1745–1765.
This pattern is the same as found on shards at Wright's Ferry Mansion.

wife Susannah Taylor, her niece who lived in the house until 1785.[30] Of the furniture values for the downstairs rooms in Samuel Bethel's inventory, the amount for the Clock Room was highest:

The Furniture in the Best Parlour	*18–9–0*
The Furniture in the Clock Room	*24–17–6*
The Furniture in the Pantry	*3–0–0*
The Furniture in the Kitchen	*12–4–0*

Although the individual pieces of furniture in this room are not given, the name of the room indicates that at one time a clock of some prominence was kept here.

Susanna Wright's father had a clock, which, grouped with a table in his inventory, was valued at five pounds; and Samuel Blunston's inventory lists "a Chamber Clock" valued at nine pounds "in the Dining Room."[31] In recalling the house in Warrington, England, where her father was born, it is the clock that stands out in Susanna's memory:

> *we were Surprisd, & Sencibly & deeply, concernd, to Read in the Gazette, an acct of the death of our Worthy friend, & distant Allie, Saml Fothergil; we are told he dyed at his own home, which was the house in which my father was Born, 105 years agoe, and where his Parents lived and Died: after my Grand fathers death, the house was purchased by my Grand mothers Brother, father to Saml Fothergils wife, as I had past many of the happyest days of my life in it, those days, unclouded by care or Sorrow, which are quickly over, and can never Return, and was Intimately aquainted with every part & Cranny of it: he was pleasd to describe all the alterations he had made, as he had in a manner rebuilt it, among other tryfling questions I askd him, I enquired after a large old Clock, that had been my Grandfathers, when my father was a Child, and which stood in my uncles parlour when we left England; he answerd it continued to go Exelently well, after having measured time to its Several owners, for a hundred years,—and alas it has now I presume, measured time to himself, to the latest hour of his valuable life,—he moralisd very Seriously upon the Subject, as I ought to do upon this Affecting Occasion, rather then Relate these uninteresting Anecdotes of a house, and a peice of its furniture; but what could I say—Such has been the decree of Devine Providence, and who Shall presume to query, why was it so.*[32]

The tall case clock displayed in Wright's Ferry Mansion is by Henry Taylor of Philadelphia. There are two other time pieces in this room, a sundial by Delure of Paris, made about 1720, and a pocket watch by Thomas Wagstaffe of London. Wagstaffe supplied silver pocket watches to Philadelphia silversmith Joseph Richardson, Sr., whom the Wrights patronized. Wagstaffe also supplied the Pennsylvania Hospital with a wall clock, which is

The Mansion's Interior: The Rooms and Their Furnishings

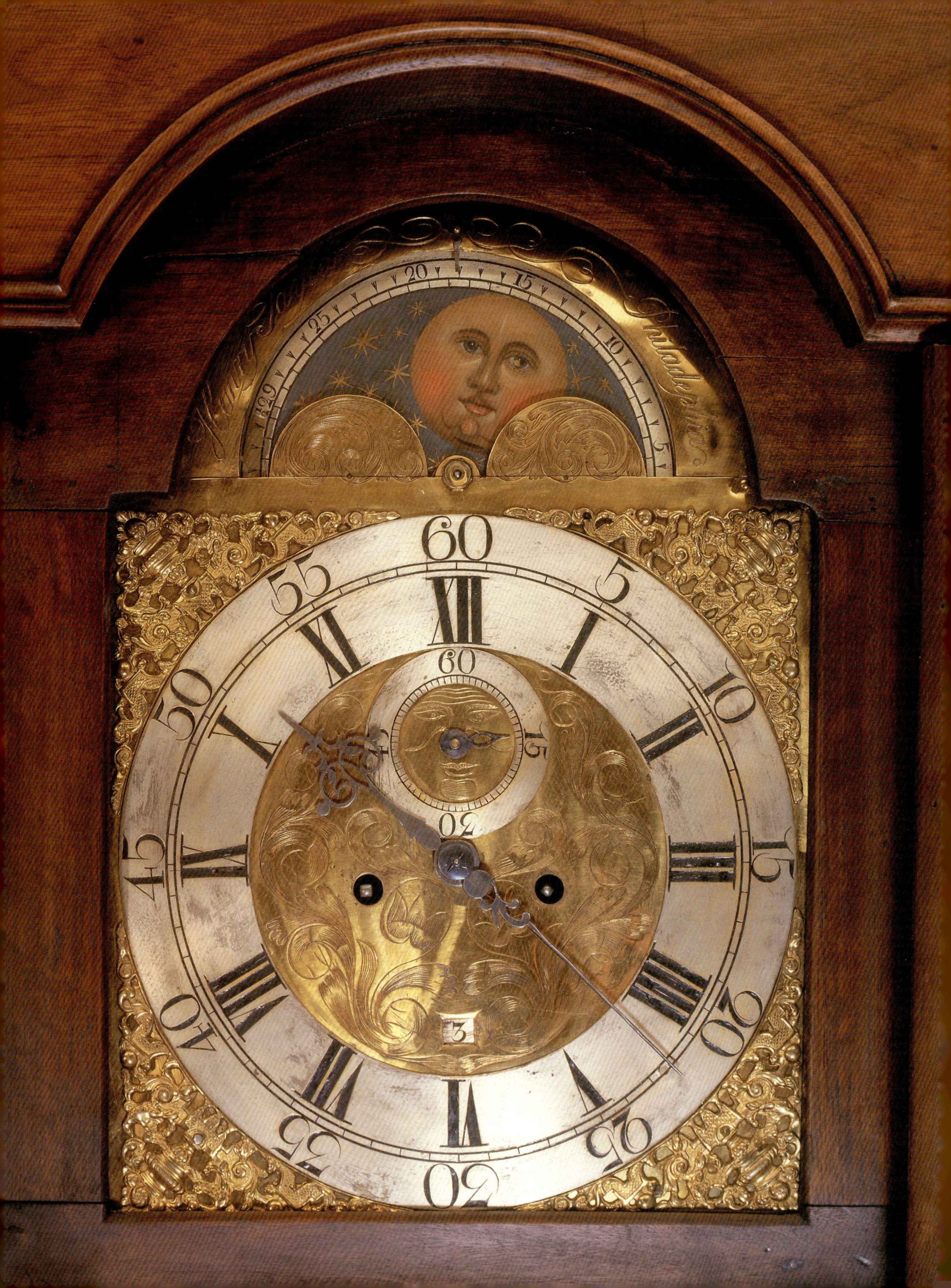
Philadelphia

Spherical horn box for holding string, England, 1740–1800; fruitwood nutcracker, probably England, 1700–1790; brass sundial by Jean-Baptiste-Nicholas Delure, Paris, 1710–1725; and English blown glass: cruciform decanter, 1730–1750; sugar bowl, 1725–1750; and wine glass, 1720–1760.

still in their collection. The Wrights contributed financially to the Pennsylvania Hospital when it was getting started in the 1750s.

Central to the house and therefore easier to heat, the Clock Room was probably used a great deal. Activities similar to those in the parlor—entertaining, studying, conducting of business, as well as dining—would have taken place in this room, albeit, with less formality. Although designating a room as a dining room was not common at this time, the term was used and appears in the inventories of James Logan and Samuel Blunston. The Queen Anne furniture in this room is more reserved, less flamboyant than the furniture in the parlor. The table in this room is a very early Philadelphia Queen Anne gate-leg table made about 1730, while the chairs with their rush seats were a very economical Philadelphia form—less expensive than the compass- or balloon-seated chairs in the parlor (which, because of the greater complexity of their construction, were costlier).

This room had undergone two major changes.[33] The original paneling had been replaced about 1790 when a new wall was constructed beyond the fireplace, utilizing space that had been part of the kitchen. The paneling installed at that time was a classic example of the period. Much of the original plaster remained in this room and provided evidence for the shape of the original cornice for the restored paneling, while the panel divisions were made to resemble the original paneled walls in other rooms of the house.

Detail of tall case clock, made by
Henry Taylor, Philadelphia, circa 1750.

OVERLEAF: Clock Room

The Mansion's Interior: The Rooms and Their Furnishings

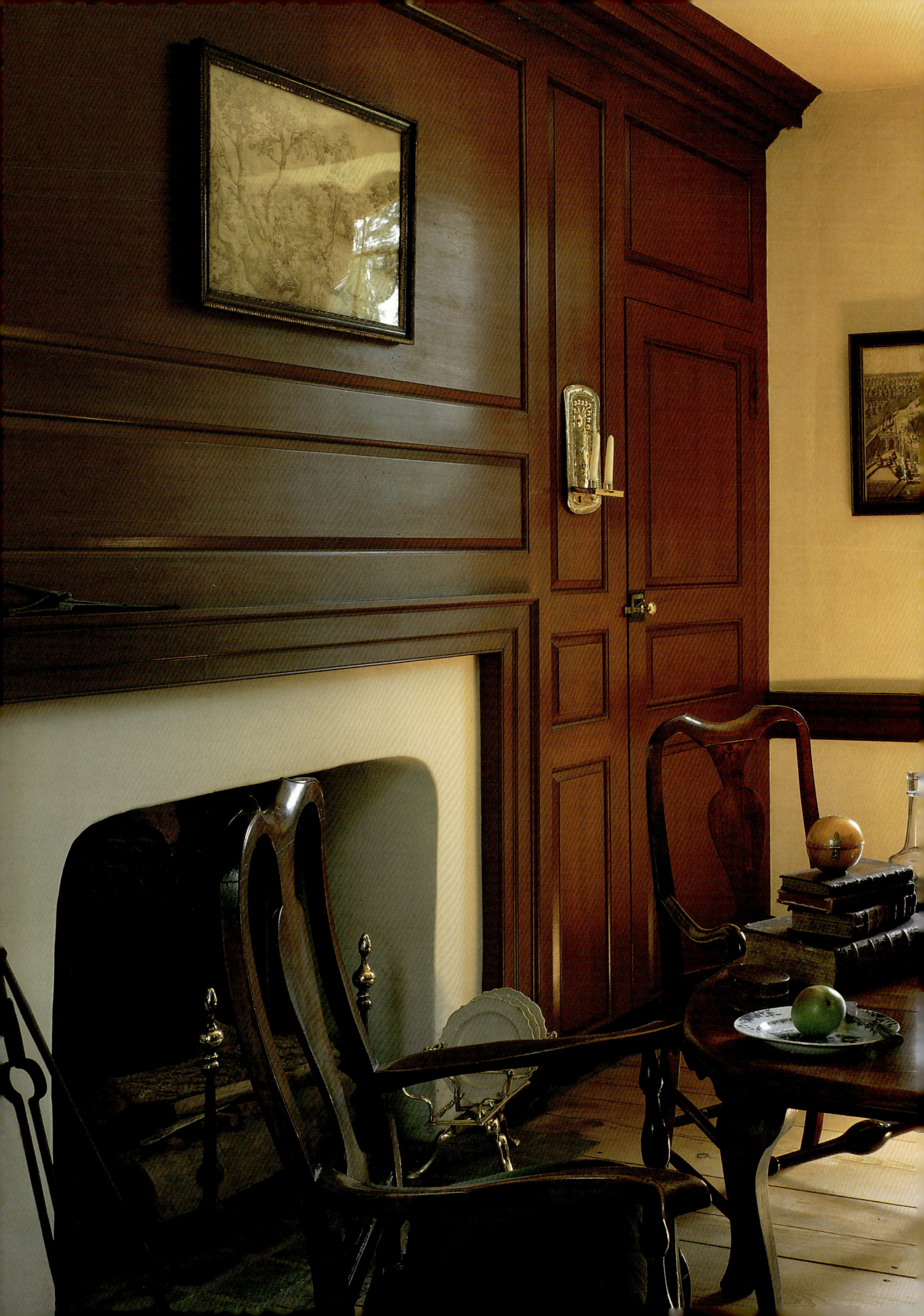

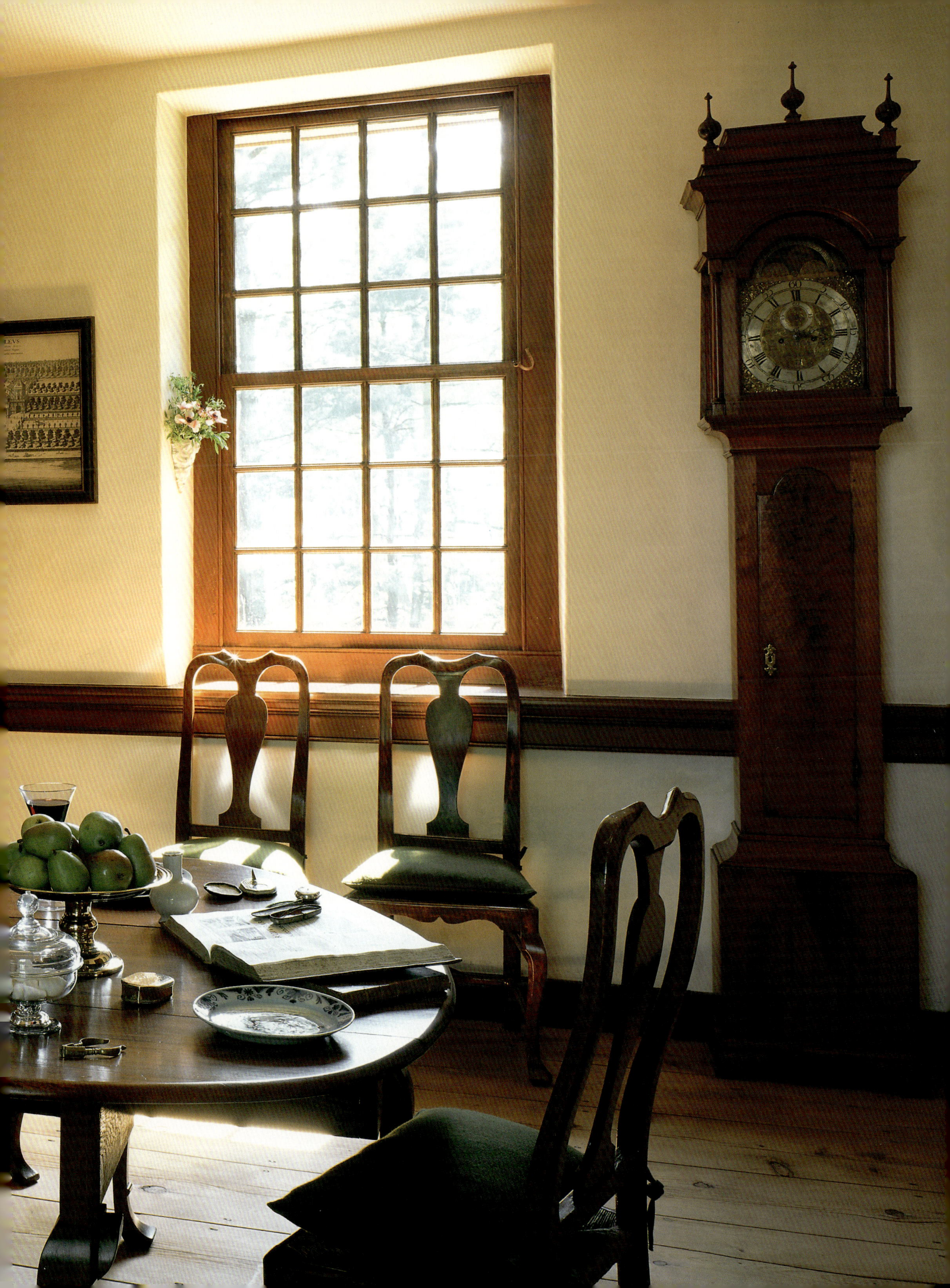

Clock Room. Built-in cupboard with door on right opening as a pass-through to the cellar. Doors in the entrance hall lead to the cellar steps, which are directly behind the pass-through.

The second change was made when the stairs in the hall that lead to the cellar were removed in the early 1800s. This affected the Clock Room because the built-in cupboard in the corner of the room was removed at that time, since it was no longer needed to provide headroom for the cellar steps. Marks in the original plaster delineating the shape of the cupboard that had been removed were used to reconstruct the present cupboard.

The Kitchen

English and European settlers coming to Pennsylvania were impressed with the fertility of the soil and the abundance of fish and wildfowl. William Penn described the enormous turkeys in Pennsylvania that weighed up to fifty pounds and he said the flocks of doves were like dark clouds they were so plentiful. Recollecting life at Wright's Ferry in the eighteenth century, Sarah Barber tells of the wildfowl and fish here:

96 *Wright's Ferry Mansion*

Closet containing early eighteenth-century English blown table glass.

> *The lower falls as they were called was a great place for hunting wildfowl. Geese & ducks were in abundance & sometimes swans. The islands & rocks as familiar by the names they had given them, and the places as well known to their fellow hunters when they described their hunt as the streets, alleys and corners in a town. There was the Big Island, now the Garden island, the Eagles Nest which had been there for years, the Big L & little Fishing Island &c &c The mud banks, High rocks, Flat rocks &c &c The currents too had their names the big shoot, the lane, and many others, not recollected. There was plenty of game from the beginning of the 10th mo[nth] until the river was frozen up.*[34]

Wright's Ferry was located on a migratory route, where even today flocks of whistling swans and Canada geese abound in winter.

In addition to local fish and fowl, Susanna Wright enjoyed the luxuries that arrived at the port of Philadelphia and then were transported over land by wagon—oranges and lemons, coffee and chocolate, stick cinnamon, blade mace, nutmegs, cloves, and sugar in

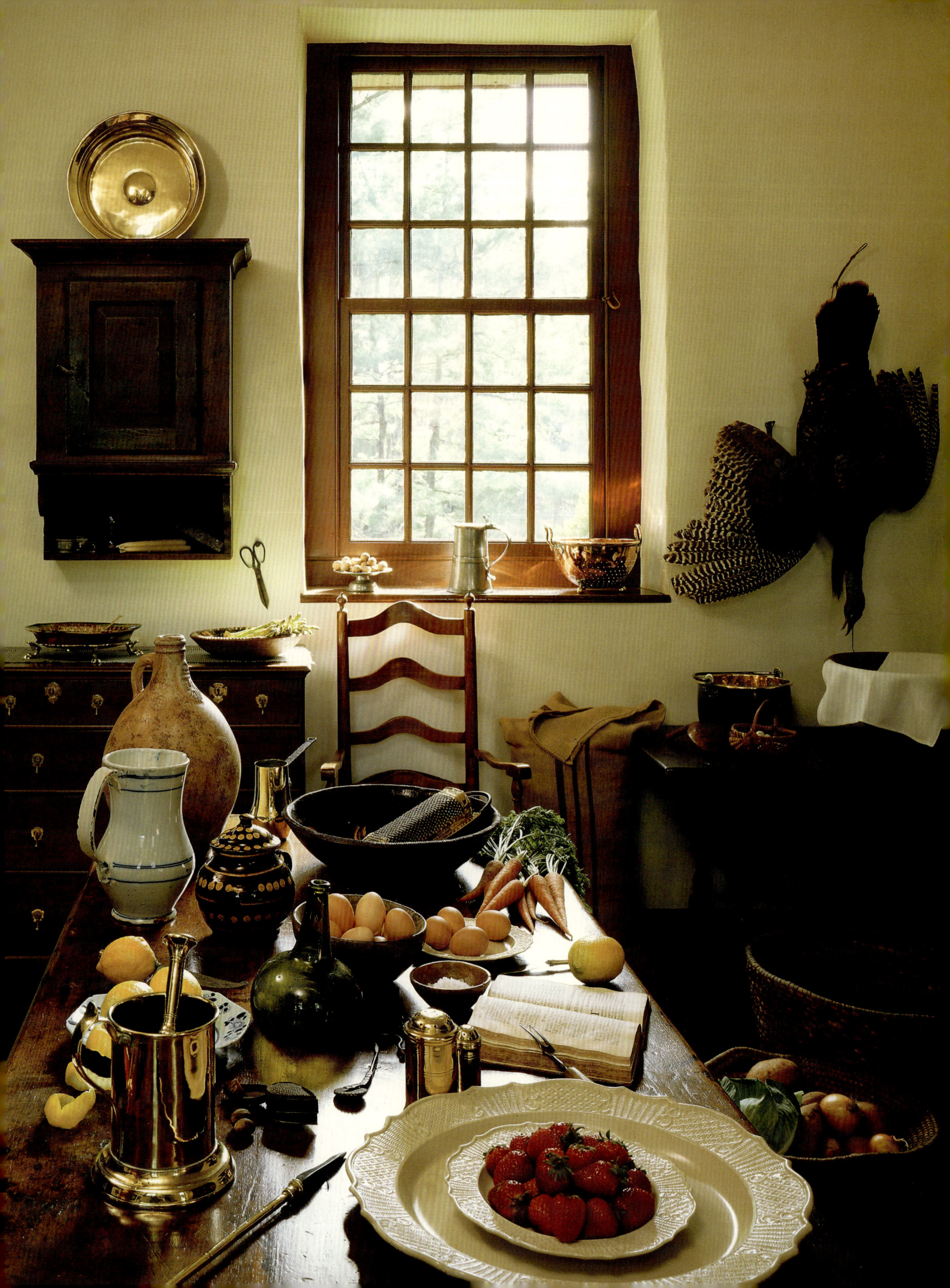

tall cones.[35] Oysters were transported from Philadelphia in casks, like the six bushels sent by Charles Norris in November of 1761.[36]

Susanna Wright and her brother Jemmy's wife Rhoda sent gifts from their kitchen to the Franklins, as the following letter written to Deborah Franklin around 1765, shows:

> *Sister Rhoda beggs your acceptance of a few of our apples, spitzbergen & pippins and a little pickled salmon (that is what we call salmon). She could not get as much of it as she wished and was forced to fill up the kegg with perch. When you have taken it out, you will please to let a serv[ant] return the Kegg to the waggoner, as it is a borrowed one and the people insist on having it again. This is ill manners, but with you our good friend, we can be quite free.*[37]

A good deal of fish was caught in the Susquehanna River, where seines and dip nets were utilized; a shad fishery was later established just a short distance below the ferry on the east bank of the river.[38]

The Franklins had a general store in Philadelphia and the Wrights would order various items from them, such as the candles mentioned in the following letter from Deborah Franklin to Susanna Wright:

> *I reseved your verey polite letter but could not anser it no more than I Cold flatter my self that I was—I wont say what I was agoing but if you think that I have aney thing in me that has the leste resemblanse of yourselef you due me honour. laste night I reseved yours by the wagoner I have got the Candels I hope thay will prove good the Chandler ses they air the most parte dears tallow I have bespoak a line & will take care to send it up as I will from time to time everey thing that you or yours shall want which may be got from Boston to South Carrolinah or else whair (is not this verey grand talk).*[39]

Since Susanna Wright worked at night, lighting was very important and she used not only the deer tallow candles but also those sent to her by Benjamin Franklin, which were probably bayberry.[40] The brass candlesticks would be brought to the kitchen to be cleaned and polished and filled with fresh candles for the coming evening.

Among other items ordered from the Franklins was a tea kettle, about which Deborah Franklin commented: "the tee Kittel was the beste Caste I saw but none of the topes did fit better and the pepel who youse them had topes maid by a smith thay air youused in all the houses I was in at Newarke at Col Skilens and at Eliz-town and much liked."[41]

Another Philadelphian, Sally Armitt, also supplied some of Susanna Wright's household needs. She provided her with basins and flat irons and even offered Susanna furniture to use if she were to rent a house in Philadelphia during the troubles of the French and Indian War.[42]

Kitchen

OVERLEAF: Walnut kitchen table, central Pennsylvania, 1740–1790; walnut armchair, eastern Pennsylvania, 1740–1775.

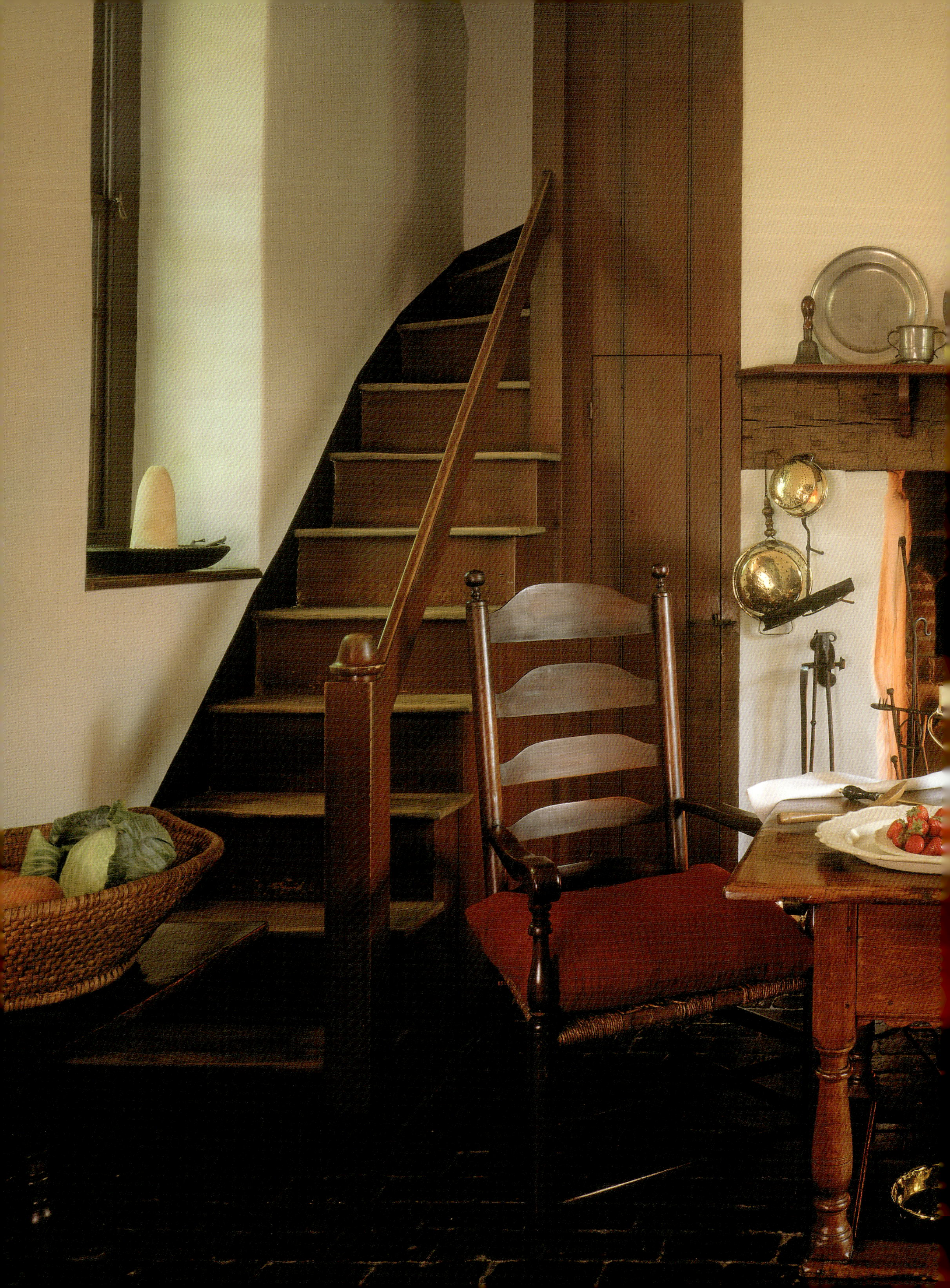

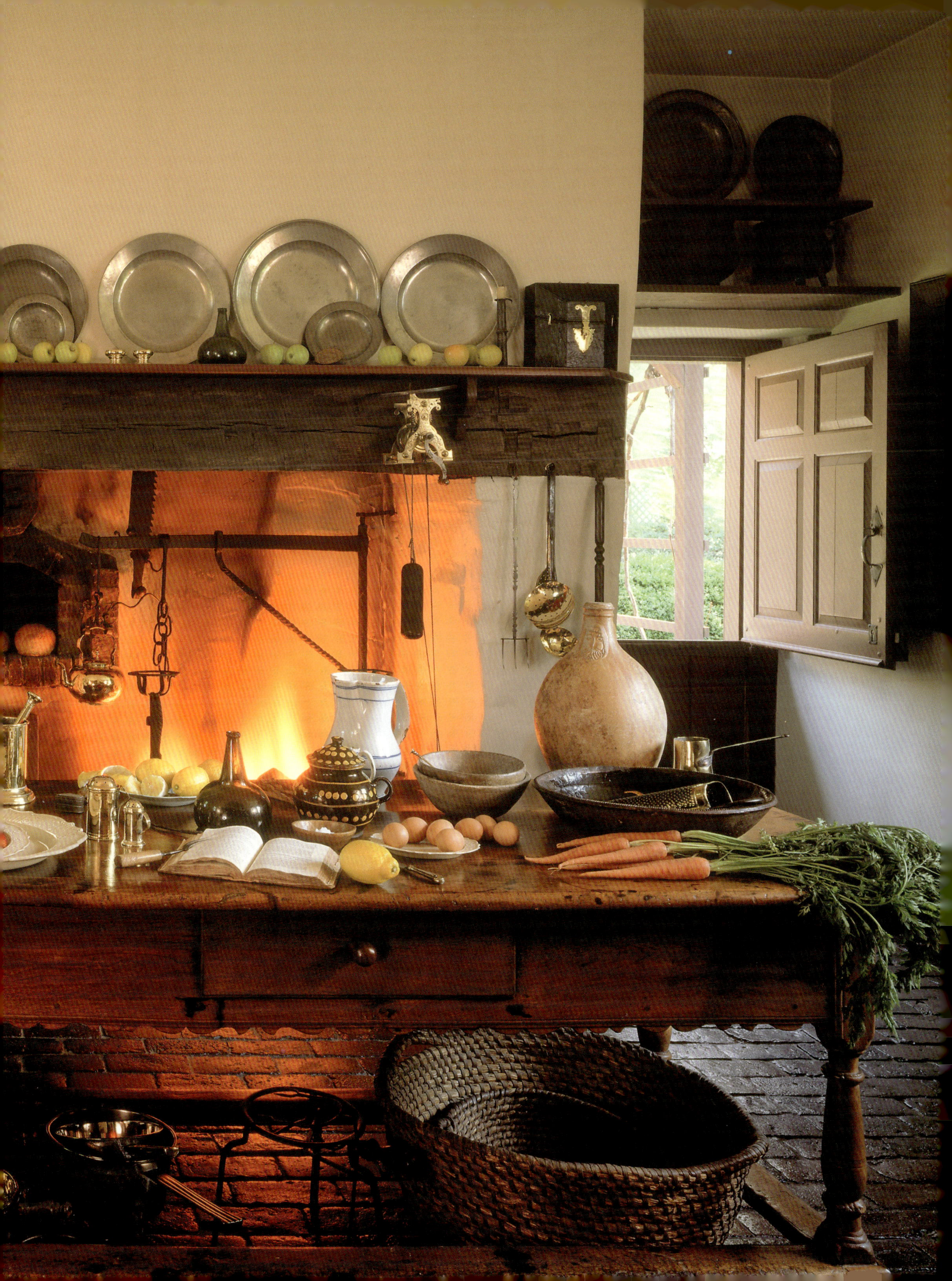

Although Philadelphia furniture predominates in the rest of the house, Susanna Wright probably would have drawn on local joiners and cabinetmakers for furnishing her kitchen with massive work pieces like the table in the center of the room. In an English household the kitchen was primarily a workroom, in contrast to the Germanic house where it was central physically to the house and most activities. In Wright's Ferry Mansion, the kitchen is placed at the end of the house and at a lower level.[43] The brick floor was a protection against fire and could easily be scrubbed down. The brick floor, the deep window entablatures (which are framed in plaster), the vertical boarded paneling, and the massive fireplace bring a seventeenth-century quality to the room. The fireplace with all its accoutrements—cranes, andirons, trammels and spits, cauldrons, posnets, spiders, braziers, and peels—also gives access to the bake oven.

The oven is attached to the back of the fireplace and extends beyond the wall of the house as a plastered dome protected by a roof. It is called a squirrel-tail oven because the curving shape of the flue resembles that form as it follows over the dome and curves upward to link with the main chimney flue of the kitchen fireplace. In the fireplace the small dark flue opening of the oven can be seen just above the main oven opening. To use the oven, a fire must be built in the oven itself and allowed to burn there for several hours until the bricks absorb enough heat. Then the ash and ember are removed and the baking is done by the radiant heat held by the bricks. Since the oven was very hot at first and gradually cooled, a sequence of baking was followed. Various dishes and preparations would be made so that advantage could be taken of every available temperature in the oven. Bread and pies would go in first while the oven was very hot; then, more delicate dishes, like cakes and custards; and finally, fruits and vegetables that could be dried by the very gentle residual heat of the oven as it cooled. The oven is equipped with a wooden door that slips into a slot beside the oven opening. Once the fire has been removed, the door can be utilized and can even be soaked with water to provide moisture in the oven, especially for the baking of bread.

On one side of the fireplace are stairs leading to the servants quarters and on the other, a door to the garden. A well lined with stone on this side of the house provided water for the kitchen.

Through time, a number of internal architectural changes had occurred to the kitchen.[44] The floor, which originally had been one step down from the Clock Room, was raised so that it would be even with the Clock Room floor. The original riser for the step down was found at the door between the Clock Room and the kitchen. Still in place, nailed against the joist, the riser was 7⅝ inches lower than the other floor. Although the original floor had been entirely removed when the level was raised, brick fragments indicated that it had been a brick floor laid typically on a tamped sand fill. Although a baseboard had been put in for the later floor when the level had been raised, there was no applied wooden baseboard in the kitchen originally.[45] Instead, the wall was simply painted black where the baseboard would be. This same treatment was also found in three of the rooms upstairs.

South side of Wright's Ferry Mansion showing the white plaster dome of the squirrel-tail oven, which opens into the kitchen fireplace.

In investigating the floor, another interesting discovery was made. A stone foundation belonging to an earlier structure was found below the original level of the kitchen floor. It ran twenty inches in front of and parallel to the kitchen fireplace and turned at each side to become part of the east and west kitchen wall foundations.[46] It was not possible to know how far to the north the earlier building extended as that evidence was destroyed when the cellar beneath the rest of the house was dug. There were also mutilated foundations of an earlier kitchen fireplace still in place, which then served as the foundation for the Clock Room fireplace. In order to utilize this earlier foundation, the builders of Wright's Ferry Mansion had to leave enough earth when the cellar was dug to support the old fireplace foundation, otherwise they would have had to remove that foundation. Thus, the cellar beneath the Clock Room extends only partially beneath that room. The cellar wall at that point then acted as a retaining wall for the earlier fireplace foundation.[47]

The fact that only the foundation of the earlier building survived suggests that the building had been either log or frame.[48] If it had been stone, it undoubtedly would have been incorporated into the present stone structure. There was no cellar beneath the earlier structure and that, too, suggests a log building, since many log houses had no cellar. There

The Mansion's Interior: The Rooms and Their Furnishings

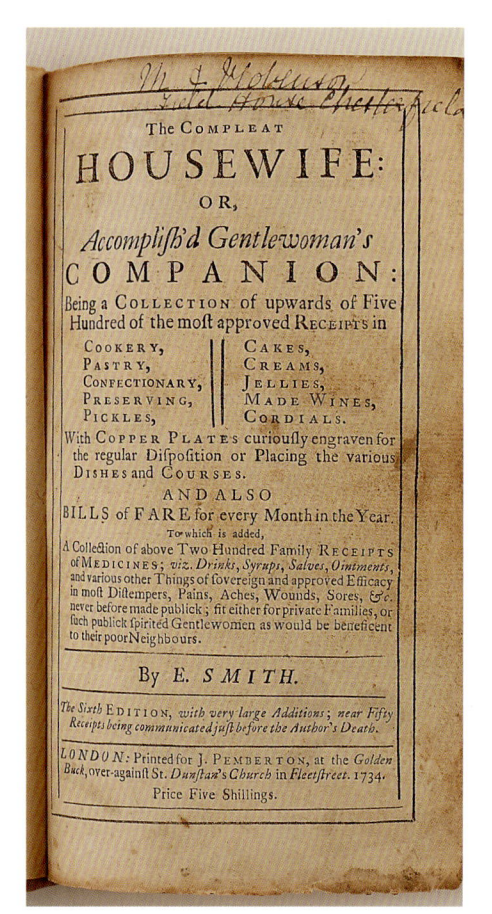

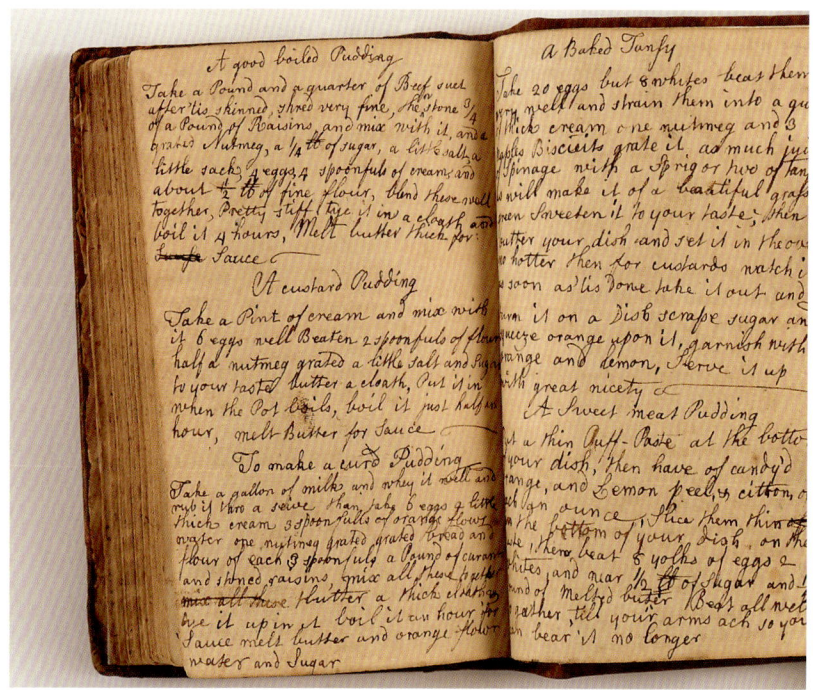

Recipes in the account book bound by William Davies (right) were copied from E. Smith's *The Compleat Housewife*.

were a number of log buildings constructed in the early settlement at Wright's Ferry, including the house belonging to Susanna Wright's father, built in 1727, which was a short distance away.

In the early 1800s, when the level of the kitchen floor had been raised, the staircase to the second floor was enlarged and a staircase at the opposite corner of the room was added, which went down to the cellar. The width of the original staircase in the kitchen to the second floor was determined by marks in the original plaster on the kitchen gable wall. Clear evidence was found on this wall of three original risers and treads and it was on this evidence that the restored staircase was based.[49]

At the time of the restoration, there was a staircase in this room that led to the cellar. The style of the millwork and the use of cut nails, however, indicated that it had been built in the nineteenth century. The masonry work for these stairs, especially the mortar in the cellar, was unlike that used in the rest of the cellar. This staircase was removed because it was not original to the house.

In enumerating the rooms downstairs, the inventory of Samuel Bethel mentions a pantry between the Clock Room and the kitchen. Based on this reference, Edwin Brumbaugh

Kitchen Pantry with (from top): English delftware flower brick, 1740–1770, and puzzle jug, 1735–1775; English salt-glazed creamer with scratch-blue decoration, 1745–1775; and English brown and yellow slip-decorated dish, 1725–1775.

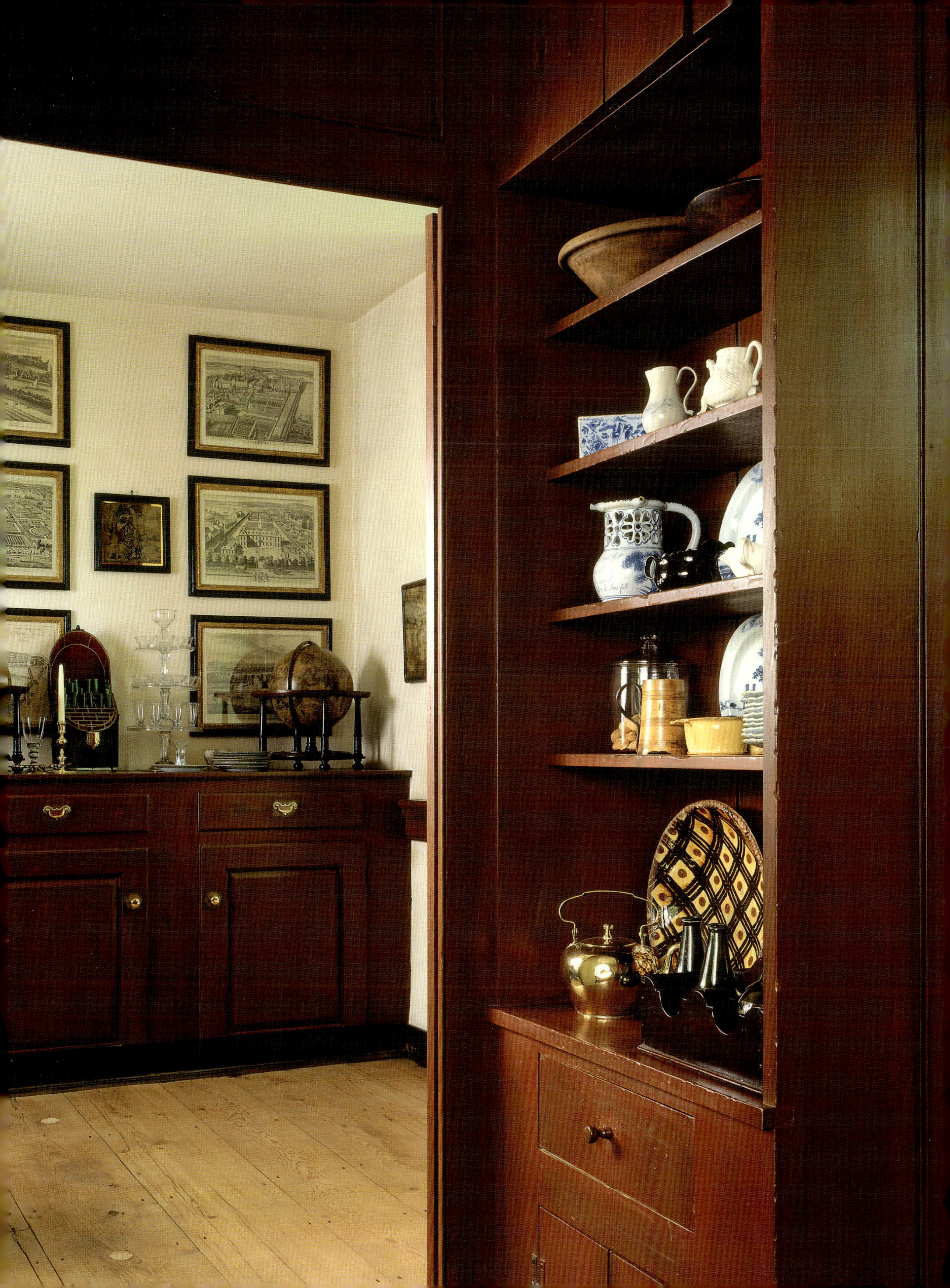

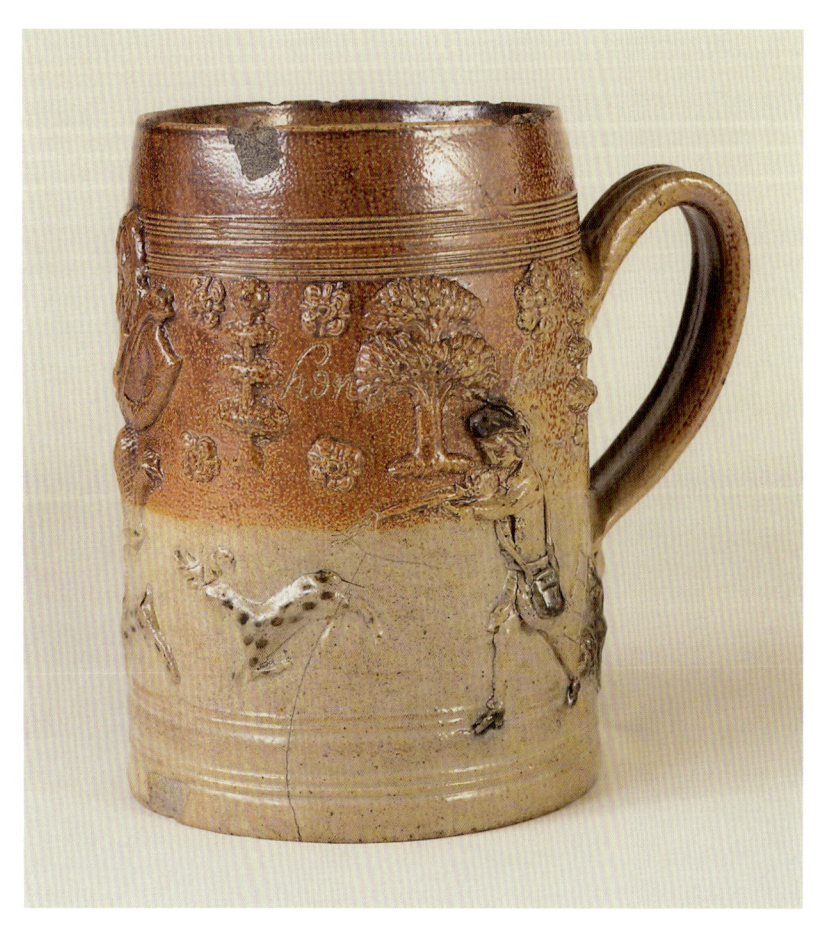

English salt-glazed stoneware mug, dated 1721, for beer, ale, or hard cider. There was a cider press at Wright's Ferry Mansion and James Wright raised hops for making beer and ale.

put beside the door between those two rooms an area of shelving with a closet behind it, providing room for display of objects as well as storage. In addition, two shelves were added above the door to the garden.

Because an addition had been made at a later time to this end of the house, the bake oven was no longer there. Its foundation was intact, however, and provided evidence for the size and type of oven that had been there originally; and it was reconstructed accordingly.

The Best Bedchamber

At the top of the staircase to the second floor is a large window that illuminates both the staircase and the long upper hall. Doors from the best bedchamber, the workroom, and the secondary bedchamber open into this hall, which has a fresh simplicity in the gently modulated plastered walls, the high ceiling, and the oak door frames with paneled doors of poplar. The woodwork here, as in the best bedchamber and workroom, is stained a soft brown. The white expanse of the walls in the hall is unbroken by the presence of a chair rail. In addition to the large window with its deep sill at the head of the stairs, illumination also spills into this hall from the neighboring rooms.

Following the pattern of the first floor, the rooms proceed in sequential order from the most elaborate and formal to the simplest. First stands the best bedchamber, directly above the parlor. Though not as elaborate as the parlor, the best bedchamber is the most elaborate of the upper rooms and is certainly striking as one enters, with the beautifully paneled wall directly opposite. Rather than the imposing elegance of the parlor paneling with its two symmetrically placed arched doors, here the paneled wall is a subtly and asymmetrically delineated pattern of raised panels. The doors to the closets flanking the fireplace virtually disappear into the paneled length of the wall, except for their definition in panel placement, and in the bold HL hinges and spring door latches with small brass knobs.

Like many houses in the Philadelphia area in the late seventeenth and early eighteenth centuries, this house is equipped with a good deal of closet space. The English technique of placing paneling against the wall where the fireplace projects into the room uses adjacent space for storage and provides added insulation. This technique has been used in all the major rooms in Wright's Ferry Mansion, creating at once a bold, yet eminently practical design, with the warmth of a hearth and a wall rich with paneling immediately confronting the gaze of the viewer entering the room.

Light fills the room from each side, coming from the elongated windows with their deep plaster entablatures that have been enlivened by a thin incised line, the carryover of a seventeenth-century feature. The poplar window sills form a continuous line with the chair rail, which encircles this room in a strong horizontal band. The sills, doors, chair rail, and paneling are all of poplar. All of the paneling in this room is original, except for a slight restoration at one closet.[50]

An interesting feature in this room on the inner wall is the chair rail, the molded element of which travels down only part of the wall beside the entry door and is carefully terminated on an angle at two ends so that only the flat part of the chair rail runs for several feet along that wall. On this flat section of the chair rail are two mortises that probably accommodated vertical supports for the canopy of a bed. Sometimes hooks were placed in the ceiling to support a canopy, as at Stenton. Here, however, the ceiling had been replaced, so evidence of further support overhead could not be determined.

The placement of the bed on an interior wall would probably provide additional warmth. Perhaps with the thought of both warmth and privacy, no window is directly adjacent to the bed and this room differs from the parlor below in having only one rather than two windows on that side of the room. Thus, careful thought went into the architectural design of this room to allow for the permanent situating of a bed on the interior wall, facing the fireplace. The simplicity in the design of the paneling allows greater attention to be drawn to the dominant pieces of furniture in the room, like the bed and the pieces of case furniture.

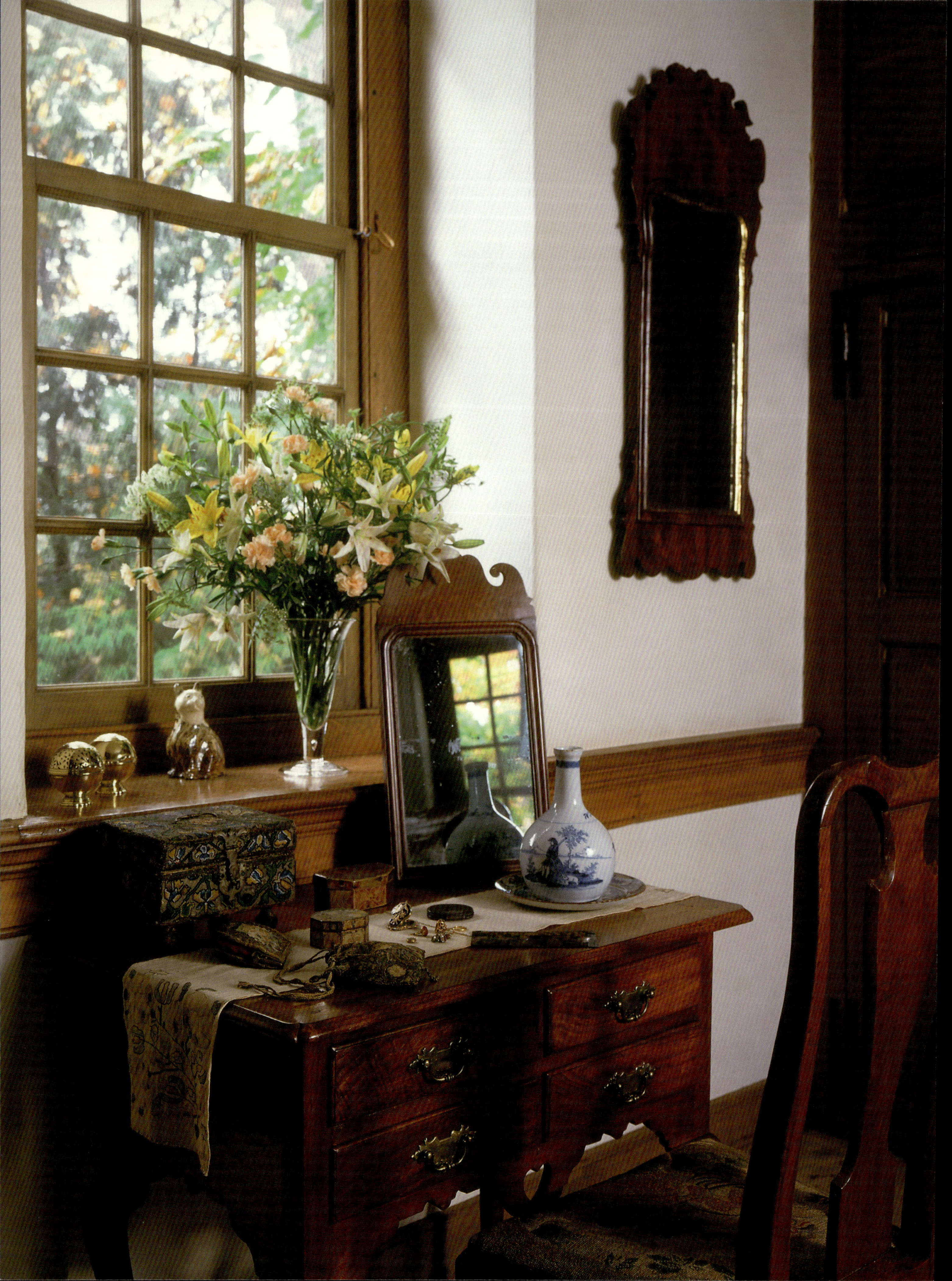

Although there is a fair amount of closet space in this room, there would undoubtedly have been pieces of case furniture here, like the high chest and dressing table. The candlestand and adjacent chairs drawn into the room show how a room like this would have multiple uses, that dining was not confined to one room, and that a more formal upper chamber was often used for receiving guests.

Liberty was taken in the myriad of needlework pictures which hang throughout the house, but which are particularly in evidence in this room. In the eighteenth century, only one or two pieces would probably have been hung but more are present here to provide a small study collection of early pieces. The abundance of textiles here reflects not only the use of the room, where clothing and linens would be stored and needlework would be done, but it also shows the great involvement and interest that the Wrights had in textiles through several generations. Thus, the collection contains examples from the seventeenth as well as the early eighteenth century.

One of the elements that gives a greater feeling of intimacy to the collection is the presence of small personal items, many of which, while very common in the eighteenth century, are scarce today. Some are rare because of their extreme fragility, like the flat hat made of beaver felt, the 1746 pin cushion covered in silk, and the clothes brush. Others, because they were elaborate and used only on special occasions, survived, like the silk brocade shoes and the kidskin gloves with silk gauntlets.

One rare survival in furnishings can be seen in the bed in this room. Although the high post bed was commonly made in Philadelphia, as cabinetmakers' account books attest, this is the only known surviving example of a Philadelphia Queen Anne high post bed. It has been placed at the spot that had been designed to accommodate a bed in the room. In this position, the bed is protected but is also a primary focal point, its bold lines accentuated by the simplicity of the paneling and the plaster walls.

The other major pieces of furniture in this room, the dressing table and the high chest, have spots seemingly made to order. The space between the two windows on one side of the room is the perfect width for the high chest. On the opposite side of the room is a small space to accommodate the dressing table, which has illumination from the window above it. Neither of these pieces can be placed against the paneling because doors to the closets run the length of the wall.

The Workroom

Next to the best bedchamber and beside the head of the stairs is a small room, well lighted by a large window. There is no fireplace in this room. The white plastered walls are unbroken by the line of a chair rail. The presence of a wooden baseboard ties this room into both the hall, into which it opens, and also into the best bedchamber rather than into the next bedchamber, which does not have a wooden baseboard.

Walnut dressing table, Philadelphia, 1730–1750.

OVERLEAF: Best Bedchamber. Mahogany bedstead, Philadelphia, 1740–1765; maple armchair, possibly Philadelphia, 1700–1730.

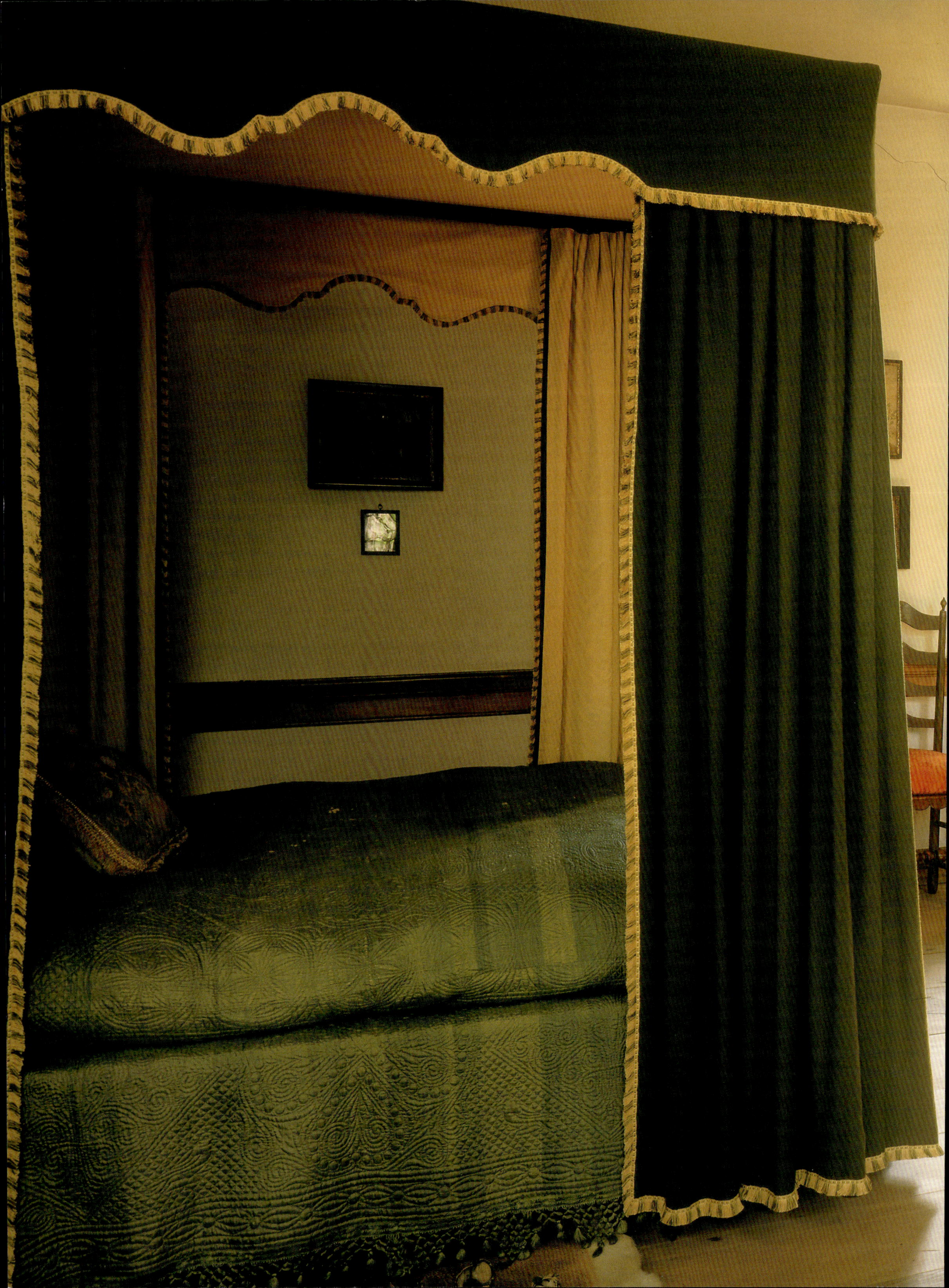

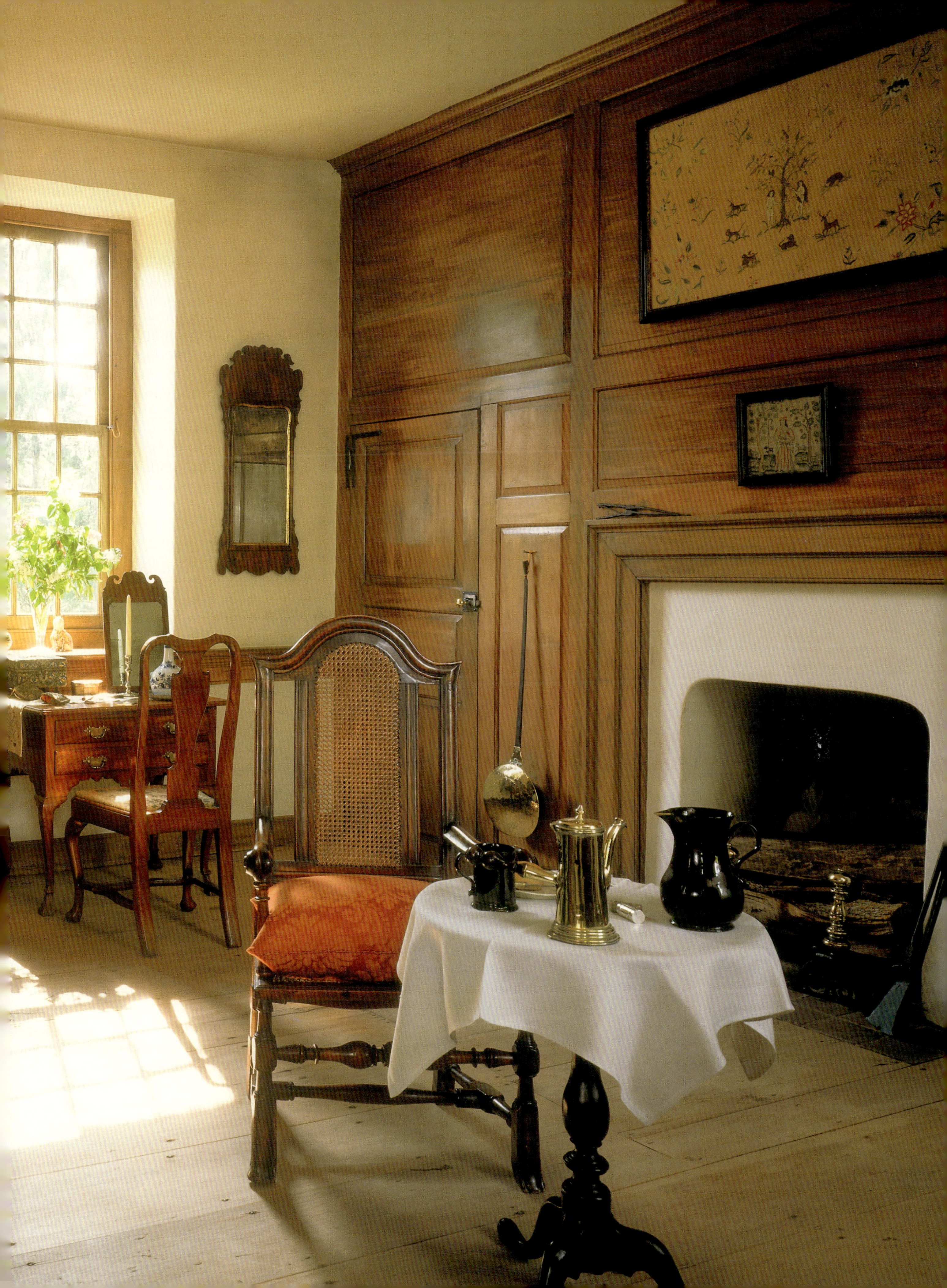

Upstairs hall with tall case clock by Joseph Wills of Philadelphia, circa 1730.

There is no indication in records or in the architecture of the room to indicate how it was used. Edwin Brumbaugh explored the possibility of its being a powder room by trying to find evidence of a board that would have been plastered into the wall to support pegs, but none was found.[51] The presence of a small, unheated room near an upper bedchamber has been noted in examples of English domestic architecture of the eighteenth century.[52] Some of these rooms were used for storage or for a private place for retiring, following the pattern of grander houses of the seventeenth century. These small rooms could also serve as a repository of rare and precious objects and specimens, the collector's cabinet, "Cabinets of Curiosities," or *Wunderkammern*.[53]

Although the original use of this room in Wright's Ferry Mansion is unknown, it is presented as a workroom, reflecting the panoply of interests that Susanna Wright had and the fascination that she shared with her friends for all the exotic natural phenomena they were encountering. The room is also evocative of the seventeenth-century collector's cabinet, where various exotic plants, feathers, fossils, and shells would be kept. Her mentor James Logan avidly collected specimens which he carefully identified.[54] Susanna Wright's brother James, at the behest of John Bartram, traveled to the Ohio River Valley to retrieve mastodon fossils. Susanna Wright collected and exchanged seeds and cuttings with her friends in Philadelphia. This little room provides a visual manifestation for her many interests.

She would have needed an area to indulge these interests, especially ones like the initial experiments with the raising of silkworms, which would not have worked well either in the more polite rooms of the house nor in a primary workroom like the kitchen. In her treatise on the raising of silkworms, she advises to place the eggs first "in a room where but little fire is," as in this room, and eventually setting them on sheets of paper on a sunny windowsill. A small room like this would be not only ideal for such activities but would have been well-nigh essential.

Susanna also experimented with dying her silks various colors. In 1771, Milcah Martha Moore wrote to Susanna Wright regarding her own experiments with colors:

> *Since my last I have been trying my Hand at shades for working with, & have sent thee a sample, but cannot promise that they will stand, they have all had several rincings in warm water, the scarlet (if I may so call it) & the Purple are both dyed with Brazilletto Salt Tartar & Allum, a very small matter of pot Ash dissolved in a cup of Water changed the scarlet when dip'd in it to a Purple—some of the same colour wash'd with hard Soap turn'd to a pretty Crimson—the Yellow is dyed with Barberry root. I never heard of its being made use of for this purpose, but as I was planting a Root of it last Summer I observed it to be of a very bright pritty yellow, upon which I boil'd some of it with a little Allum, and was much pleas'd with the colour it produced, I have sent thee a few of these Chips, also a small Phial of my blue dye. Two or three drops in a Wine Glass of Water will be sufficient for dyeing a small skein of silk of a light colour—it may be rinced out in a few minutes, but if its wanted dark, must stay in a qr. of an hour, I am not sure that this will stand any more than the rest, & shall now give thee the History of it—thee must know the Ladies make use of something of this kind to dye their old White Ribbons, shades, &ct that are soil'd—it is brought from N. York & sold in some of our Shops here at a great price. I had seen some of it, & had a very great inclination to know of what it was made. ('tis pritty lucky for me that I have a Doctors shop so handy) I try'd almost every thing I cou'd think of—at last hit upon some Spt. Salt or Vitriol. I'm not sure which & mix'd it very well with Prussian blue finely powder'd, this I found to have exactly ye appearance of that I bought and seems to answer the purpose quite as well, it*

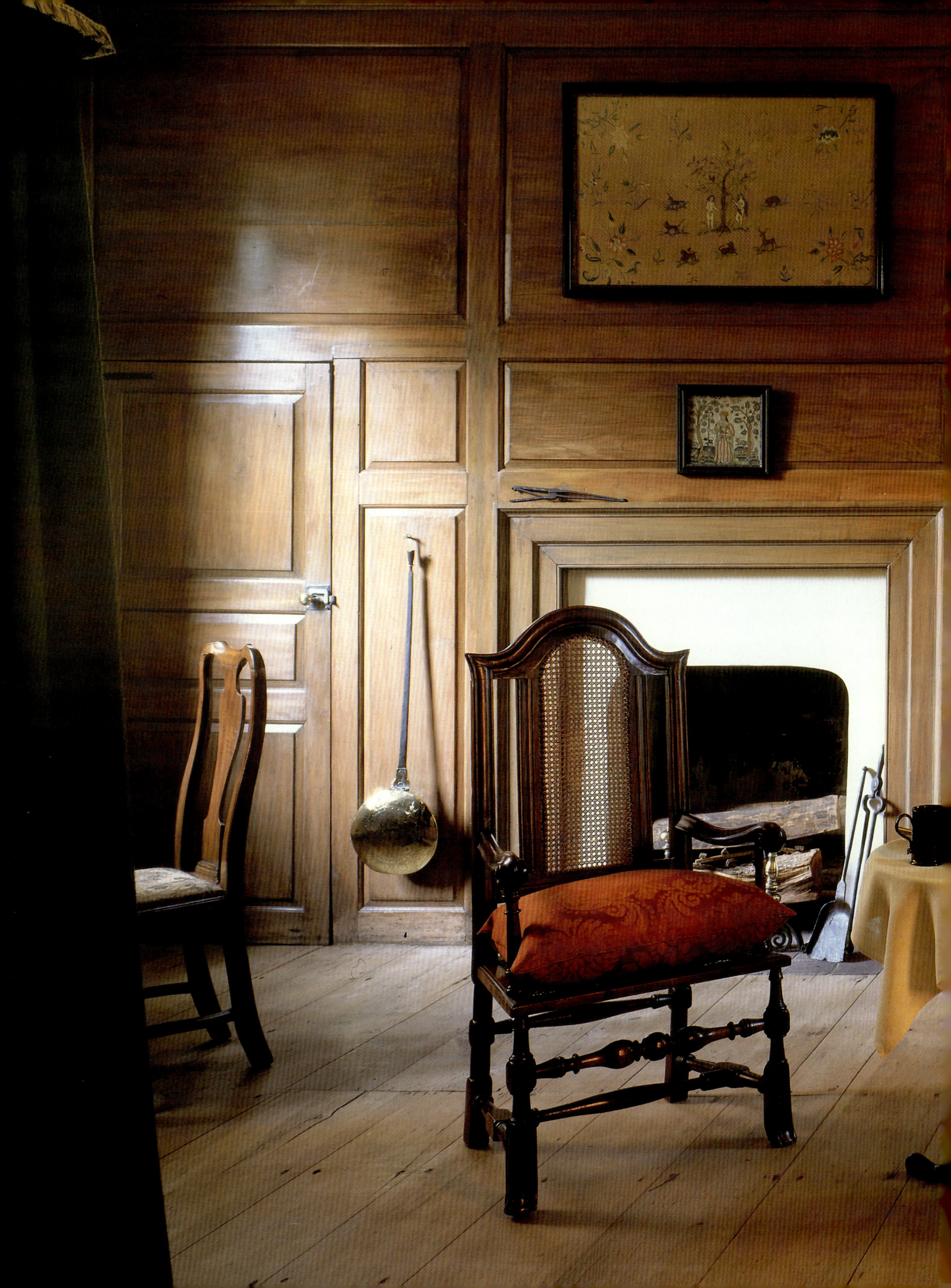

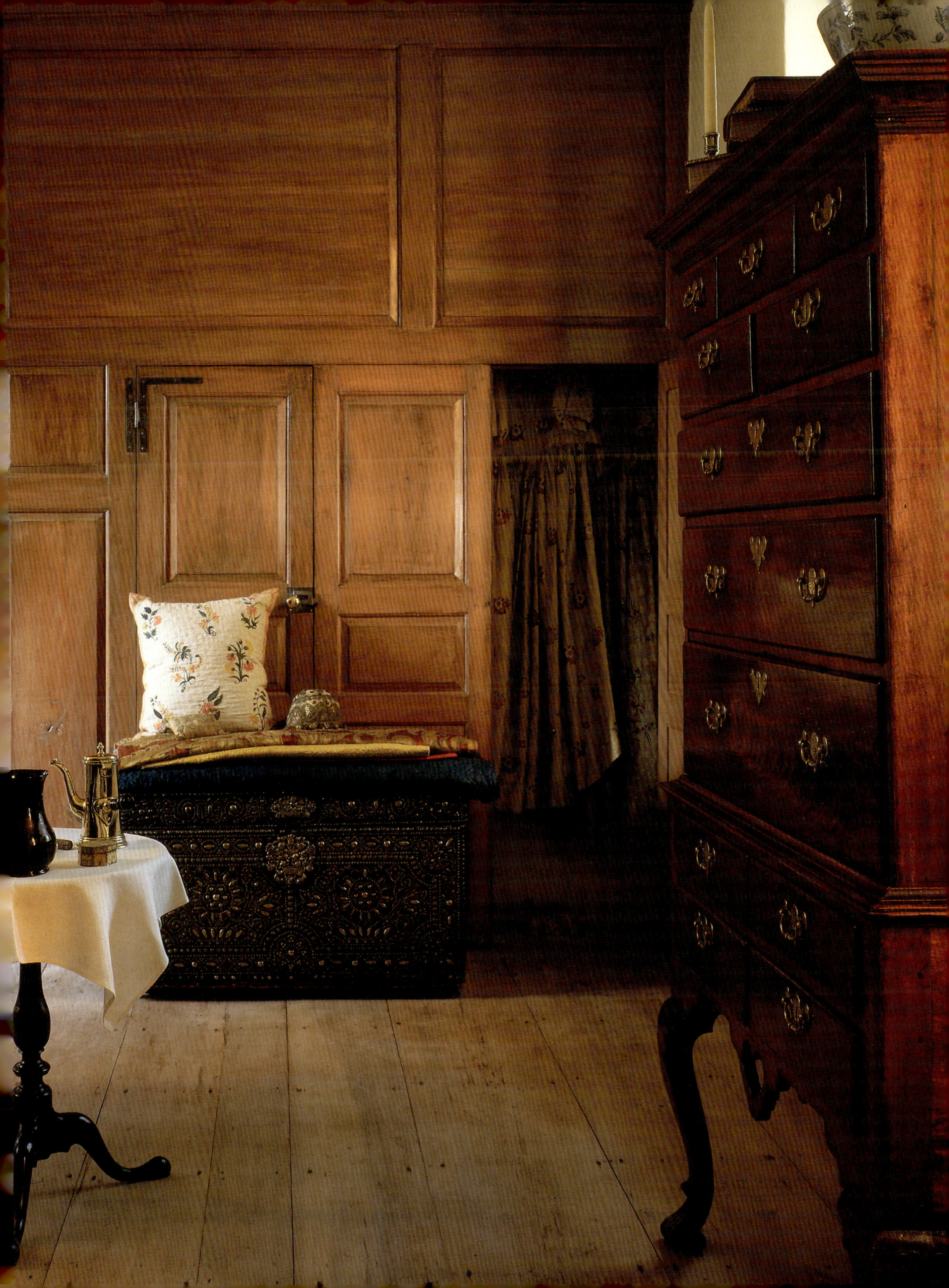

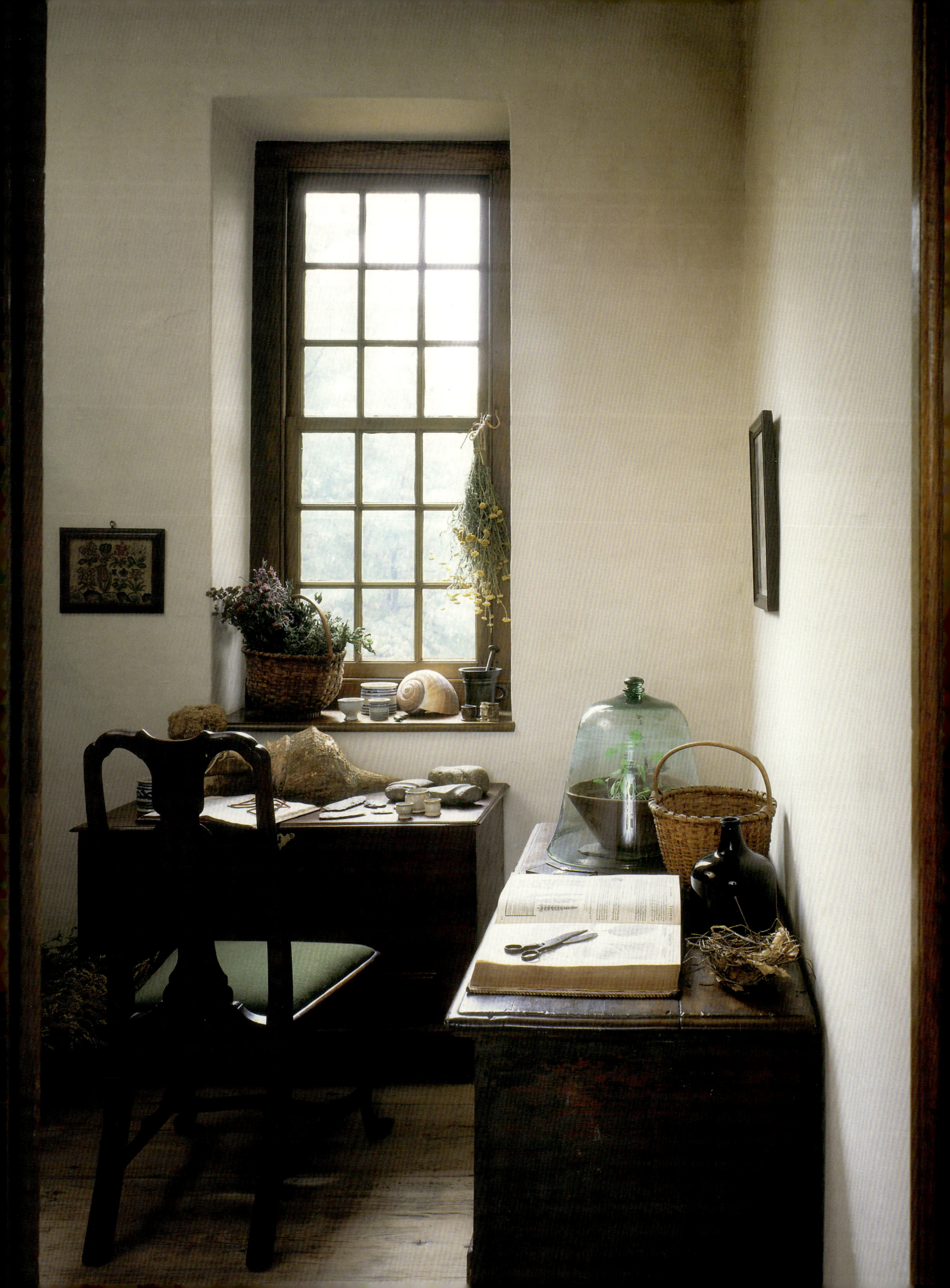

must be carefully used, as a single drop without Water will eat a hole in silk . . . after the silk is dyed with this if dip'd in the yellow it turns to a beautiful Green. I shall be very much obliged to thee for the exact receipt for dyeing the colours thee sent me, particularly the yellow Cotton, my Sister has tried it, she thinks exactly as thy Brother directed, but cannot get it to fix in Cotton I find an Orange colour the most difficult to dye, what I've sent thee was first a light yellow & then dip'd in the red dye. If I cou'd get an oppo. would send thee a pound or two of the Barberry root, it is very scarce here, my Sister got a friend of hers to write to N. England for some of it where I'm told there's great plenty. I'm almost afraid the colour will not stand, as I think such a pritty thing wou'd not have lain so long unnoticed had it been good for much.[55]

In the exchange of seeds and cuttings of plants with friends, Susanna Wright requested what was probably eggplant:

I must add a few words about a fruit, or whatever you call it, that Jemmy has told us about, which when sliced & fried, is vulgerly calld pork stake, he either did not

Copperplate engraving from *A Compendious Account of the Whole Art of Breeding, Nursing and The Right Ordering of the Silk-Worm*, by Thomas Boreman, London, 1733, showing the life cycle of the silkworm.

OPPOSITE: Workroom. Walnut side chair, Philadelphia, 1735–1750; needlework picture, England, 1700–1720.

PREVIOUS: Best Bedchamber. Walnut high chest, made by Isaac and Richard Moss, Philadelphia, 1740–1755; leather traveling chest, England, dated 1683.

The Mansion's Interior: The Rooms and Their Furnishings

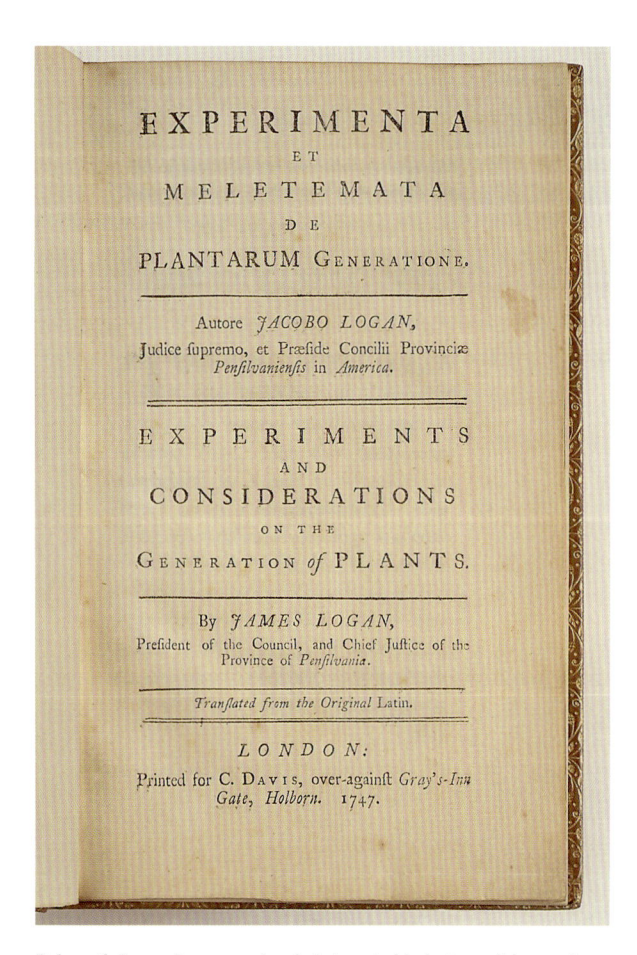

Polymath James Logan, seriously interested in botany, did experiments with maize, which he published with a Latin text in Leyden, where it drew the attention of Linnaeus.

hear, or forgot, the technical name of the plant or its produce, if it is propagated by seed, we must entreat you to save us some, if any other way, pray advise us of it, and put us in the method of procuring wherewithal to get the precious animal plant into our garden where at present we have nothing but mere vegetables— I have been very desirous for some years past, to endavour by some means or other, to get some of the Myrtle wax plants brought up, and tryd if we could propagate them in any Soyl we have, or could make, and added to what our garden already furnishes us with, if we could have Somthing resembling animal food, and Candles, I think I should be easy—as to Garden affairs.[56]

In March 1753, Charles Norris commented on some "Colly fflowr Seed" that had been sent to the Wrights and added, "We have Pease & Beans and Asparagrass too." The Norrises received beech kale and clover seeds from Susanna Wright in April of 1761.

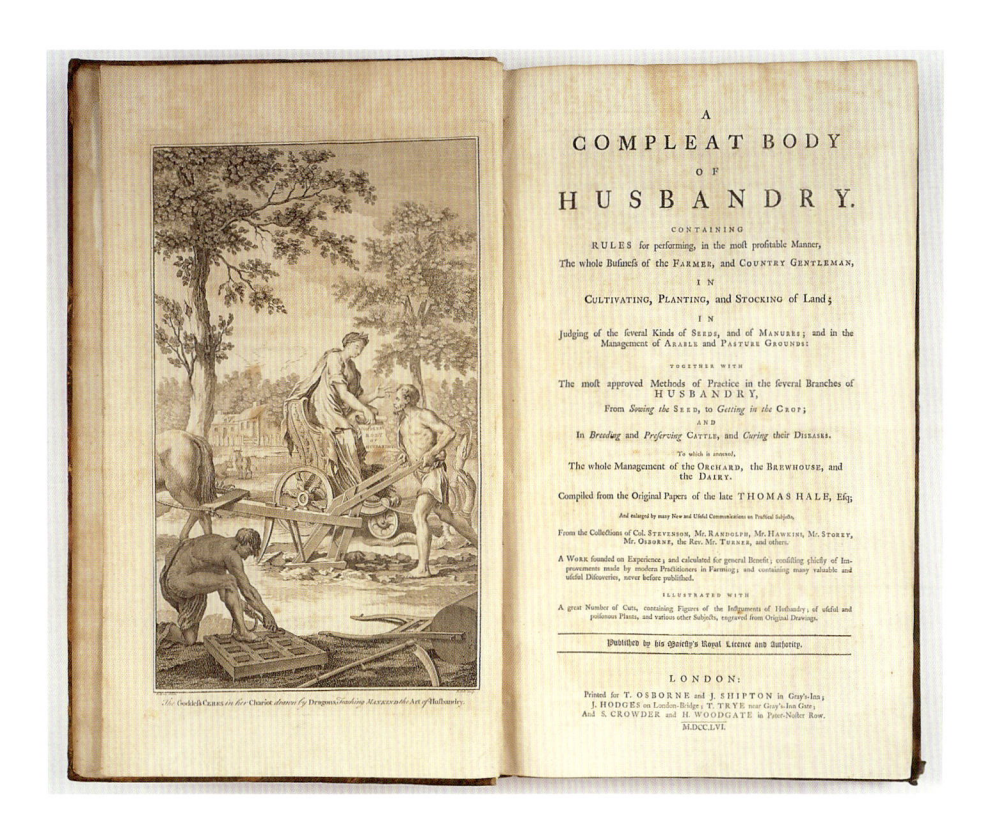

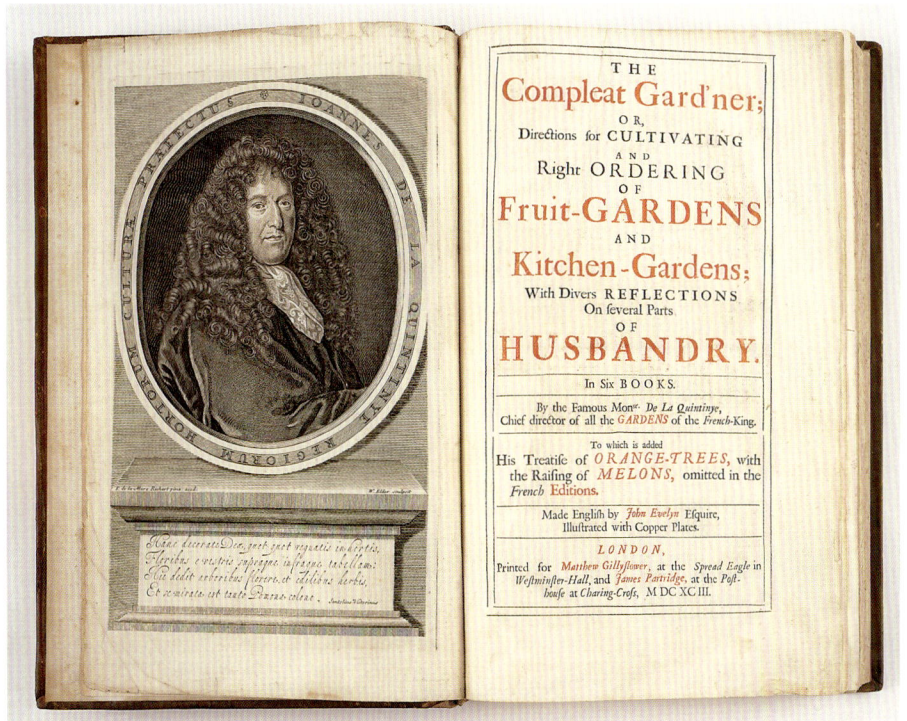

The property at Wright's Ferry Mansion was farmed with hops, hemp, mulberry trees, and orchards, and books like these above have been obtained for the collection to reflect this interest.

The Mansion's Interior: The Rooms and Their Furnishings 119

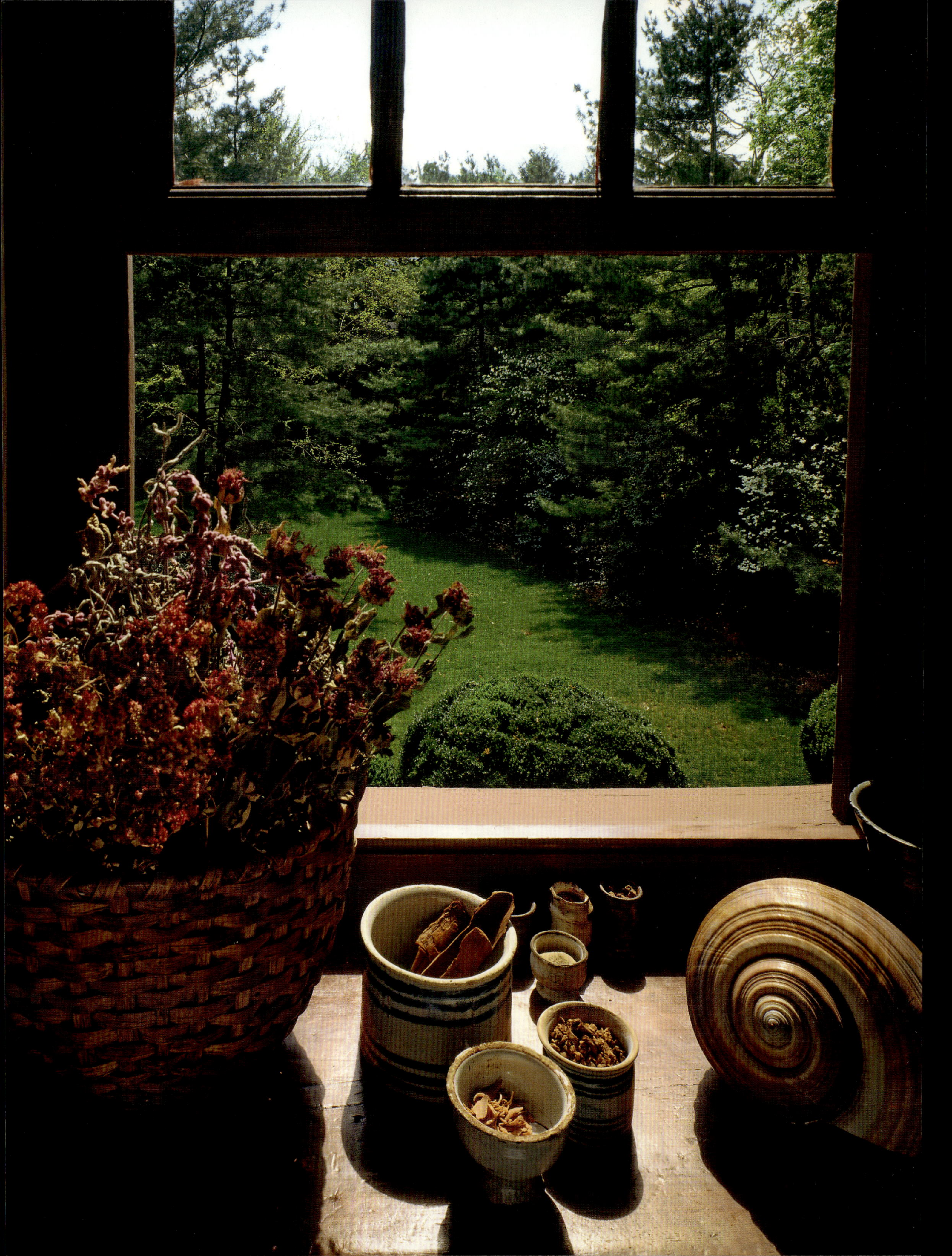

Pennsylvania walnut *schrank*, 1740–1760, designed to be disassembled for moving. The telescope, 1725-1747, was made by Matthew Loft of London. Next to the telescope stands a glass cloche used for starting seedlings in a garden.

OPPOSITE: A view toward the Susquehanna River from the workroom.

In addition to reading the latest in scientific horticultural works, Susanna Wright also was interested in current garden design. Within five years of its publication, she ordered the revolutionary garden plans designed by Alexander Pope.[57] When in London, Franklin sent her a book on husbandry. In this room is a copy of a book that James Logan loaned to her, William Wollaston's *Religion of Nature Delineated*, which particularly intrigued him because of the author's theory about the sexuality of plants.[58] As a result of reading this, Logan did a very controlled experiment with corn in his garden, and published the experiment in Latin in a periodical in Leyden. It was read by Linnaeus, who was so impressed with the work that he began a correspondence with Logan and even named a family of trees and shrubs *Loganaceae*.[59] Logan's work with hybridization helped to revolutionize the production of corn in this country.

The particular volume of Wollaston's work that was obtained for the collection actually belonged to a friend of James Logan's, Dr. Richard Mead, a fellow bibliophile, for whom this volume was specially bound. Dr. Mead was a physician in England who was involved in experiments for inoculation against small pox, a topic that drew much interest in Philadelphia. Fear of the contagion was great. Children of Susanna Wright's friends in Philadelphia were inoculated. In one of her letters, she describes how a woman whose

The Mansion's Interior: The Rooms and Their Furnishings 121

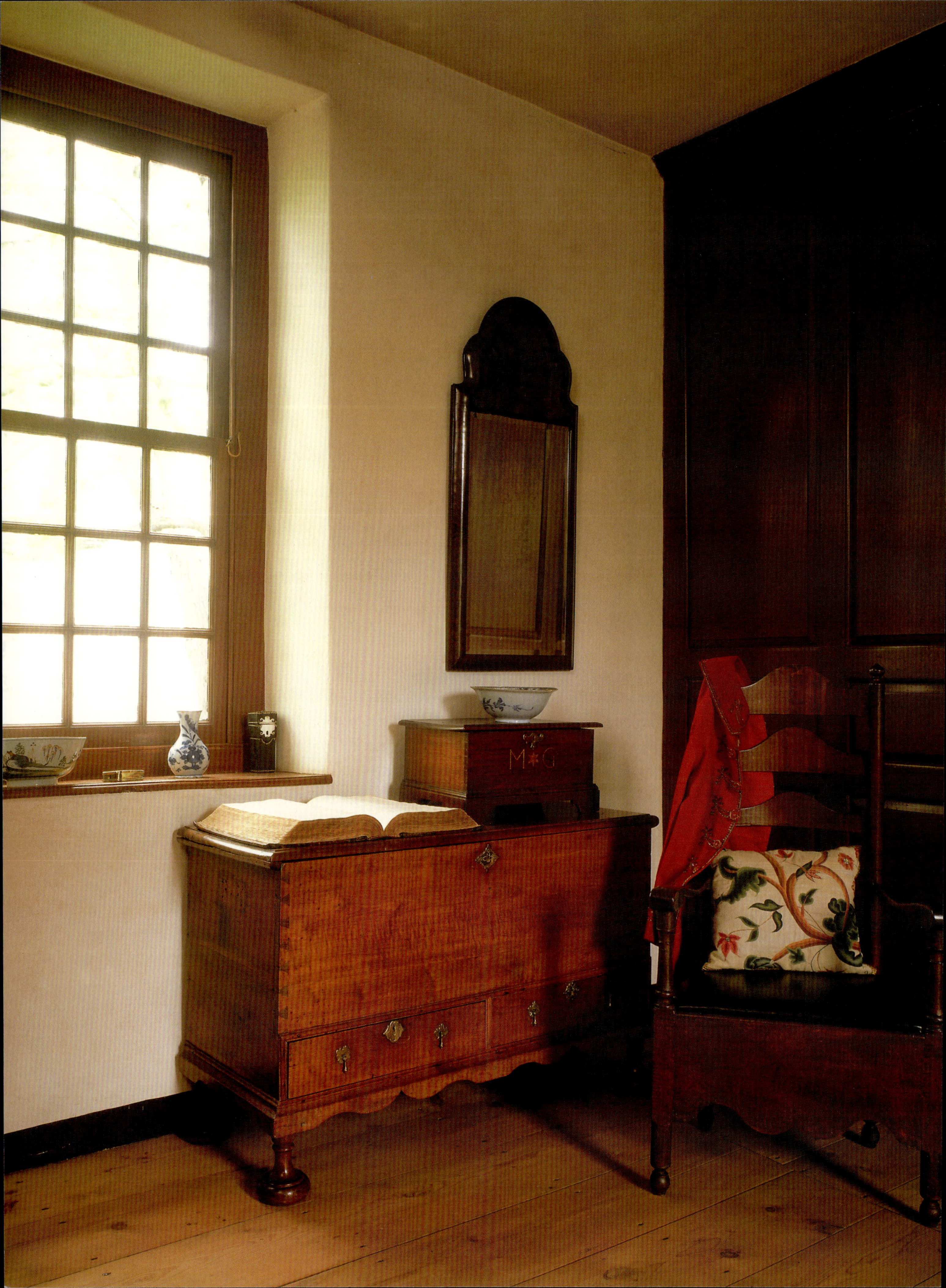
M G

children were sick with small pox had visited her and how, after the woman left, Susanna took the chair the woman had been sitting in outside to let it air, in hope of lessening the chance of exposing her nieces and nephews to the disease.

Susanna Wright used plants for medicine and, as Deborah Norris Logan said, "she was often resorted to as a physician by her neighbourhood."[60] Plants were used so extensively at this time for medicine that the study of botany was a requisite for a doctor's training. Letters to Susanna from Doctors Lloyd Zachary, Samuel Preston Moore, and Charles Moore give instructions for treating the ills of her neighbors.[61] Susanna made some medicines, like True Turlington's Balsam, a "phyal" of which she sent to Charles Norris in 1761 along with the recipe.[62]

The English delftware galley, or ointment, pots and the seventeenth-century bronze mortar and pestle were important for such preparations, as were reference books like the folio on the chest, John Parkinson's *Theatre of Plantes*, published in 1640; this volume illustrates and describes hundreds of plants—the first comprehensive systematic catalogue of plants to be published in English.

Astronomy was another interest of both Susanna Wright's family and friends. James Logan wrote a treatise on a comet he observed and had the latest works on astronomy in his extensive library. He even made corrections to Edmund Halley's astronomical tables, which Halley eventually incorporated in his work. Interest in astronomy heightened in the 1760s with the approach of the transit of Venus, especially with Philadelphia's involvement in the international scientific endeavor to observe the phenomenon. The Wrights owned a telescope, which is listed on Samuel Wright's inventory. Richard von Hess acquired a telescope for this room, made by Matthew Loft of London, 1725–1747.

In addition to astronomy, botany, and natural history, Susanna Wright enjoyed drawing and creating "little works of fancy," an interest which is reflected here in the mahogany box containing watercolors in ivory wells, an ivory-handled brush, and an ivory palette.[63]

These small rooms were also for storage. In grand houses in the seventeenth century, a small room closely associated with the main bedchamber was called the "garde-robe" and was used for storage of household linens.[64] In this small workroom, a wonderful *schrank* dominates the far wall with its design of raised panels and distinctive molded corners. The interior is equipped with shelves and drawers on the left and pegs on the right. These large storage pieces, so typical of Pennsylvania, were designed to be disassembled so that they could be moved more easily. This example is comparatively small, others being more massive. Filling the wall in this small room, the *schrank* creates an architectural effect, evocative of a paneled wall.

The Secondary Bedchamber

This room was probably the room of Susanna Wright's brother Jemmy, who was seventeen years younger than she was, the youngest of the siblings, and the first of the family to be

OPPOSITE: Maple chamber armchair, Delaware Valley, 1740–1765; walnut chest, Philadelphia, 1720–1740; shagreen razor box, England, 1720–1730 (left).

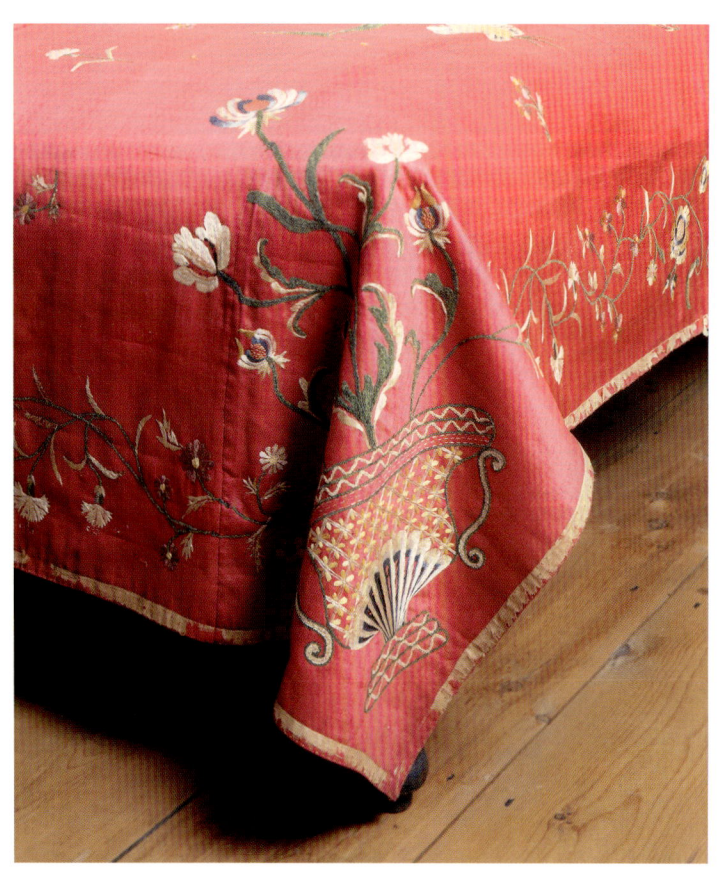

Detail of English calimanco coverlet, embroidered with silk and couched with chenille threads, 1730–1740.

born in the New World. He was not even twelve when the Wrights moved to Shawanah town on Susquehanna, and was twenty-four when Wright's Ferry Mansion was being built; he undoubtedly helped. James could perhaps view the ferry from this room, since there was a cleared expanse to the river.

Like the Clock Room beneath it, the secondary bedchamber is less formal than the parlor and the best bedchamber. Asymmetrically positioned, the fireplace is flanked by two doors, one leading to a shallow closet and the other to a large storage space. A little over half of the paneling on this wall is original and the rest (the east half), restored.[65] The fireplace retains its original brick tiles.

A greater simplicity can be seen in this room in its lack of both chair rail and baseboard. There is no applied wooden baseboard in this room, the original plaster going straight to the floor and painted black where a baseboard would be, just as it is in the kitchen and in the servants room.[66] The floor in this room had to be replaced, as one can see in the subtle shift in color from the hall floor, which is original, as are the floors in the workroom and best bedchamber. The entrance door to the middle bedchamber retains its original plate latch.[67]

Palampore made on the Coromandel Coast in India, 1740–1750, which descended in a Philadelphia Quaker family.

To the right of the entrance door is an alcove, ideal for situating a bed. The low-post bedstead, in keeping with the simplicity of the room, has two coverlets used alternately for display: a calimanco coverlet and a palampore. Both coverlets, bold in color and design, give great vibrancy to this room and also imbue it with a personality distinctly different from the best bedchamber.

The raspberry calimanco bedcovering is made of a very fine, glazed wool fabric that has been embroidered with silk and chenille threads. In his *Universal Dictionary of Trade and Commerce* of 1751–1755, Malachy Postlethwayt describes calimanco as: "(A worsted) stuff . . . (with) a fine gloss upon it. There are calamancoes of all colours, and diversely wrought; some are quite plain; others have broad stripes, adorned with flowers; some with Plain broad stripes; some with narrow stripes; and others watered."

Throughout the eighteenth century, calimanco was used for dressing beds and windows, for upholstery, and for clothing. It was a fabric that could well have been used in this house, since 36¾ yards of calimanco are listed for the year 1751 in an account book of Susanna Wright.[68]

OVERLEAF: Secondary bedchamber. Walnut side chair, Philadelphia, 1700–1720; walnut joint stool, Philadelphia, 1700–1720; walnut desk on frame, Philadelphia, 1700–1725.

The Mansion's Interior: The Rooms and Their Furnishings 125

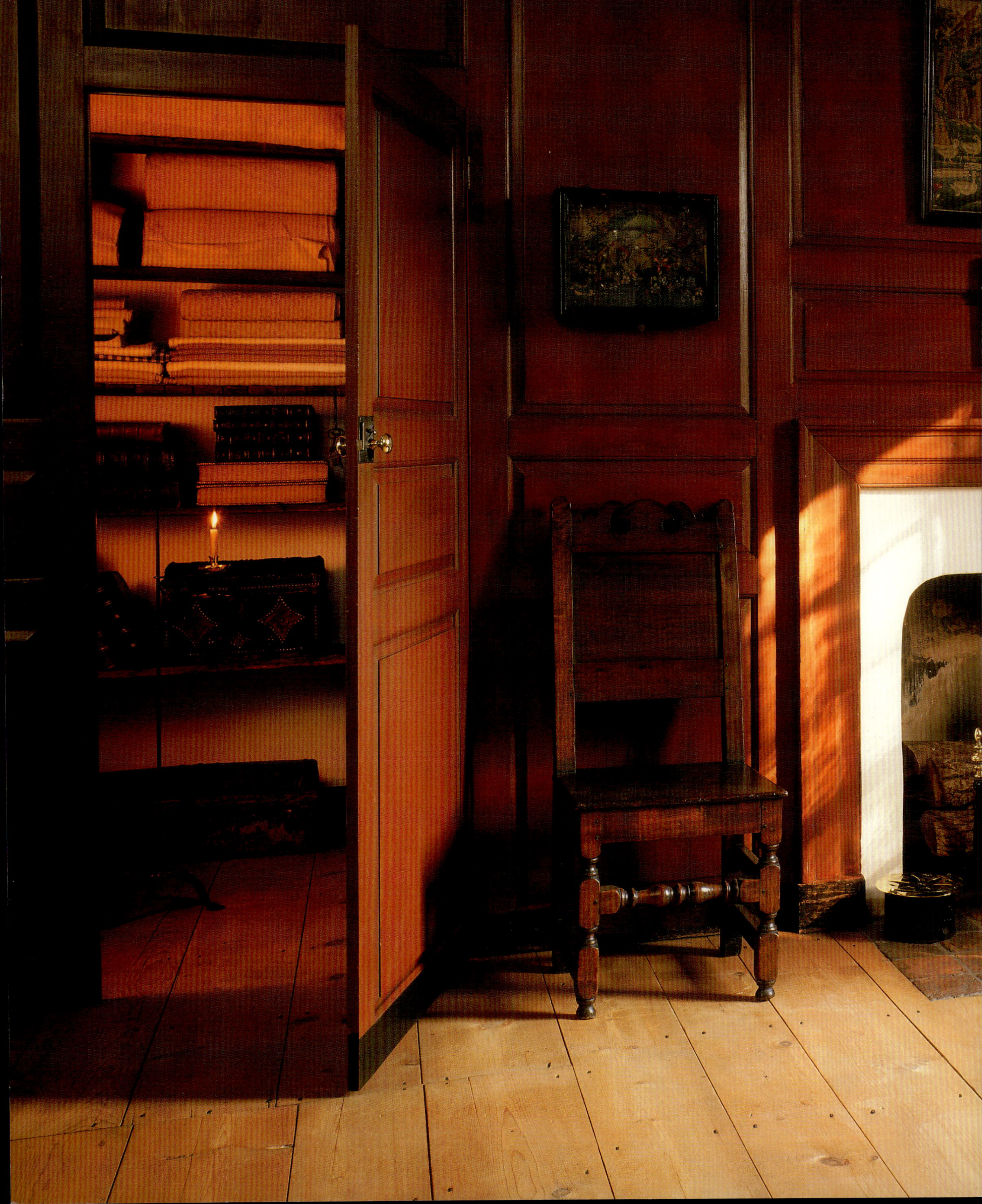

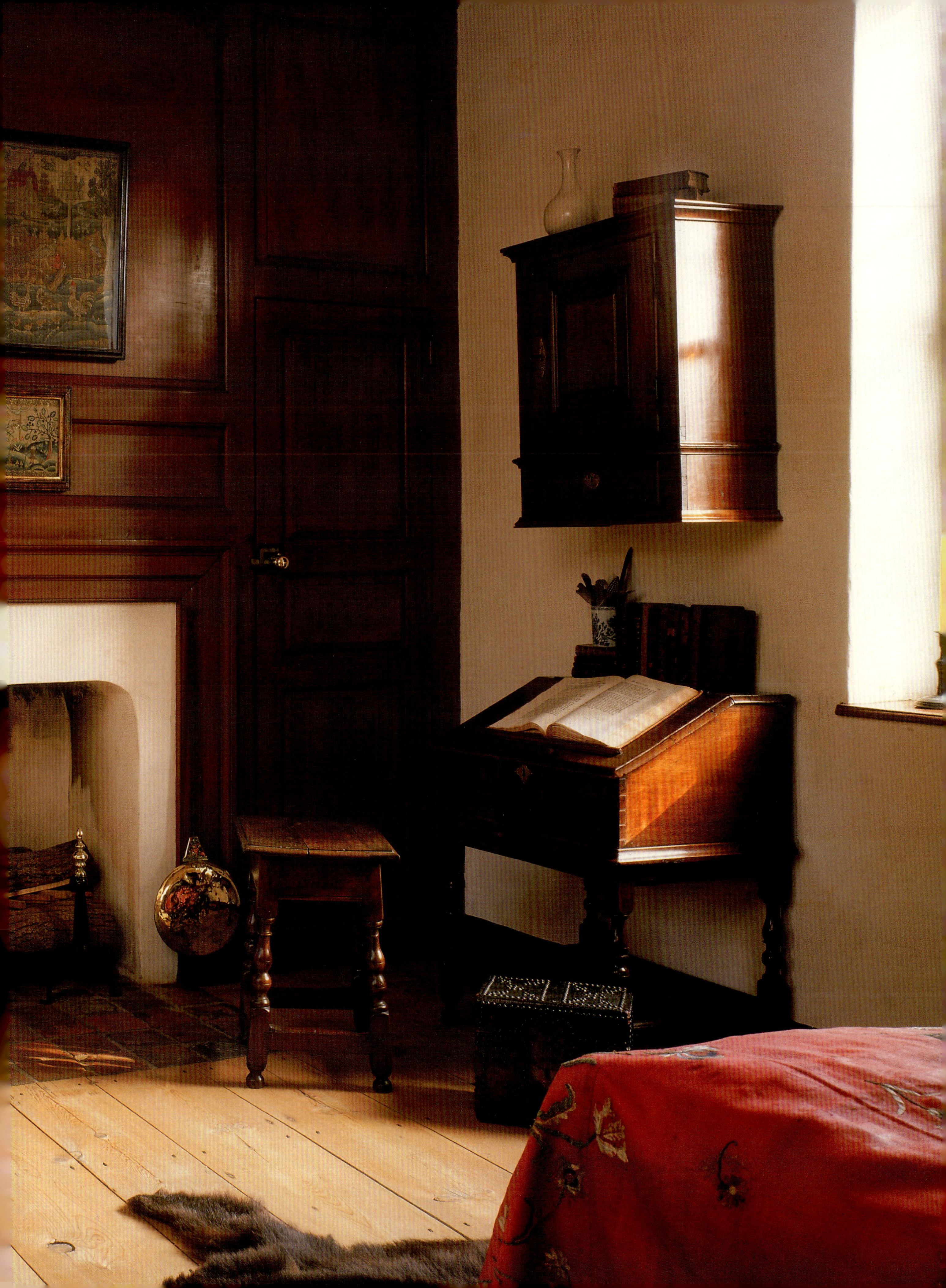

Shelves holding homespun linens, traveling cases, and books are illuminated by a rare wrought iron and brass candlestand, possibly made in Philadelphia, 1710–1750.

In rich browns and russets against a cream ground, the palampore is dramatically decorated with a bold tree of life filling the entire central space. Delicate borders of patterning fall where the bedcovering is tucked in beneath the bolster and at the sides of the bed. This palampore was made for the American market about 1740 and descended in a Philadelphia Quaker family.

Beside the bed is a black bearskin used as a small carpet, a New World *descend du lit*, a welcome comfort on icy mornings, since eighteenth-century bedchambers in winter were undoubtedly cold. Furs were used like this in households and, of course, also in clothing (like Franklin's fur cap). Furs were also extremely important for trade with England and the Continent, and the large Indian trading post at Conestoga was an outlet for this trade. The fur trade was instrumental in the whole development of Pennsylvania, since it was one of the major features that drew settlers there from its inception. Black bears were still prevalent in the immediate vicinity, as the following letter of Susanna's shows:

> *Now I think I have spun out my letter, without being able to recolect any thing further to add, except about Bears, & somthing Relating to my past Corespondence with thee my dear frend: We have had an Innundation of those Savage Creatures come down amongst us, almost famishd, by the mast being mostly destroyd, they Eat peoples hogs, be fright women & Children; a great many of them have been shot, some of our family were on the river, & met with one upon a Rock, they had no gun & Killd it with poles,—this is pretty news to write to a Citty Lady, but this is Country news.*[69]

Like the entry downstairs, this room is dominated by earlier Philadelphia furniture, dating from the first quarter of the eighteenth century—the desk-on-frame, the joint stool (another very rare form in Philadelphia furniture), the panel-back chairs, and the blanket chest, which, with its scalloped skirt and ball feet, relates to the desk and chest-on-chest in the parlor. The ladder-back chair with its bold scalloped skirt conceals a Chinese export porcelain chamber pot.

As in the best bedchamber, small personal objects help to make this room more intimate, like the man's silk cap tucked back on the blue corner shelves, and the shagreen-covered razor box with its elegant silver mounts, as well as other practical items, half-hidden or set aside on top of a chest or cupboard, like the salt-glazed chamber pot beneath the bed, the salt-glazed water bottle high on the top of the wall cupboard, and the basin for washing.

The large closet or storage space, which opens off this room, contains shelving stacked with homespun linen sheets and table covers, large bolts of linen that could be fashioned into sheets or table linens, extra bolsters, traveling cases, and books. Flax for linen was raised extensively in eighteenth-century Pennsylvania, and Benjamin Franklin especially encouraged its production. Susanna Wright raised flax and did her own spinning but then had the thread woven into cloth, as an account book shows, with a payment for two pounds, eight shillings, and six pence for weaving ninety-seven yards of linen.[70] In 1728, she received a request from James Logan, "My wife desires thee to send her 30 lbs of that fine flax she hears you have to dispose of."[71]

Just prior to the Revolution when trade was restricted, Susanna wrote that, "as Non Importation is agreed upon" her nieces "must be Industrious in Spinning, or content themselves with thin Clothing."[72] A blanket rack is nestled in at the side of the closet. A cobweb brush of beautifully turned yew wood hangs from a nail beside the shelves, beneath a small veneered looking glass.

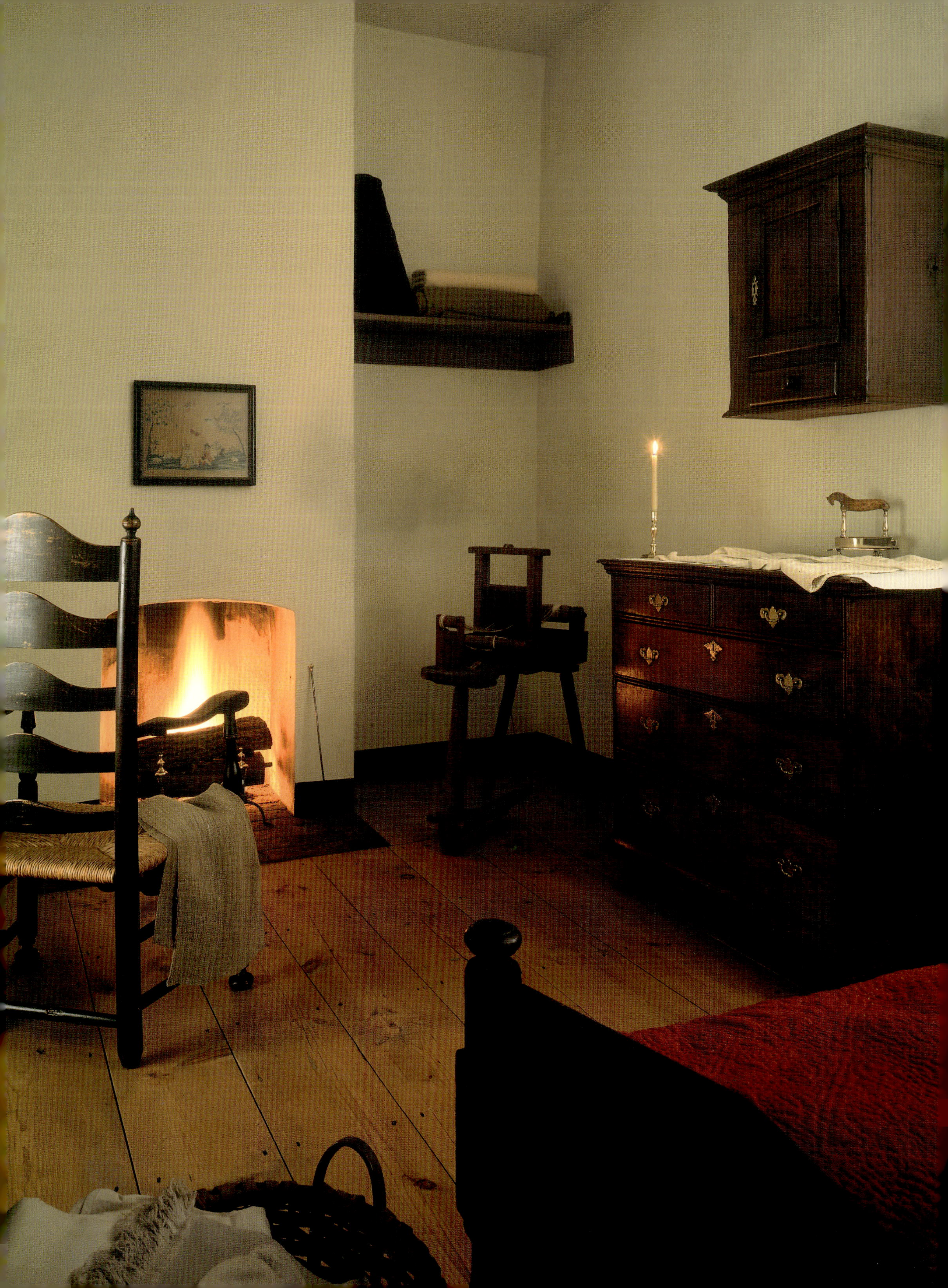

Originally, the only access to this closet was from the middle bedchamber. Now, however, there is a door opening from the closet into the servants quarters. When the building was restored, this door was added to provide easier access to the servants room for visitors.[73]

The Servants Room

Above the kitchen are two small rooms, the narrow stairs beside the kitchen fireplace originally providing the only access. Today, however, access has also been provided by a door in the adjacent large storage area that opens off the middle bedchamber, which was added during the restoration. This type of arrangement, with a staircase from the kitchen leading to a separate section of the house for servants, can be seen in the English eighteenth-century house form, identified as a two-unit house with an extra bay. In this form, the house is one room deep with a living kitchen and parlor, as R. W. Brunskill describes, with the following use for the extra bay:

> *The extra bay could conveniently serve as a kitchen or as an additional parlour but, in east Yorkshire at least, and probably in other lowland counties, the extra bay became a "men's end," i.e., the room on the ground floor was a mess room for the unmarried labourers while the room above, reached by its own staircase, was their bedroom. Access to the "men's end" was usually from the farmyard, at the side or back of the farmhouse, and this distinguishes the provision from the separately occupied cottage, which was sometimes attached to a farmhouse as an extra bay but which had a doorway at the front.*[74]

The Wrights had hired laborers to help on the farm and they undoubtedly had domestic help as well. The small room into which the staircase leads is unheated and could have served for storage of foodstuffs, such as grains. (Again, there are English precedents for rooms of this sort.) The room is lighted by a large window. Above the stairs from the kitchen, there was evidence of a small trap door in the ceiling, which opened to the attic. A ladder leading to the trap door was provided in the restoration of the building to give permanent access to the attic. The attic was never a proper room, since it did not even have a floor, just loose boards leading to the chimneys. The small room at the head of the stairs leading from the kitchen is now used as an office.

This small room leads to another room that is slightly larger and contains a tiny fireplace (with appropriately diminutive andirons and fire tools), cut directly into the plaster in an arched form with no embellishment of any sort.[75] Like the workroom, this room is appealingly austere in the white expanse of walls, the lofty ceiling, and the large window, which keeps this room filled with light. There are two additions to this room that were not here originally, a small shelf added to the niche beside the fireplace, and an opening in the plaster wall showing the original hand-split oak lath attached by rose-headed nails to the upright supports. This opening in the wall also shows how the plaster was applied so that it would seep through the cracks in the lath, forming "keys" that held plaster and lath tightly together. Animal hair, and also in some areas in this house, rye straw, provided the plaster with fibrous strength. About seventy-five percent of the plaster in the building is original, with replacement primarily in the ceilings. There was never any chair rail or applied wooden baseboard in this room; instead, as in the middle bedchamber, the area where a baseboard would be is painted black.

A simple low-post bedstead stands against the interior wall, the rich russet of the wool quilt giving a warm glow to the room. A Philadelphia chest of drawers made in the first quarter of the eighteenth century is set against the outer wall and shows how an older piece of furniture might be relegated to a secondary position in the house.

On top of the chest is a marvelous brass smoothing iron with a handle of burl elm carved in the shape of a horse. As paintings of the period attest, ironing during this period would be done on the top of a piece of furniture protected by a linen cloth.[76] Beside the chest is a basket filled with homespun linens ready to be pressed and stored with fragrant herbs, like the lavender nearby. Fabrics were extremely important in the household, where they were accorded great care. No scrap was wasted, older pieces of clothing being refurbished to a more current style, made to fit someone else, or converted to another use. Household linens also were readapted. An instance of this can be seen in the russet quilt in this room, where an old blanket dyed with indigo was reused as the batting for the quilt.

By virtue of its small size and its situation directly above the kitchen, this room was probably the warmest of the bedchambers in the depth of winter.

The Attic

The attic was an unfinished space with only a few loose boards leading to the chimneys, allowing access to the roof for emergencies and maintenance.[77] Access to the attic was through a small trap door in the ceiling above the kitchen stairs, reached by a tall, removeable ladder.[78] Not only was there no floor, there were no windows in the attic. The masonry of the gables showed no evidence of having had windows and the original rafters yielded no trace of early dormers. The dormers present at the time of the restoration had been added during the early Federal period.[79]

When the house was restored, the architects inserted trap doors in the roof near the chimneys, following the example of other early houses, which had them for emergencies and maintenance.[80] To give light to the attic, the restoration architects also inserted an eight-inch by ten-inch piece of glass into these trap doors.

The Cellar

The cellar shares the spaciousness and simplicity of design that characterize the rest of the house. With whitewashed stone walls and oak beams, the cellar is a long narrow structure with ceilings surprisingly high for such a space. One enters the cellar through two narrow paneled doors located in the entry beside the door leading to what was originally the back of the house. The cellar stairs are directly beneath the staircase leading to the second floor. Descending these stairs, one can see the shelf that acts as a pass-through to the Clock Room. Also observable here is a cut to the first floor joist to improve headroom when going down these stairs.[81] These stairs, and the shelf for the pass-through, had to be reconstructed using plaster marks and even changes in the composition of the plaster as a guide.[82]

A short distance from the foot of the stairs is one of the stone end walls of the cellar, since the cellar did not extend beneath the kitchen and part of the clock room. The cellar is composed of three large spaces corresponding to the rooms that are directly above, except for the first space in the cellar, which runs under only part of the clock room. In this section, there is a door with steps leading to the outside.

The next space is beneath the entry, where overhead one can see the stones that support the brick floor of the entry and the massive oak beams and cross beams that provide support. This part of the cellar, entirely surrounded by stone, was probably used as a cold room for food storage. At each end of this room is a large door, so the room could be closed off to keep in the cold. Sometimes cold rooms like this had a spring running through them; Brumbaugh examined the cellar very carefully for evidence of a spring, however, but found none.[83] The door leading into the section beneath the parlor is the original walnut door, an unusually fine wood for use in a cellar.

The space beneath the parlor is the largest of the cellar chambers. Above, one can see the original oak beams and the underside of the parlor floorboards. The beams, or first floor joists, are "not much more than barked trees with the tops leveled."[84] Like the stone walls, these joists were originally whitewashed. No whitewash, however, was used on the underside of the floorboards to the rooms above, which the restoration architects found somewhat unusual. In the center of the end wall is an arched support for the masonry of the chimney above it. In the restoration of the building, modern conveniences were installed here to accommodate visitors.

NOTES

1. Susanna Wright to Mary Norris, September 22, 1772. For Isaac Norris I, see Susanna Wright to Hannah Griffitts, April 5, 1762, "the first Intimacys I contracted, and the happyest hours I ever enjoyed Since I left my native land, were in thy Grandfather Norris's house"; see Appendix in this volume.
2. Nancy Goyne Evans, in *American Windsor Chairs* (NY: Hudson Hills Press, 1996), pp. 83–84, compares these banisters to the work of Francis Trumble, who supplied chairs to Charles Norris, ibid., p. 81.
3. Historic American Buildings Survey, Pa.-139, 7/15/40, sheets 1 and 14, Library of Congress.
4. The Glebe House has an unheated entry with a staircase to the second floor, which is central to the building and is flanked by a parlor and dining room, each of which has a fireplace and closets at one end.
5. G. Edwin Brumbaugh, "The Architecture of the Wright Mansion," unpublished manuscript, p. 16 (hereafter cited as *Architecture*).
6. The Wrights bought land in Chester from two carpenters, James Hendricks and John Owen, and knew Philadelphia joiner Stephen Armitt and Cornelius Verhulst of Lancaster; see Appendix in this volume, p. 271.
7. Cornelius Verhulst's estate inventory lists over thirty-five planes and only one entry for turning tools. Cornelius Verhulst, estate inventory dated February 6, 1740/1, Court House Records, Lancaster County Historical Society.
8. Debit accounts also appear in the account book, bound by William Davies, for the years 1731 to 1735, itemizing payments made on behalf of Cornelius Verhulst by Samuel Blunston. These include loans of cash and payments for services and goods, including "4 yds Frieze," "files & Locks," "Saw, Plain Irons & Compasses," and "6 lb of nails." The total, well over forty pounds, exceeded the value of Verhulst's estate inventory of 1740, which amounted to a little over thirty-eight pounds. These debit accounts, therefore, perhaps reflect a joint business venture between Cornelius Verhulst and Samuel Blunston. In 1735, Verhulst had purchased lots in Lancaster to build houses on to sell and even at the time of his death in 1740, he owned "a Lott & Timber on it for building a house." See Jerome H. Wood, Jr., *Conestoga Crossroads: Lancaster, Pennsylvania, 1730–1790* (Harrisburg, PA: Pennsylvania Historical and Museum Commission, 1979), p. 11.
9. G. E. Brumbaugh, *Architecture*, p. 14. See also Albert F. Ruthrauff, "Report on the Restoration of Wright's Ferry Mansion" (unpublished manuscript, 1976), p. 13 (hereafter cited as *Report*).
10. A. F. Ruthrauff, *Report*, p. 19.
11. Ibid., pp. 25–26.
12. Letter fragment from Susanna Wright, April 5, 1765, WFM 83.18.13.
13. G. E. Brumbaugh, *Architecture*, pp. 16–17. A. F. Ruthrauff, *Report*, pp. 19–20.
14. A. F. Ruthrauff, *Report*, p. 26.
15. Ibid., p. 6.
16. Peter Thornton, *Seventeenth-Century Interior Decoration in England, France and Holland* (New Haven, CT: Yale University Press, 1983), pp. 83–85 (hereafter cited as *Seventeenth-Century Interior*).
17. F. B. Tolles, *Meeting House*, p. 133.
18. Charles Norris to James Wright, March 3, 1747/8. Norris Papers, misc. vol., p. 12, Historical Society of Pennsylvania.
19. Anna Brightman, "Window Curtains in Colonial Boston and Salem," *The Magazine Antiques* (August 1964): 184–87.
20. Rodris Roth, *Floor Coverings in 18th-Century America* (Washington, DC: Smithsonian Press, 1967), pp. 58–59.
21. Hermione Sandwith and Sheila Stainton, *The National Trust Manual of Housekeeping* (London: Allen Lane, 1984), p. 73.
22. J. F. Watson, *Annals*, vol. I, p. 205.
23. L. W. Labaree, et al., eds., *Papers*, vol. 4, p. 336.
24. Newton D. Mereness, ed., *Travels in the American Colonies* (New York: Antiquarian Press, 1961), p. 411.
25. D. N. Logan, *Susanna Wright*; see Appendix in this volume.
26. Ibid.
27. L. W. Labaree, *Papers*, vol. 6, p. 23.
28. J. F. Watson, *Annals*, vol. I, p. 204.
29. Samuel Bethel, inventory dated June 17, 1777, Court House Records, Lancaster County Historical Society.

30. Susanna Wright, will dated January 28, 1782, Will Book E, vol. 1, Court House Records, Lancaster County Historical Society.
31. Samuel Blunston, inventory dated October 31, 1745, Pearson Family Papers, Historical Society of Pennsylvania.
32. Susanna Wright to Mary Norris, September 22, 1772; WFM 83.18.104; see Appendix in this volume.
33. G. E. Brumbaugh, *Architecture*, pp. 14–15. A. F. Ruthrauff, *Report*, pp. 17–18.
34. S. Barber, *Extracts*, p. 4.
35. WFM, Vellum Portfolio, 83.18.1, p. 15.
36. Charles Norris to the Wrights, November 3, 1761, Norris Papers, misc. vol. p. 34, Historical Society of Pennsylvania.
37. The "salmon" was perhaps pike. George L. Heiges, "Benjamin Franklin in Lancaster County," *Journal of the Lancaster County Historical Society* 61, no. 1 (January 1957): 5.
38. S. Barber, *Extracts*.
39. Deborah Franklin to Susanna Wright [n.d.], private collection.
40. L. W. Labaree, et al., eds., *Papers*, vol. 6, pp. 23–24; see Appendix in this volume.
41. Deborah Franklin to Susanna Wright, July 14, 1757; *Publications of the Pennsylvania Society of Colonial Dames of America*, vol. 1 (1905), pp. 12–13; see Appendix in this volume.
42. Sally Armitt to Susanna Wright, November 8, 1755; Autograph Collection, Case 19, Box 5, Historical Society of Pennsylvania; see Appendix in this volume.
43. Compare the Glebe House, built in 1698, (Historic American Buildings Survey: Pa.-139, 7/15/40, sheet 1), in which the kitchen is a step down from the adjacent dining room. It, too, has a squirrel-tail oven opening off the back of the fireplace, a door leading to the outside, and narrow stairs beside the kitchen fireplace to the floor above.
44. G. E. Brumbaugh, *Architecture*, pp. 12–13. A. F. Ruthrauff, *Report*, pp. 15–17.
45. G. E. Brumbaugh, *Architecture*, p. 17.
46. Ibid., pp. 12–13. A. F. Ruthrauff, *Report*, p. 3.
47. A. F. Ruthrauff, *Report*, p. 3.
48. G. E. Brumbaugh, *Architecture*, p. 13. A. F. Ruthrauff, *Report*, p. 3.
49. A. F. Ruthrauff, *Report*, p. 16.
50. Ibid., p. 22. G. E. Brumbaugh, *Architecture*, p. 17. When the house was restored, the architects carefully examined this paneled wall to discover whether a verbal tradition were true of a hidden passage leading from here through to the parlor closet below and from there down to the cellar with a tunnel to the Susquehanna River. Brumbaugh and Ruthrauff found this tradition to be totally false. On both floors the original joists and flooring boards were still in place and had no opening, nor was there ever an opening in the cellar wall to allow for a tunnel. Mr. Brumbaugh had encountered a similar tradition that also proved to be false, regarding Washington's headquarters at Valley Forge.
51. A. F. Ruthrauff, *Architecture*, p. 22.
52. R. W. Brunskill, *Houses and Cottages of Britain; Origins and Development of Traditional Buildings* (London: The Orion Publishing Group, 2000), p. 202 (hereafter cited as *Houses and Cottages*).
53. P. Thornton, *Seventeenth-Century Interior*, pp. 296–302. See also Arthur K. Wheelock, Jr., *A Collector's Cabinet* (Washington DC: National Gallery of Art, 1998); and Patrick Mauries, *Cabinets of Curiosities* (London: Thames & Hudson, 2002).
54. Jack L. Lindsey, *Worldly Goods: The Arts of Early Pennsylvania, 1680–1758* (Philadelphia: Philadelphia Museum of Art, 1999), pp. 34–35.
55. Milcah Martha Moore to Susanna Wright, February 20, 1771, Library Company of Philadelphia, no. 17, 9.12.13.
56. Susanna Wright to Charles Norris, n.d. [1763?], WFM 83.18.17; see Appendix in this volume.
57. Invoice from Charles Norris, n.d. [about 1750], Norris Papers, misc. vol., p. 38, Historical Society of Pennsylvania; see Appendix in this volume, p. 269.
58. Edwin Wolf 2nd, *The Library of James Logan 1674–1751* (Philadelphia: Library Company of Philadelphia, 1974), pp. 525–26.
59. F. B. Tolles, *Meeting House*, pp. 216–17.
60. D. N. Logan, *Susanna Wright*; see Appendix in this volume.

61. Dr. Lloyd Zachary to Susanna Wright, October 8, 1744; Dr. Lloyd Zachary and Adam Spencer to Samuel Blunston, September 18, 1744; see Appendix in this volume.
62. She also sent the recipe to Elizabeth Coultas, which is in the *Elizabeth Coultas Receipt Book 1749–1750*, Manuscript Collection, Winterthur Library.
63. D. N. Logan, *Susanna Wright*; see Appendix in this volume.
64. P. Thornton, *Seventeenth-Century Interior*, p. 299.
65. A. F. Ruthrauff, *Report*, p. 21.
66. Ibid., pp. 21–22.
67. Ibid., p. 22.
68. WFM Vellum Portfolio, p. 1.
69. Susanna Wright to [Mary Norris?], October 8, 1774; WFM 83.18.175; see Appendix in this volume.
70. WFM Vellum Portfolio, p. 13.
71. James Logan to Susanna Wright, June 18, 1728; *Publications of the Pennsylvania Society of Colonial Dames of America*, vol. 2 (1906), p. 10.
72. Susanna Wright to [Mary Norris?], October 8, 1774; WFM 83.18.175; see Appendix in this volume.
73. A. F. Ruthrauff, *Report*, p. 21. In the ceiling of this storage area, a large trap door was also added when the house was restored. This trap door had not been there originally but was needed to service mechanical equipment located in the attic.
74. R. W. Brunskill, *Houses and Cottages*, pp. 80–81.
75. G. E. Brumbaugh, *Architecture*, pp. 17–18. A. F. Ruthrauff, *Report*, p. 21.
76. P. Thornton, *Seventeenth-Century Interior*, pl. 283.
77. A. F. Ruthrauff, *Report*, pp. 7–8, 22–23.
78. G. E. Brumbaugh, *Architecture*, p. 15.
79. A. F. Ruthrauff, *Report*, pp. 7, 23.
80. Ibid.
81. G. E. Brumbaugh, *Architecture*, p. 14.
82. Ibid.
83. G. E. Brumbaugh, *Architecture*, p. 14. A. F. Ruthrauff, *Report*, pp. 13–14.
84. A. F. Ruthrauff, *Report*, p. 13.

*A*PPENDIX

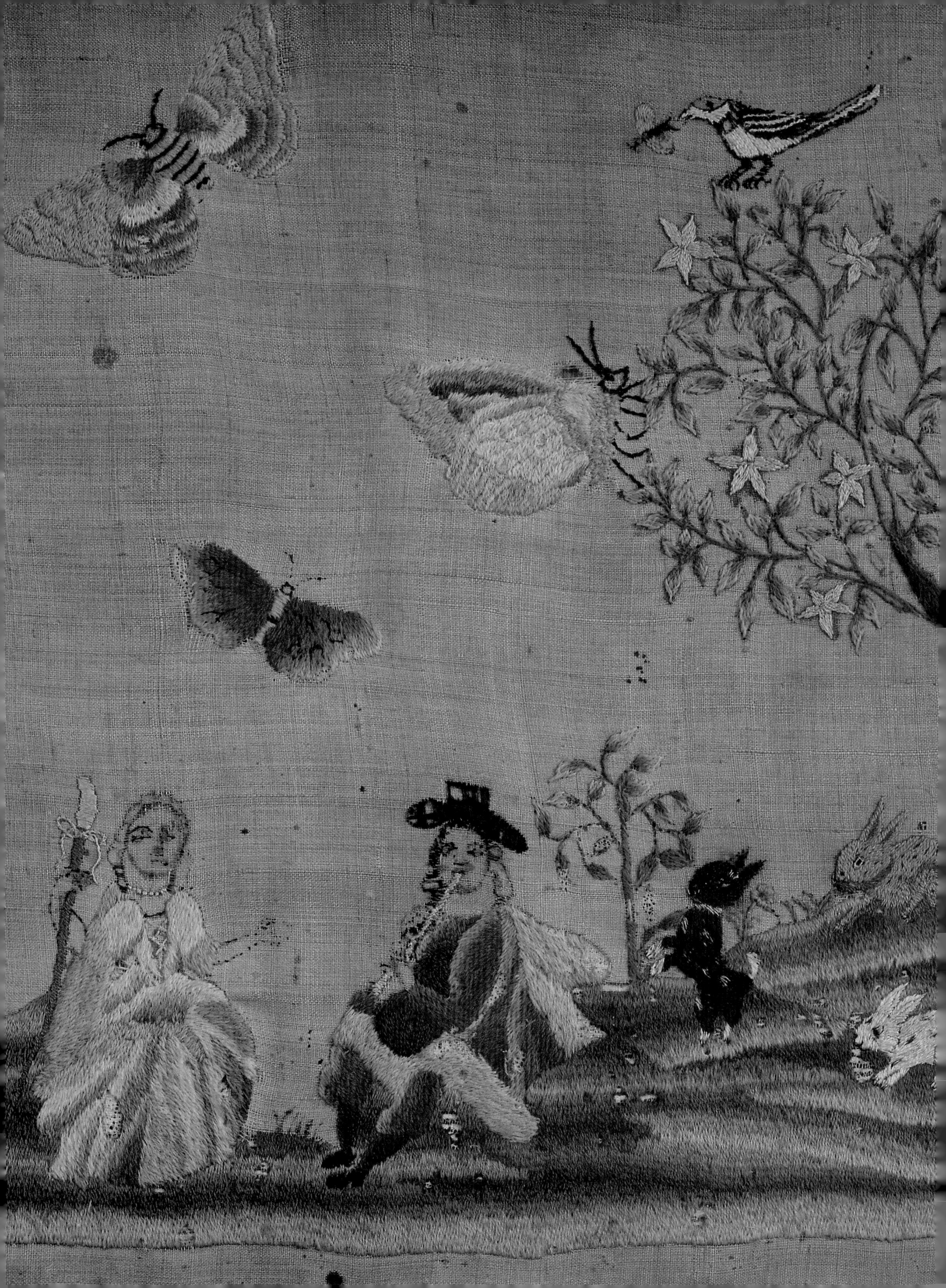

SELECTED LETTERS

She was well acquainted with books, had an excellent memory, as well as a most clear and comprehensive judgment; she spoke and wrote the French language with great ease and fluency; she had also a knowledge of Latin, and of Italian, and had made considerable attainments in many of the sciences. Her letters written to her friends, were deservedly esteemed for their ingenuity. She corresponded with James Logan, Isaac Norris, and many other celebrated characters of that period...[1]

Deborah Norris Logan included these words in her description of Susanna Wright, who had been a close friend of both the Norris and Logan families for four generations and had corresponded with them for well over half a century. Letters were an important link in friendship. Through letters, Susanna Wright was able to be an active part of the vibrant intellectual milieu of Philadelphia. Letters were also part of her literary expression. She enjoyed the published letters of Alexander Pope, Lady Mary Wortley Montague, and Madame de Maintenon and carefully composed her own letters to her friends, as surviving drafts show. The selection here makes clear the quality of her writing, the range of her correspondents, and the breadth of her interests. These letters also reflect a remarkable time period from 1714, when she journeyed to America as a sixteen-year-old girl and saw Philadelphia in its infancy through the Revolutionary War, when she admonished her nephew who was about to abandon his Quaker ideals to take up arms. Susanna Wright's letters reflect the "vivacity and spirit of her conversation," which Deborah Norris Logan described as "the best judges of such merit affirm they had seldom known to be equalled." The letters included here are both to and from her friends to convey that conversational spirit and to give intimate voice to the individuals who have been mentioned throughout this volume. Many of them were accomplished, learned individuals like Benjamin Franklin, James Logan, Charles Thomson, and Hannah Griffitts.

Where possible, the text of the letters presented here was taken from the original manuscripts, maintaining the original spelling and punctuation. Use of "thee" and "thou" was distinctive to the Society of Friends. Also distinctive was their method of giving dates prior to 1752 in the Julian calendar dating by the number of the month, the first month being March rather than January, the tenth, December. Brief explanatory information is given before each letter and the source of the text used for the transcription in the notes. Wright's Ferry Mansion has a small collection of original letters that are presented here, identified as "WFM." Although some of these were published in the *Publications of the Pennsylvania Society of Colonial Dames of America*, vols. 1 and 2 in 1905–1906, alterations there were made to reflect standard spelling and punctuation.

Susanna Wright to William Croudson, Jr., July 1, 1714[2]

fathers & mothers dear Love
to you all—

              Philadelphia ye 1 5$_{mo}$ 1714

Dear Cousin

 By these thee mayst understand we all got safe to this place this day only father who Stays a few miles off on some business. We sail^d from the rock at Liverpool the 15 of the 2 mo & arrived at Cork the 19. Sail^d from thence the 25. We met with nothing extraordinary ~~only~~ in betwixt England & Cork only mist our course about 10 Leages. We were driven by Contrary winds that on the 8 3$_{mo}$ Saw the Island of St Michaels Latitude 38. The next day Saw St Georges Lat 39, Gresaria 39–[20?] & Pico Latitude 38. I saw pico several times, tis so high it lookt higher then the Clouds. 23 Saw a sea Spout ahead of us, the wind SW our Cource WNW, the wind being brisk drove it to the norward before it reached us. The 21 caught a torteise. The 26 Caught another weighed 44 lb. The Same day Saw a Ship Call^d the Carrolina Gally, Capt Geffery Coman^r; & as they were hoisting out the boat to go on board her, one Roger Perry a Sailor was unfortunately drown^d. We saw Several Dolphins & caught 2, one on the 5 the other on the 13 of the 3 month. They Look the prettiest Creatures as the Swim & the finest Coulers as tis posable anything Can bee. When the are out of the water they are as fine Coulers as before. We Saw Several flying fish. There was one in one of the dolphins & in that flying fish a creature about an inch & ½ Long, hard on the back, ½ an inch broad & a cloven tail, 14 feet & Every foot a very Sharp Claw Like a bird. We Saw abundace of Sherks—4 together—but Caught none. We all had our health very well only pacy who was Let blood & recovered. We were 168 people on board & none dyed but one of the Captains Servants, a woman. We have had abundace of rain Sometimes & 2 Storms & Some Short gusts, but in the whole have had a very good voiage. In the Storm the Ship rould the End of her main yard in the water & broke her foreyard & losoned the main mast & broke the main top gallant mast. I was asitting in the great Cabin & See came in Just on mee & wet mee almost all over. We have had the cabin swim with water Several times & our Close cabbin broke down. The ship would rowl & tumble us all to one End of the cabbin & tumble us out of bed; but all the hardShip we Endured I hope will be maid up with the pleasanties of this Land. Tis Certainly the pleasantest Country as Can be—always Clear wether & a wholesome air. Along as we travel'd in the woods betwixt Bohemia & apequeny in penselvania twas the pleasantest as can be Imagined. Abundance of sweet Shrubs & Charming trees with abundance of birds Singing—twas Extream pleasan. Then we came up a creek into deleware bay & so to this place, all very pleasant. They Say now tis as hot as at any time; tis very Little Hotter then In England. Indeed the country & Citty answers what we have heard of it. We saw Several Ships but Spoke none but a Philedelphia Sloop & a Liverpool Ship which kept us Company to the Capes of Virginia. The 17 4$_{mo}$ we sounded & had 16 fathom & the next day Saw Land. We smelt the sweet pines before we saw them. We entred Cape Henry & sailed up the capes to oxford. From oxford we went to bohemia in a Sloop; from bohemia to apequmeny by Land & from thence to this place. Tis a very pleasant Citty. We have had a prosperes voige withall our La[?] & healths which, with all other mercys, I hope we Shall never forget. The Sea Spout which we Saw was Like a great black twisted Cloud reached betwixt the Skie & Sea. Had it L[?] on the Ship which it was very near doing had we not Seen it & [ ] about to prevent it. The wind favoring, it had be almost Certain to have Sunk us. We had one on board that was in one as a spout fell on it, Shav'd the deck into the hould & fil'd them full of water; but they being Light Loden & nere Land Land got alive to Land. It is indeed a charming Country & Citty—more frds then other people in it & 2 great meeting houses. I hartily wish if all was easy the [here?] but dare Say no more of that dear Cousin. Be sure thou write as often as opertunity will permit. News sent in this Citty is reasonable. Please to give my dear Love to unkle & aunt & Cousins with all that may ask after mee. I must conclude my paper's done & am with Sincere Love to thy Self thy truly afectionate Cousin—   Susanna Wright

I writ a Letter from Cape Henry but Could not Send it. S W

[*In margin:*]
I often think of all my relations & frd Left in England but cant think of Seing England any more. The pleasantnes of this Country & the toyle of the Sea Journey will hinder mee. I must once more bid the farewell but hopes not forever. Thy truly Loveing Cousin, tho at this distance—thee in one quarter of the world & I in one.

[*Addressed:*]
For
William Croudson Junior
Warrington in Lancashire
Great Brittain
Europe

James Logan to Susanna Wright, April 12, 1723[3]

Philaphia 12th 2mo 1723

Dear Susy
Last night at my Return from Burlington I mett with thine dated last first day evening in which thou shews a Concern by much too great for the Subject, and the two first pages of thy Lettr will very justly fall under thy well-grounded reflections in ye last which I read with very great Satisfaction because most solidly true.

Upon the whole this certain Observation may be made that hap=piness in this Life depends not in any proportion so much on out=ward Circumstances as on the inward Disposition of the Mind and the composition of the Animal Spirits, which in some persons I have often thought are so Smooth Soft and fine as to be always easie without admitting almost any thing to ruffle or disturb them, while others Seem to be rather corrosive that not only frett themselves conti-nually, but doe the Same by every thing that comes near them. This I acknowledge is carrying the matter too far, yet I doubt there is but too much Justice in the thought. It is our Duty however to labour their correction but the unhappiness is that by means of themselves only we can not work their Correction.

I Shall however be so plain here as to lett thee know my Un=
easiness has arose from an excess of a very commendable quality
in it Self: a tender Love of my Countrey (I mean not this Province)
of whose future State I have such present Views as pall all other
Enjoym^ts It is a weakness that I am labouring against to the
utmost of my Power, and was not many nights Since very much
relieved by a Dream that made a very strong Impression on me
(thou sees my further weakness in these trifling freedoms) wch was this
I thought I was Sitting very mournful in a Meadow or field by the
Side of a very great River when something appeared on my right
hand above me disswading me from my anxiety & shewing me
a Track [ ] in which I had come out of that River that I had only
so much farther to goe into the same into the River again
and then all would be entirely over with me I awaked upon
this and made a great many very pleasing Reflections upon it
to my self not without a great deal of Gratitude to the Genius or
whatever it was that gave me so seasonable an Admonition.

I must further observe hereupon that it is not the want of know
ledge that makes mankind unhappy but the want of power to
apply it Most people know their Duty but they want a right Dis=
position of Mind to putt that knowledge into practice. I could
at this time and at most others in my Life Say or write a
great deal on these subjects to shew the folly of Such an Anxiety
not only from the precepts of others but from my own reasoning
upon it. The old Testam^t furnishes us with large Materials both
in precept & Example to this purpose and the Doctrine of ye New
will render such a fruitless Concern absurd in the highest degree
Nor is it only the Scriptures that will afford instructive Lessons against
the folly but even pagan Authors will doe it in Abundance. I have
almost continually before me a few Lines of Horace; wch I wish
I could quote to thy Understanding in his own Words but the sense
of them is that the Wise God wraps up the events of futurity
in his inscrutable Mind and laughs at man if he pretends to
carry his apprehension beyond the stint allow'd to him. Know
it is thy Duty to make the best of the present All the rest
rolls on like a River Sometimes Smooth & quiet in its Channel
Sometimes overflowing its banks carries Buildings flocks and
herds before it. He is the only happy man who can say I have
lived to day Lett God Send what he will to tomorrow & with

Selected Letters

more to the Same purpose in that excellent Ode ye 29th of ye 3^d
Book of which I hope thou hast a Translation.

    I shall further here Send thee some Reflections I wrote now
almost 20 years agoe upon a particular occasion wch was this
Wm Trent & I having been reading the public News together
just then come in Stept into a Tavern where he began being
somewhat inclined to the same kind of Melancholy with my self
to make his Observations upon it. I took up the Philosophers part
and we reasoned together upon that & the like Subjects till our watches
lett us know ye time we had spent upon them wch was at least two
hours more than we had imagined Late as it was when I went home
I resolved to digest what I had there said & committ it to writing
wch I did in 3 sheets that night and the next day or day after but
never farther prosecuted it. what was done remains (as thou wilt see it
uncorrected) ~~for~~ I was unwilling to destroy it because it possibly might
be of Service to me. But I think I once Shew'd it thee before.

    I have in this told thee my own Distemper and proceeded upon it
as if I were prescribing to others. thou sees therefore that I am not
ignorant of proper remedies but as I Said before It is not knowledge
that is wanting to redress the evils of this World, but Will & Power
wch certainly depend on some thing very different from what is commonly
Imagined. If thou ever touches this Subject Pray lett it be with as much
of the heart & as little of the head as possible, for I very much admire thy
Poetick Lines of ye first sort. being the proper talent of yor Sex, but in
the other ours often outdoe you. Pray think not of me on any [ ] in
relation to thy self, but as thy faithful unchangeable friend & therefore
laying aside at all times all apprehensions & scruples consider me such
as I really am without Reserve & what [?] Pray fail not to return my
sheets by a Safe hand   ever professed to thee.
    J. Logan

[*In margin:*]
    If thy father can help me to some good flour it would Oblige me
    J L

Isaac Norris II to Susanna Wright, April 18, 1728[4]

    Barely to State the question leaves me at least a labour'd Epistle In advance, but when my hearty good wishes can congratulate anything conducive to your happiness or pleasure, I forgo the formalities wch might otherwise be necessary to retain while we converse with a part of the World, now made polite (please to let me say) since your remove among them.

    I must not omit to give all the Joy you can expect In part[g] with both the Girls; Bettsee my old friend has a very particular share in my good wishes, And my Chester Journeys may one day give me an opportunity in proper person to bid Pacie a Long Felicity.

    And now we have removed these from thy Care & conducted them thro ye nicer rules of feminine life pray give me one excuse why I may not expect to hear from thee at least once a Year, since at this time, If you are Indeed farmers, the brush must be burnt up, the grass seed sown, and phaps.: the verdant Meads wth Intermingled flowers
              Inspire new Joys & Cheat the flying hours.
Thus to live, In the midst of Rural pleasures as they are most natural, I've always believed them most lasting And on This consideration I pay a due Deference, to thy last & beautifull discription of your Parradise, now Infinitly more so, on the Return of this Season, since, you might have reason with Justice to conclude It had bid you A final Adieu, and when I shal find leasure and proper encouragement to write Our History I (as Burnet Says) will not fail to mention you with a great regard, and some very extraordinary notes on the Winter 28—

    To propagate civility, good Sence, Reason, & Good maners, to propagate Moral Justice, & Erect a Church, In a Land 'till then Barbarous is a Revolution of some Importance & may make some future Age Inquisitive into ye truest motives of such Change, this shall be my full light and the shades shall add to it all their additional Lustre—for years as formerly; a Citty Sett upon a hill whose light cannot be hidd.

    I know with What ill grace anything Intervenes when peoples heads are full of Matrimony, and at this time relise

Selected Letters 145

with all ye circumspection, and care that may be necessary to wish you all as it becomes your choice a long Sucession of Happy years when yokd. down to the comforts of this life.

    I am with much sincerity,
    Thy Assur'd frd.
    Isaac Norris Jun[r].

[*Addressed:*]
Philada. Apl. 18th 1728
April 1728
Isaac Norris
to
Susy Wright

James Logan to Susanna Wright, December 19, 1735[5]

                  Stenton 19th 10th 1735.

My friend Susie

    This afternoon I recvd thy obliging lettr of ye 7th inst together with another kind one of ye 9th from S. Blunston wch I have just answered, and now must Say Something to thine which having no Rhimes in it but my own or at most but half-one more may be somewhat the easier dispatched. I need not now tell thee I suppose how very often and very much I have with regret considered the uneasiness of thy Circumstances and Situation there: yet to be very free with thee I really think all thou hast said on that head is not a sufficient apology for a Silence if I mistake not of 4 months at least. however as it is in my power to make up its deficiency forever by forgiving all the rest I shall for this time take it for paymt.

    I know not what Construction to put on ye conduct of that man in Maryland but either that he is resolved to bully and frighten us wch I hope will not be in his power, or that he is mad with what is So. But I hope a few months will at least give us quiet by an Injunction from the Chancery, which with any proper application I can't think they will fail of obtaining nor doe I at all doubt but all due measures will be taken for it.

As to thy notion of the Author of the Distichs I must leave thee to ye enjoymt of thy own, having sufficiently acquitted myself on that head in ye print.

It had run in my head thou hadst seen the rough draught of ye 2 first books I had by me for about 25 years before it ever entered my thoughts again to finish or take any further notice of them, but if I mistake not in the Lettr wrote with ye Print from Philada I gave thee a particular ansr how they happen'd to be compleated. I may however hint this farther that if thou really hast a copy of any number of them as first Seen here, thou wilt on comparing them I believe find them somewhat improved.

I really know not what to say to thee about Books. I Suppose thou knows I very rarely buy an English one and as rarely french, and thou hast seen all I had about 2 years Since. I am forced indeed if I want one in other Language to buy or goe without them, but those others when I can I borrow my self and while thou hast Morery's (or Collier's) & Chambers' great Dictionaries by thee wch contain the Substance of all History, Geography & Philosophy I cannot imagine unless thy memory is so prodigious as to retain all thou hast once read, how thou canst be so greatly at a loss: however I have got one new history that I lent in town before I had ever read 2 leaves in it my self wch when W. Allen has done with it I shall endeavor to get to thee if another who also has the promise of it does not prevent it. Yet this would be unreasonable for there is no good book I should send there but what I would naturally expect (nor could I be agst it) should be twice read over, that is by 2 persons, before it is returned, and then when must I ever see a folio again? not in my life who want not above 10 months of entring my grand climactery. But my paper bids me have done my [ ] & therefore with kind Love to thy Self, father &c I end this from

                                         Thy affectionate frd

                                         J. Logan.

Drs. Lloyd Zachary and Adam Spencer to Samuel Blunston, September 18, 1744.[6]

Sir

We are of opinion that Nature was Kind to you in endeavoring to discharge ye Redundancy of Blood which your sanguine Constitution is Subject to. You live well and no doubt like other men you are apt when in agreable company to leap over ye Bounds of strict Temperance both in Eating and Drinking. It is a misfortune we are all liable to and unless our Depletions by Exercise or other means be in Proportion to our Repletions we ~~are~~ must succumb to ye direful Effects of Plenitude. We are talking to a man of sense or otherwise we would not thus freely tell you our Sentiments. According to ye Proverb Contraria contraris curantur, you therefore acted to your own Prejudice and against Nature in stopping so suddenly ye Flux of Blood. For tho' ye Discharge even became a Disease yet it ought to have been restrained very gradually by ye most gentle methods and not at once by so strong an Astringent as ye Juice of green Yarrow. You did however well in letting blood and living low which on considering ye Symptoms have hitherto prevented an Apoplexy or Palsy of your right Side. We now proceed to Advice. Take four of ye Pills sent you every morning and Evening and now and then ye Quantity of a Nutmeg of ye Electuary about ten in ye morning in case ye Pills procure you not at least two or three stools every Day. At ye same time strictly observe ye following Regimen:

1. Eat of such meats only as are young and of easy Digestion, with a sufficient Quantity of well baked Bread.
2. Chew your victuals thoroughly and drink at your meals water with a little wine.
3. Eat little at a Time tho' you should oftner, but sparingly at Supper
4. Abstain from Pork, salted meats, Greasy sauces, ye skin and Fat of meats, and in short viscid Foods.

Lastly, use ye Flesh Brush every morning and moderate Exercise on Horseback.

We are
    Your Friends and humble Servants
        A. Spencer
           Ll Zachary.

We could not gett an oppt Sooner
After considering thy Letter. 7th:18:1744

[*Addressed:*]
ffor Samuel Blunston
with a small packett

by the farm of
James Webb			Lancaster

Doctor Lloyd Zachary to Susanna Wright, October 8, 1744[7]

Respected ffr^d—

Susan^a. Wright.

 I think ffr^d: Sa^r: Blunston should in the first place, have her stomach settled, before anything else is proposed. And as she has already taken a Vomit, & still—continues vomiting never the less. I think the use of what I now send her in the bottle (as is there directed) will be helpfull to her & fortify her Stomach—& indeed is very good against the Intermitting feverish disorder.
 Also Spread a pretty large plaster of the salve I now send & apply it to the stomach If the smell does not offend her I beleive it will be serviceable also the box of Gummy pills, of which she may take 3 of them, twice a day to allay the Hysterick Symptoms.—and afterwards an Infusion of the bark, with Camomile flowers & Gentian, may be safely used.—A Blister to her back might I think have good service on Acc^t. of y^e: inequality of her Spirrits. If thou please to send down word sometime hence how they do. I shall be glad to hear of their being better
 Remember my Love to thy Father & S: Blunston

I am with much respects—
Thy ffriend.
Lloyd Zachary.

8th: 8br—1744.
The Town is very sickly—
& I am pretty much hurried
excuse my bad writing.

Benjamin Franklin to Susanna Wright, November 21, 1751[8]

Madam   Philada. Nov. 21. 1751

Your Guests all got well home to their Families, highly pleas'd with their Journey, and with the Hospitality of Hempfield.

When I had the Pleasure of seeing you, I mention'd a new kind of Candles very convenient to read by, which I think you said you had not seen: I take the Freedom to send you a Specimen of them. You will find that they afford a clear white Light; may be held in the Hand, even in hot Weather, without softning; that their Drops do not make Grease Spots like those from common Candles; that they last much longer, and need little or no Snuffing. I may add, what will be another Recommendation of them to you, that they are the Manufacture of our own Country, being wrought at Marcushook.

In the Magazine of August, I find that the magnificent King of Portugal has rais'd his Marble Aqueduct near 100 Foot higher than your Chicaselungo. It must be a most stupendous Work. I send you the Prospect of it.

Accept an Almanack for the New Year, with my hearty Wishes that it may prove a happy one to you and your Friends. I am Madam Your obliged humble Servant

                                                              B Franklin

Benjamin Franklin to Susanna Wright, July 11, 1752[9]

                                                   Philada. July 11. 1752

Madam

I should sooner have answered your Favour of the 27th past, but that I have been in daily Expectation of getting home the Piece you desired which is lent to a Friend. I hope to have it ready for the next Post.

In the mean time I send you two Pamphlets in which you will have the Pleasure to see a most impudent Imposture detected, and the Honour of our great Poet vindicated.

I send also *Christianity not founded on Argument*, a Piece that has made a great Noise, and received many Answers, on a Supposition that it favours Infidelity under the Guise of recommending Faith.

We have had excessive hot Weather now near two Weeks. My Thermometer has been almost every Day at 94, and 95, once at 97, which is but 3 Degrees short of the hot Sunday June 18, 1749. This Town is a mere Oven. How happily situated are our Friends at Hempfield! I languish for the Country, for Air and Shade and Leisure; but Fate has doom'd me to be stifled and roasted and teaz'd to death in a City. You would not regret the Want of City Conversation if you considered that 9/10ths of it is Impertinence.

My Wife joins in tendering our best Respects to you and your good Brothers. [John and James]

Your intimating to me wherein I can serve you needs no Apology, as if it were giving me Trouble, for it really affords me Pleasure, and is therefore a Favour for which I [must] acknowledge myself

Your obliged Friend and Servant

B Franklin

Benjamin Franklin to Susanna Wright, April 28, 1755[10]

Monday morning. [April 28, 1755]

Dear Madam

I thought from the first, that your Proposal of calling the several Townships together, was very judicious. I was only at a Loss how to get them call'd by some Appearance of Authority. On the Road from your House hither, I considered that at the Court of Oyer and Terminer here, there would probably be Constables from most of the Townships, and if the Chief Justice could be prevail'd on to recommend it from the Bench, that the Constables should immediately call the Inhabitants of their respective Townships together, perhaps the Business might by that means be effectually done. I know not whether he will think a Person in his Station, can, in Court, regularly intermeddle in such Affairs; but I shall endeavour to persuade him to it, as strict Forms ought, in my Opinion, to be disregarded in Cases of Necessity.

The Dutche Advertisement is composing, and will be printed in two or three Hours, as Mr. Dunlap tells me. I have taken the Liberty of detaining your Servant so long, after enquiring and being inform'd by him, that his immediate Return was not absolutely necessary. I am, with the greatest Esteem and Respect, Madam Your most humble Servant

B Franklin

[*Addressed:*]
To/Mm Susanna Wright/Sasquehanah

Benjamin Franklin to James Wright, June 26, 1755[11]

Philada. June 26. 1755

Dear Friend

I am glad to learn that the Flour is mostly if not all got up to Conegocheeg, and that you have so good a Prospect of getting Waggons to forward it to Wills's Creek.

The Governor has sent down the Bill and proposes to pass it with about 30 Amendments, of which one is that the Commissioners named in the Act to dispose of the £5000 for Roads, Indian Expenses &c. shall lay out none of the Money without his Consent. Another that the £10000 given to General Braddock with the £5000 be sunk in 5 years. Another that the Money arising from the Excise during the remaining 5 years be not disposed of without the Governor's Consent. Another that the Treasurer S. Preston Moore, be named in the Bill to continue till another be appointed by Act of Assembly &c. &c. &c. The House adhere to their Bill, and will send it up again tho' without any Hopes of its Passing. They are pleas'd however to find that the Mask is now forc'd off and that not one word is mentioned of King's Instructions which have long been made a Pretense to harass us, but the Governor is willing for a Bill to make Paper Money without a reclaiming Clause &c. provided we comply with the Proprietary Instructions, and agree not to chuse our own Officers nor make use of our own Money without his Consent. We should not have had this Clearing up of Things, if we had not sent him the original Royal Approbation of Gov. Thomas's Act, which deprived him of all the old Subterfuges. My Love to all the Good Folks on both sides the River.

I am with sincere Esteem and Affection Dear Sir Your most obedient humble Servant

B. Franklin

I shall be glad to hear of Johnnys Success.
Mr. James Wright

Charles Thomson to Susanna Wright, July 21, 1755[12]

Philada July 21th. 1755

I was disappointed of writing to you by the Post last time, by his setting out some Hours sooner than usual. But as I had a Letter ready, I sent it by a Waggoner & I hope it got safe to your hands. The Indians are all gone out of Town. The two Alleghenians expressed a great desire that some white Man should go with them. By that they said their People would be convinced of the sincerity of the English of their willingness to be at Peace with them & if once they were convinced of this, they said they were sure they would all withdraw from the French, deliver our Prisoners & their young Men would join with us. This was not said in public but private. The Moravian who went with me before offered to go but he wanted a Companion. As I was greatly concerned for the poor Captives & had good assurance there were upwards of 200 in one Town which might be delivered up at once, I offered my service, not doubting at this critical time of being instrumental towards bringing home the Captives, & perhaps some farther service to my Country. However the Gov & Council taking my life in Consideration were of opinion I should not be permitted to go for fear it seems I should mention something to the Indian of Land Affairs. They are conscious of Guilt and afraid of an Enquiry. Notwithstanding the Danger & fatigue I should have been satisfied to have gone, but as they have prevented me I am content. And having ever found as kind a Providence in what I might deem disappointments, as when things succeeded to my wish I rest satisfied that whatever is, either is, or will be ordered by the best.—The Moravian is gone. We have been greatly distracted this week with various Accounts from the Army before Ticonderoga. Every Day we had some blind acc'ts & every day our hopes & fears variously raised. The most certain accounts you have in this Days Paper.—It appears that the ill success of the army was occasioned by their too great eagerness as they attacked the Lines sword in hand, without waiting for the Cannon or making any regular approaches. The Highland Regiment called the Highland Watch, three times mounted the Lines and made great Havoc among the French but not being supported they were as often drove back. This it is said has been the most severely handled, some acc'ts mention their having lost 7 of their officers & a no. wounded. The same acc'ts mention the Death of several French namely Col. Lieut. Majors and particularly Major Rutherford and Major Tulehin & Lieut & Col Shaw of the Jersey Regiment. Next week's Post will we expect bring more certain accounts and we hope more agreeable News, as it is said the Army intends again to return to the attack.—I have said nothing of the Business of [ ] as it is in my last letter. I long to hear how everything goes on to the Westward. I expected some news from my friend John Wright on his return from Carlyle, but he has forgot to write. My love & Compliments to all Friends, I am with Esteem

yr. affectionate Friend

Chas. Thomson.

[*Addressed:*]
Susannah Wright at Hempfield

Michael Gross to James Wright, October 30, 1755[13]

Lancaster ocdober 30 Day 1755

Mr James Wright I hobe you Will not Take it amis that I am So Boll and Sent To you for alitle money I my Selve ben lying Seke and kant go Know Wher if you Woot too me this favour and Lit William Bawsman have as much money as you Can Spare for m[?] I Shall be vary much aplight to you and I Shall be raty to pleas you any Time again Your Whol acount is £33:16:0: Iron and Still Cam by it Selve £30:11:11:½ and the rest is all for nails £3:4:0½: out of that I received two Tupluns £10:16:0: and then ther is Some hobs against me I have a vary groid Sum to pay next Weke and I am In Such awant of money as I Never Whos afor I hobe you Will too as much as you Can and his reced Shall be your tis geary this from your frent

Michael Gross

October the 31 1755

  Received of James Wright
the Sum of ten pounds of the Within account
for the use of Mical Gross

£10.0:0   William Bawsman

Rct William Bowsman for Mical Gross

For Mr James Wright at Susquahana River

Sally Armitt to Susanna Wright, November 8, 1755[14]

         Philadelphia November ye 8 1755

Dear Susy

 It is [impossi?]ble to express the uneaseness that I am under on the Account of your Family, I wish you would come to town, as it must be more dangerous on the river, dear Susy we have Several Spare rooms which you Shall be very welcome to and we Shall take it as a favour, I know the would not chuse to be in a Family, were the could not make free, dear Susy the Shall be as if at home in our House, but if you chuse not to be with your Friends, and would take a house, we have a great deal of new furniture that was made before my daddy dy'd, which you Shall be exceeding welcome to while you are in town. many of the people in town are much frightned and Some think nothing about it, dear Susy Please to give my love to all your Family, I conclude with my Sincerest wishes for the Health and happin[ess] of your Kind Family, and am dear Susy thy very

Affectinate Friend

Sally Armitt

Susanna Wright to James Wright, 1755/1756[15]

4th day night [1755/1756]

Brother Jemmy

    We have been much concerned at the bad weather you had down, I hope Surely Johny has put away his thred Stockins—I had quite forgot that money Wm ffranklin sent, I think it was 27 dollars or £10-2-6 (but whatever it was, he Knows) that thou should have been made debter for I supose that might be what the speaker mentioned to Johny Wright, for it was put along with the other public money,—

    I hear Sam Tayler is to set off to morrow, but as his motions are so very uncertain, if he should not go down while thou stays, & Johny & his Master should agree, and he can be bound without his father, as Both Johny W & thy self can give Evidence that he is consenting to it, it wil be necessary thou should Know his age, Johny Tayler was 16 years old the Second day of July last

    Except this day, I think it has raind ever since you went, and has [?]ed our business a good deal—we have had almost the whole hospital of soldiers the 2 last nights—the poor creatures complained they could get nothing at the tavern, not even bread, for their money, we gave them what bread we had and we baked them up a bag of flour, and gave them every thing they wanted, for they were almost starved with wet & hunger, we cleard out the bake house for them, & laid them straw, they were Exeeding civil & thankful, a great many of them were English, several from Lancashire & Cheshire, & one from Manchester— we are all very well, Sam is got quite hearty as to any Sickness, and has a good Stomac, but is some pain yet with his teeth, & Remember mustard, Caleb Low desires thee to bye him a ¼ Cask of Good powder at any price—be sure write the post All our Very Kind love to you both and to all with you

> thy Affect^e Sist^r
>
> S Wright

To James Wright in Philadelphia
by Robert Barber
No 2. No date [*Written in a later hand*]

Susanna Wright to Benjamin Franklin, February 28, 1757 [16]

Coppy of a letter to B Franklin

> Febr^y 28th 1757

Give me leave among the Number of your more distinguished Friends, to express my hearty Concern, that the Necessity of the Times requires your taking a long and hazardous Voyage, to serve, and perhaps to save your Country: Personal Regard and private Friendship, make us think of your leaving this Province, and the Dangers you may be exposed to, with great and unfeigned Regret; but as Members of Society, and well-wishers to it, we rejoyce the Assembly has made so prudent a Choice, and confide in the Providence of Almighty God, that so disinterested, so laudable an Undertaking as yours, will meet with all the Success our warmest Wishes can form, both as to the Welfare of our Country and your safe and happy Return, which indeed have a most near Connection.

My good Friend your Son, has my sincerest Desires for every Blessing this World can afford:

I return the Books you was pleased to lend me, and beg the Favour of you, or Billy Franklin, to lay out a Guinea in pamphlets for me:—I desire Mrs Franklin and Sally to accept my respectful Compliments; and Condolance:

I am,

My worthy Friend with repeated good Wishes,

Your truly obliged and affectionate

Friend

S. Wright

Deborah Franklin to Susanna Wright, July 14, 1757 [17]

July 14–1757

My verey kind freind

this day I reseved your and it was the more except-
able as I have bin verey unwell I have had a bad
cold and fever it did not leve me for 48 ower &
gave me much pain indead but is gon of a gen
thank god for his mersey to me
I have bin in much pain fer sum day on a Counte
of my Husband for by this time he is as I supose
near the lands end of England and of Corse in danger
of being taken which I pray god prevent but at
this time I am in as much nead of the asistans of
my freinds as I ever was and I find myself verey
week indead I am not abel to bair the leste thing
in the world I hope I have the prayers of all
our freinds my Mrs Smith is gon ought of
town on a visit to Gray hom Kerney as was and
I mis her indead her Daster was well-abought
three days ago my nees is well so is Mr Dunlap
and Master Frankey Salley Franklin shall write
to you and I shall a deem it a verey graite
faver if you will write to her agen shee is
larning French. I had no desire of Larning that
Language but Shee desired it herself and her
master ses shee is a good garle shee has bin
4 week to day at it Shee will give you an

a Count of it her self I have not seen C
Thomson for several days he is verey unwell
and looks badly; I hope you air not in aney
dainger of the enemey what a deal of badness
thair is in the paper this week I hope god in
mersey to us all will put a stop to it my love
to all the famely on bouth sides the river to Sister
Taler and Mrs Rodey Write I am sorry I mis-
touk the name but will [ ]the tee Kittel was
the beste Caste I saw but none of the topes did fit
better and the pepel who youse them had topes
maid by a smith thay air youshed in all the
houses I was in at Newarke at Col Skilens and
at Eliz-town and much liked

                I am your freind and Servant
                       D Franklin

Susanna Wright to Hannah Griffitts, April 5, 1762[18]

                               April the 5th

Thou Canot be Sencible, nor can I My Dear ffriend tell thee, the
degree of delight, thy Obliging Letter, and very Elegant Coppy of
verses gave me; In the Situation I am, any thing truly Exelent of the
Kind, is Grateful to me beyond Expression, for tho I live in the most
conversable manner among a number of good Neighbours, yet they
are of those who are not to my tast, other then what is Included in the
resiprocal dutys of humanity,—after I have own'd these truths, I have
only to express my desire that [I may] be Enabled to make a propper
use of the Sentiments thou has favord me with, by endeavoring in the
best manner in my power, to answer the Character thou has too partialy
been pleasd to draw, and to attach the end of those pious wishes thou
has so harmoniously breath'd out for me,—these enclosd lines were not
wrote in emulation of thine I sincerely assure thee, they were indeed
occasiond, and if I may without venturing to make use of that expression,
Inspired by them, and my Sole view in sending them to thee, is to give
thee the earliest and Strongest Instance I can give, of the estimation
I have for whatever I have seen of thy writing—and if I must tell the

whole truth, an Introduction to a Sight of more I have [?]ed many times concluded I had done with mimicking poetry forever, and as often begun to do it again, but for the greater part have prudently committed all my foibles of that Kind to the fire, after a vacant hour had been amused, how I hapned to put the coppy thou art pleasd to notice, into My friend Charles Moore's hand, I canot well account to my Self, I knew he was a Critical Judge of writing, so no Suitable person to Entrust with any of mine and indeed I was under great anxiety for what I had done, when it [ ] and [ ] to P[?] self m[?]ng on the generosity of his mind, for[*line missing*]de, yet I have seen [ ] thee [*line missing*] conduct thro it, being conected in [*line missing*]g that paper, with all his Inacurcys, into his hands, as he is thy Relation and friend, I wil make no appology for these remarks—but I ought to make one for the manner in which this letter wil be finishd, it is candle light, and the children wil play round me, and every now & then give my table a drive,

    I take my Kind friend, thy good Aunts Remembrance of me as a favor, as I shal do the Remembrance of every one of the name, or descended from them for give me leave to tell thee, the first Intimacys I contracted, and the happyest hours I ever enjoyed Since I left my native land, were in thy Grandfather Norris's house, the Strongest friendship I formd there, was only dissolvd by death which must sooner or later break every human tye, the obligations stil continue to be Confe[?] on your part, and the Sencibility of gratitude wil never be lost on ours, the degree [of] Intimacy my Brother is Indulgd in, by thy Worthy Uncles and their Engaging fa[milies] are the most agreable reflections I am now in possession of, but many [ ] tranquility over my mind Just at this time, for Jemmy tell [ ] Summer with the additional favor of [ ] no Body Bribe the persons

No 9 Apl 5 1762

a coppy of a Letter to Hannah Griffits 1762

James Wright to John Bartram, August 22, 1762[19]

Respected friend

    Pursuant to thy request, I have made as particular an Enquiry relating to those bones thou mentions, as I possibly Could, from two

Sencible Shawanese [Shawnee] Indians, Assisted by an Interpreter, And the Substance of what they Say is as follows—the place where they lye is about 3 miles from the Ohio, salt & moist, as well as I could judge by their description of it seems to contain 30 or 40 Acres, in the Midst of a large Savannah, 4 days Journey Below the lower Shawanese town, on the East Side of the river, that there appear to be the remains of 5 Entire Sceletons, with their heads All Pointing towards Each other, And near together, supposd to have fallen at the same time; when they were desired to describe their several parts, they began with their heads, of which two were larger than the rest, one of these, they said a Man Could but Just Grasp in Both his Arms, with a long Nose, And the Mouth on the under side, they next mentiond the shoulder blade, which when set on End, reached to their Shoulders, And they were both tall men, What they Call'd the Cup (or socket) of this bone, was equal in size to a large bowl, the thigh bone when broke assunder, would admit of a little boy's Creeping into it—they were askd if they had seen those long bones they Call'd horns, they Answered they had, And by the distance from where they stood to the door, Showd them to be 10 or 12 feet long, And added that by the Bones, they Judged the Creature when Alive must have been the Size of a Small house, pointing from the Window to a Stable in Sight;—I askd them if the Place where they lay was Surounded with Mountains, So as to admit a probability of its Ever having been a lake, they Answered, the place was salt and Wettish, And by having been much trod & Licked, was somthing lower then the adjacent land, which however, was so level, to a prodigious Extent, that the lick, as they Calld it, Could never have been coverd with water; And that there were many roads thro this Extent of land, larger & more beaten by Buffalas and other Creatures, that had made them to go to it, than any Roads they saw in this Part of the Country on being Questiond if they had seen such bones in Any other place, they said they had seen many such, Scattred here & there in that large tract of land mentiond before, some upon the Surface, and some Partly burned [buried?], but all much more decay'd by time, then those they had been describing, and not Any Entire Sceleton; I Askd if they had Ever heard from their old men, when these 5 were first observed, or if they, or their fathers, had Ever seen any such large Creatures living, as these bones were suppos'd to have been a part of, they Answered they had never heard them spoken of, other then as in the Condition they are at present, nor ever heard of any such creature having been seen by the oldest Man, or his father—that they had indeed a tradition, such mighty

Selected Letters 161

Creatures, once frequented those Savannahs, that there were then men of a size proportionable to them, who used to kill them, and tye them in Their Noppusses And throw them upon their Backs As an Indian now dos a Deer, that they had seen Marks in rocks, which tradition said, were made by these Great & Strong Men, when they sate down with their Burthens, such as a Man makes by sitting down on the Snow, that when there were no more of these strong Men left alive, God Kiled these Mighty Creatures, that they should not hurt the Present race of Indians, And added, God had Kill'd these last 5 they had been questioned about, which the Interpreter said was to be understood, they supposed them to have been Killd by lightning—these the Shawanese said were their traditions, and as to what they knew, they had told it—the Man who Interpreted, was well Acquainted with their language, and as I have known him from a boy, I am Confident he would do it faithfully, I shal be pleas'd if what smal Information I have gain'd wil be agreable to thee, And shal be glad to oblige thee at any time to the Utmost of my Power,

I am thy Assured friend

James Wright

August 22nd 1762
John Bartram

Susanna Wright to [Charles Norris?], [1763?] partial text [20]

—one whole page, wrote from the top to the Bottom, in a fair Elegant hand, containing Eight ~~whole~~ compleat lines, and two pieces of lines, the whole consisting of one hundred and Eight words, Including Innitials, which stand for persons or things, Monosylables, and Abreviations, much in the Tast of Chancery Scribes; yet for this favour, My Good friend, Singular as it was, I hold my Self a Great deal obliged, as it bears testimony that you have us still in remembrance and a great deal rejoyced, as it gives us Inteligence of your welfare, which we wish again, and again, to be gratifyd with, as often as convenience will permit:

—we See by the paper of last week, the Alarming Situation your Citty was in, first day in the afternoon, but that thro the great mercy of Providence, no Damage, beyond terrifying the Inhabitants was the Consequence of that most tremendious phenomena of nature, and conclude every right turned & sencible mind, must be affected in a propper manner, with the greatness of the mercy—we see also in the paper, the Genl Comotions, and preperations for war, in Europe, and how nearly our native Country seems to be threatned with being again Involved in it, and it further seems apparent, that if the hand of Providence will not Sweep off a whole people at one Stroke, they Encline to destroy one another with all the dispatch they can.—But that Article of 2 or 3 vessels being gone up St Lawrence's River with warlike Stores for the Indians, affects me a great deal; the Strongest hopes we had under Providence of speedily seing an end of their Ravages, was their want of amunition, But if that Article is fact, those hopes can have no foundation. I always dreaded having (that is having previously taken such measures as would as would of consequence render all theses Savage Nations our Enemies, whenever we Should have another ffrench war, which could not rationaly be expected at any great distance from us,—But what have I to do with politics,— If indeed any thing at present transactions now in England, or in English America, merits that name, ought to be calld politics,—But we learn further by the p[?] you have a new Govr. the paper Informs us—As he is of the Name we read by the papers & family of Penn if he would Condescend to Search for, and tread in the foot Steps of his Worthy Grandfather, (again) if By a long Course of years, and a long course of—those footsteps are not so totaly Obliterated, that they can never more be recovered, if he would act an upright & friendly part with such of the natives as could yet be found reclaimable, and Could by that means restore mutual Confidence, and peace & Safety to his Province, what a Blessed change would the poor frontier Inhabitants be favour'd with,—we may at least pray for these things, and for peace, and May the father of Mercys Grant them to us

all our Relations, friends & neighbours, as far as I know, are favor'd with health, Jemmy, his wife, & Sister, affectionately Salute you all, you have our Kindest respects, complim^{ts} wishes respects and Compliments, which are desired to be delivered, Generaly, & particulerly, in town, at fairhil, & Somerville,—but how are your pretty children,—the Smal pox, spreads about us, and is very favorable, and we think we should be well Satisfyd our little boy took it, yet we are Shockd whenever we apprehand Any degre of the Infection is near him, yesterday a neighbour, whose children were lying in the distemper, came into the room where we were Sitting at Dinner, as soon as Rhoda Saw her enter, she pickd up her boy, and Carryd him off with the utmost precipitation, the woman Sate down to dinner, but as soon as she was gone, the chair she had sate in, was taken out & set to air—Alas what poor timerous mortals we are, but such we are, and such we must be, and canot help it.

—I tho[t] I had done, but I must add a few words about a fruit—or whatever you call it, that Jemmy has told us about, which when sliced & fried, is vulgerly calld pork stake, he either did not hear, or forgot, the technical name of the plant or its produce, if it is propagated by seed, we must entreat you to Save us some, if any other way, pray advise us of it, and put us in the method of procuring wherewithal to get the precious animal plant into our garden where at present we have nothing but mere vegetables—I have been very desirous for some years past, to endavour by some means or other, to get some of the Myrtle wax plants brought up, and tryd if we could propagate them in any Soyl we have, or could make, and added to what our garden already furnishes us with, if we could have Somthing resembling animal food, and Candles, I think I should be easy—as to Garden affairs

Susanna Wright to Charles Norris, September 4, 1763[21]

[I] sit down this 4th day of September with full Purpose of heart to write a long letter, so arm thy self with patience, my good frd & read on

The first Part of thy Polite favor by Thom[s] Minshal would flatter my vanity very Sencibly, If I had any Vanity to be flattred, but—but what? was that woman ever born, Absolutely destitute of it,—however mine is Sufficiently Indulgd, ~~by having a Permission to write such in Being Permited to~~ in having letters—such as these, ~~and having them~~ taken notice of in the obliging manner they are, And I want no other fine things, as what I have ~~got mentiond~~ already rec[d] are fine as may be

I am thankful for the Books, I knew they would be high, but I should not complain of the Price, if one had a little more for their money, and I am of Mess[rs] the Reveiwers mind, (who have given some extracts from them) that whoever reads these letters, must wish the number of them had been Greater multiplied,—she is a Sprightly Easy writer, and lets us into the manners & Customs of nations, very Imperfectly describd by

other travelers, But with much aquired Knowledge, which ~~must~~ could
have been Procured ~~with~~ by no Smal degree of Aplication, she Seems
to have been a good deal carryd away with the love of Pleasure, and no
wonder, ~~to~~ in a Person of her lively turn; she was in the laughing time of
life, and from her high station & affluence, had oppertunitys of Indulging
every temptation to it,—I see in a late magazine she dyed last year,
or the year before, I dont recolect which as I have them for Both years,
and So much for Lady Mountague,—yet I seem Sorry after reading
those Pritty letters she wrote to Pope, that two Persons of such fine
understanding, should quarrel as they did, and Publish their quarrels
to the World,—Surely if I had a friend I could not Regard in that light
any longer, I would drop their aquaintance and Say no ill of them;—
after one Person has Publickly Profest ~~an high~~ the highest esteem
for another it is a Poor Compliment to their own Judgm^t. to tell all
mankind how unworthy their ~~were~~ friend was of it—Both the Admired
writers are now no more, and their Readers must follow them, and so
on, (as thou observes) to the end of the generations of men

the next Article of thy letter mentions a few Books you have of mine;
Surely thou Could not Possibly Imagine any thing I wrote about my
own Careless noncence had the most distant alusion to those which
are Safer then if thy were in my own hands,

Thom^s Minshal seems to Say you express some doubt whether your
Brother Realy Recruited or not, but that he did not grow worse,—in his
weak State, if he dos not grow worse, he must Certainly Grow Better,
at least such are our hopes & earnest desires, Pray Remember us kindly
Respectfully to him, and to the Good Familys at fairhill & Somerville,—
It is with Pleasure we observe the worthy old Gentleman your Daddy,
Remembers & thinks so Kindly of us, as to Intend us the favor of a visit,
if he shal be able to Perform ~~it~~ the journey, I am certain all sides will be
highly Pleasd, Provided we shal be able to Perswade him to Stay with us
till he shal have Recovered the fatigue of ~~his Journey~~ it—from a Principle
of Self love, I have felt a great Deference for advanced age, and every
now & then I am thinking thou art too young to be a Correspondent,
and I wonder at thy Patience—but I seem to be growing younger my
Self then I have been for some months Past—as Jemmy Continues
Recovering his ~~usual~~ former health very fast, and is somtimes whole
days without any return of that tedious Pain in his side, tho he feels it
occasionaly after riding or any fatigue, I Beleive the Soap he took was of

Selected Letters

Singular Advantage to him, tho he has taken none for sometime ~~Past~~— we are truly Obliged to Our Kind friends, Both the Doct[rs] Moore and Jemmy will I hope in a few weeks be able to Acknowledge in Person, both thy Good Offices & theirs

how dare I say this when I reflect I have lately entred my 67th year— and very sencibly feel the Effects Length of days neccessaryly Produce what I mean is that the Goodness of devine Providence has removd a great weight from my Spirits by Indulgently permitting my Brother Recovery beyond what I had Hoped

Thou art Pleasd to give me notice of thy Self thy Son & daughters Journeying to Chester and an Agreable Jaunt I dare Say it was with their Pretty Prattle; ~~but understandings~~ our Judgments may be Informd by the wise Sayings & Elaborate discources of Riper years, But these dawnings of ~~Reason~~ understanding, are like the chearful dawn of a fine morning, like the first ~~Soft~~ gay appearance of Spring, like—Somthing that affords a Pleasure not to be describd, permit me to give an Insignificant Instance Johny Lowdon had put yokes upon some a number little Pigs yesterday and this morning they came very Abruptly to our Door, Jemmy Expressd ~~a good deal of displeasure at it~~ no smal degree of anger at it, when our little boy said very good humourdly, um comes here daddy, only to Show how fine um is, this Paliation occasiond the Poor Pigs to be dissmissed with more temper then they would otherways have been,—from Pigs I could naturaly make a transition to Rabbits, and tell a Story that would not be unentertaining to Isaac & Debby if I was where they are, as how about 5 months agoe the Dogs chased a Doe Rabit from her nest in the meadow before our door, and left 6 little orphans a few days old, how in Pure Compassion we took them in, fed them with milk, weand them, and that now they are the Prettyest tame Pets Imaginable, as Clean & Innofencive as English Rabits are the Contrary, Stand up on their hind legs when they are calld, and eat our little boys bread & fruit out of his hand, lye down to be Patted & stroakd,—and are Purposd to ~~be~~ become in due time, the Progenitors of a numerous & flourishing family—But I Perceive my letter is already Become too childish for even Infancy it self to Read, if Infancy could read a letter, so from Pigs & Rabits Ile ascend—no, I will Descend, to Politics & Popular comotions—our Back countys are in great agitation, Preparatory to the Ensuing Election, one day last week, not fewer then 40 ministers & Elders, deputed from their Respective congregations (some from your Citty) with sevral hundred of their Adherents, assembled in Lancaster, what they did there I canot say, only made long speeches, from thence a Part of the whole of the Principals, Proceeded to York & Carlile, all other Societys are Prodigiously Alarmd, some Say they will carry all before them, some Say they will be able to Do very little—I wish they may not take it into their heads to riot again, and that no Inocent People may be Endangerd, the leading men of every Sect who wish to Oppose them, teize Jemmy Perpetualy to let his name be made use of, which he prudently & absolutely Refuses—some friends in Particuler are very earnest with him, if he could realy do the Society any Service, he would hold it his duty to do it, and would Comply without hesitation, but as he is very Sure he canot, on the Present occasion, he can be under no tye to oblige them, merely for the Sake of obliging them, who have so disgracefully, & without any reason, discarded him from their comunity—the truth is, they are at a loss for a man who they have reason to beleive has the Same Intrest in the County that he has— But let them try their Possibles without him, he Purposes to be with you at the day of Detirmination—I wonder if thy wife is returnd from chester—wherever she is, she has our Affectionate Remembrances & Best wishes, so has thy sister—so has thy Children, so has thy self, from Jemmy in Particular—for all this is such a long & foolish letter, I am sitting on thorns all the while I write, what must thou sit upon to read it, I ought to be Spinning twine ~~tho~~ to Sow drying cloths—to which I now return—a more Justifyable Employm^t then writing tryfles & noncence, for all which I beg thy excuse and am &c

Sept-4-1763

No 8—no date

Susanna Wright to [Charles Norris?], November 26, 1764[22]

[date in later hand 1764]
Nov: 26th at night

My Good Friend

We receiv'd thy first notice of the death of our worthy old friend Jane Hoskins, without Surprise, as we had expected it for some time Past; and indeed, without that deep sence of Sorrow, too frequently claimd on Such an Affecting occasion: we Should have Rejoyced, and have been thankful, if Providence had Spared her longer to her friends, an Example of Piety, and a Sencible & useful member of Society; if she might have been favord with health to have enjoyd life with any degree of Comfort; and we Reflect upon her Kind Sentiments towards us in this Place, with gratitude to her memory; But at the same time consider her advanced age, her long Suffrings under the Pains of Distempers, esteemed incurable at her years, and (What must have great weight with mee in Regard to that Important Period) that she was not Entangled & chaind down to this Life, by those many tender Connections, the Breach of which, must constitute the Most Painful Part of quitting it; and that to crown the whole of these consolatory Reflections, we have Reason to hope & beleive she was well Prepared for her change,—yet with all these Considerations, the death of a friend we have long esteemed, will leave a Serious & meloncholy Impression upon our Spirits, that ought not to be Sudenly Obliterated, and yet in which we feel a Sincere Satisfaction, in the good account thou gives of your Sevral familys, thy Brother is Recruiting, thy Neice H Harrison recovering, the Remainder in Good health,—how much to be valued are all these mercys & Blessings, but alas how Precarious is their Continuance, and what creatures of a day we are, yet to have a mind turnd for Enjoying this <u>Present</u> good, without Imbittering it with anticipations and fears for the future, is still an aditional Blessing:—the familiar & agreable account thou gives of thy children, very Sencibly delights us all, and more Especialy, as some of us are verging towards that State of Imbecility a Second time,—thy friend Jemmy Bo[t] himself a pair of Spectacles last night;—whenever he had occasion to Read or write by Candlelight, he has been obliged to borrow one of my 3 Pairs, (for I have so many in dayly & nightly use, one Pair which magnifys the most, for sowing, one to write or Spin with in the day time, & the third & clearest for night) but the youngest of my Glasses drew his eye so near to the Paper that I had no Patience;— and whether from a dislike of Appearing an old man abroad, or from forgetfulness, I never could Perswade him to look out for any, so I sent to Lancaster for a Cargoe that he might chuse to his liking, which he did, & reads in them today with great tranquilty, tho he declares he dos not want them when the Sun Shines, his wife, out of Complaisance I supose, or to be in the fashion, has likewise taken a Pair; and declares how well she can see in them, and not to be wanting to my Self, I have added one more Pair to the 3 I had already, which makes their number exceed that of my Gowns, of which however I have Plenty as to Jemmys Journeying to Phil[a]. and having his Spirits Rousd by Public Buissiness, I am so fortunate to think Just as thou dos, no Smal complim[t] to my own Judgm[t], But the Engaging company he will meet with there, has great weight with me, in the Salutary Effects of those Journeys,—which how he will be able to Perform, is yet a Secret to us; his own riding horse can travel no longer, and to Go in his Carriage, he aledges would Slide him into a libel;—I propose that he should engage the noo york members, and James Webb, all Intimate aquaintance, tho of different Sentiments in Politics, to accept seats in the Same vehicle; and see who will be hardy Ennough to Libel a whole waggon load of assembly men—If this will not do, Comply with the advice of your obliging friend Charles Norris, and take down your wife & children, sure no body can cencure that laudible measure,—however some way or other I suppose he will get down at the appointed time, if himself and his family shal be favord with health, and his new homespun coat can be got ready,—I often ask this ~~Brother of mine~~ him to let me be of his company to Phil[a], which he never objects to, and Indeed the transient Imagination of seeing my Self once more among those friends I so truly love & honnour, gives me a momentary Pleasure, but I no sooner feel it, then It vanishes, with a Short Sigh, on Reflecting, those gratifications are all ~~Past & gone~~ at an end, that I have already had the share aloted to me of that Eligible Part of the feast of life, and am not to expect to have it again—But am in Possession of many other good things, one of which is, these Perplexing children, that drive about me & shake my table & candle, tho they have another table & candle at a little distance to themselves, if they would stay at it—But Poor things, I know not how to be angry with them, they are fine Promising children, a little too much Petted, but I ought not to complain—Sams Mammy is Perswaded he never told her an untruth, or usd a Bad word in his life. He reads well & writes a Pretty hand, and has made a considerable Progress in arethmetic, he has a good stock of Spirits, & is very Inquisitive, and I hope will make a Good sort of a man, if he may be Spared to that Period,—Bets is 6 years old, as wild as a young filly, But she reads well, & writes a Pretty hand, of which her Daddy is to take down a Specimen for your Inspection, John, who is my Present favrite, is realy a fine Sencible child, but alas he is Somthing ungovernable, tho he is Got into Leather Britches made of a fawn Scin, we have not been yet able to perswade him to conform to Scool hours, and we canot use Compulsion, as he has not yet had the Smal Pox; my little namesake is a Pretty Sprightly Girl,—Pray excuse this Chitchat—Jemmy has a Return of the coldness in his legs & feet, this late, & Present Severe weather, which he canot well avoid Exposing himself to, more then I fear is Consistant with his Safety, otherways he appears to be Pretty well

the water course that Supplyd our Still house & Kitchen has been some time so out of order, that there was a neccessity of Repairing it, and a good deal of Plank was wanting for that end, & the Springs were so low, the Saw mill could not cut them til a few days agoe, and now they are cut, Jemmy canot get a workman that has docitude [ ] to do any thing right except he is with him, So that he realy Suffers a great deal of cold, but I hope will not wet his feet, Thom^s Minshal Bro^t him up, I Beleive, a very good flesh brush, the Best Wilkinson could make, and I hope the use of it may be attended with Benefit

Jemmy desires you may all, and every one, in town & at fairhill & Somerville, accept his Kindest Grateful Respects, Rhoda & my Self have many, many thanks to Return for your Kind Invitation, which her youth, and my Age, equaly render our complying with Impracticable, while she has a number of children to take care of, & one to nurse, she is confind at home as Securely, as if she was enclosd within the walls of a fortress, and for Reasons still stronger more unsurmountable, I am the Same, but we both Present our Kindest love Respects & Complim^{ts}, as above; I must say one word of my obliging friend Hannah Griffitts, I am ashamd, but I canot help it, I love, and esteem her, and if she Knew as much as I do, she would excuse me, as would thou my Indulgent friend, for this Scribled Paper, and for every other failing as I am with great Sincerity & affection

           thy truly obliged friend

             S Wright

I think we have only one old friend & Contemporary left in Chester, Joseph Parker, he has not reachd us the late Summer, Pray mention him when thou favors us again, and when you have an Oppertunity, Remember us to him in the Kindest manner; and further oblige us, by Daddy Mammy & Aunt in town giving each of your Dear Pretty Children a Kiss for, an on Behalf of Daddy Mammy & aunt at Susquehanna

Sally Franklin to Susanna Wright, March 14, 1765[23]

Philada, March 14, 1765

Madam,

When our good Friend was in Town I told him as soon as we heard from my Father I would write. We have had no letters yet, but a paragraph in the London News by way of Cork, has made us all happy by telling us he arrived the 10 of December.

Mamma desires with me to be remembered to Mr. & Mrs. Wright and all our Susquehanna friends and claims the promise you made her in a letter to Cousin Dunlap.

I am, with great respect

Your obliged friend

Sally Franklin.

[*Addressed:*]
To Miss Wright.

Susanna Wright to Mary Norris, February 16, 1766[24]

To Mary Norris

Susanna Wrights Letter to mee No.1

February the 16th 1766

Give me leave My Dear friend, to Add one more letter, to the number, I have heretofore been Permitted to adres^s into your good family: But alas & with what diferent sensations do I now Sit down to write; I had then, only Contratulations to offer, and the delightful Prospects of being Indulged with returns, that always afforded me the most Sencible Satisfaction and pleasure,—and now, what shal I say, I need not—I cannot tell thee, how deeply we mourn the loss of that Dear Husband, father, Brother, and our Justly Esteemed and Beloved Friend, nor how Sincerely we mourn with you all: thy own late tender Connections, demand the first place in our Sympathizing hearts, all our Dear friends most affectionate family, Claim

Selected Letters

our tears, But when I think of your Sorrowing Sister Debby, who had lived
with her Worthy Brother, almost from his Child hood, to his latest hour,
I canot help making her case my own, if the same hard lot was to befal me.
—and now, what have I further to write, I have indeed no words to express
what I feel upon this mournful occasion, any more then I have to express
my Surprise at the first tydings of it, as I never had the most distant
Apprehension, that the life of our Late Exelent friend, was in any
Imediate danger; the last letter I ever receivd from him,—the last
I ever can Receive—which was but three posts before one which Brought
us, the winding up of all, mentions a difficulty of Breathing, & Swelling
of his legs, But Adds, the Physicians Say the Swellings are not dropsical,
and that his lungs were Sound, and that upon the whole, he thought
himself upon the mending hand;—he had in other late letters, mentiond
a lowness of Spirits, and Various Complaints, which are not unfrequently
the consequences of too Sedentary a life, and Checkd Perspiration; And
as I had Known Several Persons, labouring under disorders Such as
I supposd his to be, and from Similar Causes, yet who had by a propper
Regimen, & frequent exercise, happily Survivd them, & Regaind their
usual health, I had no doubt for him, and in this Persuasion, I am
conscious, I wrote many things in the cource of my Impertinent letters,
that were highly Presuming and Impropper,—I Know not what
to Say in my excuse, but this I Know, that I was ever anxous for the
welfare of my friend, and for that of every branch of his truly valuable
family,—what would I not have done, and at what hazard, had any
thing been in my Power to do, that would in any degree, have contributed
to that desirable end: as I mentiond, I had seen such evident good Effects,
from exercise & change of air, in some deplorable cases, I must own I
repeatedly recomended them, in a manner unsuitable to my Situation,
I shal be eneasy under your Just Censures, upon this account, yet Pardon me,
for adding, it can be only a Secondary weight upon my Spirits,—I cannot
reconcile my mind to the Irreparrible loss you my Dear friends have
Sustaind, nor Permit me to add that we have Sustaind, along with you,
[?]y less Solemn consideration then that Such was the will of God
and that in Patiently Submitting to this Divine will, we must look for,
Consolation, and may expect to find it, with the further Infinite advantage,
that every Painful Event, shal be Sanctifyed to us;—in the Present case,
we have only our Selves to be concernd for, the whole tenor of the life
we lament the Period of, must ascertain to us, the Present, and future
well being, of the Exelent man who liv'd it,—as he is taken from
the many Blessings, So is he taken from the many Evils, (and they
are many) which this mortal State is lyable to,—
—these, are no other then trite, and comon observations, on Similar

occasions, and I Know I write Incoherently, for I canot write without tears, But they are a Smal tribute to the memory of a friend, who's departure I shal Regret, to the latest hour of my life,

As we have for Some happy years, been favourd with frequent Inteligence from you, and your united familys, the Knowledge of your welfare is Become Essential to that of our own, and we must be anxous and uneasy if we can but rarely hear of you; My Brother tells me he Requested as a favour, that Jemmy Johnson, at least, might sometimes be Directed to write to us, it was a Request I thought of making, Before I Saw my Brother, But I have further to add that I should esteem the favour Still greater if he Shal be directed to be Particuler, when he mentions the State of health of Every Individual of you, in town, and at fairhil, and As Explicitly as Possible about your Amiable Children,—Dear lovely Creatures, & May Devine Providence Bless and Protect them, Continue the life of their Affectionate Mother, and every other Parental Relation, til themselves shal attain to years of understanding, capable of feeling the value of Such Inestimable Blessings aforded to them, and by their Sencible & virtuous Conduct, Be as Inestimable Blessings to that Dear Parent, and those tender Relations, Solace their advanced age, and Attain, and Preserve, that most amiable and Worthy Character, their Dear father so deservedly Sustaind, thro the whole cource of his Benevolent life— you will all Cherish his memory, and think of him as (for any thing we know to the Contrary) ever Rejoycing in the felicity of those Dear Pledges he left upon Earth.

Jemmy tells me thy father is very low and weak, at his age no other can reasonably be expected; I Know by Experience, thy Situation in Regard to him, is a Painful one, and that, added to one yet more Sencibly so, demands the tender Commiseration of every friend, thou has mine in a very feeling manner, thou has that of my Brother & Sister, So have you all, Our Dear af licted friends; when thou shal see thy Good father please to tell him he has the Kindest Remembrance of his Old friends in this Place—

thy truly Affectionate and Sympathising
friend

S:Wright

Susanna Wright to Mary Norris, May 28, 1767[25]

Susanna Wright's recd:
May 28th. 1767.

To Mary Norris
in Chesnut Street*Postmark:*Lan:2:O
Philadelphia

Second day may 25th

I have been a long time without writing one line to thee,
My Dear, Greatly Sufferring friend, but it has been my Misfortune to
have had such very broken health ever Since some days before my Brothers return
home, that I had no Power to write, and now, that I find my Self a little
recruited, I have to condole with you afresh, upon so distressing an occasion
and indeed so unexpected, that I want words to express my Sorrowful Sense
of it.—I canot mourn for the dead, they are removed from a State
subjected to such a variety of evils, that they ought not to be mournd
for; As we humbly trust every dear friend we feel the loss of, is taken to
the mercy of God, we have only to mourn our own deprivation of the
comforts & Blessings we enjoyd, so long as Providence was Graciously pleasd
to Spare them to us, and to Submit with that Christian Resignation we are
taught dayly to Pray for, to these affecting Separations, whenever that Same
wise Providence shall ordain them to Befal us,—Indeed when I
look back upon the Situation of your late happy family, to no very distant
Period, happy in your Selves and in one another, and the Subject of rejoycing
to your friends, and upon these repeated Severe Strokes of Mortality, I am
distrest for you beyond what I can describe,—but this can avail neither you
nor my Self; May the Mercyful Providence of God, Support Bless & Protect
you, direct all your ways to your Present Solace and Comfort, and be your
Eternal Reward.—I am highly Sencible of the the considerate
tenderness my friends expressd, to have Saved my unacountably weakened mind,
from the painful Effects of a Sudden notice of your dear lamented Sisters death,
But your Singular Kindness was accidently defeated,—My late Brothers Eldest
son, who has been for some time in an ill state of health, was lying almost in
extremity in a dangerous Sickness, & Jemmy was over the river when Jn° Lowden
recd H Griffith's Letter, he gave it to Rhoda, & told her the Purport of it, but She
said nothing to me, expecting Jemmy home, but he did not return til bedtime.
I saw her dejected & Sorrowful the whole afternoon, and Kept asking her
questions, which she Stil Evaded, in the mean time the Gazette was bro^t in,

which I lookd over, and all at once came upon that Surprising article, the Shock it gave me seemd almost to deprive me of life, as soon as I was capable of Reflection, I found my head Affected in So Strange a manner, and Beat so violently, that I was quite terryfyd, I could not shed a tear for the world thro the whole evening.

however that discomposure is now over, and I have found the Salutary releif of tears, and have to beg thy excuse for this long detail of a weakness that that probably I ought to be ashamd of, yet such as is not in my power to get the Better of, But I am gratefully Sencible of your humanity and friendship, in Rememb'ring me in the Kind manner you did, when you were so deeply Suffering your Selves—the Poor young man our nephew continues still extream ill, & Jemmy is over the River all day—and what has added to the tremor of my hand Just now is, a number of Docters have Just been Opening a large protuberance, of what kind I Know not, upon the forepart of the neck of a Child of one of my neices, and I have been in terrors all forenoon, least I should hear the Child had Perishd under their hands, But I am told this minute the Operation is over, without any aparent present danger—I have been taking Bark in Substance in Smal doses, & riding in the waggon (for my arm dissables me from riding any other way) for about a week past, and think I have found Benefit—if my life may be continued, I shal ever think I owe it under Providence, to the advice of my Kind & worthy friend Doct^r Moore,—pray give my Kindest Regards to him and his good wife,—our family are thro mercy well, pray let us hear of yours—I am Concernd, and wish to learn what friend or Companion thou has in the house with thee, besides thy dear engaging children, for tho when mourning friends are together, they canot render one another chearful yet they Seem to assist one another in Bearing their Burthens, and being quite alone, is the worst of any thing,—pray give my Affectionate remembrance and Sincere condolance to the whole united familys,—I have great Obligations to Polly Norris, I am truly Sencible of the Confidence She has reposd in me, I will not abuse it, and acknowledge it as Soon as as I am able—the Same to Hannah Griffitts, Kiss your Dr Children for us, take Comfort in them, dont Sink under Reiterated afflictions, take an Especial care of thy own health, and always Keep in mind how much depends upon the preservation of it,—the Bearer to the Post waits for my letter—farewell my Dear friend

    thy truly Obligd Affect Frd
    S:Wright

Rhoda Presents her Kindest Remembrance

Selected Letters

Susanna Wright to Mary Norris, July 5, 1767[26]

S Wright's letter July 5th 1767 La:2:0
To Mary Norris in Chestnut Street Philadelphia

July 5th 1767

My Dear Friend
If it had been in my power to have done otherways, I Should
esteem my Self Inexcusable for not having enquird after your
welfare before this time, but I have been more amiss Since I rec^d
thy last Kind favor, then (I think) I had been at all. the Perpetual
changes of weather, Storms, and Excessive heat some time agoe,
were almost more then I was able to bear, but at present thro mercy
I am better,—the poor young man, my Brothers Son,
who I mentiond in my last to be dangerously ill, dyed at the end of
ten or Eleven days, his Sickness was a bilous fever, he was in his
26th year and an Engaging person, but had unhappily livd too
fast, he was tenderly belovd by all his Relations, and no one's
Enimy but his own—poor young man
Jemmy & Rhoda have both been Amiss, but are Recovered, and
Buisy in the midst of a large harvest,—But what Shal
I say to My Dear Obliging friends at Fairhill,—what can
I say, I am highly Sencible of their favors, but I am good for
nothing,—Charles Thomson crossd our River on his way to Virginia
and said he should Return in two weeks, on which I detirmind to
send my whole Packet by him; and tryed thro those two weeks to
have it ready,—that is I tryd in my mind, for I never touchd
a pen, and if I had, I could only have laid it down again, the
causes of this Confession give me a Sencible Concern, but I realy
can Scarcely exert Spirrit Sufficient to Scribble these few
Incoherent lines to thee, tho I am full as well to day as I have
been for Seveal months Past,—however I comfort my Self
with hope, that my Indulgent friends will not quite discard
me, as my Seeming Negligence is not my fault but my
Misfortune
what Benefit I have found, has been from Riding, which my Good
Docter Moore Strongly advisd me to, and Since the heat has
moderated, I have traveld almost dayly, and always find my
Spirits Releivd by it, But it seems a Strange thing to me, who
never went much abroad in any part of my life, & for a long

course of years not at all; I have been twice at Lancaster
within this week or two, where I had been no more then twice
Before, for betwixt 20 & 30 years Past, but I stopt at a friends
house at this end of the town, & paid not one visit; we are badly
Situated for Roads for a Cariage, the river, & Broken land & high hills
are 3 Sides, and the Public Road is only travelable, where [*letter torn*]
ashamd to be seen riding, like a Creature of no use in the wo [*letter torn*]
would Submit to mortifications for Breath,

Be So Kind my Dear friend to let us hear from you; and
Be particuler how you all are, and about your Engaging
Children, we always long for it, and give us leave to Present
our Kindest Respectful love & Compliments to every one of
you in town & Country—one by one, as if they were named
we offer them with great Sincerety and Affection,—we have
not heard of Wm Logan a long time, we hope heisRecovering [*letter torn*]
I can write no longer, only to add pray excuse this whole letter

    thy truly Obliged friend
    S Wright

Susanna Wright to Mary Norris, September 22, 1772[27]

Susanna Wrights [*in later hand*]
Septr. 22^d. 1772.

To Mary Norris

Sept 22nd 1772

My Dear Friend

    I hope it is quite unnessessary to assure thee, the acct of your Genl welfare, in thy favour by polly Hart, was most welcome to us;—we have not had the pleasure to hear of you Since: we thankfully acknowledge thy care & Kindness Relating our Billet.
    as we expected to hear of Ruth Thomsons departure, it was no Surprise to us; her late long & meloncholy Situation, had been such, that had Providence permitted her Recovery from this illness, it was probably to be feard, she might have relapsed into the like Constitutional misfortune a Second time, and in that apprehension, who can Regret her being removd into a Security from those, and all other Evils:— But we were Surprisd, & Sencibly & deeply, concernd, to Read in the Gazette, an acct of the death of our Worthy friend, & distant Allie, Saml Fothergil; we are told he dyed at his own home, which was the house in which my father was Born, 105 years agoe, and where his Parents lived and Died: after my Grand fathers death, the house was purchased by my Grand mothers Brother, father to Saml Fothergils wife, as I had past many of the happyest days of my life in, it those days, unclouded by care or Sorrow, which are quickly over, and can never Return, and was Intimately aquainted with every part & Cranny of it: he was pleasd to describe all the alterations he had made, as he had in a manner rebuilt it, among other tryfling questions I askd him, I enquired after a large old Clock, that had been my Grandfathers, when my father was a Child, and which stood in my uncles parlour when we left England; he answerd it continued to go Exelently well, after having measured time to its Several owners, for a a hundred years,—and alas it has now I presume, measured time to himself, to the latest hour of his valuable life,—he moralisd very Seriously upon the Subject, as I ought to do upon this Affecting Occasion, rather then Relate these uninteresting Anecdotes of a house, and a peice of its furniture; but what could I say— Such has been the decree of Devine Providence, and who Shall presume

to query, why was it so. I have quite forgot what was Sam Fothergils age
when he was with us, But I think I concluded, he must be several years
younger then his wife; when we left her, I was betwixt 16 & 17, and
She wanted only two years of my Age, so that if she is still living
she must now be 73, an Age I presume he did not attain to; when he
Marryd her, she was a fine Girl, very pretty, and had a Valuable fortune,
and now is without doubt a disconsolate widdow,—they had not any
Children,—I Ramble on as if I Knew not when to leave off, but our
family is Gone to bed, & I have no Sleep in my Eyes, neither is my mind
easy Ennough to Indulge it, if it was otherways, my Brother & sister
are Both greatly Indisposd; Rhoda was taken about a week agoe, with
Symptoms of an Interm[?] by propper remedys, the fever left her, But a
Constant depression of spirrits and a number of other complaints, have
dissordred her so much, that we have sent this Evening to request our
Doctr to visit her in the morning, I would hope she is not dangerou ill,
but I can give no account how she is, only I Imagine she is Injured
by Suckling beyond her Strength, and which she would not have
done, but in Consideration of a great mortality that has been among
children in Lancastr, and that the distemper is now come into our very
near neighbourhood;—Jemmy was taken last first day, with a voilent
defluction upon his lungs, & an uncomon bad Cough, headake, Great
soreness in his Breast, and an universal Lassitude—he Keeps up,
but is realy extreamly out of Order,—indeed the weather has been so
changeable & I think so unfavourable to health, that I wonder almost
every one is not affected by it—my Eyes grow dim—I have only to
present a General Salutation, with great Sincerity Affection & Esteem,
from Every one of us, to Every one of you, as if named

            thy truly Obliged Friend
              S: Wright

Susanna Wright, October 8, 1774[28]

My Dear ffriend   Oct 8th 1774
  I canot express how much I was delighted & obliged,
by thy last Kind favour; I had been so long without one line
from thy hand, that I was quite uneasy: we all rejoyce to hear
of your welfare, & that thy dear son is So fully recovred: we
are Sincerely Concernd at thy good Sisters Broken state of health
she has our warmest desires for amendmt, and our Respectful

and affectionate Remembrance;—may the purposd Inoculation at fairhill, be attended with all possible safety & Success, yet I could have wishd Sally had passd thro it, a year agoe, for it seems now as if the anxiety must be doubled, yet when it shall be once happily over, as we all most sincerely wish & hope for, every thing will have been right; we hope our valued ffriend Hannah Moores Neice has been Spared to her, tho with the loss of her Infant, for in these parts, the Season has been very unfortunate to young women in her Situation: Our family are thro Mercy in health, I have been a good deal Amiss for some time past, but am at present as well at my age I can expect to be, and thankful I am as well as I am.

 Our Girls receive thy Kind notice as a great favour, and w^d Rejoyce to Embrace it, but their Station in life, must confine them at home, they were at the yearly meeting in Lancast^r, but longer Journey are at present Impracticable; Sally Bethel is pretty well, & now weaning her mother's Child, & Betsy is always buissy; as a Non Importation is agreed upon, they must be Industrious in Spinning, or content themselves with thin Clothing; our young people were Inexpressibly happy, on receit of their pretty letters & pictures, the latter, will be Speedily framd & glazd, & hung up in triumph,
We Sincerely wish Patsy Moore may find all the Releif from traveling, that can be expected or hoped for, from that most Salutary Exercise; the Same for thy agreable neice Thomson, I warmly wish health, & every Blessing, to every one of my friends, and that is all the service in my power to render them.

 Thou art pleasd to mention their Intended future Journeys, in a manner as if they were to be at a Considerable distance from you; we Should be obligd if thou could learn, if they [have] any Kind thoughts of Obliging their friends in these parts with a Visit, and when about it would probably be; we wish this both for their Sake's & our own; people in our station, are often in what is calld the Suds; and we would wish; if any of our good fr^{ds} should favour us with their Company, to render their stay with us as agreable to them, and as little disreputable to our Selves, as every thing in our power, & a hearty welcome could render it—But thro this, & thro every thing I think or write about, I never lose Sight of a hope, to see thee & thy dear children next spring; I supose my Brother must go to Phil^a in that season, & that he will take the Journey, at whatever time will best suit you to return with him; I must, I will, continue

to cherish that hope, & leave the Event to Providence,
Every one of our family, desire to be remembred to Every one
of yours, in town and Country, in the most affectionate
gratefull & Respectfull manner; our Children desire to
present their Compliments & many thanks to yours, they
are often Comparing their letters, & disputing which is the
prettiest, but all agree with Better Judges, that all are pretty.

 Now I think I have spun out my letter, without being able to
recolect any thing further to add, except about Bears, &
somthing Relating to my past Corespondence with thee my
dear frend: We have had an Innundation of those Savage
Creatures come down amongst us, almost famishd, by the
mast being mostly destroyd, they Eat peoples hogs, be fright
women & Children; a great many of them have been shot,
some of our family were on the river, & met with one upon a
Rock, they had no gun & Killd it with poles,—this
is pretty news to write to a Citty Lady, but this is Country news.
—what I am about to write has vext me a good deal,—when
I do not meet with a Convenience by a private hand, which is
not often, I write by the post without Scruples, as I always
wish thee to do; I never think much of the tryfle of a Single
letter to thee, such as thine always are to me; & I took care
to write no other,—but the paper we had in the house was
thick, & of Consequence heavy; I tho^t a Single letter was a Single
letter; But Jemmy Rec^d Just such an one the other day ch[argd]
by weight 1^s-8^d—now one Shilling & 8^d as Swift says, is a
Serious thing, & most of my letters I supose have been So
chargd to thee, But I will never more write by the post
upon such expensive paper; and I sincerely beg thy excuse,
letters such as mine, must be dear at the Lowest price,
farewell My Good friend we all desire to Salute thee & thy
dear Children with all possible affection & tenderness
 thy truly Obliged
 S Wright

we desire the favour of Phebe Chandler to get 150 more
of such needles, as She sent by Jemmy Ewing,
only that she would please to get a few of
them of finer Sizes; Several of our friends are
in Such want of good needles, that if we do not

get a further Supply for them, we must want
for our Selves, the Bearer Nat[1] Barber will
repay her what she lays down for them,

Susanna Wright to John Lowdon, July 18, 1775[29]

July 18th 1775

Cosen Johny

    If in your present Military Situation, you will own Relationship with a family of peace, be pleasd to accept the Kind Remembrance & good wishes of all ours.
    We were much Surpris[d] at the news of your present Expedition, & can by no means aprove of it, if your design is other then to visit the camp of our Brave Countrymen, & Satisfy your own Curiosity, & then return, as other Gentlemen from this province will, I presum, wisely do. you canot possibly be wanted where you are, and by the obligations to God & nature your presence will be necessary to the welfare of your five pretty Children, who, such of them as are able to Reflect, are Inconsolable for your absence. But I hope & trust, you will Reflect, & not be carryd away with an Inordinate military Enthusium, to get your Self shot thro the head, when you have realy no call to it. Transfer your valient marksmen to some other comander, and come home like a wise man, and take care of your Childrens valuable property, which you have with so much fatigue procured for them, and which, with a Small degree of foresight, we may presume, they will never be the better for, should any misfortune happen to you; Remember the wise assertion of Old Homer—"the day that to the shades the father sends,
    "Robs the poor Orphan of his fathers friends,
we have here our share of Aflictions & Evils, your poor Aunt Rhoda has had a Severe Stroke of the Palsey, She is much Recovred, yet still is in a State to be lamented; your Relation & old friend Saml Bethel, Dyed very Suddenly, three weeks agoe, Suposd to be by a Stroke of the same Kind, in one hour after he receivd it, tho the Doct[r] was in the house with him, if any assistance could have been given But the angel of Death allowd no Respite.
    Sammy Bethels family are left in a most forlorn Situation, except in point of fortune; your unhappy & most distrest cosen Sukey, is excedingly

to be pittyed, & if you have not lost the feelings of humanity in your military Character, you must find pitty take place of any remains of Resentm^t that you might have harbourd towards her; added to her heavy Sorrows, she has been very much harrassd by that Infernal servant woman she had such a partiality for; the time was Elapsd which She expected to serve her own wicked purposes by, & then she began such a howling as extreamly disturbd Her Sick master & all the family; in a week or two more; she aquitted every person she had Scandelisd, & laid her Infamy to a marryd man of credit & fortune in Lancaster, and wanted a majestrate to tender an oath to her, but as none was at hand, she persisted in her assertion with Imprecations, til in due time she produced a very dark mulattoe, & then honestly laid it to a negro fidler; which piqud her pride so sencibly, that the family have feard she would murder it;—I should not have wrote this, but to paint the heavy Burden your unhappy Cosen Sukey labours under. your friends here & Children are well except Rhoda, who as I said is Recovering; and if they Knew I was writing, they would all send their love & good wishes—once more my Dear Cosen Johny, let me adjure you to return without delay, shedding human Blood, & Especialy that of our Countrymen, however neccessary, is a most Meloncholy thing, & happy are they who have no absolute call to it; such must run a double risk, a Risk of having their own Shed, & of not finding mercy for shedding that of others, and in that Light you appear to me. I pray god to preserve you from both, & so send you Safe home to your motherless Children, & to your friends & family, & in particuler

    to your truly afectionate Aunt

S: Wright

Susanna Wright to Jasper Yeates, January 18, 1776[30]

                                          Jan^ry 18 1776

Respected ffriend

    Please to Excuse me for troubling you with a line, as it may probably Expedite the good office I have to request. An Orphans Court will be desired to meet on monday next, to appoint Gaurdians for the Children of my late dear Brother; for which purpose, his Eldest son, & our Relation Robert Barber, will wait upon you Early in the day in hopes of having it compleated before night, as there is no Settlem^t, then meerly apointing gaurdians; the persons who are desired, are John Dickinson, whos permission to be named one of them, he sent us in writing, the Childrens mother Rhoda Wright, their Elder Brother Sammy, Robert Barber, & my Self, or the Survivors of them: the names of the Children under age, are, Betsy, John, James, Susana, William & patience, the Gaurdians are to be in Comon to all the Children; I am so particular, as you may perhaps have leasure before monday to prepare any neccessary writing with more convenience, then you could do at an hours warning,

 My Sister Joyns with me in Desiring our Respectfull complim^ts and Kindest Remembrance, to our worthy friends M & Mrs Shippens and to your Good Wife.

       I am with Esteem your Aff Friend

           S Wright

p Yeates

Isaac Norris to James Wright, undated[31]

To James Wright at Hempfield   by Charles
This morning we have sent up A Bill for giving Sixty thousand
Pounds to the Kings use to be Struck in Paper Bills and sunk by
taxes of Six pence per[ ] pounds and ten Shillings per[ ] Head for Four Years
and in Order to Obviate any objections the Govr. might make to the
passing the Bill we have added the Clauses herewith Sent. The Mony
is to be drawn out of the Trustees Hands by Jo Norris Saml Hamilton
John Mifflin Joseph Fox John Hughs and Evan Morgan or a Majority
of them with the Consent of the Governor so that we have now
taken in every Objection the Govr made to our former Bill except
the Property Estate only and by these Clauses we have referred even
that to the decision of the Crown   But as our Treasury is now
exhausted and mony must be had if the Govr should still refuse this
Bill (I may say to thy Self) I believe the House will send him an
Excise Act on his own terms, with a protestation reserving their Rights
for as much mony as that Fund will produce

[Icuronyouda?] and And [Montour?] with Jayreu & Conrad Weiser are now in Town and intend to Speak to the Govr ab^t half an hour hence to which Conference the Govr has invited the House and we shall attend accordingly   We all extreamly pitty your Circumstance and you may depend upon every thing in our power to assist & relieve you

8. Novr ha past 2 PM in hast

Thy Affect Frd
Isaac Norris

We are much Concernd for the Circumstances of our Friends Your Way In Particular, & for the Country in General   We have been Expecting yr Women & Children Several days past, as there was a report of their being on the Road, As Soon as you may think it Necessary to Remove them, Let them Come to their Frds Who Will do all in their power to Aleviate their distress Which Such A Separation must Occasion. My Frds Lets be of Good Chear & Trust in God for his deliverance some way Or Other
[A few words are broken and illegible at end]

NOTES

1. D. N. Logan, *Susanna Wright*; see Appendix in this volume.
2. Library of the Religious Society of Friends, Friends House, London, England. Published with kind permission from the Library of the Religious Society of Friends.
3. Logan Family of Stenton Papers, vol. I, XR: 825.4, Historical Society of Pennsylvania. Published with kind permission from the Historical Society of Pennsylvania.
4. Family Letters, vol. 2, p. 42, Norris Papers, Historical Society of Pennsylvania. Published with kind permission from the Historical Society of Pennsylvania.
5. *Publications of the Pennsylvania Society of Colonial Dames of America*, no. 2 (1905), pp. 12–13.
6. From a nineteenth-century transcription (WFM 83.18.133) of the original document. "A. Spencer" is probably Dr. Adam Spencer, who was lecturing in Philadelphia in 1744 and who first introduced Benjamin Franklin to the study of electricity. See F. B. Tolles, *Meeting House*, p. 219.
7. The text is from the original manuscript (WFM 83.18.4) and a nineteenth-century transcription. Doctor Lloyd Zachary (1701–1756) was among the most distinguished Quaker physicians in early eighteenth-century Philadelphia. He was the grandson of the patriarch and progenitor of the Philadelphia Quaker aristocracy, Thomas Lloyd, and friend and physician to Susanna Wright and her family. See F. B. Tolles, *Meeting House*, pp. 120, 122. Despite Dr. Zachary's care, Sarah Blunston died December 13, 1744, and Samuel Blunston the next year. As early as 1730, they had provided land for burial ground, where their property adjoined the Wrights' land, and enclosed it with a wall. Samuel and Sarah Blunston were buried there and their graves marked with marble tombstones as indicated in a list of the burials in the cemetery from 1730–1750, which is included in this Appendix.
8. L. W. Labaree, et al., eds. *Papers*, vol. 4, pp. 210–11. Published with kind permission from Yale University Press.
9. Ibid., pp. 335–36. Published with kind permission from Yale University Press.
10. L. W. Labaree, et al., eds., *Papers*, vol. 6, pp. 23–24. Published with kind permission from Yale University Press.
11. Ibid., p. 90–91. Published with kind permission from Yale University Press.
12. *Publications of the Pennsylvania Society of Colonial Dames of America*, no. 2 (1906), pp. 36–37.
13. WFM 83.18.174.

14. Autograph Collection, Case 19, Box 5, Historical Society of Pennsylvania. Published with kind permission from the Historical Society of Pennsylvania.
15. WFM 83.18. 9. John Taylor was born to Susanna Wright's sister Elizabeth and Samuel Taylor on July 2, 1739. "Sam" at the end of the undated letter is probably Samuel, the son of Susanna's brother James and Rhoda Wright, who was born May 12, 1754.
16. WFM 83.18.176 (an eighteenth-century transcription).
17. In private collection.
18. WFM 83.18.11 (an eighteenth-century copy).
19. George Gaylord Simpson, "The Beginnings of Vertebrate Paleontology in North America," in *Proceedings of the American Philosophical Society*, vol. 86, no. 1 (September 1942): 140. Published with kind permission from the American Philosophical Society.
20. WFM 83.18.17.
21. WFM 83.18.12 and 83.18.14. In the collection, there are two original drafts of this letter to Charles Norris, which had been part of a body of documents numbered by a later hand. This draft was number 8 and the other draft number 4, both with subtle refinements to the text. At the time of composing this letter, Susanna Wright had been reading the letters of Lady Mary Wortley Montague, which Charles Norris had ordered for her and which perhaps inspired the special care exercised in composing this letter. Earlier, Charles Norris had ordered Alexander Pope's published letters for Susanna Wright, and Benjamin Franklin had sent her the letters of Madame de Maintenon. The text of the letter, with minor variations was published in *Publications of the Pennsylvania Society of Colonial Dames of America*, no. 2 (1906), pp. 29–33.
22. WFM 83.18.107. Part of this text had been published in the *Publications of the Pennsylvania Society of Colonial Dames of America*, vol. 2 (1906), p. 34. This letter was addressed perhaps to Charles Norris. The friend mentioned in the opening, Jane Hoskins, whose maiden name was Fenn, was born in London in 1693. Compelled from an early age to come to Pennsylvania, she arrived in 1712, her passage having been paid by Robert Davis, who was coming with his family to Pennsylvania. Although she was going to repay the money through her earnings here, Davis insisted that she bind herself for four years as a servant to him. When she would not do that, he had her arrested for debt. She was thrown into prison but was released by Quakers who paid the claim and employed her in their families as a teacher of their children. Impressed with their kindness, she joined the Society of Friends and eventually became extremely active as a minister, traveling to England and Ireland from 1727 to 1730. When she returned, she continued with her work as housekeeper for David and Grace Lloyd. David Lloyd was a Chief Justice of Pennsylvania. On October 8, 1738, at Chester Meeting, Jane Fenn married Joseph Hoskins (1705–1773), who was a Chief Burgess of Chester and, in 1758, a justice of the peace. See H. G. Ashmead, *Historical Sketch of Chester, on Delaware* (Chester, PA, 1883), pp. 113–14.

    The friend that Susanna Wright mentions in the postscript, Joseph Parker, came to Chester, Pennsylvania, in 1714, the same year as the Wrights, to be near his uncle, the noted Quaker preacher John Salkeld. Joseph Parker worked in the office of David Lloyd and succeeded him as Register and Recorder of Chester County. In 1724 Joseph Parker became Prothonotary of the Courts and Justice of the Peace in 1738. In 1730, he married Mary, daughter of James Ladd, of Gloucester County, New Jersey. She died the following year, leaving a daughter, Mary, who married Charles Norris in 1759. See Ashmead, p. 75.

    In 1733 Joseph Parker purchased the Wrights' former house and land in Chester and lived there for a short time. The deed for 221 acres and 70 perches, dated May 1, 1733, from John Wright to Joseph Parker stated: "All and singular the Messuage or Tennement & plantation where the Said John Wright lately Dwelt and the Said Joseph Parker now Dwells." "Jemmy," Susanna Wright's brother James (1714–1775), traveled to Philadelphia with frequency because he was a member of the Pennsylvania Assembly and so was able to maintain the close friendship that the Wright family had had for many years with the Norris family and its various branches. In 1753, he married Rhoda Patterson (1728–1798) and, at the time of this letter, had three children: Samuel, born in 1754; Elizabeth, born in 1758; John, born in 1760; and, the baby Susanna, born in 1764. Susanna Wright and her brother James' family lived together and when James died in 1775 Susanna became a guardian for the children. The love and care she had for the family is evident throughout her writing. It was to Samuel that Susanna Wright bequeathed Wright's Ferry Mansion and most of her land. On a portion of the land Samuel established the town of Columbia in 1788.

23. *Publications of the Pennsylvania Society of Colonial Dames of America*, no. 1 (1905), p. 14.
24. WFM 83.18.106. This letter was written at the death of one of the Wrights' closest friends, Charles Norris.
25. WFM 83.18.103.
26. WFM 83.18.105.
27. WFM 83.18.104. Information on houses and furniture occurs rarely in Susanna Wright's letters. Here she recalls the house and clock belonging to her grandparents and uncle. Her grandparents, James and Susannah Wright lived in Warrington, England, and had died in 1688, almost ten years before Susanna Wright was born. At that time, clocks were expensive and found only in affluent households. Samuel Fothergill (1715–1772) was a noted preacher of the Society of Friends, who married Susanna Croudson, the daughter of William Croudson, brother of Susanna Wright's grandmother. Susanna Fothergill died in 1773, the year after her husband.
28. WFM 83.18.175.
29. WFM 83.18.177.
30. Stauffer Collection, 31:2429, Historical Society of Pennsylvania. Published with kind permission from the Historical Society of Pennsylvania.
31. WFM 83.18.108.

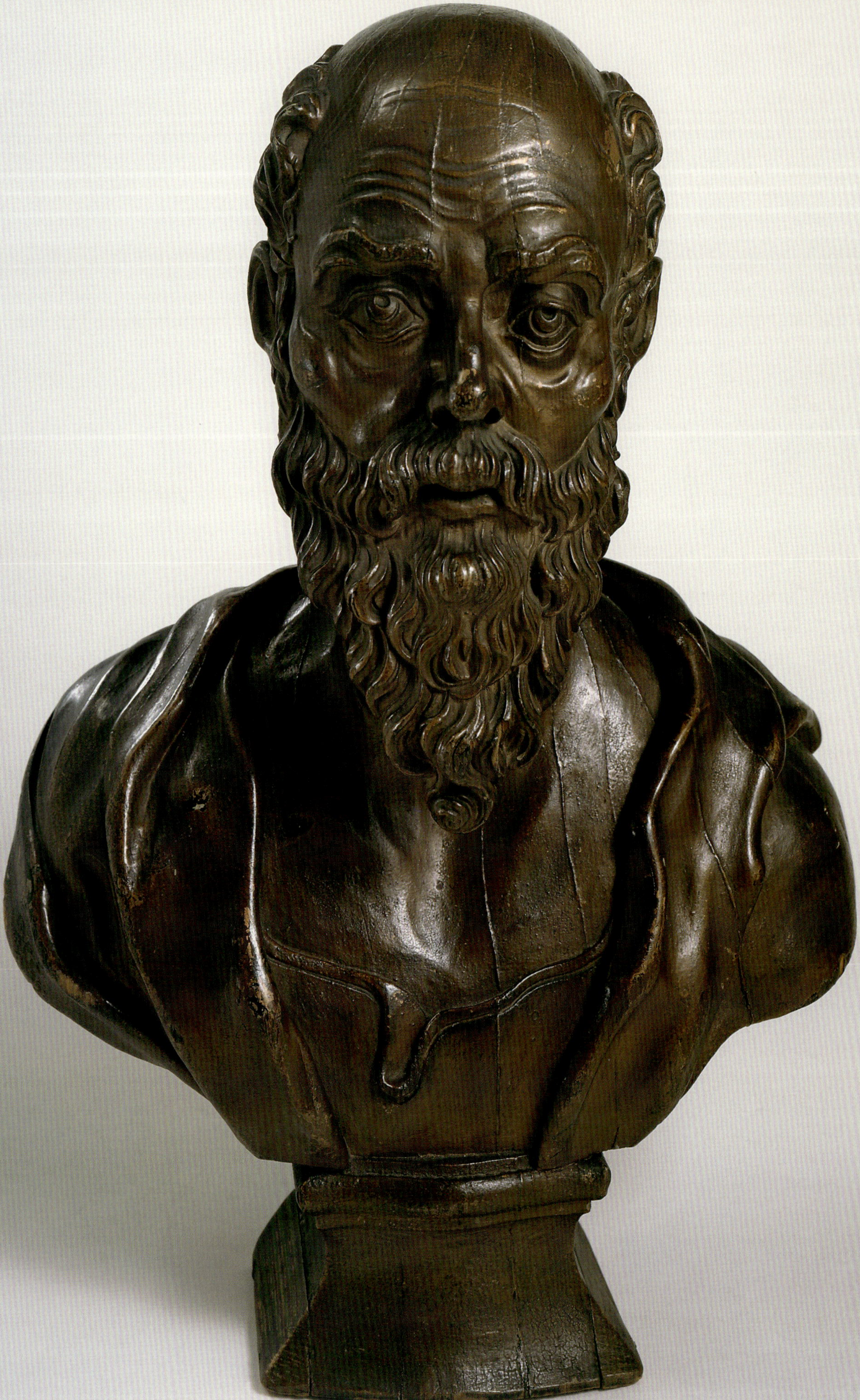

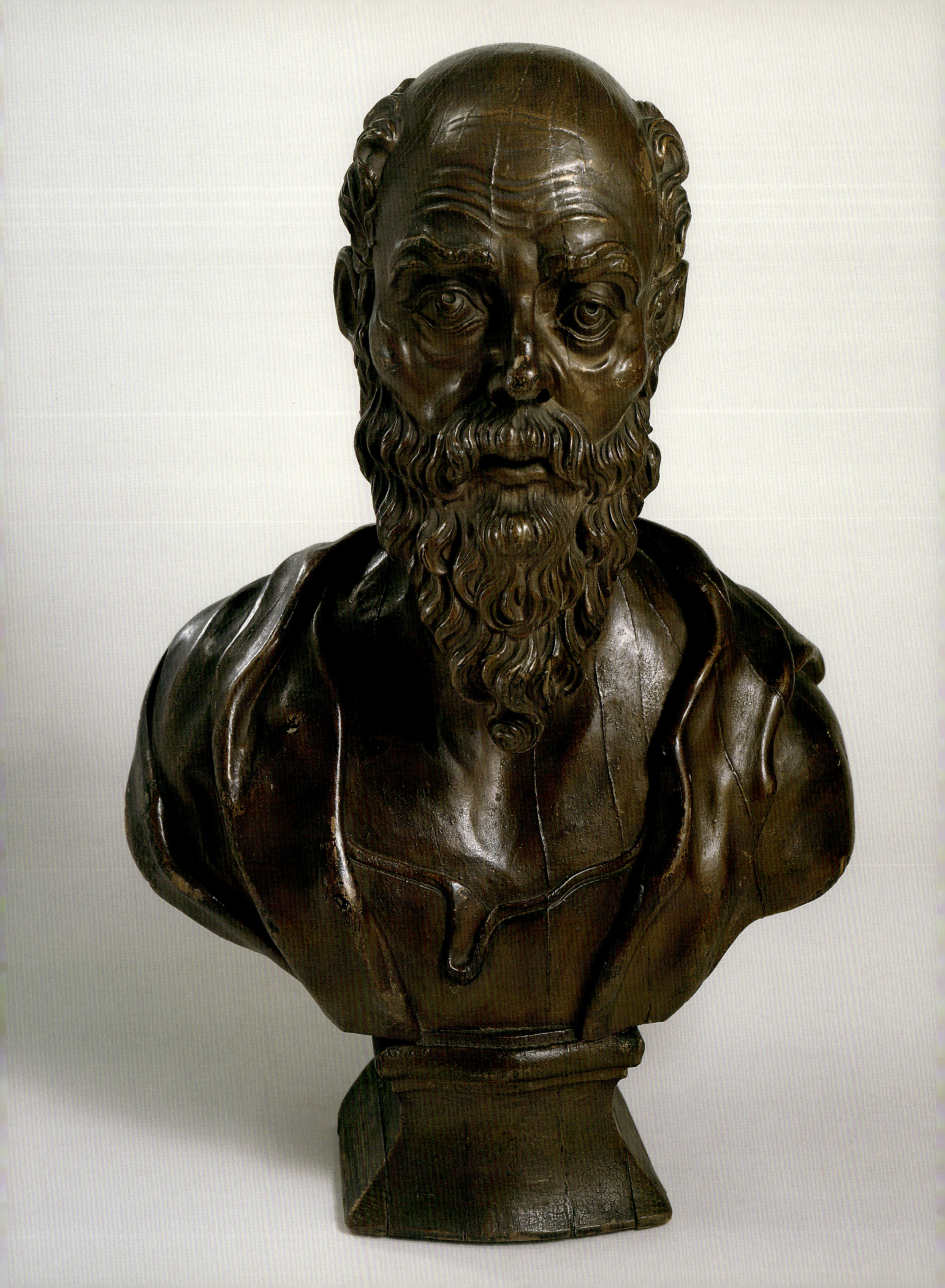

POETRY

𝒫oetry pervaded Wright's Ferry Mansion—the words of Homer accompanied the Wrights and Blunstons to the wilderness as they embarked upon their personal odysseys, lines from the *Iliad* inscribed in the very account book in which they recorded the logs that were hewn for the houses they inhabited. Benjamin Franklin included lines from John Milton in his morning devotions, "our beloved Poet," as he referred to him in writing to Susanna Wright of pamphlets he was sending. Poetry was used to unravel misunderstandings in a friendship and Charles Norris even used verse in his letter discussing the vegetables they were raising in their gardens. With a subtle, refining intellect, Susanna Wright was permeated by the best in literature and her poetry reflects the influences of Dryden, Pope, and Milton. Classical in style with a sparse, dense use of language, her poetry reveals a dramatic talent and narrative skill.

James Logan, one of the brilliant men in the colonies in the first half of the eighteenth century, was receiving poems from Susanna Wright very soon after her arrival in Pennsylvania, saying: "Tho' thy last with thy short flight at Poetry once more, requires my acknowledgement, yet I would not give thee one line were it not that I wish barely to tell thee that I had thy promise to visit us this fall. . . ." At least as early as 1723, and continuing for many years, Susanna Wright sent James Logan poetry along with her letters. His knowledge of Greek and Latin literature (some of which he translated) as well as contemporary literature was formidable and is reflected in his library, now at the Library Company of Philadelphia, from which he would lend Susanna Wright volumes. In his letter of April 12, 1723, he said, "I have almost continually before me a few Lines of Horace; w[ch] I wish I could quote to thy Understanding in his own Words." He paraphrased them for her: "Know it is thy Duty to make the best of the present," since time "rolls on like a

River Sometimes Smooth & quiet in its Channel Sometimes overflowing its banks carries Buildings flocks and herds before it...."[1] This poem perhaps was mentioned in conjunction with Susanna Wright's poem "On Time." Her exchanges with James Logan, and with her other literary friends like the Norrises, undoubtedly encouraged and inspired her talents, which were so highly esteemed that she was numbered among the important poets of early Pennsylvania. Today she is regarded as one of the most significant poets in colonial America.

A spiritual quality pervades Susanna Wright's poetry, clearly springing from her Quaker beliefs. These were rooted in her family almost since the inception of the Society of Friends, when the visionary George Fox, seeing everything as a new creation, wanted to return to the purity of the early Church. Fox's works as well as those of William Penn and the French spiritual writer Fénelon are strong influences in her writing. Her poem "To Eliz[a] Norris at Fairhill" extends to revolutionary proportions the Quaker belief regarding equality of men and women in the statement "No right has man his equal to control." As in the Pauline injunction in I Corinthians 7:8, 34 which places celibacy above marriage, this poem is also remarkable in upholding the unmarried state as one of fulfillment and completion in which one can "shine yourself, the finish'd piece you draw."

In Wright's Ferry Mansion, poetry was created; some, however, was consumed in the fire of the hearth. Susanna Wright herself refers to "committing most of my foibles to the fire." Deborah Norris Logan said of Susanna Wright:

> *It was in the productions of her pen that she most excelled they were deservedly admired whilst she lived, and would abundantly satisfy the world of her merit could they now be produced; but as she wrote not for fame she never kept copies, and it is to be feared but little is at this time recoverable.*[2]

Fortunately, some did survive which we have presented here as a collection of twenty-seven poems.

The most extensive collection of Susanna Wright's poems has been preserved in the *Commonplace Book of Milcah Martha Moore*, wife of Susanna Wright's physician, friend, and correspondent, Dr. Charles Moore. Following twenty-four poems by Susanna Wright, Milcah Martha Moore notes:

> *The foregoing poetical Pieces are copied from the Authors original MSS—I have seen a Copy of the last p[s]. with several Alterations as may probably be the Case with several or all, the others—but as I had not any of them I chose to follow the Originals.*[3]

Only a few "originals" (versions in Susanna Wright's own handwriting) have been located. They include "On the Death of a Young Girl—1737" in the Historical Society of

Pennsylvania and a collection of five poems at Wright's Ferry Mansion. Susanna Wright Cook presented them to Wright's Ferry Mansion where they are a treasured part of the collection, poetry as a "distillation of the spirit," an essence of the original inhabitant of Wright's Ferry Mansion. With the fragile, fragmented pages sewn together, only two of the five poems are complete, "My Own Birth day August 4th 1761" and "Tis wel there are new worlds of light in store," with fragments of the poems "To live alone amidst the busy Scene," "[To a Friend—On] Some Missunderstanding," and "—„Lo all things are but alter'd, nothing Dyes." The text of these five poems is printed here with missing portions supplied from the *Commonplace Book of Milcah Martha Moore* and the Historical Society of Pennsylvania. Three poems not included in the *Commonplace Book* are printed here: a poem written in 1726 when Susanna Wright moved to the banks of the Susquehanna, "From all the social world estrang'd," which was published in the *Literary Magazine and American Register* in 1804; "To Polly Norris"; and "To Eliza Norris at Fairhill."

The sequence of the poems in the *Commonplace Book* has been maintained here, since it appears to follow a rough chronological arrangement. The three poems not in the *Commonplace Book* that have been printed here have been incorporated chronologically into the collection, with "From all the social world estrang'd" first and "To Polly Norris" and "To Eliz[a] Norris at Fairhill" last.

As she sent poems to her mentor James Logan in her early years, so in later years Susanna Wright sent her poems to two young aspiring poetesses, Milcah Martha Moore (1740–1829) and Hannah Griffitts (1728–1817), who circulated copies of the poems among their friends. Both of these ladies, as well as Deborah Norris Logan, were related to each other through Thomas and Mary Lloyd, who were their great grandparents.

I acknowledge with gratitude the assistance of Dr. Timothy C. Miller for the literary insights he has provided regarding Susanna Wright's writing and for his guidance in the editing of the poetry as well as the documents presented throughout the Appendix.

[Untitled][4]

From all the social world estrang'd,
    in desert wilds and woods,
Books and engaging friends exchang'd
    For pendant rocks and floods;

Nature's uncultivated face
    A varying aspect wears;
But every charm and every grace
    Are sunk in stronger cares.

Each morning dawn to labour calls,
    Through noontide's sultry sun,
And when the dew of ev'ning falls,
    The task is but begun.

Lamps (wont to guide calm midnight hours
    O'er the amusing page,
Of poetry th' enchanting pow'rs,
    The wisdom of the sage)

Now gild the midnight hours of toil,
    'Till weary nature fails,
'Till glimmering they have spent their oil,
    And balmy sleep prevails;

'Till morning dawn renews the day,
    And with the day its care;
So pass the hours of life away
    Through the unvarying year.

Ah! how unlike those days of peace
    By earlier prospects given!
But hush, my heart, thy murmurs cease,
    And take thy lot from heaven.

With spirit act thy painful part,
    Subdue thy erring will,
Thy passions regulate, thy heart
    Guard from each thought of ill.

Then shall thy waining hours of day,
    (If life such hours shall bring)
Pass like a cloudless eve away
    To an eternal spring.

Meantime enjoy this season fair,
    And every joy that's given;
Shake from thy mind this weight of care,
    And bless indulgent heaven.

Behold the trees their leaves resume,
    The shrubs and herbage rise,
Unbidden flowers the groves perfume,
    And all serene the skies.

Behold the morn and evening sun
    The rock and water-fall,
Retract the wrong that thou hast done
    To scenes that never pall;

A scene the hand of nature drew
    With all surpassing skill,
Keeps through a thousand ages new
    Its pristine glories still.

The morning sun revives and warms,
    In native splendour bright;
And evening soft, with wonted charms,
    Leads on the shades of night.

The moon as pure her beams can shed,
    And stars as brightly glow,
As when yon arch of heaven was spread
    First o'er this world below.

Behold the morn and evening sun,
    The rock and water-fall,
Retract the wrong that thou hast done
    To scenes that never pall.

A Meditation[5]

For as Jonah was 3 Days & 3 Nights in the Whales Belly, so shall the Son of Man be 3 Days & 3 Nights in ye Heart of ye Earth.

Where shall I this unfathom'd Secret find
Of what thou art? O my mysterious Mind,
Where learn what Crimes committed heretofore,
Exact a Course of Punishments so sore
In present Ills & one great Risque of more?
Would Heaven all wise, all merciful & just
Have chang'd this intellectual Soul to Dust
If she no State of Pre existance knew?
If all these Ills were not her righteous Due?
Not one small Movement of herself she knows,
Involv'd in Darkness & oppress'd with Woes,
Whoes Weight our vain Inquietudes increase,
Strangers alike to Knowledge & to Peace,
'Till the full Expiation overpast,
(By Means in Heavens eternal Volume wrote
Surpassing all Extent of human Thought)
Peace, Light & Knowledge may be gain'd at last,
So when the Prophet his Obedience fled,
And the directed Lot mark'd his devoted Head
Aghast he plung'd amidst the broken Wave,
The living Tomb yawn'd dreadful to receive,
He enter'd & in solid Darkness lay,
The unweildy Monster roll'd his Bulk away,—
Down to the Bottom of the boundless Flood
He bore the Rebel from his angry God;
Through shining Plains & coral Groves he pass'd
Thro' Groupes of Beauties all around him cast;
But what avail'd, the Seer imprison'd lay,
Secluded every chearful Beam of Day;

'Till after three collected Nights of Pain,
Had cleans'd his Soul from her rebellious Stain,
He landed on his native World again.
Shadow & Type of him who long foretold,—Gen:3
Consol'd the patriarchal Sires of old,
Whose Day by Faith enraptur'd Abraham saw,
Completion of the Prophets & the Law,
With boundless Grace & unexampled Love
He left the Heaven of Heavens all Heights above,
Except the Throne supreme—
On this dark Orb a Veil of Flesh to wear,
And ev'ry Woe of human Nature bear,
Beneath the Weight of Heavens dread Wrath to groan,
To expiate Transgression not his own,
For the lost Tribes of Adams erring Race,
To gain Probation & an Hour of Grace,
Fulfill'd the hard Conditions of his Birth,
And took his Lot with all the Sons of Earth;
'Till three long Days, & 3 long Nights past o'er,
The mighty Sufferer must endure no more,
First born of them who from the Dead shall rise
He all triumphant sought his regal Skies.

Lost & confounded in the amazing Plan
A God! subjected to this Reptile Man
For his wild Passions & unguarded Fall
Great Sacrifice! was offer'd once for all,
A Sacrifice sufficient full & great
For Crimes of any pre-existant Date,
When those of this frail Life are added to their Weight.

Anna Boylens Letter to King Henry the 8th[6]

From anxious Thoughts of every future Ill
From these lone Walls which Death & Terror fill,
To you great Sir! a loyal Wife from hence,
Writes to assert her injur'd Innocence,
To you, who on a Throne supremely great
Look down & guide the partial Hand of Fate,

Who rais'd your Subject to a royal Bride,
To the imperial Purples gaudy Pride
And glowing Gems around these Temples ty'd,
You glowing Gems your Dazling Rays rebate
And fade thou purple, at thy wearers Fate,
To Grandeur rais'd, to Misery cast down
And mourn my sad acquaintance with a Crown,
My Life & Fame must join the Sacrifice
The last alone all peaceful Thought denies,
Renews my Anguish & o'erflows my Eyes.
For Life & Crown with Patience I forego,
There's no such Charm in filling Thrones below
My Name alone, tis Anna Boylens Name
With whose low Station & unspotted Fame
All innocent & happy Days I'd seen,
This harmless Name exalted to a Queen
Is handed infamous to future Times
Loaded with Falshoods, blacken'd o'er with Crimes
Y.r infant Daughter her sad Part must bear,
And with her Mother's Heart her Suff'ring share,
Poor lovely Offspring of a wretched Bed
What are thy hapless Mother's Crimes that shed
This baleful Influence on thy harmless Head?
Thy Father sternly casts thee from his Knee,
Whilst each licentious Tongue that rails at me
Points o'er thy opening Years with Infamy,
All Hopes on Earth with Patience I forego
But thee—poor Child left in a World of Woe
May thy dear Life in smoother Channels run
Secure from Ills thy Mother could not shun
All this in Pain, but nothing of Surprize
This Fall I look'd for from my fatal Rise,
From that unhappy Day, my Person pleas'd y.r Eyes.
Such slight Foundations never lasting prove
Where Fancy only lights the Torch of Love,
I see another Fair assume my Place
Who's in your Eyes what Anna Boylen was,
Beware triumphant Beauty how you shine
Those charms, those Vows & ardours all were mine.
Look on me & beware for as you see,

Wright's Ferry Mansion

What I am now, that you shall surely be,
But since my Death & nothing less will do
To bring you to the Bliss you have in View,
May bounteous Heaven the mighty Sin forgive
And not repay, the Injuries I receive,
Yet think, O! think what Crimes will wound y^r. Soul,
When your dim Eyes in search of Slumber rowl,
When Lamps burn blue & guilty Tapers fade,
As by your bridal Bed I glide a ghastly Shade,
While sanguine Streams from purple Fountains drain
And all around the gay Apartment stain.
From conscious Guilt will these Illusions rise,
And haunt your Steps & fill your watching Eyes,
For ever raising Tumults in your Breast,
But fear me not for I shall be at Rest.
But at that Day when the last Trumpets Sound,
Shall reach the dead, & break their Sleep profound,
Bones long sepulchred burst their narrow Rooms
And hostile Kings rise trembling from their Tombs,
When nor your Heart, nor mine can lie conceal'd
But ev'ry secret Sin shall stand reveal'd,
Stand full reveal'd that God & Man may see,
How Fate has err'd, & you have injur'd me.
When, but alas all Arguments are vain
To bring your royal wand'ring Heart again
What Innocence unaided & oppress'd
Could do, I've done, but who can Pow'r resist.

I've but one Wish but one Request to make
Let not my Friends be Sufferers for my sake,
All Innocent, humane, & kindly good
May their dear Lives be ransom'd by my Blood,
For ev'ry one the Price I'd freely pay
So many Times could Life be drain'd away,
By what I once have been by what you are,
Happy & great,—by all y^r. Joy & Care;
By all things sacred, all your Love forgive,
My Friends their harmless Crimes & let them live.

Lo! on her bended Knees thus asks y[r]. Wife,
On terms, you see, she would not ask her Life,
With this I cease, to trouble your Repose,
A few short anxious Hours the stormy Scene will close.

[Untitled extract dated September 1, 1721][7]

—Now never more, you my auspicious Stars!
I'll blame for Anguish, or a Life of Cares,
For Friends deserted, Fortune's Goods decay'd;
One happy Gift, has all those Wrongs o'er paid,
Rich in Possession, I despise my Fate,
Be but the Joy as lasting as 'tis great,
But you too short, my slender Thread design
Ah, since so short—permit it to be fine!
Crowd y[r]. promiscuous Pleasures where you'll give
A length of Years the Relish to outlive.
None but your chosen Blessings I desire,
And with so exquisite a Thought admire,
That winding up my Days, one step I rise,
To taste the Bliss of your imperial Skies.

[Untitled extract dated July 24, 1722][8]

For they who've taken an extensive View,
Of all that Raphael or that Titian drew,
With the same Fire, & the same Judgement,—Fraught,
As the immortal Workmanship was wrought,
Can they admire the cold & dull Design,
Of Pieces where no Master touches shine,
Where all's unlabour'd, Light & Shade confus'd
The colouring artless, & the Strokes abus'd,
E'en the Design (tho' cold & dull at first)
By accidents still alter'd for the worse,
And plac'd far from that advantageous Light
That gives to all a Tincture of its white,
A transient View must tire the curious Eye

Which for Relief will pass regardless by,
And kindly let the Faults neglected dye.

A Congratulation on Recovery from Sickness[9]

When thro' this Land, impetuous Sickness ran,
And sacrific'd the brittle Life of Man,
When burning Syrius like a Fury stood.
With purple Spots, & Arrows dipt in Blood,
And from his Magazine of Death & Pains
Shot scorching Fevers thro' our labouring Veins,
Then not a Life in sober Temperance spent
Warded the Blow, or hinder'd the Event,
But Infancy, & Youth, & bending Age,
All sunk alike beneath the Conqueror's Rage,
Learning & Wit, & every powerful Charm,
Prov'd all too weak the Tyrant to disarm,
When thou my Fr[d]. his Rage must undergo
'Till pale & faint, & sinking with the Blow
We saw—what every forward Fear cou'd show,

Then what avails it, mortal Men to rise
'Till high exalted to their kindred Skies,
Their Souls impatient, every Day refine
'Till bright as their own native Heaven they shine,
If we so early must resign our Claim,
While they remount the Regions, whence they came,
It has been so, & must be so again
Tho' thus refin'd they are but mortal Men,
For Addison & Garth resign'd their Breath,
Nor can a worth more strong, repel the Arms of Death.

But better News, these dark Reflections crost
That thou My Friend, regain'd the Health, thou'd lost.
In thy fair Consorts joys a Part we bear,
As in her Griefs, we had a real Share.

Late—so Brittannia saw the Sun arise
To bless the Earth & beautifie the Skies,

But as he shone in all his Strength of Light
Thick Shadows spread & veil'd him from their Sight,
And antient Night on mighty Wings uprose.
While silver Stars their feeble Lights disclose—
Each Beast of Prey, from out his Den appear'd,
And Birds of Night their screaming Voices rear'd
With Fear & Wonder every one drew nigh
To see such Omens threaten from on high,
But how their Hearts exulted, when they saw;
The Sun appear, & vanquish'd Shades withdraw,
'Till like himself, he shone again confest,
"With all his Arrows arm'd, in all his Glory drest."

On the Benefit of Labour[10]

Adam from Paradise expell'd,
Was drove into a Locust Field,
Whose rich luxuriant Soils produce,
Nor Fruit, nor Plant, for human Use,
'Till clear'd by Toil, & till'd by Art
With Plenty chear'd his drooping Heart.
'Twas thus Relief our Father found
When sent to cultivate the Ground.
For God who knew what Man could bear,
Form'd not his Sentence too severe,
A Life of indolent Repose
Had been the Plan of greater Woes;
While tir'd with Ease too dearly bought,
He past the tedious Hours in Thought,
For Labour only causes Rest,
And calms the Tumults in the Breast.

More leisure to revolve his Fate
Had added Sorrow to the Weight,
Of his unhappy fall'n State.—
While Memory drest the gaudy Scenes
Of Edens never fading Greens,
Of Trees that bloom without Decay,
Where Storms were silent—Zephyrs play.

And Flowers their rifling Sweets bestow,
On all the gentle Winds that blow,
With ev'ry Charm that crown'd the Place
Design'd for Adam & his Race:
Our Sire too weak for such a Stroke,
Had sunk beneath the heavy Yoke,
Had on his Breast the Sentence try'd,
Let out his tortur'd Soul & dy'd.
But kindly to suspend his Doom
For sake of Ages yet to come,
A Life of Action was decreed,
And Labour must produce him Bread;
His Hands the artful Web prepare
To screen him from inclement Air,
And equal Pains a Tent provide
To turn the beating Storm aside.

These necessary Toils & Cares
For present Wants & future Fears,
Joyn'd to the Curse, a Blessing grow,
And lessen or divert our Woe.

[Untitled extract dated October 1728][11]

Thus whilst in Hope of better Days
    The present Moment flies,
And Fancy with Ill-fortune plays,
    The Fool deluded dies.

[Untitled][12]

Neither knoweth any Man the Father save the Son & he To whomsoever the Son shall reveal him. Matthew:

What Means yet unattempted can I try
To still this anxious Searcher in my Breast
These fond Enquiries—whence had I a Being?
What am I now?—what shall I be hereafter?

I owe this Being to one powerful Cause,
But what thou art I cannot comprehend,
Or learn thy incommunicable Name.
I search & fain would gain some happy Knowledge
Fain would I gain some faint Ideas of thee
Invisible, Almighty, uncreated.
I am taught thy Temple is the Heart of Man:
But in this vain polluted Heart of mine,
Only a Consciousness of thee can dwell,
And that too weak.—O! strengthen thou who made me,
And placed me here upon a Stage of Wonders;
But to what End, 'tis thou who made me knows;
Sure to enjoy some fuller Good hereafter,
For here I'm toss'd upon a troubled Sea
With Knowledge just enough to guess at Error,
But not enough to fix unerring Truth—
In this Perplexity of Thought I am lost,
While tyrant Passions sway me here & there.
Just God! this is not sure my only End.
—So in his shatter'd Bark the Sailor fares,
When cheating Calms & smiling summer Seas,
Have tempted far on the unfaithful Deep;
Aghast! he sees the Tempest round him rage
Nor aught avail his Hopes nor aught his Art
So near to Death in the devouring Flood,
'Till pitying Powers above, rebuke the Storm,
And the directing Star shines full & clear:
Thou sov'reign Wisdom cast a gracious Ray
Of living Light on my benighted Soul.
Save the enquiring Fugitive from Ruin
And let me not transgress whilst I demand
What art thou, reasoning Principle within,
Thou something which I cannot comprehend.
I call thee Spirit, immaterial Being,
But tell me what is immaterial Being
And tell me what is Spirit—what thou art.
What e'er thou art reveal thee to thyself
What has thou been a thousand Ages past,
What shall thou be a thousand Ages hence?

What art thou now?—involv'd in Clouds & Tempests
Thou pants & labours for Eternity,
Beneath a heavy Weight of finite Cares,
Though weary of Existance yet thou fears,
A falling into nothing—thus oppress'd,
With num'rous Cares, variety of Ills,
I bend beneath a Weight that is not lasting,
But oh!—tis this Futurity confounds me.

[Untitled][13]

So Man lieth down & riseth not, 'till the Heavens be no more, they shall not awake nor be raised out of their Sleep.—Job. And he said unto me, my Grace is sufficient for thee.
Corinth:

To live alone amidst the busy Scene,
Of busy Cares & hear thy God within,
Say by what Means from human Eyes conceal'd
Can those celestial Beauties be reveal'd
Which my chill'd Breast with potent Charms may fire
Calm & refine, prepare & the inspire?
For whiter Days to future Worlds I trust,
When this weak Frame shall moulder into Dust,
When my last Debt to Nature shall be paid,
And the soft Soul, rise in new Robes array'd;
Mean while with Patience, as our God commands,
I wait each kind Chastisement from his Hands,
Full well appris'd that Sorrow, Care & Pain,
Correct our Steps o'er Lifes uneven Plain,
Where Adams Sons in erring Paths have trod
Far from their Interest Duty & their God—
Hope to survive & patiently to bear,
The common Ills of Sorrow Pain & Care,
And more, shou'd more be sent;—but where to find
The tranquil Bliss of an unruffled Mind
By what deep Art the Tempest to controul,
When Clouds of doubtful Reasonings crowd my Soul;

When the long Views in solemn Order spread,
Fill all my Breast with wonder & with Dread,
How shall I plunge amidst the numerous Dead?
What, shall I be unbodied?—how & where?—
Instant—will those tremendous Scenes appear?
Or must I sleep unnumber'd Ages o'er?
'Till Nature sink & Time shall be no more?
Elude all Search, & each Enquiry fails
Though our first Parents curious Crime prevails.
Then tell me O!—ye Messengers of Peace
(Your gospel Tydings of the World to come
Our Hope, our Rest, our long expected Home!)
What angel Voice can charm the Soul to cease
Her fruitless Wanderings in a Path unknown,
Conceal'd from Man, & clear'd by Death alone.

—Since death alone these misterys can explore,
I thou enquiring mind Enquire no more:
but all to weak the vain Injunction proves,
from thought to thought Incessantly she roves,
there neither peace or Knowledge can attain,
fruitless each search, and each enquiry vain
She flys to thee O God
As Order [calm'd Confusion's] dreadful storm
when thy almighty word calld forth the birth of form,
and chaos groan'd to see his throne destroyd,
whilst light came darting thro the mighty void,
So calm the tempest's labouring in my Soul,
Each view contract, each daring search controul,
with faith and patience arm my wavering breast,
and let thy Grace conduct my steps to rest,
then tremb'ling reason shal confess thy power
[And low in Dust, lye pros]trate and adore
[Shall in thy Light her narrow Limits see,
And own that none are great & wise but Thee.]

On the Death of an Infant[14]

I praise the Dead with undissembled Voice,
    Who in that Sleep too deep for Dreams remain,
'Till happier, waking to immortal Joys,
    They find one Pleasure unallay'd with Pain.

In Thoughts like these I vainly seek a Groan,
    Or Words of Woe to form the plaintive Song,
Death & the Grave have challeng'd as their own,
    The soft the sweet, the sprightly & the young.

If judging as the vulgar World, we mourn,
    To thee, dear Child, how many Tears are due?
From Life & Peace & Joy untimely torne,
    Thyself & each surrounding Object new.

But change the Scene—see the gay Colours fly—
    And true to Nature be the Portrait Just;
Shade it with Woe from the soft Infant Cry,
    'Till hoary Cares shall sink the Wretch in Dust.

Fair Innocence!—first & all envied State!
    Wisdom may err, & Virtue fall oppress'd;
But who untainted meet this Stroke of Fate,
    An angel wafts them to eternal Rest.

To Flowers that open with the morning Sun,
    (As gay & fragrant as the Babe we mourn)
E'er to his Noon-tide Height of Glory run,
    By wanton Hands from their fair Borders torne.

Of blasting Death endure the stern Command,
    And turn their gaudy Heads & droop & die,
Each fading Charm owns the Destroyers Hand.
    And closing Bells are thrown neglected by.

When Phoebus self, who ting'd their Leaves so gay,
    (E'er Ev'ning Falls or noxious Vapours rise,
To blast & darken the Remains of Day)
    Exhales their Souls into the painted Skies.

A Meditation: August 1735[15]

For I know that thou wilt bring me to Death & to the House appointed
for all the living—Job:
For God created Man to be immortal & made him to be an Image of
his own Eternity.—Wisdom.

I call to Mind those Ages that are gone,
Whose fleeting Hours their Periods hurried on.
And well remember this precarious Breath,
Shall meet the Blast of all subduing Death,

Resolv'd to Dust this mouldering House of Clay,
Shall lie forgot, the Trifle of a Day;
Then why so anxious by what unknown Doom,
I'm mark'd to fall this Victim to the Tomb;
All different Paths but to one Centre tend
On which Death waits us to our Journey's End.
A frightful Spectre—or a gentle Friend:
A welcome Visit to the Wretch he pays,
Lulls Pain to Sleep & ends his tedious Days;
But smiling Fortune in a bridal Dress
Chills with the Thought, & dreads his meagre Face
Thinks the calm Grave but comfortless & cold
A Lodging suited to the poor & old,
Exults in Manhood, fondly treads the Stage
Fearless, unconscious of Disease or Age;
Fancy bewilder'd! can the Wretch forget,
To live is only running more in Debt;
A Debt all animated Beings owe,
'Till summon'd back to shady Realms below,
The hard Conditions of our Birth fulfill'd,
To which thro' strong Necessity we yield.
'Tis one Release from all this World of Woes,
Here Care & Sorrow sink into Repose
And the last Scenes of human Action close.

Then let no smiling Hours alure thee on
To childish Fears of what thou cannot shun
Or angry Fates urge thee to seek thy Doom,

From thy own Hand impatient of the Tomb,
An unknown Solace of that World to come:
But calmly wait the grand deciding Blow,
Of this kind Friend—or unrelenting Foe;
Nor the great Father of Mankind distrust,
But stand the Shock & mix with common Dust.
This Share of blended Elements resign;
Which have been once, & may again be thine;
Natures fix'd Laws inviolable stand,
The mighty Work of an unerring Hand,
And thou a Part of the stupendous Frame,
Art still to be, but whether still the same,
Or chang'd to what new Form, if reasoning Mind
Its Source to Matters purest Parts confin'd,
Of if (without Ideas) we believe
Our Souls shall immaterial Beings live,
Trust thou in God, who form'd them what they are,
Will still preserve them with paternal Care
Through Ages infinite they shall endure,
A Part of his Creation most Secure.

On Time[16]

Since Moments past are as a Dream,
    A fleeting Evening Shade,
Which close like a divided Stream
    Like dying Tapers fade.
Enjoy the Present & be bless'd,
    While yet they're in y^r. Power,
Nor Place Y^r. Happiness or Rest,
    On any future Hour.
But know the Present will be gone
    And leave the Soul no more,
To feed its craving Wishes on,
    Than what you now deplore,
Enjoy the Present, but secure,
    The future as you go;
Alone the Future must endure
    A Happiness or Woe.

It will be present in its Time,
    But never can be pass'd
To an eternal Now you climb
    Which must forever last.

On the Death of a Young Girl—1737 [17]

The little bird, at break of day
    that wak'd us with its Song,
And fondly hoppd from spray to spray
    the music to prolong

E're evening came illfated fell
    struck by a hand unseen,
resign'd that breath which pleasd so well,
    and flutt'red on the green.

the lambs that wont to bleat and play,
    and bask in sunshine air,
that danc'd the fleeting hours away,
    and Knew not want or care,

As night her Sable curtain spread
    fell to the wolf a prey,
and here—and there, (disperc'd & dead)
    the Scattred fragments lay

the Blossoms which to vernal air
    their fragrant leaves unfold,
and deck the spreading branches fair,
    In purple, white, and gold;

Defuse their Sweets, and charm the eye
    and promiss future Store,
Nipp'd by a frost, untimely dye,—
    and shed perfumes no more:

t'was thus, the poppet ceas'd to breath,
    the Small machine stood still,
the little lungs no longer heave,
    nor motion follows will,

No more that flattring voice we hear
    Soft as the linnets Song,
each Idle hour to Sooth and chear
    which Slowly rolls along;

that Sprightly action's past and gone,
    with all its tempting play,
Sprightly as lambs that tread the lawn
    along a Summers day

The dawn of reason we admir'd
    as opening Blossoms fair;
now to the Silent grave retir'd
    its Organs Moulder there;

flowers on thy Breast, and round thy head,
    with thee their Sweets resign,
Nipp'd from their tender Stalks, and dead,
    their fate resembles thyne,

Just as their charms alure the Eye
    and fragrant leaves unfold,
closd in Eternal night they lye
    to mix with Common Mold,

Thy harmless Soul, releasd from earth
    a Cherub Sings above,
Immortal in a Second birth
    by thy Redeemers love.

From the Athaliah of Racine[18]

High Adoration & perpetual Pray'r
To thee whose Works ten Thousand Worlds declare!
Tho' back to an Infinity we run,
We find thy Empire fix'd e'er Time begun.
And tho' our active Thought should roam,
Ten thousand Ages yet to come,
Ten thousand thousand Ages more
Thy Throne unshaken as before
Can never know a late Decay,
Tho' Time & all his Works shall pass away,
Tho' not a Track of where his Wheel had run,
Shall tell the wond'rous Race was e'er begun.

On Death[19]

We know we once must dye, by sev'ral Ways
The same Decree has swept all Ages past,
Then oh! how vain to ask a Length of Days!
Each big with anxious Wonders of the last.
For the first Moment our frail Lives begun
Th'unalterable Period was ordain'd;
In vain would Man the righteous Sentence shun
No Art has ever one short Moment gain'd.
From a deceitful World to be remov'd,
From present Evils & from those to come,
From Objects too, too fading to be lov'd,
To the long Rest of an eternal Home.
With every blooming Virtue in its Spring,
Each Faculty full in its Strength & Prime,
Free from those Clouds, which Age & weakness bring,
O'er the declining Evening of our Time;
Will more than recompense the scanty Day
Allow'd us, our allotted Race to run,
Then who would strive, so rugged is the Way
A happy Period of their Toil to shun?
'Tis true, Amazement fills each Thought of Death,
'Tis not to be no more—'tis Fear—'tis Pain,

'Tis but a Step in yielding up our Breath;
From Life to Death—from Death to Life again.—finis.

A second Thought on the Soul.[20]

"Sees infinite & in that Sight is lost"—Prior's Solomon Book 1st.

I contemplate thee Work of Art divine,
Thou glorious Being, subtle, strong, & pure
That bears the fair Impression of a God!
So vastly high can thy Conceptions rise,
Thou takes the whole Creation at a View,
Grasps Worlds on Worlds, & ranges thro' them all;
To that vast boundless Space where Matter ends,
Passes the mighty Void, that separates
Invisible—and visible Abodes:
There forms Ideas of unnumber'd Hosts
Which stand before the overflowing Light,
But far above where all Conceptions rise,
Beyond the utmost Stretch of human Thought
To an Infinity of Height, enthron'd
The great Creator—the first Cause of all,
Impenetrable sits—in vain we strive
To rise—for none shall see his Face & live.

On the Death of two infant Nephews.—1736[21]

The darling Babes for whom these Tears we pay,
So early gone to join their kindred Clay,
Unknowing what they were,—or were to be,
With nervous Pangs, but with a Conscience free,
Have paid that Debt amidst the fatal Storm
Which Nature owes to animating Form.

Had they surviv'd unto a further Date,
Ten thousand Troubles might have crown'd their Fate;
And when the long revolving Train was past,
They must have mix'd with kindred Clay at last.

[Untitled][22]

Tis wel there are new worlds of light in store
for the Opres't the wrecked & the poor
for Sufring al their rigid fates, [or]dain
thro Many rowling years variety of pa[in]
thro a false world Just to its Self alone
A World where faith nor Gratitude are known
Where freindship's Basely made a trade an Art
~~Our freinds are kind while~~ that holds but while on the Gaining part—
—But hear & let your Conscious Soul Confess
the Goods which God permits you to possess
(fatal Efects of humane happiness)
make you forget you are no more then man
Amidst them al your Life is but a Span
& I ~~you now for my misfortunes~~ whom now you as beneath you Shun
Ere ninety years their fleeting Course have run
Shal have as much as you of all your Stone
A Quiet tomb, & you Can have no more
By Death your Judgem[t] Rectifyd you'll See
no Odds Betwixt your mighty Self & mee
for all you of the Late Low world possest
& I with none of all her treasures Blest
then shal apear to y[r] Enlightned Eyes
the Only Diference which must arise
Consist in this—in this & nothing more
of pious works who has the Greatest Store
of Justice, temperance, Charity & Love
Safe with their heart reposited Above

[Untitled][23]

—„Lo all things are but alter'd, nothing Dyes
then Spirit to the world of Spirit flyes
not useless Long the Severd Body Lyes
turnd & over turnd—mix'd in the Common Mas
in flowers shal Glow or freshen into Grass
the painted Beds & yellow meads adorn
Delight the Eye & Chear the Opening morn—

„So from Coruption Nature's Seeming wast
New Charms Shal rise Each Yealding to the Last
til after Num'rous Diferent Changes past
a Change to fix it Evermore the Same
Comes rouling onwards in a flood of flame
[til exalted moun]tains Level with their plains.
[One mighty Mass of liquid F]ire remains,
[Each scatter'd Atom, shall no l]onger roam
[But ev'ry Part fly to its pr]opper home
["Till all refin'd & pass'd the searc]hing flame
[Is fix'd & incorruptibly the] Same—
[If Souls must seek their kind]red Clay Again
[They thus refin'd, may rise immortal] men

[To a Friend—On] Some Missunderstanding[24]

[When desp'rate] Ills to Such a Crisis rise
as the Physicians utmost art Despise
Both Likely & unlikely means hee tryes
if after al[l his] painful Labours past
hee Chance to find the happy Cure at Last
hee Sets it down the Sovreign of his Skill
a future med'cine for a future ill
thy Strange unkindness Carryd much to high
has made me fondly Every method trye
to work a Cure & every dress essay
the haughty, Supliant, Serious & the Gay
But as I fondly Every method tryd
it mockd my hopes & unsuccessful Dyd
uneasy Stil another way Ive Chose
to Be a Jest in rime as wel as prose
for if Resentment freindship must outlive
& Injurd Love forbids thee to forgive
Be Angry, Be Cencorious, be Severe,
Who feels the worst has nothing more to fear
But if as much I hope Yet Scarce Beleive
this artless verse may all my fears Deceive
thee happy ~~verse~~ muse I almost Shal Adore
thee but harmonious folly heretofore

but never now harmonious folly more
Should Every painful il of Life Encrease
Ide Chuse thy Charms to Soothe[m] all to peace
think what was humane Nature in us Blooms
Ere Adam fel or Death Became his Doom
weak was his Reason & his Wil was Strong
Short were his veiws of that Eternel wrong
hee fell not unaprisd—his fate he knew
[Yet on his Race, their long Destruction drew.]
Where the Colected weakness finds a place
of that first father of our hapless race
whence must perfection & foreknowledge rise
which are requird to Be Exactly wise
for a Defect in Every thing Beside
by a Defect in Knowledge is Implyd
& this Defect Can never Be denyd
we Canot Love or Cencure as we ought
unless we had a more ~~extensive~~ exalted thought
of Every Cause th[e real Merit] recl[ ]
Could Say that [this is false, & this is true.]
whoever humane[Nature better drest]
has never been [impartial to his Breast]
there numrous [Passions, num'rous Folly's reign,]
a Constant Long [& solitary Train.]
Our pressent thou[ghts judge those already gone]
& those to [come will push the Contest on,]
Stil I [judging, still condemning, still the same]
Stil [blaming, still creating Work for Blame.]

On Friendship[25]

While I, too daring, such a Subject chuse,
As might demand an Angel for a Muse,
(For I these elevated Tasks pursue,
To write of Friendship & to write to you)
Do thou, oh! sov'reign Flame, each Thought controul,
And fill the vast Recesses of my Soul!
Thou can be sung, by no inferior Pow'r

As Music only Music can explore.

When the Creator did his Law unfold
By his distinguish'd Delegate of old,
"I am"—he said, but what he was remain'd
Behind the Viel—not then to be explain'd;
But when this hallow'd Earth, Messiah trod
And Men beheld, the Actions of a God,
He condescended further to explain,
The mystick Wonders of his peaceful Reign,
Mankind, he with a clearer Prospect blest
And what he was the Deity exprest;
When his enlighten'd Servant from above
Inspir'd—declar'd that God himself was Love.
—What Angels are, no Mortal can explore,
They mock the utmost Search of our enquiring Pow'r.
That they're possess'd of an unfading Bloom,
In human Form, our active Thoughts presume
There's the benevolent, the perfect Friend,
Thus far our weak Ideas comprehend,
But what's their Conversation, how convey'd
Thro' the bright Choirs, which ask no Organs' aid,
Our Reason's dumb, & our Enquiry vain
For Things of which we no Ideas gain
No human Understanding can attain,
But this we know—of the refin'd above,
Their most exalted Attribute is Love.

The Soul a Being—whether increate
(So justly worthy its eternal State)
A Part of him in whom we live & move,
Bright Essence of, Immensity of Love!
Which tho', a Time, its fetter'd in a Chain,
Shall be united to its Source again,
Or if it is created—'tis so fine
So free from Parts, so glorious, so divine:
Bears such exact Impressions of a God,
And form'd a Temple for his bright abode,
(That loving it, I part of God, adore
Or honour him in his creating Pow'r;)

Tho' its Original from Heaven it prove,
The highest Pitch it can attain to's Love,
And more we of this best of Passions know,
The more of Heaven's reveald to Men below.

As Souls no Sexes have, I claim a Right
To love my Friend with that refin'd Delight
With all that Warmth, with all that pleasing Fire
A most harmonious Being can inspire.

What's Life, unless a Friend the Measure fill?
Tasteless its Good—unsufferable its Ill,
A Night of Shades, a ling'ring slow Disease.
A Course of Sorrows o'er unfaithful Seas,
But if a Friend, we're suffer'd to possess,
It colours all our Days with Happiness;
Improves the Relish of Neglected Joys,
And ev'ry potent Ill of Life destroys;
Inspires—enlivens, now, e'en now, confest
The vast Idea fills my labouring Breast.
Be still, ye murmuring Thoughts! that dare complain
Forever dumb—there's no such Thing as Pain,
I'll lead you where eternal Pleasures reign!

To the still Grove where opening Buds declare
The genial Spring, in all its Beauty near;
Where Silence reigns, not e'en the breathing Wind
Or creeping Streams—the close Retirement find.

There thou, my Soul, thy secret self regard,
Thy Origin—thy Actions—thy Reward!
In an Existance, which shall never end,
All doubled in a kind & faithful Friend
This one good Thing, O! may I long possess!
In Lieu of all the World calls Happiness;
But if my Friends too dang'rous Blessings prove,
And I grow giddy with excess of Love,
Or if they change,—which too, too much I fear,
For Frailty is to human Nature, near,
How shall I stand a Tryal so severe?

When of my Friends, or of their Love, depriv'd,
I'll all resign—for long enough I've liv'd.

But why this strange Emotion in my Breast
Why all this Passion, all this Care exprest?
For Things of which I may be dispossest.
'Twas Natures mighty Author gave the Soul
Desires beyond what Reason can controul,
Something with their full Bent, they must pursue
And while we keep created Good in View;
While from Lights great Original, we turn
Unsatisfied, our anxious Cravings mourn
But who can all Things visible despise,
And to this Source of Love & Beauty rise?
Their vitiated Sentiments refine,
And own no Passion but for Things divine,
In their capacious Souls shall know no void
No anxious Cravings mourn unsatisfied?
For he must all Things fill, who's infinite,
And all enlighten who created Light.

—The great Ideas, in such Throngs arise,
Fain would I speak, but weak Description dies.
Oh! thou supreme Director, Life & Light!
Before thee may my Ways be found upright!
What most of all I fear, oh! grant I flee
Of loving thy Creation, more than thee.

To the Memory of Charles Norris[26]

When Woes unfeign'd the human Breast assail,
And Tears the first Resource of Sorrow fail,
The pensive Muse her soothing Aid extends,
To mourn thee! best of Men & best of Friends!
To mourn thee! late so blessing & so bless'd,
Thy Hopes all crown'd & every Wish posses'd;
Now vanish'd as a baseless Vision fled!
And thou art number'd with the silent dead;
Yet of thy Life & Worth, nor Time or Place,
Nor varying Scenes the Memory shall deface.

While health was thine, prime Bliss beneath ye Sky
Peace & Delight beam'd gently from thy Eye;
Thy placid Mien fair Image of thy Mind,
Where all was just, benevolent & kind,
No more expressive of that heavenly Ray,
Is veild & shrouded from the Face of Day.
Thy Mind fair Image of those Seats above!
Serene Abodes of Harmony & Love,
Is now restor'd to its congenial Clime
Beyond the wild Viccissitudes of Time
Beyond the Grave, where human Sufferings cease,
And thy Remains rest in Eternal Peace.

You orphan Children! & thou widow'd Wife!
Balm of his Cares & Solace of his Life,
While Life was lent—our bleeding Hearts deplore,
The Husband & the Father now no more,
No more, with ever sympathetic Power,
To sooth the pain'd or gild the social Hour,
No more his infant Offspring to survey,
Meet their Caress & smile their Tears away;
One fatal Stroke dissolv'd these tender Tyes!
But who shall say, Almighty & All Wise!
Why was this Friend of Human kind remov'd,
So amply bless'd, so honour'd, so belov'd,
When Thousands of thy Creatures, from their Birth,
Unbless'd, unblessing, still are found on Earth?
Presume not to enquire, or to repine,
For not our Will, All Wise! be done but thine.

You weeping Sisters! & each sorrowing Friend!
Who knew his Worth, & now lament his End,
Console your Minds, through Natures mournful Strife,
In calm reviews of that all blameless Life,
That stedfast Honour that unblemish'd Truth,
That Sanctity of Manners from his Youth,
Thro' Manhoods Prime, thro' ye licentious Days
That Fear of God which guarded all his Ways,
Prepar'd him this tremendous Change to try,
Prepar'd—at the appointed Hour to die.

O Bliss! to be desir'd by all who live,
Beyond what Wealth, beyond what Kings can give;
Nor Wealth nor Power one Terror can defeat,
Or gild the Gloom, or light the dark Retreat;
Virtue alone & all supporting Grace,
And Faith & Hope cou'd conquer in the Race,
The Prize of Immortality attain,
And bear him safe thro' Death to Life again.

My Own Birth day August 4th 1761[27]

few and evil have the days of the years of my life been.　　　Genesis

Were few and evil, calld the Patriarch's days,
extended to a length of years, unknown
in this luxurious age, whose Swift decays
alow to few, as many as my own;

and what are they? a vision all the past,
a bubble on the [water's] shining face
what yet rem[ain, Till] the first transient blast
shal leave no more remembrance of their place.

Still few and evil, as the days of Old,
are those allotted to the race of man,
and threescore years, in Sounding numbers told
where's the amount? a Shadow and a span.

look back thro' this long tyde of Rolling years,
Since early reason gave reflection birth,
Recal each sad occasion of thy tears,
then Say: can happyness be found on earth.

pass former strokes—the recent only name,
a Brother whom no healing art could save,
in life's full prime, unnervd his manly frame,
from wasting pains, took refuge in the grave.

A Darling child, all lovely, all admir'd
Snatchd from our arms in youth's engaging bloom.
a Lazar turnd e're his short date expir'd
And laid a piteous object in the tomb.

*

your memory from my breast shal never stray,
should years to Patriarchal age extend:
thro Glooms of night, thro Social hours of day,
the Starting tear stands ready to descend:

But tho I mourn, not w[ithout ho]pe I mourn:
Dear Kindred shades—tho all unknown your place,
tho' to these eyes you never must return,
You are Safe in the Infinitude of Space:

Our alldisposing God who gave you birth,
that life sustaind, which his Good pleasure gave,
then cut you off, from every claim on Earth
is the same Guardian God, beyond the grave.

tho by I[mpenetrable Dar]kness veild,
your Seperate [State lyes] hid from mortal sight,
the Saviour, friend of [M]en, Messiah hail'd
brought life, and Imortality to light.

Rest then my Soul; in these appointments rest;
and down the Steep of age pursue thy way:
with humble hope, and faith unfailing bless'd
the Mortal, shal Surpass the natal day.

*

a Sister, who [lo]ng causeless anguish Knew,
a tender parent, and a patient wife:
calmly she bore, the bitter lot she drew
and closd her sorrows with her close of life

[Untitled][28]

Dear partial Maid, where shall I find,
    One Spark of Fire divine,
To warm my dissipated Breast
    And make it glow like thine?
Where learn the soft seraphic Strains,
    Of thy enchanting Lay?
To charm our Cares, our Sorrows sooth,
    And steal our Souls away.
When ebbing Spirits languid flow,
    And Fancy's drooping Wing,
Unplum'd by Time no more can rise,
    To seek a second Spring,
The Evidence of Things not seen,
    Faiths bolder Pinions gain,
And gentle Hope unceasing smiles
    To soften human Pain.
By these sustain'd the immortal Mind,
    Unconscious of Decay,
Feels all her Powers of Action strong
    Thro' Life's declining Day.
'Till that shall close in endless Shade,
    Each lenient Art engage,
To temper Nature's rugged Cares,
    And smooth the Path of Age.
The social Hour, the enlighten'd Heart,
    That entertains & binds,
The endearing Intercourse of Friends,
    Bless'd with congenial Minds.
Such once—but long the Vision's past
    My Honour, Bliss & Pride!
Thy Mothers social Hour was mine,
    As kindred Minds allied.
Such wou'd thou be, cou'd youth to Age,
    The engaging Hand extend;
Such wou'd I prize the tender Tye,
    And fondly call thee Friend.

To Polly Norris[29]

In Memory of her Amiable Sister

When hoary Age Resigns its feeble Breath,
and unreluctant, meets the arms of Death,
for dissolution, Ripened by decay;
We own the Common Lott; and pass away.

Not So, when youth with health and Beauty Crownd,
And every opening Virtue blooming Round,
Of all this flattering World can give, possess'd,
with friends, with fortune, love and honour Bless'd,

when these, the unrelenting Angel calls,
heavy and sad, the dread Contagion falls,
Amazement seizes Every trembling breast,
and Anguish Stands in Every Eye Confessd:

Such is the tribute, dear Lamented Maid
to thy Invaluable Memory paid;
Such are our feelings:—Strangers mourn thy fate,
thy Suffering lott, and life's untimely date.

O Early lost! Sad Victim in thy Bloom
to dire disease, and the Insatiate tomb?
Our tears await thee to that Bed of Peace,
where human cares, and human Sorrows Ceace,
where all the fair, the wise, the learn'd, the Just
Rest from their Labours, and Repose in dust,
when the Short tryumphs of life's transient day
are Vanish'd, and their Splendours passd away;
—Yet what are these? and what has life to give,
for which a Reasoning Beeing Sighs to live!
In youth, gay Gilded promises of Bliss,
Enchanting prospects of unbroken Peace;
But years on years, Shal undeceive the mind,
and Show a dreadfull train of woes behind;
friend after friend, the Shadowy path Explore,
'til all we love, these Eyes must meet to more;

fresh wounds Inflicted, while the Recent pain;
our tortur'd hearts will bleed from Every Vein;
fullness of days, this troubled View Extend,
and Closing life alone, the Conflict End.
thy lot has drawn a portion of this truth,
Inur'd to Sorrows thro thy Bloom of youth;
then fortify thy mind, dear Sufferring Maid,
call Reason, call Religion, to thy Aid,
Remember Heaven's Allrightious will is done;
By Resignation, make that Will thy own:
hard task, to drain this Bitter Cup of Woe,
and Nature Shrinks, and human Sorrows flow
to drain without Repining; yet that Power
which call'd to Birth this tribulating hour,
can Calm thy Anguish, bid the tempest Ceace,
and Sooth thy Agonizing Soul to Peace:
give thee to See, with faith directed Eyes
Mansions of Bliss beyond these Azure Skyes,
for Such prepar'd, who Virtue's path have trod,
fear'd and Obeyd, their father and their God,
thro the Probation of this Mortal day;
And when His Wisdom Summon'd them away,
Resignd and Patient, waited to fullfill
the dread decrees, of his Eternal Will:
Who life's alurements nobly could despise;
Its Strong Connections, fond Endearing tyes
with fortitude foregoe: hopes heavenly Ray
that Better hope, gave Earnest of a Day
Approaching, on time's Rapid Wing Convey'd,
when thou Lamented, dear Departed Maid
Shall meet thy mourning friends, to mourn no more,
Shall meet thy Kindred Spirits, Gone before,
made perfect; In the Saints Serene Abode,
with Peace, with Immortality, and God.

To Eliz^a Norris—at Fairhill[30]

Since Adam, by our first fair Mother won
To share her fate, to taste, & be undone,
And that great law, whence no appeal must lie,
Pronounc'd a doom, that he should rule & die,
The partial race, rejoicing to fulfill
This pleasing dictate of almighty will
(With no superior virtue in their mind),
Assert their right to govern womankind.
But womankind call reason to their aid,
And question when or where that law was made,
The law divine (a plausible pretence)
Oft urg'd with none, & oft with little sense,
From wisdom's source no origin could draw,
That form'd the man to keep the sex in awe;
Say Reason governs all the mighty frame,
And Reason rules in every one the same,
No right has man his equal to control,
Since, all agree, there is no sex in soul;
Weak woman, thus in agreement grown strong,
Shakes off the yoke her parents wore too long;
But he, who arguments in vain had tried,
Hopes still for conquest from the yielding side,
Soft soothing flattery & persuasion tries,
And by a feign'd submission seeks to rise,
Steals, unperceiv'd, to the unguarded heart,
    And there reigns tyrant—

But you, whom no seducing tales can gain
To yield obedience, or to wear the chain,
But set a queen, & in your freedom reign
O'er your own thoughts, of your own heart secure,
You see what joys each erring sex allure,
Look round the most intelligent—how few
But passions sway, or childish joys pursue;
Then bless that choice which led your bloom of youth
From forms & shadows to enlight'ning truth,
Best found when leisure & retirement reign,
Far from the proud, the busy & the vain,

Where rural views soft gentle joys impart,
Enlarge the thought, & elevate the heart,
Each changing scene adorns gay Nature's face,
Ev'n winter wants not its peculiar grace,
Hoar frosts & dews, & pale & summer suns,
Paint each revolving season as it runs,
The showery bow delights your wond'ring eyes,
Its spacious arch, & variegated dyes.
You watch the transient colours as they fade,
Till, by degrees, they settle into shade,
Then calm reflect, so regular & fine.
Now seen no more, a fate will soon be mine,
When life's warm stream, chill'd by death's fey hand,
Within these veins a frozen current stands;
Tho' conscious of desert superior far,
Till then, my friend, the righteous claim forbear—
Indulge man in his darling vice of sway,
He only rules those who of choice obey;
When strip'd of power, & plac'd in equal light,
Angels shall judge who had the better right,
All you can do is but to let him see
That woman still shall sure his equal be,
By your example shake his ancient law,
And shine yourself, the finish'd piece you draw.

NOTES

1. Logan-Fisher-Fox Papers, XXIV, 8, Historical Society of Pennsylvania. The quotation is from Horace Bk 3: Ode 29.
2. D. N. Logan, *Susanna Wright*; see Appendix in this volume.
3. *Commonplace Book of Milcah Martha Moore*, p. 23, Quaker Collection, Haverford College Library.
4. This poem was prefaced by the following note: "For the Literary Magazine. A Copy of Verses, Written by Susannah Wright, on removing from Chester to the banks of Susquehannah, in the year 1726; where she afterwards lived near 60 years." Published in the *Literary Magazine and American Register*, vol. II (Philadelphia, June 1804): 191–92.
5. The introductory lines are from Matthew 12:40. *Commonplace Book of Milcah Martha Moore*, pp. 5–6, Quaker Collection, Haverford College Library. Published with kind permission from Haverford College.
6. Poem dated 1720. Ibid., pp. 6–8. Published with kind permission from Haverford College.
7. Ibid., p. 8. Published with kind permission from Haverford College.
8. Ibid. Published with kind permission from Haverford College.
9. Ibid., pp. 8–9. Published with kind permission from Haverford College.
10. Ibid., pp. 9–10. Published with kind permission from Haverford College.
11. Ibid., p. 10. Published with kind permission from Haverford College.
12. The opening lines are from Matthew 11:27. Ibid., pp. 11–12. Published with kind permission from Haverford College.

13. The opening lines are from Job 14:12 and 2 Corinthians 12:9. Most of the text is taken from *Commonplace Book of Milcah Martha Moore*, pp. 12–13, since there is only a fragment in Susanna Wright's handwriting in WFM 83.18.18. The text from that fragment is used here for lines 38 through 54 with brackets denoting missing text that has been supplied from the *Commonplace Book of Milcah Martha Moore*. Missing text published with kind permission from Haverford College.
14. Ibid., pp. 13–14. Published with kind permission from Haverford College.
15. The opening lines are from Job 30:23 and Wisdom 2:23. Ibid., pp. 14–15. Published with kind permission from Haverford College.
16. Ibid., p. 15. Published with kind permission from Haverford College.
17. This text is from a version in Susanna Wright's handwriting, located in the Library Company Manuscript Collection, 7422.F.2, MSS of Hannah Griffitts, Historical Society of Pennsylvania. The copy in the *Commonplace Book of Milcah Martha Moore*, pp. 16–17, Quaker Collection, Haverford College Library, contains minor differences in word choice, punctuation, capitalization, and spelling: These are "charm'd" instead of "wak'd" (verse 1, line 1); "As Ev'ning" instead of "E're evening" (verse 2, line 1); "When" instead of "As" (verse 4, line 1); "With" instead of "In" (verse 5, line 4); and "Or" instead of "nor" (verse 7, line 4). In addition, Susanna Wright's own version is dated 1737, whereas Milcah Martha Moore's is dated 1735. Published with kind permission from the Historical Society of Pennsylvania.
18. *Commonplace Book of Milcah Martha Moore*, p. 17, Quaker Collection, Haverford College Library. Published with kind permission from Haverford College.
19. Ibid. Published with kind permission from Haverford College.
20. Ibid., p. 18, where the poem is identified as "A Fragment." Published with kind permission from Haverford College.
21. Ibid. Published with kind permission from Haverford College.
22. The text is a draft in Susanna Wright's handwriting (WFM 83.18.18), with the missing parts in brackets from *Commonplace Book of Milcah Martha Moore*, pp. 18–19. Missing text published with kind permission from Haverford College.
23. The text is the version in Susanna Wright's handwriting (WFM 83.18.18), with missing parts in brackets from *Commonplace Book of Milcah Martha Moore*, p. 19. The inverted quotation marks are original to the manuscript. Missing text published with kind permission from Haverford College.
24. The text is from a version in Susanna Wright's handwriting (WFM 83.18.18), with missing text in brackets from *Commonplace Book of Milcah Martha Moore*, pp. 19–21. Missing text published with kind permission from Haverford College.
25. This poem was, in all likelihood, the poem James Logan referred to in his letter to Susanna Wright, dated February 7, 1726/1727, writing, "I design'd my Letter wherein the chief po[int] was to crave thy excuse for not answering thy last obliging Lines both in Prose and Poetry Sooner the latt[er] truly answers thy a[cct] of it, that is, it shews the height [of] friendship wch is carried to a height." James Logan had loaned Susanna works by Fénelon, whose "Dissertation on Pure Love" (xliv and xxxvi) is echoed here, as well as William Penn's "Some Fruits of Solitude" (Part I, No. 94). *Commonplace Book of Milcah Martha Moore*, pp. 21–23. Published with kind permission from Haverford College.
26. Charles Norris's wife, Mary Parker Norris, was probably born in the Wrights' former house in Chester, which her father had purchased in 1733 and where her family was living in that year till they moved to another house in Chester. Her children, all under the age of six at the time of their father's death, included Deborah, who became a writer and historian, composing a biographical portrait of Susanna Wright; see Appendix in this volume. Charles Norris's sisters included Marry Norris Griffitts, whose daughter Hannah was a noted poetess and a correspondent of Susanna Wright; Hannah Norris Harrison, whose son-in-law, Charles Thompson, was a correspondent of Susanna Wright; and Elizabeth Norris, for whom Susanna Wright wrote the poem, "For Elizabeth Norris at Fairhill." Susanna Wright's letter to Mary Norris, dated February 16, 1766, at the death of her husband Charles, is included in "Selected Letters" in this Appendix. *Commonplace Book of Milcah Martha Moore*, pp. 23–24. Published with kind permission from Haverford College.
27. The text (WFM 83.18.18) is in Susanna Wright's handwriting, with losses in the text, in brackets, from a copy of the poem dated April 1767 in the Library Company of Philadelphia MS Collection 7422.F.14, MSS of Hannah Griffitts, Historical Society of Pennsylvania. There is a second copy with variations in

that collection; a third in the Society Collection, Poem of S. Wright, 1761, Historical Society of Pennsylvania; and a fourth in the *Commonplace Book of Milcah Martha Moore*, pp. 24–25, Quaker Collection, Haverford College Library.

The brother "whom no healing art could save" was John, who died in 1759; and the "Darling child" was probably Charles Wright, son of her brother James. The seventh verse, with the asterisk placed at the end, was evidently added later in 1761 after Susanna Wright's sister Elizabeth died in October of that year. Missing text published with kind permission from the Historical Society of Pennsylvania.

28. As is indicated by Milcah Martha Moore, Susanna Wright's poem, "My Own Birth day August 4th 1761," inspired Hannah Griffitts to write a poem in response. Susanna Wright, in turn, replied with this poem. Hannah Griffitts's mother was Mary Norris, sister of Charles and Isaac and wife of Thomas Griffitts of Jamaica, who became mayor of Philadelphia. In her letter to Hannah Griffitts, April 5, 1762, Susanna Wright wrote: "the happyest hours I ever enjoyed Since I left my native land, were in thy Grandfather Norris's house." It was a house filled with books, a love of literature and learning, and "kindred minds allied," which extended to the next generation—Hannah Griffitts, Deborah Norris Logan, and Polly Norris. *Commonplace Book of Milcah Martha Moore*, pp. 26–27, Quaker Collection, Haverford College Library. Published with kind permission from Haverford College.

29. This poem, in the Library Company of Philadelphia 7421. F.61 Francis Logan Collection, Historical Society of Pennsylvania, is in the handwriting of Susanna Wright, although her name at the end is in another hand. Nicknamed "Polly," Mary Norris (1740–1803) was the daughter of Sarah (James Logan's daughter) and Isaac Norris. Polly had two brothers, Isaac and James, who died in infancy, and her only sister, Sarah, who was four years younger, died at the age of twenty-five. In 1770, the year after this loss, Polly Norris married John Dickinson. Through them Isaac Norris's wonderful library was given to Dickinson College. Published with kind permission from the Historical Society of Pennsylvania.

30. This text from the Library Company of Philadelphia Collection, 7423.F.102, MSS of Hannah Griffitts, Historical Society of Pennsylvania, had a note at the end: "I Copied the above Lines, from a very Torn Copy, In SW hand, Addess'd to Eliz Norris, (but without any Date)." Elizabeth Norris (1703/1704–1779) was one of fourteen children born to Mary (Lloyd) and Isaac Norris I. Of the ten who lived to adulthood, only four married (Mary, Hannah, Charles, and Isaac), not uncommon in large families in the eighteenth and nineteenth centuries. This remarkable poem affirms choice of the unmarried state for religious and, perhaps, even secular reasons, to allow self-realization of one's abilities that otherwise might not be obtained. Published with kind permission from the Historical Society of Pennsylvania.

A R

SEMPER EADEM

WILLS AND INVENTORIES

Although not fully representative of the contents of a house, wills and inventories are, nevertheless, basic tools for investigating what an early house might have contained, as well as elucidating familial relationships and professions. Arranged chronologically, the wills and inventories presented here reflect households that Susanna Wright knew—those of her relatives in England, her father and close neighbors at Wright's Ferry, and two later inhabitants of Wright's Ferry Mansion, Samuel Bethel II and Samuel Wright. The English documents clearly show the involvement with both textiles and farming that continued with Susanna Wright and her brother James at Wright's Ferry Mansion. The documents also show the diversity in the family from modest farmer to prosperous mercer, illuminating an otherwise obscure part of the Wrights' lives. For providing a genealogy of the seventeenth-century Wrights, as well as copies of the original seventeenth-century wills and inventories, I thank Thomas Woodcock, Somerset Herald of the Royal College of Arms.

Will of William Wright of Cadishwallhead, April 11, 1685, proved May 24, 1685[1]

In the name of God Amen. I William Wright of Cadishwallhead in the county of Lanc^re Husbandman being weak and sick in body but of good and perfect memory praised be God for the same but knowing that death is certain but the time thereof uncertain do therefore ordain and make my last will and testament in manner and form following And first and principally I commit and commend my soul into the hands of Almighty God my maker trusting assuredly through the merritts death and passion of my blessed Lord and Saviour Jesus Christ to have free pardon and remission of all my sins, and my body I committ to the earth to be buried in such decent and Christian manner as by my Executors hereafter named shall be thought meet and convenient And as for touching and concerning all such temporall estate wherewith it hath pleased God to bless mee I give devise and dispose thereof as followeth And first my will and mind is that my debts and funerall expenses be first paid and deducted out of my whole estate And as for touching and concerning my messuage and Tenement which I hold by a Lease and grant from Richard Calverley Esq for the terme of ffourscore and nineteen years If I, and Dorothy my wife should soe long live and is of the yearly rent of Two and twenty shillings and eleven pence with other boones specified in the same Lease I doe hereby devise grant and assigne the same unto Thomas Hartley of Martinscroft in the said County of Lancaster husbandman and Peter Robinson of Liverpoole in the County aforesaid Silkweaver and Their heires and the survivor of them and his heires from and Immediatly after my death and deccase for and during so many of the said ffourscore and nineteen years as shall be then unspent run up and unexpired Nevertheless in trust that they the said Thomas Hartley and Peter Robinson and their heires and the survivor of them and his heires shall yearely and every yeare pay unto the said Dorothy my now wife soe much, or such sum or sums of money as can or may be raised thereout or therby above all changes and Reprizes for and during the Terme of her naturall life in case shee marry not. But if shee marry again then onely the moyety or one half of such yearely sum as shall or may be raised, and the other moyety or half of such yearly sum to be paid imployed and disposed of for the use benefit and behoof of the Children of Thomas Parrin my brother in law Item I give and bequeath unto my brother James Wright the sum of fforty shillings Item I give and bequeath to my sister Margaret Bray fforty shillings Item I give to my Niece Mary Parrin fforty Shillings Item I give unto Jane Robinson wife of said Peter

Robinson Twenty shillings Item I give unto my brother in law Abell Owen
Twenty shillings and all the above mentioned Legaties to be paid within the
space of one yeare after my decease And if it happen any of the above mentioned
person or persons to dye before his her or their Legacy or legacies shall or may
become due and payable then my will and mind is that such Legacy or legacies
which should have belonged to him or her so dying shall be paid to my said
sister Margaret Bray and if shee should also be dead then to such children of
the said Thomas Parrin as shall be then living share and share alike And if any
of the said Legatees shall be anywayes quarrelsome, or use the least disturbance
towards my executors hereafter named, or the said Dorothy my wife the same
person shall have onely twelve pence in lieu of such Legacy Item I give and
bequeath unto my said wife Dorothy all and singular my goods both quick and
dead of What kind or qaullity soever And lastly I doe make ordain & constitute
the said Thomas Hartley and Peter Robinson executors of this my last will &
testament revoaking all former will or wills by mee heretofore made In witness
whereof I have hereunto set my hand and seale the Eleventh day of Aprill Anno
Dm 1685:

Sealed and Published in the presence of us.

William Foles	William Wright
John Yeats	his marke

Send these from   John Gerard

Will of Abel Owen of Liverpool, June 11, 1694, proved June 3, 1695[2]

In the name of God Amen the eleventh day of June in the year of our Lord
Christ one thousand six hundred ninty ffour, and in the sixth yeare of the raigne
of our Soveraigne Lord and Lady William and Mary by the grace of God King
and Queen of England Holland ffrance and Ireland Defenders of the faith &c
I Abel Owen of Liverpoole in the County of Lanc[er]. Tobacconist being aged
and weake yet praised be the Almighty of a Sound pfect and disposeing memory
Do make and ordain this my Last will and testam[t]. And first and principally
I committ my soul into the hands of God who gave it me And my body to
the earth whence it came to be buried in decent and Christian manner at the

discretion of my Exrs herein after named And now as for and concerning all such temporall and worldly estate wherewith God of his goodness hath blessed me after my just and proper debts funerall expences and probate of this my last will and testam.^{t} are first paid and discharged out of the same, I do hereby will, give, devise and bequeath the same as followeth That is to say I give and bequeath to my Exrs the sume of one hundred pounds in trust and to the intent that my Exrs shall yearly & every yeare during the naturall life of my dear and Loving wife Anne Owen Imploy & dispose the interest benefitt increase and improvem.^{t} of the said one hundred pounds to and for the maintenance and Lively hood of my said wife And my will is that if in case the sd interest benefitt increase and improvem.^{t} yearly comeing growing or ariseing by the s^d one hundred pounds will not amount or extend to maintain my said wife, that then my Exrs shall convert imploy and dispose so much yearly of the s^d one hundred pounds during my s^d wife her naturall life as will amount or extend to maintain my said wife what or so much as the said interest or increase falls short therein. And my will is that my s^d wife shall or lawfully may give and dispose the sume of ffifty pounds of the said one hundred pounds to whomsoever she shall will or please to give the same in or by her last will and testam^t. Item I do hereby will and appoint the further Trust that my Exrs immediatly after the death and decease of my said wife do and shall imploy improve and put forth for interest all such residue and remainder of the s^d one hundred pounds as shall remaine unspent over and above maintenance of my s^d wife and payment of the said fifty pounds ffor my daughter Margrett Blease and the children of the body of the said Margrett begotten or to be begotten as my Exrs shall think most meet Item I give and bequeath to my said wife Anne all my Linnen, Item I give to the children of Margrett Owen on her body begotten by my Kinsman Richard Owen Taylor the sume of fifteen pounds, to be put forth for interest by my Exrs for the s^d children till they respectively attaine to their respective age of one and twenty years and so improved for and distributed amongst them as my Exrs shall think fitt, Item I give to the said Margrett wife of my s^d Cousin Richard Owen the sume of five pounds. And as for my messuage & tenem^t. wth the appurts situate and being in John's street in Leverpoole afores^d I do hereby give divise and bequeath the same and all Leases grants & writings to me apperteining concerning the same to my s^d Exrs in trust and to the intent that my Exrs shall let the same to for or under a full and just yearly rent to my son in Law John Blease before any other but upon his refusall all such said yearly rent by my Exrs be put forth for interest and converted and imployed to and for the equall use and benefitt of the children of my said daughter Margrett on her body begotten or to be begotten And after the death and decease of my s^d daughter Margrett I give and bequeath my s^d messuage and tenem^t. Leases or grants thereof as afores^d. equally to use amongst the children on the body of my s^d daughter Margrett begotten or to be begotten during the residue of all my estate terme or termes and interest therein or thereunto Item I give and bequeath all the rest residue and remainder of my said temporall and worldly estate whatsoever remaining over the payment of my said just and proper debts—funerall expences probate of this my Last will and the bequests afores^d equally to the use and behoofe of my s^d daughter Margrett and such her children as aforesaid And my will is that if my Exrs shall in their judgm^t and directions after my decease think meet to change or put in any pon or psons life or lives in a new grant or Lease of the s^d messuage & tenem^t. that then they shall & may Contract for the same to the intents herein before limited of and concerning the s^d messuage and tenem^t. And for want of moneys to pay the fine or fines for any such new Leases or grants to pceive receive and take the clear yearly issues and profitts of the said messuage and tenem^t. yearly for so long time as like such fine or fines and all reasonable Counting out charges therein be fully raised and paid And of this my Last will and testam^t I do hereby notate & ordain my brother in law Peter Robinson Robert ffleetwood of Leverpoole afores^d merchant & John Pemberton the younger of the same Apothecary Exrs not doubting their care and faithfullness in the disposition hereof In witness whereof I have hereon to set my hand & seale the day and yeare first above written

Sealed and published
in presence of
Tho. fford   Abell Owen
John ffells
Peter Eaton
Will: Gandye

Abel Owen's Will

Be it known unto all men by this psent writing that I Abel Owen testator in the wthin written will named do hereby give and bequeath to Ann my wife my best bed wthall its furniture and my new trunke a little square box wth the lock and

Key thereto, the Sitting which a large box wth the lock and Key thereto, three pewter plates & spoons, All my late earthen ware the little glasses, Cupboard in the buttery one looking glasse, the Smoothing iron and heaters and my pockett watch, And whereas in my sd will I gave to my Cousin Margrett Owen and her children the sume of twenty pounds I do hereby will, give and bequeath the said twenty pounds to my Kinsmen Zechariah Owen & John Owen sonnes of my s^d Cousin Margarett Owen equally to be diveded betwixt them the said Zechariah & John Owen not wthstanding any thing in my fores^d will to the contrary of this my Codicill witness my hand & Seale hereto set the fourteenth day of November An regni Gulielius et Maria Rx, et Regina Angl et sexta Aug diu 1694

Sealed and Published   3.rd Juny 1695.   Abell Owen
in prsence of   Jurati fuere Execur p supranoiat
Margarett   Perrin   de bene et in cui forma juris
       her marke   Coram me
Will: Gandye   Tho: Wainwright

Inventory of Abel Owen of Liverpool, March 28, 1695[3]

An Inventorie of the Goods and Creditts of Abel Owen late of Leverpoole in the Countie of Lancaster Tobacconist deceased Appryzed by Edmund Livesy Roger Richardson John Crane & John Blundell the Eight & Twentieth day of March Anno domini: 1695.

	£	s	d
Imp^{rs}. in the House in Pewter	01	03	04
" in Brasse	00	08	09
" Two Iron Potts	00	05	04
" one Iron grate & other Iron ware	00	17	02
" In Tinn ware	00	02	04
" one little Jack & Materialls	00	05	00
" one Clock and Case	01	10	00
" one looking glasse & Stayes	00	03	04
" Twelve Chaires Nyne Stooles & ffive Cushions	00	18	08
" In Wooden Ware	00	14	02
" Two little Tables	00	05	06

"	one presse & Two brushes	00	12	08
"	Two Chists & ffoure boxes	00	06	02
"	In Severall Books	01	00	00
"	Two bedstidds Cords Matts & one shute of Curtaines	01	00	06
"	Two ffeather bedds & one bolster	02	12	10
"	one Chaff bed, a bed Case & Two bolsters	00	08	04
"	Two Ruggs & Three blanketts	01	02	04
"	in Severall Sorts of Tobacco	126	06	03
"	in Paper and Twine	02	11	00
"	one chist boxes Casgue & a Stoole	01	04	08
"	in Sives & working Boards	00	05	06
"	one Tobacco Skrew, Iron Croe & Tobacco Iron	01	10	03
"	one Tobacco presse and one Stalk Milne	02	10	00
"	one Tobacco Ingin & Three Wheeles for Rowle	01	01	00
"	one Grindle Stone Turne & Trough	00	04	00
"	In Beames Scailes and Waights	01	03	00
"	In moneys good and bad	33	12	00
"	In debts Sperate & Desperate	61	07	11
"	In the decedents wearing Apparell	01	05	00
"	In od Implements	00	01	00
"	one small Tenement in Leverpoole for one & Twenty yeares after Two lives ow in being	10	00	00
	Sum Tot(al)	256-	18 —	0
		ccLvi[L]	xviii[S]	

Will of Peter Robinson of Liverpool, June 9, 1703, proved June 24, 1703[4]

In the Name of God Amen I Peter Robinson of Liverpoole in the County of Lanc[re]. Mercer being Sick and weake in body but of Perfect Sound mind & Disposing memory Doe make declare and Publish this my Last will & Testam[t]. in writing Revoking and annulling all other will & wills by me at any time heretofore made and this onely to be my Last will & Testam[t]. in manner & forme following ffirst and Principally I Comitt my Soul into the hands of Almighty God my Creator trusting in him through the meritts and mediation of my Redeemer Jesus Christ assuredly to be saved & my body to be Decently buryed as I have given Some directions to Some of my Exect[rs]. hereafter named And as for and

Wills and Inventories

Concerning Such Temporall Estate as it hath pleased God of his goodness to bless me withall I give and Dispose of the Same as followeth (that is to Say) that all my Just Debts funerall Expences & the Probat of this my will Shall be first raised p^d. & Defray'd out of my whole Estate And whereas my brother John Robinson is Really & bona fide indebted to me in the Summe of Twenty Pounds which Said Summe I doe Desire my Exects to Call in & receive with what Convenient speed they can & when Soe done to deliver and pay the Same unto my Sister Margrett Hand and I doe evenly give the Same unto her accordingly Item I Give unto my Brothers John Robinson Josue Robinson and Joseph Robinson the Summe of ffive Shillings apeice Item I Give devise and bequeath all the rest Residue and Remainder of my said Personall Estate of what nature Kind or Quality Soever Together wth the Closse of Land upon Leverpoole Common which I now hold by Lease from the Corporation of Leverpoole aforesaid & all my terme and Estate therein unto my Loveing wife Jane Robinson And Lastly I doe hereby nominate and appoint my Said wife and John Wright of Manchester in the s^d. family Yeom Together with John Plumbe of Leverpoole aforesaid who I desire will give the best assistance he can to be my Exect^rs. of this my Last will hopeing they will See the same performed as my trust is in them Reposed In witness whereof I have hereunto Put my hand & Seale the Ninth day of June In the Second yeare of the Raigne of our Soveraigne Lady Queen Ann over England et Annoq Dm 1703;

Sealed Signed Delivered Published as my Last will & Testam^t. In psence of

Jn° Marsh	Peter Robinson
Marg^t. M Charrock	his marke
her marke	24. Junii 1703.
Risley Browne	Jurator fuit Jana Robinson Vidua Executorum supra nominat de bene &c (potate Johanni Wright & Joi Plumb alteris Executorum reservata) Coram me
	Tho: Leftwicke

Inventory of Peter Robinson of Liverpool, June 21, 1703.[5]

A full & perfect Inventory of all & every the Goods & Chattells Debts Rights and Creditts which Late were of Peter Robinson Late of Leverpoole in the County of Lanc: Mercer and Valued & apprized by William Hurst & James Townsend Mercers & Thomas fford & Timothy Whitthe four Indifferent Neighbours   This Twenty ffirst day of June Anno Dm 1703; as follows viz.

No:		l	s	d
1:	Im primis One peice of Broad Cloath Number: j: containing ffive yards at 6:^{s}p	01	10	00
2:	Itm another peice ffive yds: at 7^s:p:	01	15	00
3:	Itm Seaven Yards Three quarters at 10^s:6^d:p	04	01	04½
4:	Six Yards & a quarter att 6^s:6^d:p	02	00	07½
5:	Eight yards att 6^s: p	02	08	00
6:	Seaven yards att 13^s: p	04	11	00
7:	Eight yards & halfe att 11^s: p	04	13	16
8:	Eight yards att 10^s: p	04	00	00
9:	Eight yards att 5^s:p	02	00	00
10:	ffive yards att 8^s:p	02	00	00
11:	Two peices ten yards & quarter att 7^s:6^d:p	03	16	10½
12:	Two yards Three quarters att 7^s: p	00	19	03
13:	Three yards att 8^d:p	01	04	00
14:	Three yards att 8^s:6^d:p	01	05	06
15:	One yard & three quarters att 7^s:6^{d}p	00	13	00
16:	Three yards & a quarter black two att 9^s:p	01	09	03
17:	One yard & a quarter att	00	09	00
18:	Eleaven yards & a halfe att 10^s:p	05	15	00
19:	Ten yards att 10^s:p	05	00	00
20:	Seaven yards & a halfe att 10^s:6^d:p	03	18	09
21:	Seaven yards & a halfe att 8^s:6^d:p	03	04	03
22:	Nine yards att 9^s:p	04	01	00
23:	Twelve yards black att 6^s:6^d:p	03	18	06
24:	nine yards & three quarters att 7^s:p	03	08	03
77	Ten pound & quarter of Belladile Stiching silk 22^{d}p	11	05	06
78	Three pound ffive quarters of Ardus Stiching 14^{d}p	02	06	04

Wills and Inventories

79	one pound Twelve ounce of Sowing Bell att 20^d.p	01	16	00
80	Two pound five ounce Light Coller att 22^{d}p	02	12	00
81	one pound seaven ounce black & Coller ardass hanke & Skeyne att 14^s.p	01	00	01½
82	Seaven ounce Raw Bell att p	00	08	02
83	Six pound white Threed vizt 3. No 26: 3^{s}4^d & 3. att 3^s.9^d.	01	01	03
84	Twenty seaven Pound of ordy Threed 18^{d}p	02	00	06
85	Eleaven pound & halfe white threed att 2^s.p	01	03	00
86	nine Grose Coat buttons mowharr att 4^s.p	01	16	00
87	Six Remnants Twenty Eight dozn att 4^d.p	00	09	04
88	Seaven Remnants twenty nine do^z.n att four pence p	00	09	10
89	Three Remnants nine doz.n & halfe gimp & haire att 11^d.p.	00	01	02½
90	one Grose of mow haire Coats att 3^s.p	00	03	00
91	Twenty nine Grose of mow haire brest buttons att 18^{d}p	02	03	06
92	Three Grose & Eight do^{z}n. flat brass buttons att 8^d.p	01	09	04
93	one grose Carved & two doz. 10^s.p	00	11	08
94	ffour Grose Round & three doz.n 5 p	01	01	03
95	ffive Grose brew att 2^s.p	00	10	00
96	nine grose bren Lachyrd att 2^s.6^d.p	1	02	06
97	ffour Grose & nine dozn. white buttons 20^{d}p	00	05	10½
98	one Grose att 14^d.p	00	01	02
99	Twelve Grose of flat folio butt^s 2^s.p	01	04	00
100	Two Boxes Remnants Coat buttons att	01	15	00
35	one peice milld att	02	02	00
36	one peice black milld att	02	02	00
37	one peice att	02	02	00
38	one peice black stript att	01	04	00
39	one peice Gray Serge att	01	09	00
40	Two peices black & white Crape both att	02	00	00
41	one peice Damask att	01	08	00

42	Eleaven peices do: from No: 42 to No: 54: at 29ˢp	15	19	00
54	one peice Damask att	01	04	00
55	one peice Damask att	01	04	00
56	one peice Damask att	00	17	06
57	one peice half silk Damask att	02	00	00
58	Eleaven peices of ffine Stuffe att 18ˢ.p	09	18	00
65	ffive peices D°: at 16ˢ.p	04	00	00
73	one peice D°: at	01	02	06
74	another peice D°.	01	00	00
75	another peice D°:	01	01	00
76	Two peices D°: at 22ˢ.p	02	04	00
79	one peice of Russell att	01	16	00
80	one peice Green stript Tammy att	00	18	00
81	one peice purple stript	01	05	00
82	one peice Stuff	01	00	00
83	one peice plod double pie att	01	16	00
84	one peice stript Calamanco att	02	10	00
85	one peice stript att	02	10	00
86	one peice Black Damask att	01	12	00
87	one peice att	01	09	00
88	one peice Collourd Russell att	01	12	00
89	one peice Crimson att	01	11	00
90	one peice black att	02	15	00
91	one peice blue Tamarine att	02	03	00
92	one peice Collourd att	01	18	00
93	one peice milld att	02	02	00
94	one peice stript att	02	02	00
95	one peice Collourd Shalloon att	02	00	00
96	one peice Tamarine att	01	18	00
97	one peice att		18	00
98	one peice Druggett att	01	03	00
99	one peice att	01	03	00
100	one peice att	01	03	00

No

1	Two peices of figured Druggett at 12ᵈ .p yd.	02	12	
3	Two peices of Toys att	01	12	0
4	Two peices of Eastimines	01	16	00

6	ffour peices of white fushton att	02	11	00
10	Eighty yards of red & blue boulter at	00	16	08
11	ffour Dozen of skins att	02	06	06
13	a parcell of buttons att	02	15	10
14	fforty five yards & half of flowrd half Silk att	03	06	11
17	Thirty one yards & half of hair Camlet 4 p	06	04	06
19	fifty nine yards of scarlet Crape att	03	13	09
21	a parcell of Caddas att	02	17	03
23	a parcell of Ribband galloon & ferrett att	16	05	06
32	a parcell of gold & silver Lace & threed att	06	16	06
33	a parcell of silk lace & mow hair fringes at	03	00	00
34	ninety three yards & half of rash & woosted plane	04	13	03
36	a parcell of stockins & hatts att	04	00	06
37	a parcell of Buckerome & fushtons att	08	00	00
38	a parcell of tapes & searing Candle att	01	12	00
39	a parcell of Linnen & Calligoes att	08	13	02
41	a parcell of bed ticks att	02	18	00
	Goods In the Kitchen			
	Clock & Case att	02	00	00
	ffifty Six pound of Pewter att 7^d.p	01	12	08
	Two dozen of Plates att	00	12	00
	Twelve Porringers att	00	03	00
	Two Tankards & four Cups att	00	05	00
	One possitt Cup & washing bason att	00	01	06
	Two salts, one mustard one Cruit att	00	01	02
	ffive Candlesticks att	00	01	03
	three brass Candlesticks att	00	01	00
	a parcell of tinn ware att	00	01	06
	a parcell of white ware att	00	01	04
	a Jack Grate & the rest of the Iron ware at	02	00	00
	a parcell of broken Arms att	00	10	00
	ffive Chaires att	00	06	00
	A Table Dresser & Shelves att	00	08	00
	Punch bowl & morter att	00	03	00
	Brewing pan & vessells att	01	10	00
	three Skellets & two Iron pots att	00	07	00
	Two Tables above staires	00	03	06

one standing bed Curtaines valance & all furniture	06	00	00
Some Shelves & a Close stool pann att	00	14	00
one pair of bed Stocks & Cord att	00	06	00
Curtaines & vallance featherbed & Rug	01	05	00
one Picture & Looking Glass att	00	06	06
one Chest of Drawers Table & stands att	01	00	00
seaven Chaires one small Deske one Grate att	00	13	06
one Bed Bedstocks & hangings att	00	08	00
one Chest & one Trunk att	00	03	00
a pair of Bedstocks Curtaines & bed att	01	00	00
Six Cushions one Tub & a pcell of wheat & rye	01	03	00
a pcell of yarn & a Table att	00	08	00
two Casks three Sieves att	00	03	00
wearing apparell & Linen att	10	00	00

    Debts Sperate   264: 9.3¾

    Debts Desperate   215.15.8½

Wm Hurst   24 Junii 1703

                                    Extim p Extores   vero &c

                                          cum   tatione &c

                                          H. P.

Timothy Whitlon

Will of Dorothy Wright of Cadishead, dated January 11, 1696/7, proved October 29, 1708[6]

    In the name of God Amen. The Eleventh day of January in the year of our Lord One Thousand Sixe Hundred Nynety, and Sixe I Dorothy Wright of Cadishead als Cadishwallhead in the County of Lancaster Widow Being of Sound Memory, and understanding (Praised bee God) And Considering the certainty of death, and the uncertainety of the time thereof Doe therefore Make, and Publish this my Last Will, and Testam.ᵗ in manner following (that is to Saie) ffirst, and principally I comend my Soule, and Spirit into the hands of my good God, and heavenly ffather by whom of his [ ] and onely grace, and mercy to mankind in Christ Jesus I Trust to bee saved, and Received into

Eternall Rest, And my body (in hopes of a Joyfull Resurrection) I Committ to the Earth To bee Interred in Such decent, and Christian manner as to my Executors herein after named Shall bee thought meet, and convenient, And as touching the disposition of my Personall Estate (which the Lord in mercy hath Lent mee) My mind, and Will is That the Same Shall bee Imployed, and bestowed as hereafter in, and by this my Last Will is Expressed (that is to Saie) First I give, and Bequeath unto John Wright of Manchester in the Said County of Lancaster Linen Draper (my Nephew) the Sume of Twenty Pounds of Lawfull English money, Item I give, and Bequeath unto Anne Owen of Liverpoole in the said County Widow (my Sister in Law), Peter Robinson of the Same Mercer, and Jane his wife (my other Sister-in-Law) Margaret Parrin of the Same Spinster (my Neece) Mary Peeres wife of John Peeres of Glassbrooke (my Neece) Anne Renshaw (my Neece) Matthew Litherland of Cadishead aforesaid husbandman (my Nephew) Richard Hey of the Same yeoman, and Ralph Hartley of Martinscroft in the County aforesaid yeoman (my Nephew) fforty Shillings a peece; Item I Give, and bequeath unto [line missing]

I Shall Owe by Law, of right, or in Conscience at the time of my decease to any person, or persons whatsoever (If any Such there bee) Together with my ffunerall Expences, and the Probate of this my Last Will Shall bee well, and truely contented, and paid, within Convenient time after my decease; Item I Give, and bequeath unto Dorothy yates my Neece, and God-daughter now dwelling with me as my Servant (after the paiem^t. of my Said Debts, Legacies, ffunerall Expences, and the Probate of this my Last Will All the then Rest, Residue, and Remainder of All, and Singular my Goods, Chattells, Credditts, and Personall Estate whatsoever; And I doe Make, Constitute, Ordaine, and Appoint the above named Richard Hey, and Ralph Hartley the Lawfull Executors of this my Last Will, and Testam^t. (Hoping they will faithfully Execute the Same as my Trust is in them Reposed; And Lastly, I doe hereby Absolutely Revoke, and make void All Wills, and Testam^{ts}. by me formerly made, and doe declare this to bee my Last Will, and Testam^t. In wittnesse whereof I have hereunto put my hand, and Seale the day, and yeare first above written.

Sealed, Signed, and Published   the Marke of

by the above named Dorothy   Dorothy   Wright

Wright as her Last Will and   29 Octobris 1708

Testam^t. In presence of Jurali fuere Extores in hoc Testm^t:notali

G: Leigh   de bene

Jo{n}: Worrall   Coram Me

Jo{n}: Leigh   Tho: Wainwright

Inventory of Dorothy Wright of Cadishead, Lancashire, June 28, 1708[7]

A true & perfect Inventory of ye goods & chattell rights debts & credits of Dorothy Wright late of Cadishead als Cadishwalhead in ye County of Lanca{str}. Widdow decd taken and appraised this 28th day of June in year of our Ld 1708 by William Peers of Glazebraugh in ye County afs{d}. yeom. & Alexand{r}. Clively of Rixton in D°. yeoman Vizt.

	£	s	d
Five Closes of Corne uncut	18:	0.	0
Four Cowes	9.	0.	0
Three heifers	4.	10.	0
One year old shirl [?]	1:	2.	6
One Weaning Calfe	0:	10:	0
One Swine	0:	10.	0
For 30 lbs Weight of Pewter	0:	17:	6
Two Brass Potts	0:	13.	4
Two D°. panns	0:	10:	0
Two Skellitts	0:	11.	6
Iron things	0:	5:	0
One Chest Table From & Dish board	0:	16.	0
A parcel of Tow	1.	0:	0
Twelve pr. of Sheets one dozen of Napkins & a Table Cloath	2.	0:	0
New Cloath and Linen Yarn	2.	10:	0
The Beddin a bove Staires	2.	0:	0
two Chests	0:	10.	0
One bed wth ye. appur{tns}. below Stairs	0:	10:	0
Appersell of Sheese	1:	10:	0
A parsell of Corn & meall	3:	0.	0
Bees	1.	0:	0

Wearing Apparell	3:	0.	0
In Im[p?]lements	0:	5.	0
In ready money	0:	7.	6
	£	s	d
A debt owing by Jnº Yate of Rixton	1:	15:	0
Dº. by Matthew LitherLand of Cadis head	1.	11.	0
Alexander Cliveley	57:	14:	4

29 Octobris 1708
Extm

Will of Ann Owen of Liverpool, July 13, 1708, proved May 7, 1713[8]

I Ann Owen of Liverpoole in the County of Lankester Widdow and Relict of Abell Owen late of Liverpool Tobacconist Being Somewhat Inferme of Body but of Sound and perfect memory, Considering the uncertainty of this life do make this my last will and Testement in mannoure and forme following I comitt my Body to the dust to be decently Buried According to the Discration of my Executor hearafter mentioned, And for these Worldly goods I am posesed of at the time of my decease I dispose of in manner and forme following—I give unto Ellin the wife of [Mundick?] Lankester in the Kingdom of Ireland Butcher the Sum of Tenn pounds, Item I give unto John Wright of Manchester Champman the Sum of Tenn pounds in Trust for the wife Child or Children of John Peers of [Holmfaire?] in the County Aforesd Husbandman or to which of them the said John Wright thinketh fitt, Item I give unto Margt Hoult Relict of Tho Hoult Distiller late of Liverpoole in the County Aforesd deceast thirty pounds Item I give unto John Wright of Manchester Chapman the Sum of Five Shills Item I give unto William Hurst of Liverpool Carter the Sum of five Shills, Item I give unto my Sister Jane Robinson one Silver watch, All the rest and Residue of my personell Estate my funerel Expences feirst being deducted Lastly I make Constetute and Apoynt John Pemberton of Liverpool Marcht my Sole Executor, hearby Revoaking all former wills by me made doe declare this my last will and Testemt in Wittness wherof I have putt my hand and Seal this therteenth day of July in the Year of oure Lord One Thousand Seven hundred and Eight

Sealed Signd Published and Decleard
In Presence of—I allsoe leave
unto Peter [Datwin?] of [Joxlath?] Park
five Shillg before the Ensealing
and Publication hearof

Harman westhead
Samuel Atkinson
Thomas Westhead

                                                      her
Ann   Owen
            marke

7 May 1713.
Juralis fuit Executore de bene &
in Coi Imis forma
coram me
Tho: Wainwright

Will of Samuel Blunston, September 22, 1745[9]

    I Samuel Blunston of Hempfield Yeoman Do make this my Last will & Testament ffirst I will that my Just debts be paid by my Executors Secondly I give to my ffriend Susanna Wright the Sum of ffifty pounds To be p^d. to her Yearly and every Year during her Natural Life I also give her all my Books & Vessells of Plate called Silver I also give her full Power & Liberty to Live on this Plantation and take and receive the Benefitt Use and Profitts of such part of the Buildings Land & Plantation as she shall think fitt during her Natural Life I also give her the Negroe Boy Tobe Til he shall arrive at Thirty Years of Age & when he arrives at that age he is to be free I also give her the Boy called Herculas 'till he shall arrive at twenty six Years of Age & then he is to be free I also give her my Chaise and the Chaise Horse all these to be first taken out of my Estate for her I do acquit and Release my ffriend John Wright from the Bonds & Debts which he may at this time be Justly Indebted to me I give to my ffriend Robert Barber ffifty Pounds over and above what he is Indebted to me on Ballance of Acc^{ts}: I give to my ffriend John Ross on Sasquehanna Ten pounds over and above what he is Indebted to me I give to the Poor of the County of Lancaster the Sum of Thirty pounds To be p^d. to such of them as the Major part of the Justices of Peace of the County shall direct & appoint I give to my ffriend James Wright The one half of

the Corn or Grist Mill with all its appurtenances & the free Liberty of the
Water To the same without Interruption for Ever (Sa: Blunston) & Liberty
of my Landing & the road to it while he shall keep the ferry I further give
to my ffriend James Wright the Sum of Two Hundred pounds over and above
anything he may be Indebted to me at the time of this writing & Impower
him to make & Assign to his Brother John a Deed of Conveyance of that Land
which I Sold to him Joyning his Tract and for which I have reced the Money To
hold to him the said John Wright his Heirs and assigns for Ever I furthermore
give the said John Wright Junr: the Sum of Ten Pounds over and above what he
is Indebted to me and to his Sister Patience the Sum of Ten pounds I give to my
Kinsman John Bown the Sum of ffifty pounds to be p^d. him by my Executors
I give to my ffriend Samuel Norris the Sum of one hundred pounds and to
his Brother Charles & Sister Debby Each of them Ten pounds in token of
acknowledgment of the Good will they have shewn to me I give to Samuel
Armitt the Son of Stephen Armitt the Sum of twenty pounds to be paid to
his ffather for his Use I Leave my Wife's Cloths to be divided between Sarah
Worrall and Hannah Barber & Sarah Low In a friendly and amicable manner
I Leave my Wearing apparrell to James Wright & Robert Barber To be Equally
and friendly divided between them I Leave to Rhoda Patterson Thirty pounds
over and above any Wages that may be due to her I give to my ffriend Susanna
Wright my Scrutoire; the Use and occupation of such other Household Goods
as she may have occasion for to furnish her rooms during her Naturall Life and
also two Milch Cows after all these Legacys are taken out and paid Excepting
also the Reservations upon the Plantation I give devise and bequeath unto
Sarah Worrall & Hannah Pearson and their Heirs and assigns for Ever all my
Psonall Estate To be divided among them in such manner as Sam:[1] Bethel when
he comes to Age shall have (Sa: Blunston) a double Share and I give full Liberty
to my Negroe Sal to be free at the End of one Year Living and Serving Susanna
Wright after the date of this or to Live w:th Susanna Wright which She shall
think fitt and I reserve out of my Estate ffive pounds a Year to be paid to the
said Negroe Sal during her Life my Negroe Harry by Contract I agreed should
be set ffree in July 1748. which Contract I order to be fulfilled all the rest of my
Negroes who are arrived at full age If they behave well I order shall be sett free
at the End of seven Years after the dates of this and all the Younger Negroes &
Mulattoes not yet mentioned shall be free at the Age of Thirty Years respectively
as near as the time can be Calculated all the remainder of my psonall Estate not

yet given I give and bequeath one half thereof To Sam.ˡ Bethel one quarter to his Sister mary and the other quarter to the Children of Hannah Pearson I do further order and appoint that if any Surveys which I have made for which I have been paid and the Surveys cannot be made out So that the Land must be Surveyed again the Money shall be returned to those who payed it I do further declare that I Sold to Samˡ: Taylor the Tract of Land which I bought of John Hendricks Containing 350ᵃ & have reced Several payments which are Entred in my Book and I order and appoint that my Exectˢ: shall make over & Convey to him his Heirs and assˢ. for ever all the right Interest & Estate I have to the same he paying the Remainder of the Money due Lastly I ordain Constitute and depute my ffriends James Wright & Samˡ: Norris to be my Exectˢ: of this my Last Will & Testamᵗ Charging (Sa Blunston) them to have a Special Regard To my ffriend Susanna Wright Signed Sealed and declared by the sᵈ. Samuel Blunston to be his Last Will & Testament this Twenty second day of September anno Dom 1745. Signed by the said Samuel Blunston w:ᵗʰ his own hand at the foot of every Page Seal In the presence of the Subscribers Robᵗ. Barber, Rhoda Patterson, Hannah Barber Philadᵃ: October 24ᵗʰ: 1745. Then personally appeared Robert Barber & Hannah Barber two of the Witness:ˢ to the forgoing Will and having first Released their Claims as Legatees as by their Instrument of Release remaing in the Regʳ: General's office more fully appears were admitted as Lawfull Evidence (Thoˢ: Pearson who Entred a Caveat agˢᵗ. the sᵈ. Will receiving Probate having first withdrawn his Caveat) and accordingly they the said Robert & Hannah on their Solemn affirmacon according to Law did declare and affirm they Saw & heard Samuel, Blunston the Testator therein named Sign, Seal, Publish & declare the same will to be his Last Will & Testaᵗ: and that at the doing thereof he was of Sound mind Memory & Understanding to the best of their knowledge.

Coram

Wᵐ Plumsted Reg Genl

Inventory of Samuel Blunston, 1745[10]

An Inventory of the Household Goods Late of Saml Blunston deced appraised by Consent & wth the approbation of Peter Worrall & Thos Pearson by Robt Barber & James Mitchell taken this 31st day of October 1745.

given by Will to Susa Wright during her Life.

In the River Chamber

a bedstead and white Linnen Curtains	2:	0:	0
ffeather Bed Bolster & 1 Pillow	3:	10:	0
pr Sheets Pillow Case & 1 Blanket	1:	10:	0
Callico Quilt & Cotton Coverlid	2:	10:	0
Callico Counterpain	0:	15:	0
Swinging Bed & Fly Curtains	0:	15:	0
2 Looking Glasses 13: 10: 0 } Tables 30/6 Leather Chairs 3	18:	0:	0

In the Stair Case a Glass	2:	0:	0

In the other Chamber

a Bed Stead & old Callico Curtains	1:	10:	0
a ffeather Bed, Bolster 2 Pillow Cases	2:	10:	0
Blanket, Callico Quilt & pr old Sheets	2:	0:	0
pr Drawers £3. Dressg Table & Glass	5:	10:	0
6 Rush bottomd Chairs	1:	4:	0
an old Tick wth a few ffeathrs in it / a hair Cott, Bolster pr ornabrig / Sheets, blanket & Cotton Cunterpain	2:	10:	0
an old Sheet	0:	2:	6

The Lodging Room below

Bed Stead wth old Curtains of Callico	1:	10:	0
old Silk head Cloth & Tester	0:	10:	0
ffeather Bed Bolster & pr Sheets	3:	5:	0
a ffeather Bed a Tick wth a few feathers	4:	0:	0
2 Pillow Cases pr Sheets one blanket	1:	4:	0

a small Quilt & a ffeather Cover	2:	10:	0
pr Low Drawers £1:15:0 a Glass £2:10:0	4:	4:	0
6 Rush Chairs 18/old Chest 5/	1:	3:	0
a Pallat Bedstead	:	7:	0

    In the Dining Room

a Large Table	2:	0:	0
a Smaller Do.	1:	0:	0
Round Tea Table	1:	0:	0
old Tea Table & Tea Chest	0:	5:	0
2 Wood arm Chairs	0:	10:	0
5 old Leather Chairs	0:	10:	0
a Chamber Clock	9:	0:	0
a Couch & small oak Table	1:	10:	0
a Glass £2:10:0. Sundy Maps & Pictures 10/in all ye Rooms	3:	0:	0
Tongs ffire Shovel & and Irons	1:	0:	0

    In the Beaufet

3 China Bowls. 4 smaller Do	1:	5:	0
7 China Plates. 6 Tea Cups & Saucers	1:	7:	0
3 Cups & Saucers, 7 Chocolate Cups &c.	:	7:	0
3 Glass Tumblers a Stone Jugg	0:	4:	0
Tea Pott & Mustard Pott	0:	3:	0
3 Earthen Dishes. 15 Plates Do	0:	7:	0
	£88:	7:	6

Bt over	£88:	7:	6

    In the Pantry

10 Pewter dishes	3:	0:	0
3 doz & 9 Plates	2:	10:	0
Cheese Plate & Ring	0:	4:	0
Shagreen Case for Spoons & Knives	2:	5:	0
old Do for Knives	0:	12:	6
10 Knives & fforks	0:	10:	0
2 Brass Chaffing Dishes	0:	10:	0

2 Box Irons, House wife & 2 fflat Irons	1:	4:	0
Warmg Pan 12/5 Iron Candlesticks 6/	0:	18:	0
2 old Tea Kettles, 2 Sauce Pans	0:	12:	0
5 Damask & Diaper table Cloths	2:	10:	0
2 doz. Damask Napkins	2:	0:	0
In ye Kitchin 1 Brass Kettle	0:	10:	0
an Iron Kettle 20/2 old brass Pots 12/	1:	12:	0
3 Iron Pots 15/Iron Dish Kettle 6/	1:	1:	0
Griddle 4/2 ffrying Pans 8/	0:	12:	0
andirons 6/Tongs 3/	0:	9:	0
2 Tables 8/Dough trough 2/	0:	10:	0
Small Iron Pot	0:	4:	0
	£110:	1:	0

Appraised by Robt Barber
      Ja Mitchell

Memorandum this 31st Ocr 1745. Robert Barber & James Mitchell the appraisers in this Inventory named Came before me & on their respective oath and affirmation declared ye appraismt therein to be Just & reasonable according to the best of their knowledge & Understanding.

Tho Cookson

Inventory of such Effects of Saml Blunston deced as were [ ] to us by the Executors of his will & called Specific Legacys.

The decd wearing apparrell includg his watch & Buttons	£ 80:	0:	0
a Scrutoire	20:	0:	0
Books 160 Vols	100:	0:	0
286 oun of Wrot Plate	143:	0:	0
a Chaise & horse	38:	0:	0
2 Negroe Boys for a Term of Yrs	30:	0:	0
Two Cows	4:	10:	0
Cash due from J. Wright upon bond	86:	0:	0
Cash due upon Ball of his acct	11:	17:	9
Cash due upon Ball from J Ross	25:	12:	0
Cash due from J Wright Junr on Ball	5:	6:	10
Cash due from James Wright on Ball	13:	16:	8
	£558:	3:	3

Appraised by Us this 1st day of Janry 1745/6.
Robt Barber
Ja Mitchell

Additional Inventory of Sundry Goods belonging to the Estate of Samuel Blunston

154 Bushells of Wheat a	20d: p	12: 16: 8
215 bushells Rye	18d	16: 2: 6
50 bushells Barley	20d	4: 3: 4
36 bushells oats	13d	1: 19: 0
Sheep in the Possession of Josha Low		2: 10: 0
5 Hives of Bees		1: 5: 0
Scantling 92 feet 8 more Do small 15 f. Boards 45 f 10/		0: 18: 0
4 Yds Hemp Linnen 6/2^{ls} Spun Cotton 5/		0: 11: 0
New Iron 10 g. £1.10.0 Iron Shovel 3/		1: 13: 0
Case of Razors & a Hone		0: 10: 0
		£42: 8: 6

Robert Barber
Ja Mitchell

I Wm Plumsted Regr General for the Probate of wills & granting Lrts of administration in and for the Province of Pennsylvania do hearby Certify that the foregoing are true Copys Taken from & Compared wth the original Papers remg in the Reg. Genl. office at Philada. In Testimony whereof I have hereunto set my hand & Seal of office at Philada the 4th March anno 1746.

Wm Plumsted Reg Genl

Inventory of John Wright, October 31, 1749[11]

An Inventory of Goods and Chattels of John Wright, late of Hempfield Decd. taken and approved this 31st day of Oct 1749

Wearing apparel and Riding Horse	20–0–0
A folio Bible & Other Books	3–0–0
A Silver Pint Can	6–0–0

A Quart Can mixd mettle	2–0–0
Two Beds & Furniture	10–0–0
A clock-a table	5–0–0
A writing desk	1–10–0
A glass-6 chairs-6 ditto	2–10–0
Andiron-fireshovel & tongs	1–10–0
Pewter	5–0–0
Kitchen furniture	2–0–0
Tubs & Casks	2–0–0
8 Cows 6 Yearlings 6 Calves	26–10–0
26 hoggs	6–0–0
Cart plow harrow & other utensils of husbandry	6–10–0
John Roune	
Robert Barber	
Cash received from John Kinsey	70–0–0

Inventory of Robert Barber, December 22, 1749[12]

An Inventory of the Goods & Chattels of Robert Barber Late of Hempfield Deceased taken & appraised Dec: the 22nd 1749 By James Webb & James Wright

The Decedts Wearing Apparel Ryding horse Saddle & brydle	20–00–0
Cash in the House	12–00–0
Bonds with Interest due on them	178–00–0
a Large Byble	1–00–0
a parcel of Hopps	113–02–0
a Negro Woman	20–00–0
three Negro Children (6 years, 4 years, 18 months old	20–00–0
Household & Kitchin furniture	21–06–0
Table Linnen	5–00–0
a quantity of Clean hemp	4–16–5

Hemp unbroke	18–00–0
Barley	2–00–0
Oats in the Straw	6–00–0
Rye in the Straw	3–00–0
Hay	2–00–0
a Waggon & Geers	5–10–0
three Working Horses	21–00–0
two mares & five Colts	12–00–0
Eighteen hornd. Cattle Including Calves	25–00–0
Hoggs	4–00–0
two pair of plow Irons, Harrow, and Crow	1–15–0
two Axes, male rings, 2 wedges, 2 weeding hoes, & a Grubbing hoe	0–18–0
	496–7–5

Signed James Webb
     James Wright

Inventory of Samuel Bethel II, June 17, 1777[13]

Inventory of all and Singular the Goods and Chattles Rights and Credits which were of Samuel Bethel late of Hempfield Township in the County of Lancaster Gentleman deceased appraised by us the Subscribers this 17th of June A Dom 1777.

wearing Aparel & watch	30–0–0
a riding horse Saddle & Saddle Bags	37–10–0
an Old Brown Mare	13–0–0
a horse Colt 1 Year old	8–0–0
3 Cows a 4-	12–0–0
7 Sheep a 7/6	2–12–6
7 Hogs a	
an old waggon & 2 Pair of Geirs	6–0–0
an old Plough & Irons & Some old Harrow Teeth	0–18–0
an Iron Crow Bar, a dung fork, an ax & a Broad Hoe	1–2–6
13 old Barrels 2 Hop Boxes and a Tub	2–15–6
a Negro Man	60–0–0
a Servant Woman	5–0–0

25 Bushl Wheat a 4/11	6-2-11
Bushl. Rye a 3/6	
the Part of a fishing Boat & old Shad Sein	3-0-0
a Canoe	1-10-0
Table Linnen	9-0-0
Plate	16-10-0
The Furniture in the Best Parlour	18-9-0
The Furniture in the Clock Room	24-17-6
The Furniture in the Pantry	3-0-0
The Furniture in the Kitchen	12-4-0
The Furniture up Stairs	34-10-0
14 Chairs a 3/	2-2-0
a writing Desk	2-10-0
an old Bible & other Books	2-12-0
4 Guns a 4	16-0-0
a Syder mill & [ ] Box	1-10-0
4 Young Hogs	1-10-0
3 Large Hogs	3-15-0
13 Bushell Barley at [ ] per Bushell	2-8-9
20 Bushell Corn at 2/9 per Bushell	2-15-0
302 3/4 Bushl. Wheat a 3/11	59-5-1
200 1/2 Bushl. Rye a 2/11	29-4-9
28 Bushl. Oats a 1/8	2-6-8

Appraised by us
Nathaniel Barber
James Barber

Will of Susanna Wright, January 28, 1782[14]

I Susanna Wright of Hempfield in Lancaster County Single Woman tho of very Advanced age Being of Sound [mind] and disposin[?] make and Ordain this my last Will and Testament in Manner and form following, to my knowledge I am not Indebted to any Person whatever I give and bequeath to my Nephew Samuel Wright Son of my Late Brother James Wright to him and to his heirs and Assigns forever all that my land and Plantation in Hempfield Township aforesaid lying upon Susquehanna River & Adjoining

to and lying betwixt Land of my late Father John Wright and Samuel Blunston
Deceas'd containing one hundred Acres with Allowance with all the Buildings
and Appurtenances whatever thereto Belonging upon the following Conditions,
to wit, that his Mother Rhoda Wright shall have Absolute Right and Priviledge
to Occupy with her Children the Dwelling house on the said Land Now Occupy'd
By Susanna Bethel with the Garden and other Conveniences appertaining to
the said house not Including the Plantation as long as she shall continue his
fathers Widow Which I hope and Believe will be to the end of her Natural life.
I give to the said Sam[l.] Wright my Escrutoire & my Silver Coffee Pot all this
I give him upon the following Conditions that he the said Saml Wright shall
make Over to his three Brothers John James and William in Equal Shares with
himself all the Buildings now in the tenure of Joseph Jeffrys called the ferry
house with the land they Occupy to them their heirs and Assigns forever
in Joynt Property with himself as Also the House Builded for a Smith to live
in with the Garden. All the Rest and Residue of my Plate I Give and Bequeath
in Equal Shares to the Children of my afors[d]. Brother James Wright directing that
their Mother shall have the use and Care of the said Escrutoire and Plate while
she shall live in the said house as aforesaid and that it shall continue to be a
home for all the Children as long as they or any of them are destitute of other
Convenient home. I need not Inforce their Brothers Kindness to them his
Afectionate Regard for every Part of his family and his Rectitude of heart will
Secure to his Mother & Brothers & Sisters every good Office in his Power
the Old Watch which was my Grandfathers & has Continued to go more than
100 years, I desire may not be Suffered to goe out of the family the Silver tweezer
which was given me by my Father, I Bequeath to my Neice Sukey Wright who
lives with me & any other tryfles which may belong to me I Give & bequeath
to the Children of my afs[d]. Brother James Wright Amongst them my Books I
leave to the disposal of my Executor, after what shall be taken out for the use
of the Family, to dispose of them as shall be most Profitable to them, And I do
most Earnestly press it upon them all that they Behave to their Mother with
the Utmost duty and Afection & Always Esteem her as she has a Right to
be Absolute mistress of the House and family. Lastly I Constitute and Appoint my
aforementioned Nephew Sam[l]. Wright Sole Executor of this my last Will and
Testament Strongly Recommending to him that in every Deficuly or Embarress-
ment he may meet with Relating to his late dear fathers or in his own Affairs
or those of his Brothers and Sisters he may have recourse to the Advice &
Assistance of the able and never failing friend of our whole family the Benevolent John Dickinson, I think it Necessary to add a few Words to prevent any

Wills and Inventories 255

Reflections on my Executor hereafter it has been Surmised & Reported that I have Amass'd Considerable Summs from the Bequest of Sam[l]. Blunston when they first came into my hands I delivered the whole to my Brother & he Suplyed me with whatever I had Occasion for & I declare I never laid by the Value of five Shillings nor have Cash or Specialtys to that amount in my own or any other hands whatever, written with my own hand & Seald with my Seal this 28th Day of January Anno Dom. 1782.

         Susanna Wright

Published & declared in the Presence of
Joseph Jefferies
Isaac Kagen
Richard Lowdon

Inventory of Samuel Wright, August 14, 1811[15]

A true and perfect Inventory and conscionable Appraisement of all and singular the Goods and Chattels which were of Samuel Wright late of the Town of Columbia in the County of Lancaster de-ceased, at the time of his death viz–

Deaceased Wearing Apparel & Watch	50.00
1 Pr Looking Glasses	20.00
1 Dining Table	6.00
2 Circular Mahogony Tables	12.00
1 Breakfast Table	2.00
2 Arm Chairs and 8 Windsor do	12.00
Arrowsmiths Map of the World	8.00
1 Carpet	20.00
1 Pr Qt decanters & 1 doz Wines	2.00
1 Set Casters	6.00
1 pr Silver Sauce Boats & 1 Soup Ladle	30.00
1 Silver Coffee pot	30.00
1 Silver Cream Jug & Small Cann	15.00
½ doz Table and 1 doz Silver Tea Spoons	12.00

1 Pepper Box & 1 Mustard pot	5.00
1 Silver Tankard	20.00
Sundry China, Glass & Queensware	8.00
4 Windsor Chairs	3.00
1 Mahogony Stand	2.00
1 Map of State of Pennsylvania	1.50
1 pr Fire Buckets	3.00
1 Bed Bedstead Bedding & Curtains	<u>50.00</u>
Amount Carried forward	$317.50
Amount brought forward	317.50
½ doz Windsor Chairs	6.00
1 Mahogony Wash Stand	4.00
1 Carpet	10.00
1 Waiter	1.50
1 Looking Glass	2.50
1 Bed	15.00
1 Hair Matrass	6.00
1 Trunk	2.00
1 Desk & Book Case	6.00
1 Small Table	0.75
2 Chairs	1.50
1 Bed	3.00
1 Clock	40.00
1 Table	2.00
1 Carpet	8.00
1 Settee and Six Windsor Chairs	8.00
2 Pr And Irons Shovel & tongs	5.00
1 Copper Kettle	10.00
Sundry Kitchen Furniture	12.00
200 lb Bacon @ 8 cts lb	16.00
1 Set of Washingtons Life	15.00
2 Volms Westleys Philosophy	4.00
Sundry Books	15.00
3 Guns	30.00
1 Ten plate Stove	24.00
10 Bushls Wheat @ $1.50/100	15.00
1 Canoe	<u>2.00</u>

Amount Carried forward		581.75

Amount brought forward		581.75
40 Bushels Oats	40 cts	16.00
1 Old Horse		10.00
1 do do		30.00
1 Three Year old Colt		60.00
1 Bay Mare, Saddle & Bridle		75.00
1 do do		140.00
2 Cows each $15		30.00
3 do do $15		45.00
2 Yearling Calves	$7	14.00
3 do do	$3	9.00
1 Poney		25.00
1 Sow and 4 Pigs		16.00
9 Pigs	ea $2.50/100	22.50
1 Wind Mill		12.00
1 Cutting Box		2.00
200 Bushels Corn More or Less	@ 4/	106.67
do Wheat		
do Rye		
do Oats		
do Barley		
4 Acres of Corn		

Appraised by us Saml. Miller
                     Calvin Cooper

NOTES

1. William Wright was Susanna Wright's great-uncle. WCW William Wright 1685, Lancashire Record Office. Published with kind permission from the Lancashire Record Office.
2. Abel Owen, who married Ann Wright in 1667, was Susanna Wright's great-uncle. WCW Abel Owen 1695, Lancashire Record Office. Published with kind permission from the Lancashire Record Office.
3. Ibid. Published with kind permission from the Lancashire Record Office.
4. Peter Robinson, married to Jane Wright, was Susanna Wright's great-uncle. WCW Peter Robinson 1703, Lancashire Record Office. Published with kind permission from the Lancashire Record Office.
5. Because of this inventory's length and repetition, a partial listing of the fabrics is given here with omissions shown by breaks in numbering. Household furnishings, however, have been listed in full. Ibid. Published with kind permission from the Lancashire Record Office.
6. Dorothy Wright was the wife of William Wright and great-aunt to Susanna Wright. WCW Dorothy Wright 1708, Lancashire Record Office. Published with kind permission from the Lancashire Record Office.
7. Ibid. Published with kind permission from the Lancashire Record Office.
8. Ann (Wright) Owen was Susanna Wright's great-aunt. WCW Ann Owen 1713, Lancashire Record Office. Published with kind permission from the Lancashire Record Office.
9. WFM 83.18.157.
10. Inventory for Samuel Blunston, 1745, Pearson Family Papers, Historical Society of Pennsylvania. Published by kind permission from the Historical Society of Pennsylvania.
11. Court House Records, Lancaster County Historical Society. Published with kind permission from the Lancaster County Historical Society.
12. Ibid. Published with kind permission from the Lancaster County Historical Society.
13. Ibid. Published with kind permission from the Lancaster County Historical Society.
14. Ibid. Published with kind permission from the Lancaster County Historical Society.
15. Ibid. Published with kind permission from the Lancaster County Historical Society.

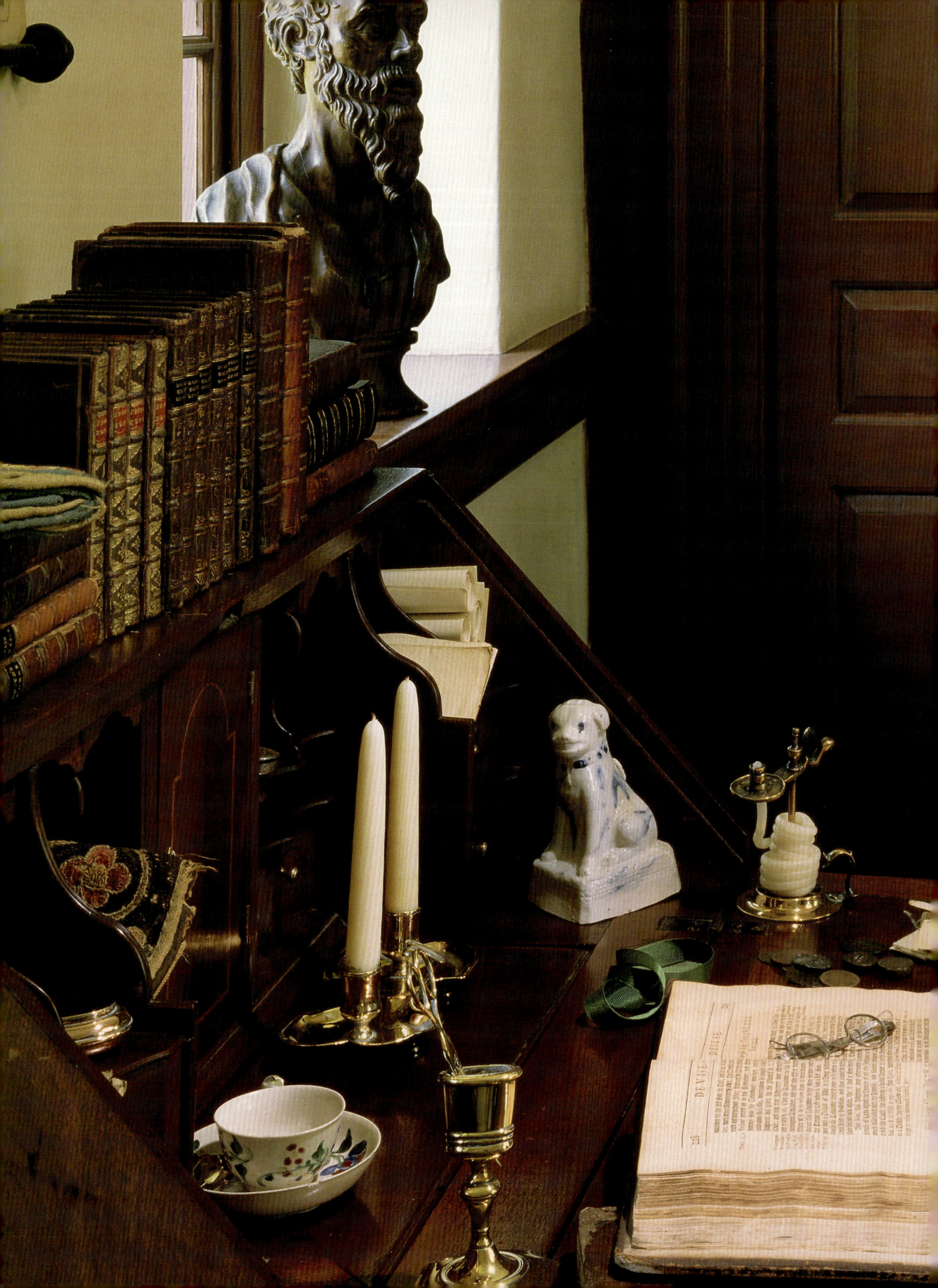

THE LIBRARY OF SUSANNA WRIGHT

Books are not only the furnishings of a house, they are also the furnishings of the mind and therefore they give us a very intimate glimpse into the owner as well as into the intellectual life of the period. In a period when literacy was limited, the presence of libraries in the colonies was limited, too. Susanna Wright and most of her close friends were avid bibliophiles and were part of the vibrant intellectual life of Philadelphia. Many of her friends—James Logan, the Norrises, Benjamin Franklin, Lloyd Zachary, the Pembertons—had notable libraries, James Logan's one of the finest in the colonies.

James Logan was Susanna Wright's mentor and guided her reading, sending her the works of Wollaston, Fénelon, Corneille, Voltaire, and many others. Just as he encouraged his children in the study of languages (even teaching his daughter Sally Hebrew before she was nine years old so she could read the Psalms in the original language), so he encouraged Susanna. In a letter of April 12, 1723, he writes to her about a passage from Horace which he regrets she cannot understand in the Latin original:

> *I have almost continually before me a few Lines of Horace; wth I wish I could quote to thy Understanding in his own Words but the sense of them is that the Wise God wraps up the events of futurity in his inscrutable Mind and laughs at man if he pretends to carry his apprehension beyond the stint allow'd to him. Know it is thy Duty to make the best of the present All the rest rolls on like a River Sometimes Smooth & quiet in its Channel Sometimes overflowing its banks carries Buildings flocks and herds before it. He is the only happy man who can say I have lived to day Lett God Send what he will tomorrow & with more to the Same purpose in that excellent Ode y[e] 29th of y[e] 3[d] Book of which I hope thou hast a Translation.*[1]

She eventually learned Latin, along with Italian, and had a great facility in speaking, reading, and writing in French.[2] She occasionally would write letters in French to the children of her friends in Philadelphia so that they could get practice in the language.

Throughout her life Susanna Wright read extensively in French, borrowing many of the books from James Logan, whose letters are repeatedly filled with reprimands for not returning his books. He complained of "such things being almost buried with thee when in thy hands."[3] In 1728 when she was in transition between Chester and her new home on the banks of the Susquehanna, perhaps with some uneasiness that the books might be swallowed up in the move, Logan writes:

> *Tho' thy last with thy short flight at Poetry once more, requires my acknowledgment, yet I would not give thee one line were it not that I wish barely to tell thee that I had thy promise to visit us this fall, that I find thy father desires it, and therefore that as I am sure it is necessary for thee I shall take no excuse whatsoever, downright sickness excepted, but shall interpret all others that can be offer'd as a direct declaration that thou art absolutely determined to renounce for Hempfield all the rest of the World, and amongst others, one who has ever since his acquaintance with thee been most strongly inclined to shew himself thy sincere and affectionate frd*
>
> *I was in hopes what I said of some Books being confined to idleness at Chester when they are much wanted here would have procured them. My Daughter is hard at her french under a Master & has occasion for fontanelle & fenelon or Arb'p Cambray. Pray let others learn also. Where is Vaugelas?*[4]

James Logan loved his books and carefully provided in his will that the magnificent collection would go to the Library Company of Philadelphia:

> *It is now above six months since thou took with thee three volumes of a work of which I have 15 more & by my will given amongst others all the 18 to the Library of Philadia . . . As for Voltaire I must refer it to thy own goodness and for Colliers Dict^{ry} I suppose thou hast prescription on thy side for it viz considerably above twice 7 years.*[5]

Despite this chiding, Collier's *Dictionary* still did not find its way back to its owner for at least another seven years, for in August of 1746, Logan wrote to Susanna, saying he "could not but think the Detention of Collier's Dictionary for above 20 Years was somewhat odd."[6]

Susanna, however, also loaned her own books. Three volumes of a set were never returned to her but rather finally ended up in the Library Company of Philadelphia.[7] Another book of hers, Claude Jordan de Colombier's *Voyages Historiques De L'Europe*, also part of a set, found its way to the library of Dickinson College among the books of Isaac Norris.[8]

The books Susanna Wright purchased from England were often bound in calfskin, which was costlier than the more common sheepskin. Usually the bindings are decorated with simple gilt decoration or blind stamping. A few of the books were bound by Pennsylvania bookbinders, like those by William Davies, Abraham Latscha, and Stephen Potts.

The following books in Wright's Ferry Mansion's collection are known to have been owned by Susanna Wright from the inscriptions:

Anson, George. *A Voyage Round the World in the Years MDCC XL, I, II, III, IV, compiled by Richard Walter. London: John and Paul Knapton, 1749.*

    Signature on fly leaf: *Susanna Wright.*

[Baxter, Andrew.] *An Enquiry into the Nature of the Human Soul: Wherein the Immateriality of the Soul is Evinced from the Principles of Reason and Philosophy. The Second Edition. London: Printed by James Bettenham for A. Millar, 1737.*

    2 vols., 12mo. Signature on title of vols. 1 and 2: *S Wright.* Signature inside cover of vol. 2: *Patience Wright.*

Boswell, James. *An Account of Corsica: The Journal of a Tour to That Island; and Memoirs of Pascal Paoli, Illustrated with a New and Accurate Map of Corsica, Second Edition. London: Edward and Charles Dilly in the Poultry, 1768.*

    12mo. Signature at top of title: *James Wright.* Bookplate of Samuel Wright inside front cover. Label on spine: *Boswell's Corsica.*

Burnet, Gilbert. *The Abridgment of the History of the Reformation of the Church of England. The Fifth Edition Corrected. Vol. II. London: Printed for J. Walthoe, B. Tooke, J. Knapton, D. Midwinter, B. Cowse, and R. Robinson, 1718.*

    12mo. Signature on title: *S Wright.* Marginal gloss, p. 226: *Joan Dudly or Lady Joan Gray.* Numerical calculations inside front cover. On spine: *2.*

Burnet, Gilbert. *An Abridgment of the Third Volume of the History of the Reformation of the Church of England. London: Printed for W. Churchill, 1719.*

    12mo. Signature on title and inside front cover: *S Wright.* Signatures inside back cover in two different hands: *Susannah Wright* [and] *Susannah Wright 1924.* On spine: *3.* Bunch of clover [found] at p. 97.

Chubb, Thomas. *The True Gospel of Jesus Christ Asserted. To which is added A Short Dissertation on Providence. London, Printed for Thomas Cox, 1738.*

    12mo. Signature on title: *S Wright*. Signature inside front cover: *Patience Wright*. At p. 197, beginning "A Short Dissertation on Providence," an 18th-century pin piercing top corner.

Freebairn, James. *The Life of Mary Stewart, Queen of Scotland and France. Second Edition. London: Printed for A. Millar, 1729.*

    12mo. Signature on title: *S Wright*. Bookplate of Samuel Wright inside front cover.

Glover, R[ichard]. *Leonidas. A Poem. The Fourth Edition. London: Printed for R. Dodsley, 1739.*

    12mo. Signatures on title: *S Wright [and] Patience Wright*.

An Historical Review of the Constitution and Government of Pennsylvania, from Its Origin; So Far As Regards the Several Points of Controversy, Which Have, from Time to Time, Arisen between the Several Governors of that Province, and Their Several Assemblies, Founded on Authentic Documents. London: Printed for R. Griffiths, 1759.

    8vo. Signature on title: *James Wright*. Bookplate of Samuel Wright and label of the Columbia Pennsylvania Library Company inside front cover.

Herodotus. *The History of Herodotus: Translated from the Greek by Isaac Littlebury. The Third Edition, Vol. II. London: D. Midwinter, A. Bettesworth and C. Hitch, J. and J. Pemberton, R. Ware, C. Rivington, J. Batley and J. Wood, F. Clay, A. Ward, J. and P. Knapton, T. Longman, and R. Hett, 1737.*

    12mo. Signature on title: *S Wright*. Bookplate of Samuel Wright inside front cover. In gilt on spine: *2*.

[John, Earl of Orrery] *Remarks on the Life and Writings of Dr. Jonathan Swift, Dean of St. Patrick's, Dublin, In a Series of Letters from John Earl of Orrery To his Son, the Honourable Hamilton Boyle. The Fifth Edition. London: Printed for A. Millar, 1752.*

    Signature on title: *S:Wright*. Bookplate of Samuel Wright inside front cover.

Latin-English Dictionary, seventeenth century, lacking title page. Bound by William Davies (1693–1740) of Chester and Philadelphia, Pennsylvania.

12mo. Signature inside front cover: *S. Wright*. Signature on page beginning section on proper names: *Saml Blunston*. Signature on pages BLA, CIV, HER, IAC, INV, and NUM: *William Blunston*. Signature on page INF: *Wm. Disney writ yet 3 day of October 1651*. Signature on page CAP: *John Blunston*. Signature on page IRA: *Wm. Martin*. On page ZIN: *Blunston Hyble Amen*. On pages ALN, COL, COM, HOS, INV, LYM, MER, and MOD: miscellaneous glosses.

Macky, J. *A Journey through England in Familiar Letters, from a Gentleman Here, to His Friend Abroad. In Two Vols., The Fifth Edition, Vol. I. London: Robert Gosling and John Pemberton, 1732.*

Signature on title: *S Wright*. Signature inside front cover: *Patience Wright*. Bookplate of Samuel Wright inside front cover. Interlinear gloss on p. 126: *See Camden's Sussex.*

Meriton, G. *A Guide to Surveyors of the High-Ways, Showing the Office and Duty of Such Surveyors. London: W. Rawlins and S. Roycroft, 1694.*

Signature on title: *J Wright*. Bookplate of Samuel Wright inside front cover.

De Pollnitz, Baron. *The Memoirs of the Baron de Pollnitz on his Travels to Germany, Italy, France, Flanders, Holland and England.*

Signature on title: *S. Wright*.

Ray, John. *Travels through the Low-Countries, Germany, Italy and France, with Curious Observations, Natural, Topographical, Moral, Physiological, &c. Also, A Catalogue of Plants Found Spontaneously Growing in Those Parts, and Their Virtues. by the late Reverend and Learned Mr. John Ray, F.R.S. To which is added, An Account of the Travels of Francis Willughby, Esq: Through Great Part of Spain. The Second Edition. Corrected and Improved, and Adorned with Copper-Plates. Vol. I. London: Printed for J. Walthoe, D. Midwinter, A. Bettesworth and C. Hitch, W. Innys, R. Robinson, J. Wilford, A. Ward, J. and P. Knapton, T. Longman, O. Payne, W. Shropshire, J. and R. Tonson, T. Woodman, R. Chandler, and J. Wellington, 1738.*

12mo. Signature on title: *S Wright*. On spine: *1*. Folding plates at pp. 4, 5. Plate on p. 6.

Ray, John. *A Collection of Curious Travels and Voyages. Containing, Dr. Leonhart Rauwolf's Journey into the Eastern Countries, viz. Syria, Palestine, or the Holy Land, Armenia,*

Mesopotamia, Assyria, Chaldea, & c. Translated from the Original High Dutch, by Nicholas Staphorst. And also, Travels into Greece, Asia Minor, Egypt, Arabia Felix, Petraea, Ethiopia, the Red Sea, & c. Collected from the Observations of Mons. Belon, Prosper Alpinus, Dr. Huntingdon, Mr. Vernon, Sir George Wheeler, Dr. Smith, Mr. Greaves, and others. to which are added three Catalogues of such Trees, Shrubs, and Herbs, as grown in the Levant. By the Rev. John Ray, F. R. S. The Second Edition Corrected and Improved. Vol. II. London: Printed for J. Walthoe, D. Midwinter, A. Bettesworth and C. Hitch, W. Innys, R. Robinson, J. Wilford, A Ward, J. & P. Knapton, T. Longman, O. Payne, W. Shropshire, J. & R. Tonson, t. Woodman, R. Chandler, and J. Wellington.

12mo. Signature on title: *S Wright*. On spine: *2*.

Rohan, Henri de. *The Memoires of the Duke of Rohan: or, A Faithful Relation of the Most Remarkable Occurrences in France; Especially concerning those of the Reformed Churches there. From the Death of Henry the Great, untill the Peace made with them, in June, 1629. Englished by George Bridges. London: Printed by E. M. for Gabriel Bedell and Thomas Collins, 1660.*

12mo. Top of title missing but vestiges of signature in hand of Susanna Wright: *ht*. Samuel Wright's bookplate inside front cover.

Sheppard, William. *The Offices of Constables, Church-Wardens, Overseers of the Poor, Supravisors of the Highwayes, Treasurers of the County-Stock; and some other lesser Country Officers. Fifth Edition. London: Printed by Ric. Hodgkinsonne, for Nath. Ekins, 1658.*

Signature on title: *S Wright*. Bookplate of Samuel Wright inside front cover.

Swift, Jonathan. *Political Tracts, By the Author of Gulliver's Travels. Vol. I. London: Printed for C. Davis, 1738.*

12mo. Signature on title: *S Wright*. Bookplate of Samuel Wright upside down inside back cover. On spine: *I*.

NOTES

1. Logan Family of Stenton Papers, vol. I, XR: 825.4, Historical Society of Pennsylvania.
2. D. N. Logan, *Susanna Wright*; see Appendix in this volume.
3. James Logan to Susanna Wright, June 18, 1728, in private collection.
4. James Logan to Susanna Wright, November 24, 1728; ibid.
5. James Logan to Susanna Wright, September 28, 1739; private collection.
6. James Logan to Susanna Wright, August 2, 1746. Logan Letterbook H, 188, Historical Society of Pennsylvania.
7. With a presentation inscription to Susanna Wright in the hand of Isaac Norris II, these were volumes I–III of *Oeuvres Diverses Du Sieur Dxxx in 4 vols* (Paris: Chez Claude Barbin, 1694), which are in the University of Pennsylvania Collection, No. 69888.0, Library Company of Philadelphia.
8. Tome VI (Amsterdam: Chez Pierre de Coup, 1712) with signature on title page: *Susa Wright*. See Marie Elena Korey *The Books of Isaac Norris (1701–1766) at Dickinson College* (Carlisle, PA: Dickinson College, 1975), p. 165.

Two volumes of the *Letters of Madame de Maintenon* possibly given to Susanna Wright by Benjamin Franklin, with inscriptions in Susanna Wright's handwriting.

(viii)

Those who look for Intrigue, may spare themselves the Trouble of reading these Letters. The Elevation of Madame *de Maintenon* had nothing in it but what was lawful and natural; and she was therefore the Wonder of the Age she lived in.

In this Collection are inserted many that were written to her by eminent Persons; not in order to swell the Volume, but solely with a View of adding to the Pleasure of the Reader: I am not certain whether every one of them may be placed in exact Order of Time.

There are other Letters of Madame *de Maintenon* (and some of Madame *de Montespan*) not printed in this Volume, which will shortly be published.

In this new Edition, the Translator has thought proper to add the 266th Letter, from the first Volume of the *Tatler*, where it was formerly published.

LETTERS
OF
Madame De MAINTENON.

LETTER I.
To Mademoiselle De St. Hermant.

Niort, ———, 1650. Ætat: 15

YOU flatter me, Madam, indeed too much, and treat me, almost, as if I were of the other Sex. Your Encomiums on me really carry more Flattery in them than those of Monsieur *De M———*: His Praises are more passionate, but they are less tender than yours: I should, in Truth, be shy of a Lover that could find a Way to my Heart with the same Address as you get Admittance to it. *Paris* would be little regretted by me, were you absent from it: You eclipse every Thing that pleases me in that City. The Tears we have shed

---

(316)

Marshal Catinat.

FEW Men knew him, for he was averse to being communicative. At Court he was not relished: His outward Carriage discovered nothing of the great Man in him. He was hardly known in *Paris*: In the Army he was adored. No Man ever had fewer Friends; but those were remarkable for a Zeal and an Admiration to be seldom found in Friendship. When he was out of Employment, it used to be said of him, that he was capable of executing any thing. He raised himself without caballing: He never sounded his own Praise: He scorned to ward off any Blow, which envious Persons, for he had no Enemies, aimed at him. He died calmly, fearing nothing, hoping nothing, perhaps believing nothing. His Merit was natural; it cost him nothing. He was above Honours. Though charged with Irreligion, he was never accused of any Vice.

FINIS.

—upon the Death of the King M. Maintenon Retired to the Abbey of St Cyr for the remainder of her Life, where she dyed April 15th 1719 and was Buried in the middle of the Choir in the Church there, in a tomb of plain black Marble, with the following Inscription upon it — the translation from the French —

Here lies
The most high & most potent Lady the Lady Frances d'Aubigny Marchioness of Maintenon, a Wife Illustrious, a Woman truly Christian, that Virtuous Heroine, whom the wise man sought in vain in his time, and whom he would have proposed to us for a pattern, if he had lived in Ours.

She was of Birth most Noble, her wit was early Commended, and much more her Virtue. Sobriety, good nature and Modesty formed her her Character, from which she never derogated, always unchangable in the various Situations of her Life; the same Principles, the same Rules, the same Virtues.

Windsor
Le Chateau
Castle
de Windsor
le Palais et Park de St. James
St. James Palace and Park

MISCELLANEOUS DOCUMENTS

Invoice from Charles Norris to Susanna Wright [about 1750][1]

    Invoyce of Books
    Mapps & C. had from
    C. Norris 12–13–0 & 6–4–0

    Sundry Books & c. Sent to Hempfield

    Susanna Wright by Charles Norris

1 Vol. Ansons Voyages	0.6
1 do Night Thoughts	0.6
1 do Miscellanious Correspondence	
1 do Plan of Popes Gardens & c.	
1 do Popes Essay on Man	0–[2?]0
3 do Popes Letters	0–9–0
2 do Plynys Letters	0–8–0
3 do Thompson's Seasons	0–15–0
7 do Gentlemans Magazines Anno 1731, 32	
33, 34, 46, 47, & 1748	2–9–0
7 Pamphlets of Gentleman's Magazines viz	
January, February, March, April, May	at 6d
June & July Anno 1749	–3–6

2 do Con. Philips Life & c. .13.0
4 Numbers do.
1 Pamphlet Suspicious Husband 0-17-0

---

22 Vol. 11 Pamphlets Pack'd in 4 Boxes Ma

Sundrys for James Wright

Alexanders Battle 9/10 The World 2
6 Views of Prospects abt. London
2 Cases 2/6 Charger Shippg
Can [&c.?] paid

[*in margin:*] Errors Ex
Chas. Norris

The Burial Ground at Hempfield[2]

"Hempfield" was sometimes used to refer to the little settlement at Wright's Ferry, since that was the name of the township where it was located. This list, which is in Susanna Wright's handwriting, names the people who were buried here between 1730 and 1750 and includes people living within a broad radius of the little settlement, some living even in Lancaster and across the river. In the manner of the Society of Friends, most of the graves had no tombstones, except for those marking the graves of Samuel and Sarah Blunston, who had given the land for the cemetery and enclosed it with a wall.[3] The property was at the far end of Susanna Wright's tract of 100 acres and is now part of Mount Bethel Cemetery. Susanna Wright was eventually buried here but with no stone to mark the grave. Because of the lack of markers for these early graves, this listing is of particular importance.

Prior to the twentieth century, mortality among the young was great. In the twenty year period that this list covers, of the seventy-eight people who died, thirty-five were infants or children. A period of great loss for Susanna Wright occurred in the six years from 1744 to 1750, when four children of her brother James died on March 12, 1744/5; two children to her brother John, on January 22,

1746/7; her sister Patience Lowdon, in 1747; her brother-in-law Richard Lowdon, in 1745/6; and her father, in 1749. Within that same period, Robert Barber, whom the Wrights had known in Chester, and Samuel and Sarah Blunston, all of whom had founded the settlement with the Wrights in 1726 and who were Susanna Wright's immediate neighbors, also died.

An Account of the Several Persons Laid In the Burying Ground at Hempfield In Lancaster County

      aged 17
John Deval—Dyed in the year 1730 the first person Buried here

Rachel Murphy
Edward Murphy ⎫
Jane Murphy   ⎬ father & mother to Rachel Murphy
Bryan Sheils
Samuel Bethel
John Bethel   ⎫
Anne Bethel   ⎬ Children to Samuel Bethel
Sarah Bethel ⎭
John Morris
Robert Wilson
James Waterman
John Waterman   ⎫
    Waterman   ⎬ Children to James Waterman
    Waterman   ⎭

    Verhulst ⎫
    Verhulst ⎬ Infant Children to Cornelius Verhulst

James Wright an Infant   ⎫ Children to Jnᵒ Wright Junʳ
James Wright aged 8 years ⎬ 1746/7 Jan 22 Dyed
    Susy Wright Infant   ⎭

Susy Wright   ⎫
John Wright   ⎬ Infants ⎫ Children to James Wright
Susy Wright   ⎭   ⎬ – Dyed March 12th 1744/5
Susy Wright aged 2 years   ⎭

Samuel Blunston } who Gave the Land & Enclosd it with a wall and are laid under ~~two~~ Marble Tombstones
Sarah Blunston } Sarah Blunston Dyed Dec 13th 1744 S Blunston Dyed Sept 30th 1745

Richard Lowdon—Dyed last day of January 1745/6
Elisabeth Sams
Richard Richards
Widow Brown
   Alison an Infant
      an Infant
    Minshal an Infant
    Mary Watson Infant
George Davis   Drounded in Susquehana River
John [M'land?]   Drounded in D°
Joseph Hall
  an Infant
John M'Daniel
M'Daniel an Infant
Joshua Minshal   27th Day of June 1746
Mackdanil
Susanah Atkinson
Hannah Barber   an Infant
Jane Minshal
Josh^a Minshal   Dec 12th 1747
Jn° Minshal
Patience Lowdon—Dec 13th aged 41 years & Six months
Tom Smith
Patrick Hayes
Hannah Ives
Rebecka Ives
    Ives an Infant
John Watson
Thomas Wilson
   an Infant
Margt Magathy
Robert Barber the Elder Dyed September the 3rd 1749 aged 60 years
John Wright the Elder Dyed the first day of October 1749 aged 82 years 5 months
Timothy Ward Buried August 14th 1750   & 15 days
woman from Rosses D° from [Tatins?] – Andrew King – Hannah Barber Infant

Wm M'manamy   [Kathrine Fhouse?] M'manamy an Infant Mary Sulwan
Lydia Bishop – Margret Wright

    Ging a Negro Man
    Phebe a Mulato Girl   } Servants to Samuel Blunston
    five Negro Children
    Prince an Indian Man

    Scipio a Negro Man
    York a Negro Boy   } Servants Belonging to Robt Barber
       Negro Girl

a Conestoga Indian Youth

NOTES

1. Norris Papers, misc. vol., p. 38, Historical Society of Pennsylvania. Published in *Publications of the Pennsylvania Society of Colonial Dames of America*, no. 2 (1906), p. 24. Published with kind permission from the Historical Society of Pennsylvania.
2. WFM 83.18.101.
3. William C. Braithwaite, *The Second Period of Quakerism* (Cambridge: Cambridge University Press, 1961), p. 417.

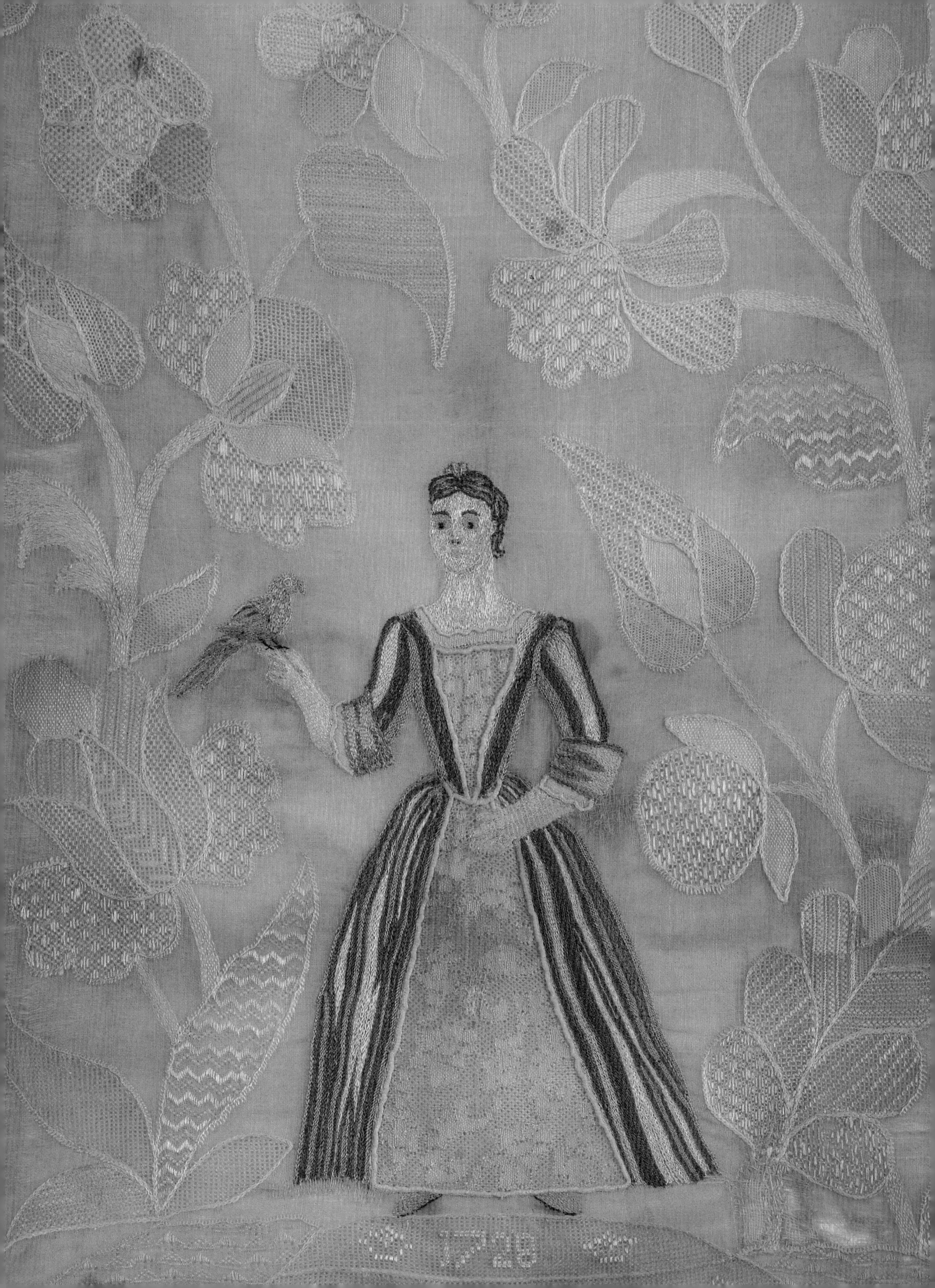
1720

DESCRIPTION OF SUSANNA WRIGHT BY DEBORAH NORRIS LOGAN

Born in Philadelphia, October 19, 1761, Deborah Norris Logan was the daughter of two friends very close to Susanna Wright, Mary Parker and Charles Norris, who were married in 1759. After Charles Norris's death in 1766, Deborah and her mother moved to Chester to live in the house where her mother had been raised. In 1781, Deborah Norris married Dr. George Logan, the grandson of James Logan, and at that time moved to Germantown to live in Stenton, the house which James Logan built in 1726. She lived there until her death in 1839. Her work as an historian was notable. Having inherited voluminous correspondence between James Logan and William Penn, she spent several years transcribing the documents which were beginning to deteriorate, so that the text would be preserved. These transcriptions were published in two volumes by the Historical Society of Pennsylvania. She derived a particularly intimate insight into the early history of this country through her close relationship with her cousin, Charles Thomson, the Secretary to the Continental Congress, who also was a good friend of Susanna Wright.[1]

When Deborah Norris Logan was born, Susanna Wright would have been sixty-four years old, so Deborah Norris Logan's recollections were of Susanna only in mature years. In addition to her own memories of Susanna Wright, Deborah undoubtedly drew from the recollection of others, since she was intimately associated with Susanna Wright's closest circle of friends who had known her for many years before Deborah's birth. In addition, she would have had access to the rich correspondence between Susanna Wright and the Norris and Logan families.[2] *The following biographical portrait of Susanna Wright was published by Deborah Norris Logan in "Analectic Magazine," vol. 5. (Philadelphia, 1815): 250–52.*[3]

Notice of Susanna Wright.

It is frequently objected to relations of particular lives, that they are not distinguished by any striking or wonderful vicissitudes. The scholar, who passed his life among his books; the merchant, who conducted only his own affairs; the priest, whose sphere of action was not extended beyond that of his duty, are considered as no proper objects of public regard, however they might have excelled in their several stations, whatever might have been their learning, integrity, and piety. But this notion arises from false measures of excellence and dignity, and must be eradicated by considering, that in the esteem of uncorrupted reason, what is of most use is of most value.   Dr. Johnson.

    As it has always appeared to me a duty which the living owe to each other, as well as to the dead, to rescue merit from descending into immediate oblivion, I have endeavored to trace the following notices of a lady, who, though she was well known, and generally esteemed, by the most eminent characters in the state of Pennsylvania whilst she lived, yet nothing, I believe, respecting her has ever yet appeared in print. What I now mean to offer is from recollection alone; but my opportunities for information were such as to enable me to give those recollections with certainty.

    Susanna Wright was the daughter of John Wright, Esq. a very intelligent and upright man, and one of the first settlers in Lancaster County; she came over with her parents from Warrington, in Great Britain, in 1714, being then about seventeen. She had received a good education, and having an excellent understanding, she assiduously cultivated her fine talents, notwithstanding the disadvantages of her situation. Her parents first settled at Chester, but a short time afterwards removed to the banks of the Susquehannah, then a most remote frontier settlement, in the midst of Indians, subject to all the inconveniences, labours, privations, and dangers of an infant establishment; here she exerted herself continually for the good of her family and the benefit of her neighbours; nor did she ever quit this retirement for the more improved society of Philadelphia but twice, when the danger of their situation from an Indian war rendered this removal necessary for their safety. She never married; but after the death of her father became the head of her own family, who looked up to her for advice and direction as to a parent; for her heart was replete with every kind affection, and with all the social virtues. She was well acquainted with books, had an excellent memory, as well as a most clear and comprehensive judgment; she spoke and wrote the French language with great ease and fluency; she had also a knowledge of Latin, and of Italian, and had made considerable attainments in many of the sciences. Her letters written to her friends, were deservedly esteemed for their ingenuity. She corresponded with James Logan, Isaac Norris, and many other celebrated characters of that period; and so great was the esteem in which she was held by her neighbours, for integrity and judgment, that disputes of considerable interest were frequently left to her sole arbitration by the parties concerned. Her advice was often desired on occasions of importance respecting the settlement of estates, and she was often resorted to as a physician by her neighbourhood. The care and management of a large family, and of a profitable establishment, frequently devolved entirely upon her; and she appeared to be so constantly occupied with the employments usual to her sex and station, that it was surprising how she found time for that acquaintance with polite literature which her conversation displayed, when she met with persons capable of appreciating it.

She took great delight in domestic manufacture, and had constantly much of it produced in her family. For many years she attended to the rearing of silk worms, and with the silk which she reeled and prepared herself, made many articles both of beauty and utility, dying the silk of various colours with indigenous materials; she had at one time upwards of sixty yards of excellent mantua returned to her from Great Britain, where she had sent the raw silk to be manufactured. She sometimes amused herself with her pencil, and with little works of fancy; but it was in the productions of her pen that she most excelled: they were deservedly admired whilst she lived, and would abundantly satisfy the world of her merit could they now be produced; but as she wrote not for fame she never kept copies, and it is to be feared but little is at this time recoverable. Her character appears to have been without vanity, and above affectation.

I had the pleasure, when very young, of seeing her, and can remember something of the vivacity and spirit of her conversation, which I have since heard some of the best judges of such merit affirm they had seldom known to be equalled.

She lived to be upwards of eighty, preserving her senses and faculties. She had been educated in the religious society of Friends, and often in her latter years professed, that she saw the vanity of all attainments that had not for their object the glory of God and the good of mankind. She died a most humble, pious, sincere christian.

In her person she was small, and had never been handsome, but had a penetrating, sensible countenance, and was truly polite and courteous in her address and behaviour. Her brother, James Wright, was for many years a representative for Lancaster county in the assembly of Pennsylvania, and was deservedly esteemed by his fellow citizens. His descendants still possess the estate where their ancestors settled, upon which they have recently founded the flourishing town of Columbia.

NOTES

1. Henry Graham Ashmead, *Historical Sketch of Chester, on Delaware* (Chester, PA: Republican Steam Printing House, 1883), pp. 75–76.
2. Now in the Historical Society of Pennsylvania.
3. See also *Publications of the Pennsylvania Society of Colonial Dames of America*, no. 2 (1906), pp. 5–8.

GENEALOGICAL CHART

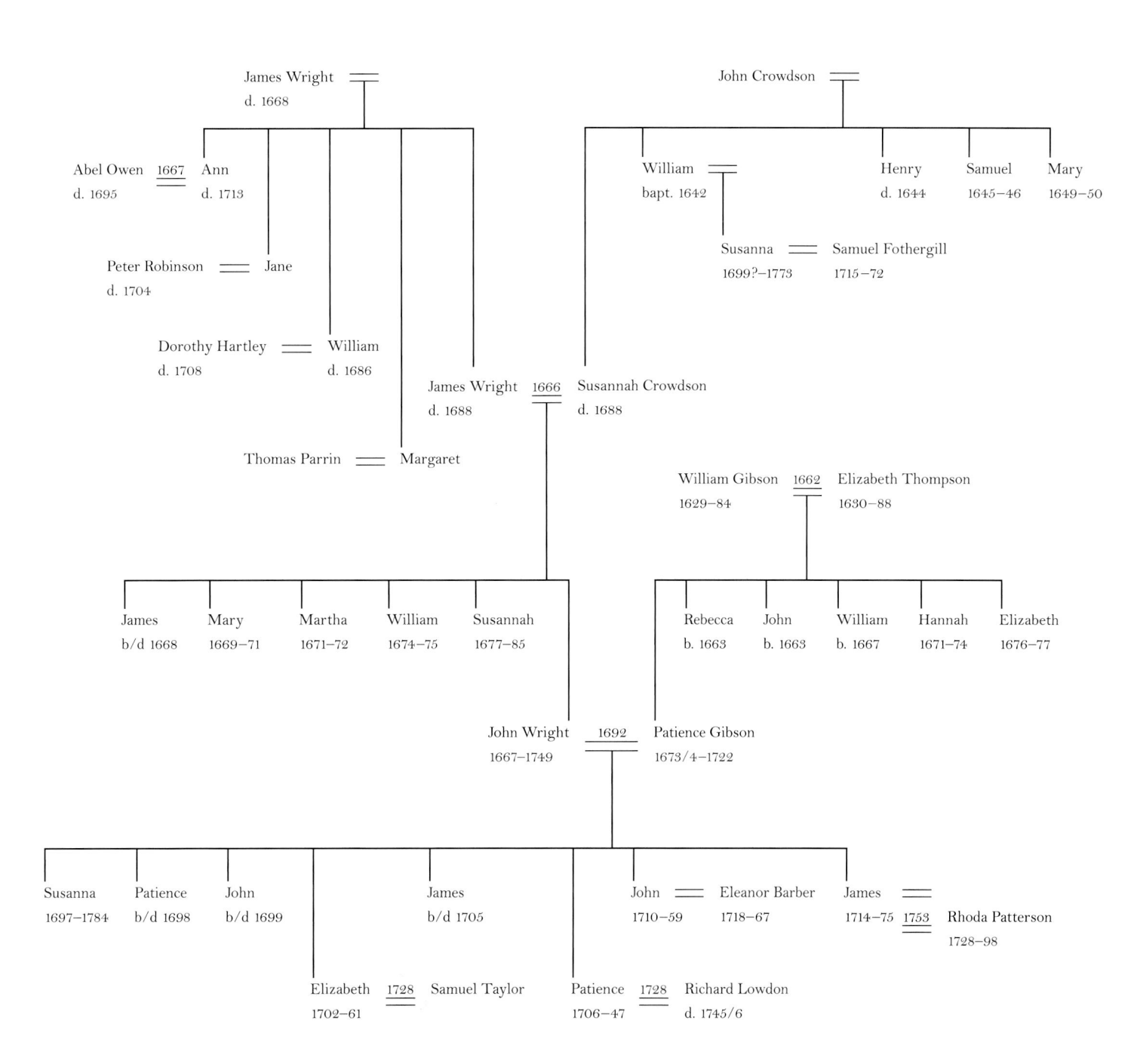

```
                James Wright                                                          John Crowdson
                  d. 1668                                                                  
        ┌───────────┬──────────┬──────────┐                    ┌─────────────┬──────────┬──────────┐
Abel Owen  1667  Ann                                       William              Henry     Samuel      Mary
 d. 1695         d. 1713                                   bapt. 1642           d. 1644   1645–46    1649–50
                                                              │
Peter Robinson  Jane                                    Susanna    Samuel Fothergill
 d. 1704                                               1699?–1773      1715–72

Dorothy Hartley  William
 d. 1708         d. 1686
                                James Wright   1666   Susannah Crowdson
                                  d. 1688              d. 1688

        Thomas Parrin  Margaret                          William Gibson   1662   Elizabeth Thompson
                                                            1629–84                  1630–88

  James     Mary     Martha    William   Susannah         Rebecca   John    William   Hannah   Elizabeth
 b/d 1668  1669–71  1671–72   1674–75   1677–85           b. 1663  b. 1663  b. 1667  1671–74   1676–77

                            John Wright   1692   Patience Gibson
                             1667–1749            1673/4–1722

Susanna    Patience   John        James          John    Eleanor Barber    James           Rhoda Patterson
1697–1784  b/d 1698  b/d 1699   b/d 1705        1710–59    1718–67        1714–75  1753       1728–98

                    Elizabeth   1728   Samuel Taylor     Patience   1728   Richard Lowdon
                     1702–61                              1706–47           d. 1745/6
```

279

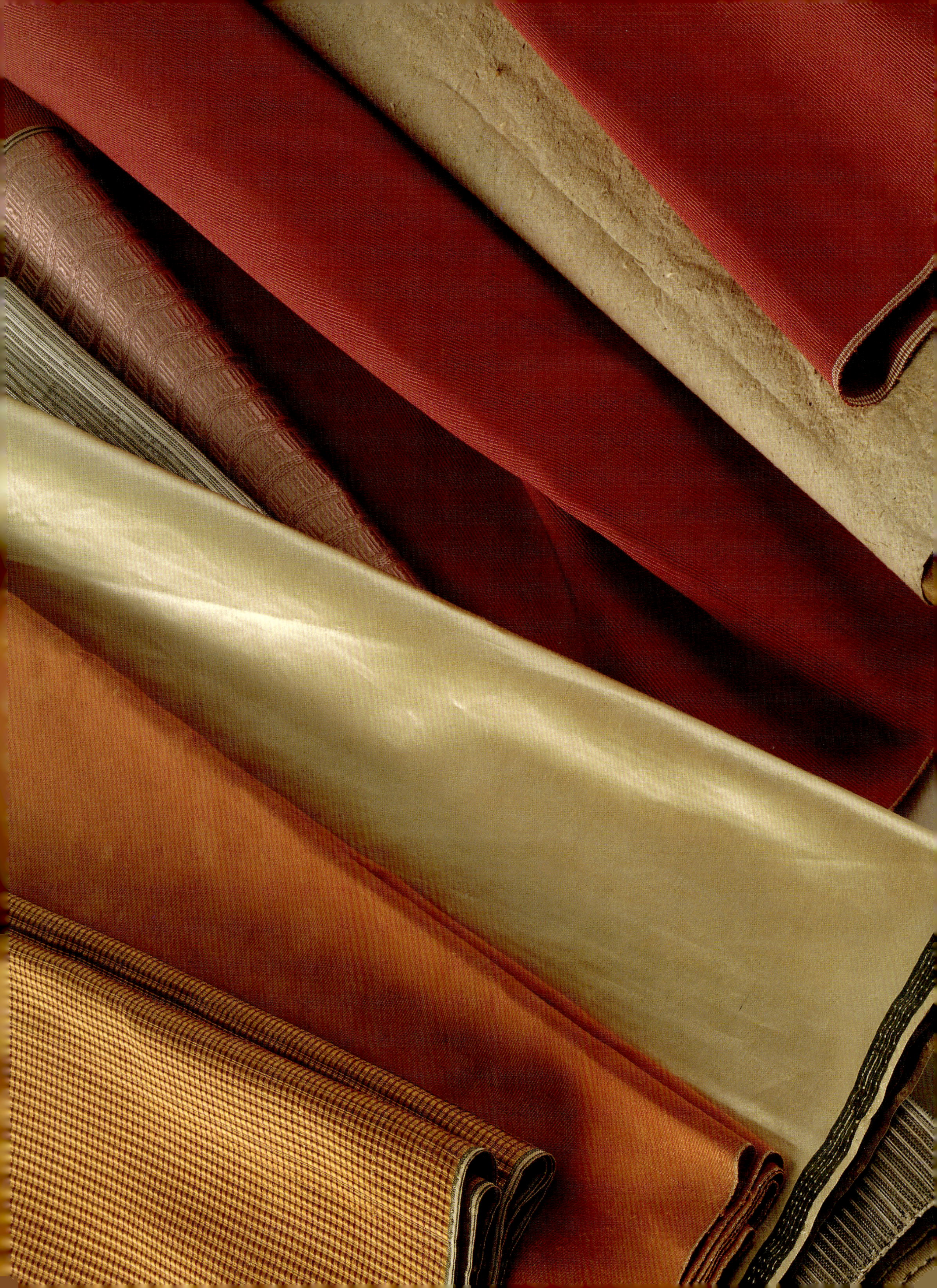

SUSANNA WRIGHT'S TREATISE ON THE RAISING OF SILKWORMS

Directions for the management of Silk-Worms[1]

Lay the sheets of eggs in folds of dry ironed linen, in a drawer, in a room where but little fire is kept. As soon as the mulberry-buds begin to open into leaves in the spring, we should bring the sheets of eggs into a warm room, and lay them in a south window, where the sun may shine through the glass upon them. We may, perhaps, do this several days before they begin to hatch; but, notwithstanding this, when we lay them by, we should not return them into a cool room.

    As soon as the worms appear, pick the small mulberry leaves from the tree, and lay them, with the under sides downwards, upon the sheets of eggs, in those places particularly where they have already hatched; and the worms will immediately begin to eat. As the leaves fill with the worms, take them up carefully, and lay them on a sheet of clean paper, which should be perfectly dry, and apply fresh leaves. The greater part of those worms, which hatch in a day, come out before evening; and we should be cautious to keep the hatchings of every day upon separate papers, that they may be prevented from intermixing with each other; and, indeed, during the whole time of their feeding, we should strictly adhere to this caution; for as the worms moult at certain periods from the time of their hatching, the sick among them would be liable to communicate the infection to the others, and thus create infinite trouble.

Whenever we intend to clean them, we should, as before, lay fresh leaves over them, and when they have pretty generally come upon them; remove the leaves upon clean sheets of paper, and brush and dry the other sheets for the next remove: it sometimes happens, that a few of the worms do not come upon the leaves; these should be taken up with a large needle.

The silk-worm casts its skin four times during the time of feeding; and at the first moulting, which is a week, or perhaps longer, from its hatching, is very small. Previous to this, the worms lie in a manner torpid, with their heads erect, and are averse from food; but, perhaps, a few of them, not so forward as the rest, may require food longer, and therefore here and there we may lay a few leaves for them; but at these times we should take care not to meddle with them at all, for when they moult they do it best by their skins sticking among their litter, by which means they creep out of them with more ease, and we should observe this through all their four moultings. After this, they eat more voraciously than before, and the better they are fed, the sooner they will spin, and make the richer cocoons; but we ought to be particularly careful when we give them the leaves, that they be free from moisture of every kind, and we should secure them from cats, rats, mice, and ants; a smaller species of this last, which is very common in Pennsylvania, is peculiarly destructive to the silk-worm.

If our worms have been accustomed to a room warmed by either a chimney or stove, and a cool rainy season should come on, it would be proper to warm the room moderately in such weather; otherwise they will be liable to droop and grow languid. When they are ready to spin, they look clear, and their skins shine; they leave their food, and begin to ramble in search of convenient places, which should be ready prepared for them. A variety of contrivances may be found for this purpose. None are more neat than paper cones; but as it is not practicable to make use of these for any very considerable number of worms, without some expence and trouble, we may procure old trunks or boxes, which we should stick full of small bushes, stript of their leaves, and so disposed that the worms can conveniently fix their threads to them. Sometimes, however, they are inclined to ramble about, and waste their silk: in this case, it will be necessary to secure them in paper cones.

In a week and one day after the worms have certainly begun to spin, we may take them down, and strip off the refuse silk, that is, such as is loose upon the cocoons, and also what we find among the bushes, &c. Whatever quantity of cocoons we mean to preserve for *seed*, should be strung upon long threads, and suspended, with papers behind them, over a table, or laid upon sheets of paper upon a table, upon which the worms will come out, and lay their eggs.

It will be proper to preserve an equal number of the round and long cocoons, as it is said these different shaped cones are each the produce of the two sexes. Such of the cones as are kept for winding, should be laid in sieves covered closely with thick cloths, and placed over kettles of boiling water, in order that the steam may penetrate the balls, and thus destroy the worms; or they may be placed in vessels in ovens after the bread is taken out. The former of these methods is, however, the best, as the steam is not so liable to harden the gum, as the application of heat in a dry form. Those balls, where two worms have spun together, will not wind: these should be cut open and boiled, with the refuse silk above-mentioned, in soap and water, until they open, and become as soft as cotton; it may then be spun out of the hand upon a wheel, but can never be carded.

NOTES

1. Published in the *Philadelphia Medical and Physical Journal*, Volume I, no. XXVIII (1804): 103–107, with the heading: "By the late Mrs. S. Wright of Lancaster-County, in Pennsylvania. It is not supposed, that this paper contains much information that is entirely new to those who have directed their attention to the subject to which it relates. But, as it may be useful, it is here presented to the public. The author was a woman of uncommon powers of mind, and directed much of her attention to the management of silkworms, and to other subjects of public utility, at a time (at least forty years ago) when she stood alone in her exertions in this way. It is to be observed, that the silkworm upon which Mrs. Wright made her experiments, was the foreign worm; and not any of the native species of North-America. These Directions are printed from a MS. account, which was found among the papers of the Editor's Father, the Reverend Mr. Thomas Barton, of Lancaster."

THEATRUM
BOTANICUM,
THE THEATER
OF PLANTES.
OR
An Universall and Compleate
HERBALL.

Composed by John Parkinson
Apothecarye of London, and the
Kings Herbarist.

LONDON.
Printed by Tho: Cotes.
1640.

ADAM.   SOLOMON.

JAMES WRIGHT'S TREATISE ON HOPS AND HEMP GROWING

The most proper Land for raising Hemp is a rich and light soil, free from Ponds and stagnated Waters. This should be broken up in the Fall of the year, which will greatly contribute to meliorate ye soil, and to render ye Spring Tillage more effectual. It should be twice plow'd in the Spring; the second Time, just before the seed is to be sow'd, which seeding should be done betwixt ye Beginning & Middle of May, though perhaps that season may prove rather too early to the Eastward or Northward of this Province, as the young Hemp cannot bear Frost, if any should happen after it appears above ground; neither should it be sown while the land is very moist, but with us it is generally sufficiently dried by that Time. To every Acre of Land we allow one Bushel and one peck of good, clean seed, of ye last year's growth; for seed that has been kept longer, however good in its kind, will never yield a Crop. We then harrow it in Smooth & well. We have observed, if heavy Rain fall a Day or two after Seeding, they sodden the Ground, and injure the future growth of ye Plant; if that should happen, we run the Harrow again lightly over it, as soon as it is sufficiently dry, provided we can be certain by examining some of the seed in the Ground, that it has not begun to sprout; but if we find that to be ye case we let it lie as ye Rain has left it. Nothing more is to be done, 'till the Hemp becomes fit for pulling. There are what appear to be two Sorts of Hemp, growing promiscuously together in ye same Field; one (improperly perhaps) distinguished by the Name of the Male & the other of Female Hemp. The first produces the Hemp we sow, the other bears a Blossom, & afterwards a Farina, that flies like a Dust over the Whole Field, after which it turns Yellow, and begins to shed its Leaves. At this Time we pull it altogether & beat ye soil clean from ye Roots of every Armful before it is laid down, taking care, in doing this, not to break ye Stalks, which would greatly injure it. Then spread it as thin over ye Ground on which it grew as the Space of Ground will admit of, every man taking a Breadth of Land to pull, equal to the Length of his Hemp, and laying it Length-Ways across the Ground he has pull'd it from. We are told, it is usual, in some neighbouring Provinces, to cut their Hemp with Instruments close to Ye Root, instead of pulling it; but this Method we disapprove, & is never practis'd with us. It should lie in this Manner a week, or a longer or shorter space, Till we find it dry, When we gather it up straight, & bind it with a few stalks of ye short Hemp in small Sheaves as thick as a Man's Thigh, striking ye Bottom of ye Roots against ye Ground to straighten them still more, and pushing the Band downwards, to tighten them.

We then set 15 or 20 of these Sheaves with their Heads pointing together, so as to support each other, in kind of Shocks, & let them stand a Day or two, except we are satisfied that they were very dry when we took them up, & then the Trouble of Shocking may be omitted. In either of these Cases, we House the Hemp, if we have Convenience, or build it up in long Stacks or Ricks, with ye Buts or Roots all outward, taking Care from ye Bottom to keep the Middle of the Stacks or Ricks the highest, & building them so as they shall widen gradually from the Bottom to the Top. The Stacks or Ricks are then to be thatch'd or covered to a considerable Thickness with straight Rye Straw, well secur'd upon them. Great care must be taken in covering these Ricks, so as there be no Danger of taking in Rain, as that would extremely damage ye Hemp. It is to stand in these Stacks or Ricks 'till ye Beginning or Middle of November, except it should have lain Abroad in a rainy season before it was first gathered up; and in that Case we let it stand in Stack a Week longer. We then spread it in even Rows upon any sort of Grass-Ground, which is not subject to be overflowed in the Winter; the thinner it is spread the better, as by that means it waters more equally. Not any kind of Creatures should be suffer'd to enter ye Fields where it lies, to tread and tangle it, & there it must lie 'till it shall be sufficiently Water'd, which generally is about the Beginning of March. But this can only be ascertained by setting up a few Handfuls against a Fence, to have it thoroughly dry, & trying it in a Break. And this Trial should be made from Time to Time, when the Watering is nearly completed, At which Time the Stalk or Hex will shake clean out, & the Rind or Harl remain strong. Great Care should be taken in breaking, to keep the Hemp straight, & not ruffle it, as by that Means it cleans with more ease & to greater Perfection, so as to be fit for a Market, for we never use any Swingle, or other Means of that kind, but twist it up from ye Break in Handfuls, & pack it in tight Bundles or Bales of 100 or 150 Pounds each.

We esteem those Winters most favourable to our Hemp, when the Snowfalls soon after it is spread, & lies till near the Time of taking it up, as the Hemp is more equally watered, and better colored, than in variable Weather, and much Rain, when the Watering is often compleated at a season of the year when the Weather is too precarious for either drying, if wet, or cleaning it. But when it is fit for the Break, about the Beginning of March, & ye Weather favourable, we take it up & set it in large shocks, without Binding, & break it in the Field without even housing; and this, where there are a sufficient Number of Hands, is the most expeditious Method. Where the crop is large, there should be 15 or 20 Hands at Work in ye Field at once, in order to get it out of the way when the Ricks are broke, before bad Weather comes on. Each man is to have his Break, which is no great Expense, as those Machines may be made for about 5s. apiece, & will last 5 years, if taken Care of. But if a sufficient Number of Hands cannot be got, we bind it in large Sheaves. With Bands of Rye-Straw, and house or stack it, taking great care to secure it from Rain, 'till we have Leisure to clean it. The Land with us, while it is fresh, or old Fields that have lain long untill'd & old Upland Meadows, sufficiently broken up by repeated Plowings, will yield from 6 to 700 Weight an acre, & sometimes much more; thinner or poorer Land made very rich with Manure, will often produce from 900 lb to 1000 lb weight. Upon the last mentioned sort of Land, 2 Bushels of seed may be allowed to an Acre, and the Hemp Will grow up regularly & mostly to an equal Height; if that Quantity of seed was sown upon Land naturally rich. Part of ye Crop would push up a great Height & Strength, overtop & smother all the rest. Planting the seed, or sowing it with a Drill-Plow, can only be of Service Where seeds is not readily to be procured, & by this Method (of which we prefer planting in Hills 3 feet apart) the Hemp will branch out, & become a little Tree, which affords a large Quantity of seed. One of these Trees will often Yield a Peck. When the seed is ripe, cut ye Stalk, or pull it, and when it is dry, thresh it upon a Winnow-Sheet, spread on the Grass, as threshing on a Barn Floor would bruise & injure the seed. We formerly procured seed by planting, but now we leave straggling on large Stalks standing near Fences, or single, and find sufficient seed from them for our Use. When this is threshed out it must be cleaned in such a Manner as the light white seed may be blown away with ye Chaff, & then laid thin, where it may have Air, or it will heat & become of no value.

Several Methods have been tried in these Parts for expeditiously breaking & cleaning Hemp both by Machines of the Mill Kind, & coarse & fine Breaks, But after many accurate Trials, and by a large Experience, they have all given Way to one simple Break of a particular Construction, which is now everywhere adopted in this Province, & in general Use. This Machine was first invented & made Use of in this county. By this one Man does what he calls rough break or crackle in the Hinder Part of it, & cleans and finishes ye Working in ye Fore Part, and all Without laying the Hemp out of his Hand. With this Break a New Beginner will clean about 50 Pounds of Hemp in one Day, but those who are acquainted with this Employment will clean, fit for the market, above 100 Pounds every day.

Method of Growing Hops

The best Soil for Hops is that which is light, deep, rich & a little Sandy. The Ground is to be broke up in ye Fall, that it may be meliorated by the Winter Snows. In the Month of March it is to be well plow'd again, & cleared of all Grass, Weeds & Roots, and every lump, or Clod, broke fine with a heavy Harrow or Spade. In this Month we begin to plant, marking out where each Hillock or Plantation is to be. We generally plant in Squares, Checquer-Wise, for ye Convenience of Plowing between the Hills. When ye Ground is Marked out we then begin to make a large Square Hole at each Mark at ye Distance of 10 Feet from each other; and having chosen the largest and best roots or Sets, with 3 or 4 Joints to each Set, we plant a set in each Corner of ye Hole, that is, 4 Sets in each Hole, throwing in a fine Compost of rotten Dung & Mould mixed together & prepared on purpose, & then raising ye Earth 2 or 3 Inches high about them. When the Hop Ground begins to get old, & to lose its Fertility, we dig about ye Roots, claw away ye old Soil, & supply them with New Hills of fresher and fatter Earth. When the Roots branch out luxuriantly & become to thick and crowded in the Hill, they must be laid bare in ye Fall, & all the Fibres & small young Roots prun'd away. As soon as the Hops begin to appear above Ground they are to be Poled. Two poles to a Hill are enough. Let them be strong,

& about 12 Feet high. To prevent ye Hops from what they call Housling, the Poles are to be set deep, taking Care not to injure ye Roots in setting them; and leaning outward towards ye South, to give the Plants ye full Warmth of the Sun. When they have sprung up 2 or 3 Feet above ye Ground, they are then to be gently conducted by the Hand to ye Pole, & tied with a soft straw or woolen yarn, but not close, which would prevent their Climbing. In ye Month of May, after a little Rain, the Ground is to be plow'd between ye Hills, in order to render it kind & mellow & to destroy ye weeds; the Hills at ye same Time are to be dress'd with a Hoe. If the Season should prove too dry, let them be Watered 2 or 3 times. About ye Middle of August the Hops are fit for gathering. Their Ripeness is known by their strong Fragrance, by being easily pull'd, by their changing their Hue to a Yellowish Cast, & by ye Seed turning a little brownish. At this Time they are to be gathered when they are neither Wet by Dew or Rain. They are to be cut close to ye Hill, the Poles pulled up carefully, & carried, with their Load of Vines about them, to ye Place of picking. Here a Frame is made by laying 4 short Poles on 4 Forks driven into ye Ground, so as to represent a Square. To These Poles a large Winnow-Sheet, Blanket or Hair Cloth is to be tacked by the Edges, so as to bag down like a Hammock. On the Edge of this Frame ye Poles, with the Hops on them, are to be laid. The Pickers are to stand at each side & pick ye Hops into ye Cloth put on ye Frame in its Place. As fast as they are picked they must be dried, which is done in a Hair-Cloth on a common Malt-Kiln, with Char-Coal made of Hickory, Care being taken to prevent the Smoke from passing through them, by conveyances made for it at ye Corners & Sides of ye Kiln. The Hops must be carefully turn'd with a kind of Shovels made of Tin, which, if handled well, will not bruise or injure them. When they are sufficiently dry, spread them about a Foot thick on a dry Board Floor, & there let them remain 3 or 4 weeks to toughen.

 Take Care that no Cats, Rats, Mice or any other vermin get among them, which will soon damage them. After they have lain thus to toughen, the next thing is to bagg them, which is done in this Manner: Cut a Hole in an upper Floor large enough for a Man to pass thro' with Ease; Then tack a strong Hoop about ye Mouth of the Hop-Bag, which is generally made of strong Oznabrigs, & something like a Wool-Pack. Let this Bag down through ye Hole, so that it may be supported by the Hoop above, well-fasten'd to it with Pack thread. Throw in a few Hops, which are to be tied at each lower Corner, with a Piece of Pack thread, to make as it were a Kind of Tassel, which serves as a Handle to lift or remove ye Bag when full. A man is then to go into ye Bag & tread ye Hops on every side, another still throwing in as fast as requir'd it be full. When that is ye Case, let ye Bag down by ripping off ye Hoop. Then sow up ye Mouth of ye Bag & tie some Hops in ye upper corner, as you did in the lower.

The Hops are now fit for Market & have been generally sold at Philadelphia at one shilling per Pound, or £5 per Hundred. An Acre of Hops in this County, if well attended, will produce from 15 to 20 cwt., which is near £100 raised from One Acre of Ground. What an immense Profit would rich Land in America yield to ye Planter of Hops, were he permitted to send them to Ireland, where they are often sold at 2l6 Sterling per Pound! In all ye Employments of Agriculture, there is scarce any Thing, which, under proper Management, yields more Advantage, or, perhaps, Amusement, than the Culture of Hops. See a fine Poem, Called ye Hop-Garden, written by Mr. Smart, where all ye Diversions & of the Hop-Gatherers are elegantly and humorously displayed.

N.B.—The above Method is pretty similar to that in England, only alter'd to ye Soil & Climate of Pennsylvania.

Published in the *Lancaster County Historical Society Journal*, vol. IX, no. 9 (1905): 285–93 and published here with kind permission from the Lancaster County Historical Society.

Watering Pot, England, Holland or France, 1690–1750, copper, iron.

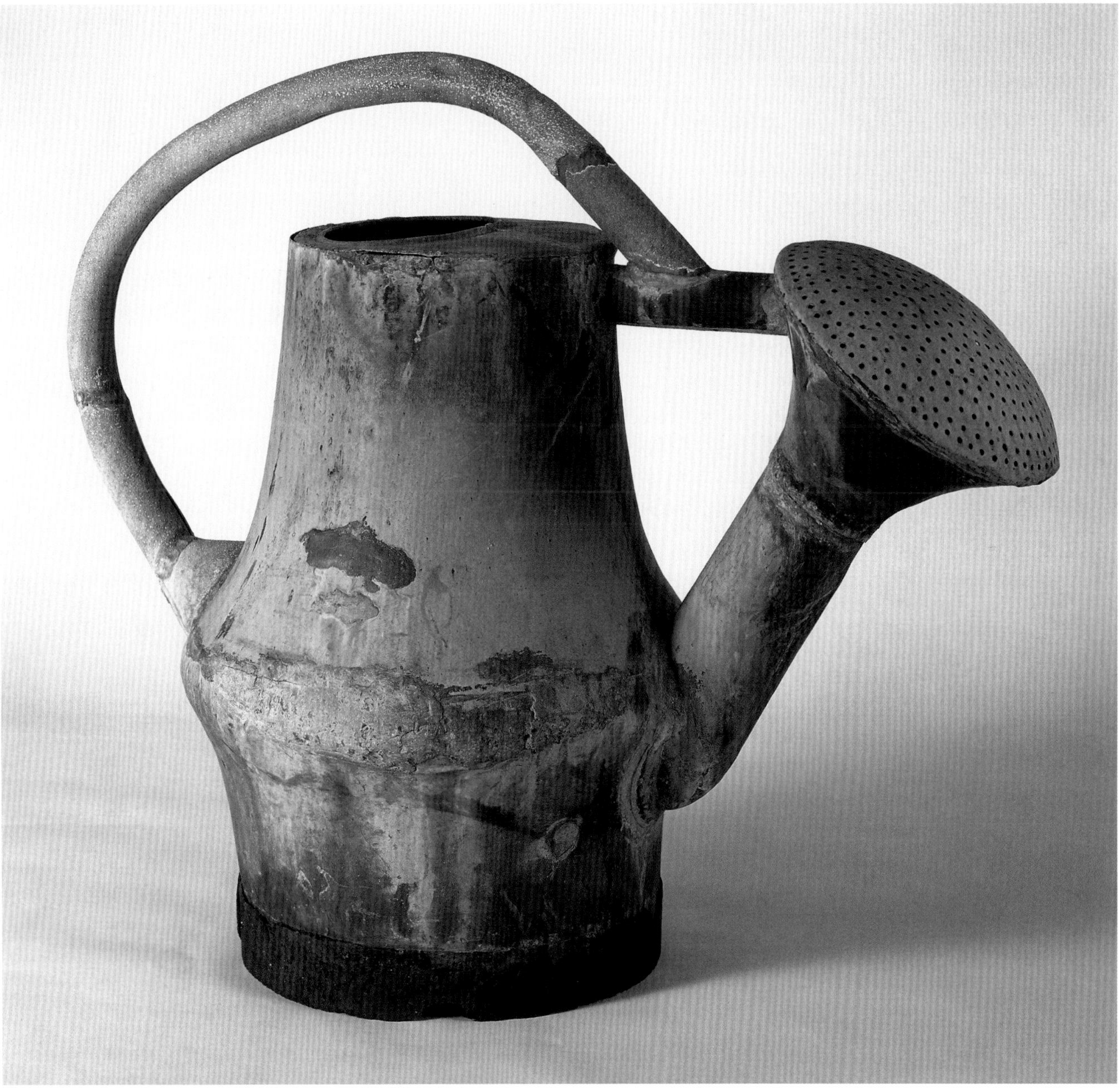

LEO

Crater,
Poculū Apollinis

SELECTED BIBLIOGRAPHY

Arnold, I. C. "Samuel Blunston—The Public Servant." *Proceedings of the Lancaster County Historical Society Journal* 26 (1922): 195–204.

Ashmead, Henry Graham. *Historical Sketch of Chester, on Delaware*. Chester, PA: Republican Steam Printing House, 1883.

Barber, Edwin Atlee. *Genealogy of the Barber Family*. Philadelphia: William F. Fell & Co., 1890.

Bell, Whitfield J., Jr. *Patriot Improvers: Biographical Sketches of Members of the American Philosophical Society*. Vol. 2. Philadelphia: American Philosophical Society, 1997.

Bell, Whitfield J., and Leonard W. Labaree. "Franklin and the 'Wagon Affair,' 1755." *Proceedings of the American Philosophical Society* 101 (1957).

Brumbaugh, G. Edwin. "The Architecture of the Wright Mansion." Unpublished manuscript, 1981.

Brunskill, R. W. *Houses and Cottages of Britain: Origins and Development of Traditional Buildings*. London: The Orion Publishing Group, 2000.

Butterfield, L. H. "Rush's Trip to Carlisle, 1784." *Pennsylvania Magazine of History and Biography* 74 (1950).

Cope, Gilbert. *Genealogy of the Sharpless Family from John and Jane Sharpless*. Westchester, PA: Dando Printing Co., 1887.

Cowell, Pattie. *Women Poets in Pre-Revolutionary America, 1650–1775, An Anthology*. Troy, NY: Whitson Publishing Co., 1981.

Dallett, F. J. "Certain Pennsylvania Settlers." *American Genealogist* 41, no. 4 (October 1965).

Ellis, Franklin, and Samuel Evans. *History of Lancaster County, Pennsylvania*. Philadelphia: Evarts and Peck, 1883.

Eshleman, H. Frank. "Cresap's War—The Lancaster County Border Struggle." *Proceedings of the Lancaster County Historical Society Journal* XIII, no. 9 (1909): 237–54.

Eshleman, H. Frank. "The Public Career of John Wright, Esq." *Proceedings of the Lancaster County Historical Society Journal* XIV, no. 9 (1910): 251–82.

Frost, J. William. *The Quaker Family in Colonial America*. New York: St. Martin's Press, 1973.

Heiges, George L. "Benjamin Franklin in Lancaster County." *Proceedings of the Lancaster County Historical Society Journal* LXI, no. 1 (1957): 3–10.

Hindle, Brooke. *The Pursuit of Science in Revolutionary America, 1735–1789*. Chapel Hill, NC: University of North Carolina Press, 1956.

Hostetter, Albert K. "The Early Silk Industry of Lancaster County." *Proceedings of the Lancaster County Historical Society Journal* XXIII, no. 2 (1919): 27–37.

Kalm, Peter. *Travels in North America*. 2 vols. Translated by John Reinhold Forster. Barre, MA: Imprint Society, 1972.

Kent, Barry C., Janet Rice, and Kakuko Ota. "A Map of 18th Century Indian Towns in Pennsylvania." Reprinted from *Pennsylvania Archaeologist* 51, no. 4 (1981).

Kent, Barry C. *Susquehanna's Indians.* Harrisburg, PA: Pennsylvania Historical Society and Museum Commission, 1989.

Korey, Marie Elena. *The Books of Isaac Norris (1701–1766).* Carlisle, PA: Dickinson College, 1976.

Labaree, Leonard Woods, William Bradford Willcox, Claude-Anne Lopez, Barbara B. Oberg, and Ellen R. Cohn, eds. *The Papers of Benjamin Franklin.* 37 Vols. New Haven, CT: Yale University Press, 1975.

Lindsey, Jack L. *Worldly Goods: The Arts of Early Pennsylvania 1680–1758.* Philadelphia: Philadelphia Museum of Art, 1999.

Logan, Deborah Norris. "Susanna Wright." *Analectic Magazine* V (1815): 250–52.

Lopez, Claude-Anne, and Eugenia W. Herbert. *The Private Franklin: The Man and His Family.* New York: W. W. Norton, 1985.

Myers, Albert Cook. *Quaker Arrivals at Philadelphia 1682–1750, Being a List of Certificates of Removal at Philadelphia Monthly Meeting of Friends.* Baltimore: Genealogical Publishing Co., 1969.

Proud, Robert. *The History of Pennsylvania in North America.* Philadelphia: Zachariah Poulson, Jr., 1798.

Publications of the Pennsylvania Society of Colonial Dames of America. Nos. 1 and 2 (1905–1906).

Ruthrauff, Albert F. "Report on the Restoration of Wright's Ferry Mansion." Unpublished manuscript, 1976.

Scharf, J. Thomas, and Thompson Westcott. *History of Philadelphia.* 3 Vols. (Philadelphia, 1884).

Sheppard, Walter Lee. "John Wright, Lancaster County, Pennsylvania." *American Genealogist* 40, no. 1 (January 1964).

Shirk, Jr., Willis L. "Wright's Ferry: A Glimpse into the Susquehanna Back Country." *Pennsylvania Magazine of History and Biography* 120: 61–67.

Thornton, Peter. *Seventeenth-Century Interior Decoration in England, France and Holland.* New Haven, CT: Yale University Press, 1983.

Tolles, Frederick Barnes. *James Logan and the Culture of Provincial America.* Westport, CT: Greenwood Press, 1957.

Tolles, Frederick Barnes. *Meeting House and Counting House: The Quaker Merchants of Colonial Philadelphia, 1682–1763.* 1948. Reprint, New York: W. W. Norton, 1963.

Tolles, Frederick B. "Susanna Wright." In *Notable American Women 1607–1950: A Biographical Dictionary*, edited by Edward T. James. Cambridge, MA: Belknap Press of Harvard University Press, 1971, pp. 688–90.

Watson, John Fanning. *Annals of Philadelphia and Pennsylvania.* 3 Vols. Philadelphia: E. S. Stuart, 1884.

Wolf 2nd, Edwin. *The Library of James Logan of Philadelphia, 1674–1751.* Philadelphia: The Library Company of Philadelphia, 1974.

Wood, Jerome H., Jr. *Conestoga Crossroads: Lancaster, Pennsylvania 1730–1790.* Harrisburg, PA: Pennsylvania Historical and Museum Commission, 1979.

Wright, James. "Hemp and Hop Growing in Lancaster County in 1775." *Proceedings of the Lancaster County Historical Society Journal* IX, no. 9 (1905): 285–93.

Wright, Samuel. "Hempfield: The Beginning of Columbia." *Proceedings of the Lancaster County Historical Society Journal* XVII, no. 8 (1913): 215–26.

Wright, Susanna. "Directions for the management of Silk-Worms." *Philadelphia Medical and Physical Journal* I, no. XXVIII (1804): 103–107.

Wright, Susanna. [Untitled Poem], *The Literary Magazine and American Register* 2 (1804): 191–92.

INDEX

Page numbers in **bold** type refer to illustrations.

account books
    bound by William Davies, **36,** 37, **38,** 39, 42, 45, 68 n.34, 70 n.98, 78, **104,** 134 n.8
    vellum portfolio, 125, 129, **228**
Addison, 199
agriculture, 60, **119,** 121, 145, 164, 176, 189, 200, 201, 285–90
    Indians and, 35
    See also crops; husbandry; orchards; silk
Alexander's Battle, 270
Allen, W., 147
almanacs, 87, 150
American Philosophical Society, 60
    and establishment of filature for silk processing, 51, 54, 70 n.96
American Society, 60, 70 n.96
Amherst, General, 52–53
ammunition, 157, 163
Anderson's Ferry, 47–48
andirons, 81, 82–83, 250, 252, 257
Anson, George, **85,** 269
    Voyage Round the World . . . , 263
ants, 282
Apequmeny, 141
apoplexy, 148
apothecary, 233
apples, 45, 46, 99
Archbishop Cambray, 262. *See also* Fénelon
Armitt, Sally, 22, 99
    letter to Susanna Wright (November 8, 1755), 155–56

Armitt, Samuel, 63, 246
Armitt, Stephen (cabinetmaker), 22, 63, 134 n.6, 246
army, 154, 156, 182–83
arrowhead, **38,** 39
astronomy, 123, **292**
Athaliah (Racine), 210
Atkinson, Samuel, 245
Atkinson, Susanah, 272
Azores, the, 27–28, **27**

bacon, 257
bags, 56, 289, 290
bake house, 156
Barber, Hannah, 246, 247
Barber, James, 254
Barber, Nathaniel, 69 n.57, 182, 184, 254
Barber, Robert, 35, 37, 43, 49, 50, 63, 69 n.51, 69 n.57, 251–53, 247
    inventory, 252–53
    servants to, 273
Barber, Sarah (daughter of Robert Barber, Jr., 43–44, 49, 96
Barber, Sarah Taylor (niece of Susanna Wright), 69 n.51, 96–97
Barber family, 19, 37, 48, 66, 69 n.57
barberry root, 113, 117
Barnes family, 30
barrels and kegs, 46, 253
Barton, Thomas, 283 n.1
Bartram, John, 60, 113
    letter from James Wright (August 22, 1762), 160–62
Bawsman, William, 155

Baxter, Andrew, *Enquiry into the Nature of the Human Soul, An*, 263
bayberry, 99, 150
Beale, George, 35
bears, 129, 181
beaufet, 249
bed coverings, 124–25, 128, 235, 241, 249
    blankets, 235, 248
    calimanco, 27, **124,** 125, 239
    palampore, **125,** 128
    quilts, 132, 248, 249
    sheets, 243, 248
    See also coverlets
beds, 26, 27, 43, **56,** 63, 233, 235, 241, 243, 248, 252, 257
    bed ticks, 240
    canopy for, 107
    chaff, 235
    curtains, 235, 241, 243, 248, 249, 257
    feather, 235, 241, 248
    hair mattress for, 257
    swinging, 63, 248
beer and ale, 27, 81, 106, 240
bees, 26, 243, 251
Belgioioso, Count Ludovico Barbiano di, 59
Benezet, Anthony, 17, 84
Bethel, Mary, 63, 247
Bethel, Samuel (I), 62–63, 271
Bethel, Samuel (II), 63, 64, 70 n.102, 88, 182, 229, 246–47, 253–54, 255
    inventory, 88, 91, 104, 253–54
Bethel, Sarah Blunston, 62–63, 246
Bethel, Susannah Taylor (niece of Susanna Wright), 63, 64, 65, 88, 91, 180, 255

295

Bethel family, 180, 271
Bible, books of, 143
   1 Corinthians, 190
   2 Corinthians, 203, 226 n.13
   Genesis, 195, 219
   Job, 203, 206, 226 n.13, 226 n.15
   Jonah, 194
   Matthew, 25, 194, 201, 225 n.5, 225 n.12
   Wisdom, 206, 226 n.15
Bible, Wright family, 25–26, 43
Bibles, 25, 26, 251–52, 254
birds, 28, 39, 96, 104, 141
Bishop, Lydia, 273
blacksmith, 255
Blaeu, J. and W. (globe makers), **27, 292**
Bland, Elias (London bookseller), 88
Blease, John and Margrett, 232
blood letting, 140, 148
Blue Rock, 69 n.53
Blundell, John, 234
Blunston, John and William, 62, 265
Blunston, Samuel, 19, 22, 35, 37, 45, 49,
   50–51, 60, 62–64, 75, 78, 134 n.8, 146,
   185 n.7, 189, 255, 256, 265, 271–73
   building of Lancaster courthouse, 37, 63
   house, 42, 43, 63–64, 75, 88, 93
   inventory, 63, 64, 91, 93, 248–51
   servants to, 273
   will, 49, 63, 245–47
Blunston, Sarah Bilton, 51, 62–63, 149,
   185 n.7, 246, 270, 271–72
boats, 47, 48, 254
Bohemia, 141
Boleyn, Ann, 195–98
bolsters, 56, 63, 235
bookbinders, 263
   Davies, William, **36,** 37, **38,** 263, 264
   Latscha, Abraham, 263
   Potts, Stephen, 263
books and reading, 20, 30, 64–65, **85,** 87,
   117–19, 123, **128,** 147, 150–51, 157,
   164–65, 186 n.21, 192, 227 n.28, **228,**
   235, 245, 250, 251, 254, 255, 257, 261–
   66, **267,** 269–70, 277, 277 n.28, **284**
Boreman, Thomas, **56, 57, 117**
   *Compendious Account of . . . Breeding . . .
   the Silk-Worm,* 117
Boston, 99
Boswell, James, *Account of Corsica . . . ,* 263
botanical works, 118, 119, 121, 123, 265, 284
botany, 121, 123. *See also* gardening
Boude, Col. Thomas, 66
boundary dispute with Maryland, 19, 35
bowls, 27, 75, **77,** 99, 240
Bown, John, 246
boxes, 53, 93, **122,** 123, 129, 233, 234, 235,
   249, 251, 253, 257, 258, 270, 282, 283
Braddock, General, 87, 152
brass, 68 n.38, 234, 238, 240, 243, 249, 250

Bray, Margaret (great-aunt of Susanna
   Wright), 230–31
bread, 53, 102, 148, 156, 166, 283
brewing pan, 27, 240
brickyard, 63
bridges, 47, 49, 66
Bright, Thomas, 28
Brown (widow), 272
Browne, Risley, 236
Brumbaugh, G. Edwin, 14, 21, 23, 75, 79,
   104–6, 112, 133, 135 n.50
brushes, 109, 148, 170, 235
Bucks County (Pennsylvania), 49, 67 n.12
buffalo, 161
Buffalo Valley (Pennsylvania), 49
burial practices, 270, 272
Burlington, 142
Burnet, Gilbert, 39
   *Abridgment of the History of the Reformation
   . . . ,* 263
   *Abridgment of the Third Volume of the
   History of the Reformation . . . ,* 263
bushes, 53, 282
bust of Homer, **188**
butcher, 244
buttery, 234
buttons, 27, 238, 239, 250

cabinetmakers, 102
   Armitt, Stephen, 22
   Moss, Isaac and Richard, 117
caddas, 240
Cadishead, near Warrington, England, 25,
   26, 241–44
Cadishwallhead, 230, 241, 243
calico, 63, 240, 248
calimanco, 27, **124,** 125, 239
Calverley, Richard, Esq., 230
Calvert, Lord (of Maryland), 35
candles, 99, 118, 150, 164, 169, 240
candlestand, **128**
candlesticks, 27, 99, 240, 250
cann, 26, 43, 241, 256
canoes, 49, 254, 257
Cape Henry, 141–42
Carlisle, 154, 167
Carolina Galley, 140–41
carpenters and joiners, 28, 78, 102, 134 n.6
carpets, use of, 81, 84, 128, 256–57
carriages, 169, 245, 250
carter, 244
Carter, Jeremiah, 28
carts, 252
cases, 128, 129, 249, 251, 270
casks, 99, 241, 252
caster, 256
Caton, England, 29
cattle, 26, 43, 45, 51, 64, 243, 246, 250, 252,
   253, 258

cellars, 43
cemetery, at Hempfield, 270–73
ceramics, 63, 234, 240, 249, 257
   Chinese export porcelain, **89,** 129
   English delftware, 75, 76–77, **88,** 104,
   105, 129
   salt-glazed wares, 88, **88,** 89, **90,** 104,
   105–106, 129
   shards, **89**
   slipware, 104, **105**
Chadeshead (Wright family home in
   Chester), 25, 28–29
chafing dish, 249
chairs, 27, 63, 81, 84, 94–95, 123
   caned, 109, **111**
   easy, 81, **82**
   ladder-back, 99, **100**
   ladder-back chamber chair, **122,** 123, 129
   panel-back, 75, 77, 125
   Queen Anne, 87, **116,** 117
Chalkley, Thomas, 31
chandler, 99
Chandler, Phoebe, 180
Charlotte, Queen, 52, 57–58, 60, **62**
Charrock, Margaret, 236
cheese, 243
   plate and ring, 249
Chekiang, China, 58
cherry, 44–46, 73, 78, 79
cherry fair, 46
Chesapeake, 19, 33
Cheshire, England, 156
Chester, Pennsylvania, 28, 29, 32, 35, 43, 75
Chester County, Pennsylvania, 37, 145, 170,
   225 n.4, 226, 262, 264, 271, 275, 276
chests, 26, **56,** 63, 235, 243, 249
chests of drawers, 88, 132, 241, 248, 249, 281
Chicaselungo, Lancaster Co., Pennsylvania,
   49, 50
Chickies Rock, 49–50, 69 n.59
china ware, 249, 257
chocolate, 63, 97, 249
Chubb, Thomas, *True Gospel of Jesus Christ
   Asserted,* 264
cider, 106, 254
Civil War, 66
Clively, Alexander, 243, 244
cloche (garden), **121**
clocks and watches, 26, 27, 43, 66, 91–93, **92,**
   144, 178, 187 n.27, 234, 240, 244, 249,
   250, 252, 253, 255, 256, 257
close cabin, 28
close stool and pan, 241
clothing, 43, 54, 56, 59, 60, 88, 109, 128, 129,
   156, 169, 180, 235, 238, 241, 244, 246,
   250–53, 256
clover field, 47
coat of arms (Wright), **26**
cobweb brush, 129

coffee, 97
coffeepot, 65, 255, 256
cold storage, 133
collector's cabinet, 112–13
Collier, 147, 262
Colombier, Claude Jordan de, *Voyages Historiques De L'Europe*, 262–63
Columbia, Pennsylvania, 35, 46, 47, 66, **71**, 186 n.22, 256, 264, 278
comet, observed by J. Logan, 123
Conegocheeg, 152
Conestoga, Pennsylvania (Indian settlement), 19, 31, 33, 35, 37, 129
Continental Congress, 275
conversation, 19, 84–85, 151
Cookson, Thomas, 63, 250
Cooper, Calvin, 258
Cope, Thomas P., 46
Cork (Ireland), 27, 140, 171
corks, 55
corn, 118, 121, 246, 254, 258
    raised by Indians, 35
    stalks used in silk production, 59
Corneille, 261
cotton, 61, 63, 117, 248, 251, 283
couch, 249
Coultas, Elizabeth, 136 n.62
counterpane, 248
courthouse (Lancaster Co.), 37, 63
courts of oyer and terminer, 151
coverlets, 63, 124–25, 248
Crane, John, 234
cream jug, 256
Cresap, Thomas, 69 n.53
crops
    barley, 251, 253–54, 258
    corn, 35, 254, 258
    hay, 252
    hemp, 60, 119, 251–53, 285–88
    hops, 60, 106, 119, 155, 252, 288–90
    oats, 251–52, 254, 257–58
    rye, 241, 251–52, 254, 258
    tobacco, 51, 235
    wheat, 241, 243, 246, 251, 254, 257–58
Cross Keys Tavern, 63
Croudson, genealogy, 279
Croudson, Susanna (cousin of Susanna Wright), 187 n.27
Croudson, Susannah (paternal grandmother of Susanna Wright), 25, 187 n.27, 279
Croudson, William (paternal great uncle of Susanna Wright), 91, 178, 187 n.27, 279
Croudson, William, Jr. (cousin of Susanna Wright), 27–28, 67 n.6
    letter from Susanna Wright (July 1, 1714), 16–17, 67 n.5, 140–42
cruet, 240
cucumber, 70 n.96
cupboards, 26, 243
cups, 240, 249

curtains
    bed, 235, 241, 243, 248, 249, 257
    window, 63, 81
cushions, 27, 234, 241
cutting box, 258

Darby, Pennsylvania, 35, 37, 63, 75
dates, method of recording, 67 n.2
Davies, Amelia, 66
Davies, William (bookbinder), **36**, 37, **38**, **104**, 263
Davis, George, 272
Davis, Robert, 186 n.22
de la Feuille, Jacob (globe maker), **27**
decanter, 256
deer, 33, 99, 162, 169
Delaware Bay, 141
delftware, 75, **76–77**, **88**, 123
Delure, Jean-Baptiste-Nicholas, 91, 93
desks, 27, 43, 63, 88, 241, 246, 250, 252, 254–55, 257
    scritoire, 63, 65, 246, 250, 252, 255
Deval, John, 37, 271
Dickinson, John, 64–65, 84, 184, 227 n.29, 255
Dickinson College, 64, 227 n.29, 263
diet, 148
dining room, use of term, 93
dining table, 256
dish board, 243
Disney, William, 265
distemper, 168, 179
distilling, 60, 70 n.98, 155, 170, 244
dogs, 53, 166
dolphins, 27, 140
dough trough, 250
drawing and painting, 123, 180, 198
dreams, 143
dresser, 240
dressing tables, 14, **108**, 109, 248
drowning, 140, 272
Dryden, John, 189
drying cloths, 167
Dunlap, Mr., 152, 158, 171
dyeing, 58, 113–17

earthenware, 104, 234, 249
East Indies, 56
East Jersey, 30
Eaton, Peter, 233
Eccles (England), 25
eggplant, 117
election, 166
English language, in Philadelphia, 84
engravings, 88, **268**
    from *Compendious Account of . . . Breeding . . . the Silk-Worm*, **56–57**, 117
    map of England by John Senex, **86**, 87
    ordered from London, 270
    Queen Charlotte, London (J. Smith), **62**
    St. James Park, London, by J. Kip, **52**
    six engravings by J. Kip, **268**

Epley, Peter, 49
escritoire. *See* scritoire
Evans, Cadwalader, 53–56, 58
Evans, Samuel, 68 n.38
Ewing, James, 48, 180
exercise, 148, 172, 180
eyesight, 168

fabrics, 26–27, 59, 60, 125, 132, 230, 237–40. *See also* silk, linen, etc.
Fairhill (Norris family home), 31, 78–79, 81, 163, 165, 170, 173, 176, 180, 190
farm equipment, 252, 253
fawn skin britches, 169
feather beds, 63, 235, 241, 248
Fells, John, 233
fences, 47
Fénelon, François de Salignaç de La Mothe-, 190, 226 n.25, 261, 262
ferries, 69 n.53
    Anderson's Ferry, 47–48, 69 n.53
    Cresap's Ferry, 69 n.53
    Wright's Ferry, 46–50, 65, 68 n.35. See also *separate entry for Wright's Ferry*
fertilizer, 287
Fhouse, Katherine, 273
filature, for silk processing, 51, 53–54, 56, 59–60
fire, 49, 75, 79, 281–83
fire arms, 240, 254, 257
fire buckets, 79
fireplace equipment, **82–83**, 234, 240–41, 249, 250, 252, 257
firewood, 47
fish, 27, 46, 96, 99, 135 n.37, 140
flats, for river travel, 48
Fleetwood, Robert, 233
flesh brush, 148, 170
floors, care of, 81
flour, 60, 62, 144, 152, 156
flowers, 23, 75, **76**, **104**, **105**
food and cooking, 96–102, 104, 164
Foles, William, 231
Fontanelle, 262
Ford, Thomas, 233, 237
forests, of Susquehanna area, 42, 43–44
Fothergill, Samuel and Susanna, 178–79, 187 n.27, 279
Fox, George, 190
Fox, Joseph, 184
fox hunting, 49
France, land claims of, 19, 35, 56. *See also* French and Indian War
Franklin, Benjamin, 46, 49–50, 69 n.59, 70 n.90, 84, 87, 99, 121, 128, 129, 139, 171, 185 n.61, 186 n.21, 189, 261, 266
    and silk industry, 53–60, 70 n.84
Franklin, Benjamin, correspondence, 19, 64
    letter to James Wright (June 26, 1755), 152–53

Index   297

Franklin, Benjamin, correspondence
  (continued)
  letter to Susanna Wright (November 21, 1751), 49–50, 150
  letter to Susanna Wright (July 11, 1752), 19, 150–51
  letter to Susanna Wright (April 28, 1755), 151–52
  letter from Susanna Wright (February 28, 1757), 157–58
Franklin, Deborah, 45, 60, 64, 99, 151, 171
  letter from Susanna Wright (undated), 45–46
  letter to Susanna Wright (July 14, 1757), 158–59
Franklin, Sally, 46, 60, 157–58
  letter to Susanna Wright (March 14, 1765), 171
Franklin, William, 156–57
Freebairn, *Life of Mary Stewart . . .* , 264
French and Indian War, 35, 62, 87, 99, 153–54, 156–57, 163
French language, 30, 36, 85, 139, 158, 262, 277
fruits, 33, 45–46, 53, 97, 164, 166
frying pans, 250
fuller's earth, 81
fur trade, 30, 128–29
furniture in the collection
  beds, 107, 109, **110**, 125, 132
  blanket chests, **122**, 123, 129
  candlestand, 109
  chairs, 75, **77**, 81, **82**, 87, 99, **100**, 109, **111**, **116**, 117, **122**, 123, 125, **126**
  chest of drawers, 132
  chest-on-chest, 129
  clocks, 91, **92**, 93, **112**
  daybed, 81, **83**
  desk-on-frame, 125, **127**, 129
  desks, **86**, 129, **260**
  high chest and dressing table, 14, **108**, 109, **115**, 117
  joint stool, 125, **127**, 129
  looking glasses, 81, **82**, **83**, 129
  schrank, **121**, 123
  shelves, **128**, 129
  tables, 75, **76–77**, 78, 87–88, 93, 99, **100–101**, 102, 109
  traveling chest, **115**, 117
furs and skins, 109, 128, 240

Gandye, William, 233, 234
gardening, 117–18, 121–23, 164, **290**
gardens, 46, 118, 121, 164, 255, 269
Garrigues, Rebecca Haydock, 59–60
Geffery, Commdr., 140
genealogical chart of Wright family, 279. *See also* Wright family
Gentleman's Magazine, 269
Georgia, 57, 58
Gerard, John, 231

German (Dutch) language, 152, 266
Germantown, Pennsylvania, 31, 75, 275
Gibson, Elizabeth (great-aunt of Susanna Wright), 30
Gibson, Elizabeth (maternal grandmother of Susanna Wright), 30, 279
Gibson, John (great-uncle of Susanna Wright), 30, 67 n.12
Gibson, William (maternal grandfather of Susanna Wright), 29–30, 67 nn.11–12, 279
Ging ("a Negro man"), 273
Glassbrooke, England, 242–43
glassware, 55, 93, **97**, 113, 234, 257
Glebe House, 75, 134 n.4, 135 n.43
globes, **27, 292**
Gloucester County, New Jersey, 186 n.22
Glover, Richard, *Leonidas. A Poem*, 264
"God is our Guide," 39
Gordon, Governor, 52
Gough, John, 29
gowns, 59, 60, 168
grate (fireplace), 234, 240–41
Greek language, 51, 189
griddle, 250
Griffitts, Hannah, 139, 170, 174, 175, 191, 226 n.26, 227 n.28
  letter from Susanna Wright (April 5, 1762), 159–60, 227 n.28
Griffitts, Marry Norris, 226 n.26
Griffitts, Thomas, 227 n.28
grist mill, on Shawnee Creek, 47, 60, 246
Gross, Michael
  letter to James Wright (October 30, 1755), 154–55

haberdasher, 30, 67 n.16
Haldeman's store, 49
Hall, Joseph, 272
Halley, Edmund, 123
Hand, Margrett, 236
Hamilton, Samuel, 184
Harrison, Hannah Norris, 226 n.26
Hart, Polly, 178
Hartley, Col., 64
Hartley, Ralph, 242
Hartley, Thomas, 230–31
Hartshaw, England, 29
hats, 27, 109, 240
Hayes, Patrick, 272
Hebrew language, 52, 261
hemp, 60, 119, 251–53
  James Wright's treatise on, 285–88
Hempfield, 19, 23 n.1, 49, 65, 84, 150, 151, 154, 184, 245, 251–54, 262, 269–71
Hendricks, Albert, 28
Hendricks, James (carpenter), 28, 134 n.6
Hendricks, John, 247
Henry VIII, 195–97
herbs, 81, 148, 149, 266

Herculas (a boy), 245
Herodotus, *History of Herodotus*, 264
Hey, Richard, 242
Hill, Richard, 35
Historical Review of the Constitution and Government of Pennsylvania . . . , 264
Historical Society of Pennsylvania, 190–91
hogs, 45, 129, 181, 252–54
Holme, Thomas, 30
Holmes, Thomas, 29
Homer, 182, 189
  bust of, **188**
honey, 148
hops, 60, 106, 119, 155, 252
  James Wright's treatise on, 288–90
Horace (Quintus Horatius Flaccus) (Roman poet), 143–44, 189, 255 n.1, 261
horses, 43, 47, 48, 148, 169, 245, 250–53, 258
  saddles and bridles, 252, 253, 258
Hoskins, Jane Fenn, 167–68, 186 n.22
Hoskins, Joseph, 186 n.22
Hoult, Thomas and Margaret, 244
Hughes, John, 184
human happiness, theme of, 142–44
hunters, 97
Hurst, William, 237, 241, 244
husbandman, 230, 241, 244
husbandry. *See also* agriculture
  book on, **119**, 121
  utensils of, 252–53
Hyble, 265
hybridization, 121

illness, 158, 163–66, 175, 179. *See also* medicine
  small pox, 51, 121–23, 163–64, 169, 180
illumination, 150, 168. *See also* candles
Indian corn, 59
indigo, 132
inoculation against small pox, 51, 121, 180
inventories and wills, 93, 134 nn.7–8, 229
  Barber, Robert, 252–53
  Bethel, Samuel (II), 88, 91, 104
  Blunston, Samuel, 63–64, 91, 93, 245–51
  Owen, Abel (great-uncle of Susanna Wright), 231–35
  Owen, Ann (great-aunt of Susanna Wright), 244–45
  Robinson, Peter (great-uncle of Susanna Wright), 235–41
  Wright, Dorothy (great-aunt of Susanna Wright), 241–44
  Wright, John (father of Susanna Wright), 91, 251–52
  Wright, Samuel (nephew of Susanna Wright), 123, 256–58
  Wright, Susanna, 22, 65, 254–56
  Wright, William (great-uncle of Susanna Wright), 230–31
Ireland, 186 n.22, 244, 290
iron, 155, 234, 240, 243, 250, 251, 253, 257

298 *Wright's Ferry Mansion*

ironing, 132
Italian language, 85, 139, 262, 277
Italian pound, 70 n.84
Ives, Hannah and Rebecka, 272
Ives, Thomas, 47

jars, 55
Jefferies (Jeffrys), Joseph, 47, 65, 256
Jersey Regiment, 154
John, Earl of Orrery, *Remarks on the Life and Writings of Dr. Jonathan Swift . . .*, 264
Johnson, Jemmy, 173
Jones, Owen, 81
Julian calendar, 139
justice of the peace, 30, 37, 186 n.22

Kagen, Isaac, 256
Kalm, Peter, 23, 45
Keatt, William (London silversmith), **26**
kettles, 53, 250, 257, 282
King, Andrew, 272
King of Portugal, 49
Kinsey, John, 252
Kip, John, engraving, **52**
kitchen
 of ferry house, 49
 of John Wright's house, 43
Kneller, Sir Godfrey, **62**
knife case and knives, 249

Ladd, James, 186 n.22
Lancashire, England, 25, 26, 28–30, 37, 48, 63, 65, 69 n.55, 74, 141, 156, 165, 230, 231, 234, 235, 237, 241–44
Lancaster, Pennsylvania, 37, 154, 167, 168, 177, 180, 183, 270
Lancaster County, Pennsylvania, 33–37, 179, 245, 253, 254, 256, 271, 276, 278, 283 n.1
Langhorne, Jeremiah, 35
Languedocian hired for filature, 56
Lankester, Ellin, 244
Latin-English Dictionary, 264–65
Latin language, 52, 85, 118, 139, 189, 262, 277
Latscha, Abraham (bookbinder), 263
leather, 55, 63, **115,** 117, 128, 129, 169, 248–59
Leigh, G. and J., 243
lemons, 97
Leyden, 118
libraries, 31, 121, 123, 261–67
library, of Susanna Wright, 20, **85,** 261–**67**
Library Company of Philadelphia, 189, 262
lighting. *See* illumination
lightning, 49
linen, 26, 53, 63, 88, 109, 123, **128,** 129, 132, 232, 240, 241, 243, 248, 251, 252, 254, 281
linen draper, 26, 59, 242
Linnaeus (Carl von Linné), 118, 121

literature. *See* books and reading
Litherland, Matthew, 242, 244
Liverpool, England, 25, 26, 27, 140, 141, 230–37, 242, 244
Livesy, Edmund, 234
Lloyd, David and Grace, 186 n.22
Lloyd, Mary, 191
Lloyd, Thomas, 31, 51, 185 n.7, 191
locks, 79, 234
Loft, Matthew (telescope maker), 121, 123
log buildings, 43, 47, 48, 49, 103–104
log house of John Wright (father of Susanna Wright), 42–44, 68 n.38
Logan, Deborah Norris, 84, 85, 185 n.1, 191, 226 n.26, 227 n.28
 description of Susanna Wright, 51, 84–87, 123, 139, 190, 275–78
Logan, Dr. George, 275
Logan, James, 17, 22, 30, 31, 32, 33, 35, 50, 51, 68 n.25, 75, 84, 85, 93, 113, 121, 123, 129, 139, 227 n.29
 children Hannah and James, 51
 dream of, 143
 Experimenta et Meletemata, **118,** 119
 as mentor of Susanna Wright, 30, 33, 189–91, 261–62, 277
 and silk industry, 51–52
Logan, James, correspondence
 letter to Susanna Wright (April 12, 1723), 142–44, 261
 letter to Susanna Wright (February 7, 1726/1727), 226 n.25
 letter to Susanna Wright (December 19, 1735), 146–47
Logan, Sally, 261
Logan, William, 177
Logan family, at Stenton, 22, 31, **32,** 75, 79, **84,** 275
Loganaceae, 121
London, 29, 30, 45, 52, 56, 58, 59, 67 n.15, 70 n.84, 75, 81, 84, 88, 171, 186 n.22, 268, 270
looking glasses, 27, 63, 129, 234, 241, 248, 249, 252, 256, 257
Loudon, Susan, 66
Louis XV, 35
Low, Caleb, 157
Low, Joshua, 251
Low, Sarah, 246
Lowdon, John (nephew of Susanna Wright), 49, 166, 174
 letter from Susanna Wright (July 18, 1775), 182–83
Lowdon, Patience. *See* Wright, Patience (sister of Susanna)
Lowdon, Richard (brother-in-law of Susanna Wright), 271–72
Lowdon, Richard (nephew of Susanna Wright), 256

Macky, J., *Journey through England in Familiar Letters,* 265
Magathy, Margaret, 272
mahogany, 44, 79, 256, 257
Maintenon, Madame de, 139, 186 n.21
 Letters, 266, **267**
Manchester, England, 25, 26, 156, 236, 242, 244
mantua, 60, 61
maps, 249, 256, 257, 270
 England, by John Senex, **86**
 Pennsylvania, **34**
Marcus Hook, Pennsylvania, 150
Marsh, John, 236
Marshall, Humphrey, 59
Martin, William, 265
Martinscroft, England, 230, 242
Maryland, 19, 35, 37, 69 n.53, 146
mast, 129
mastodon fossils, 60, 113, 160, 161–62
Mazzei, Philip, 70 n.84
Mead, Dr. Richard, 121
medicine, 51, 123, 140, 148–50, 157, 165, 170, 175, 180
meetinghouse, Quaker, 42, 66
mercer, 25, 26, 67 n.16, 235, 237, 242
merchants, 233, 244
Meriton, G., *Guide to Surveyors of the High-Ways . . .*, 265
Mifflin, John, 184
milk, 166
Miller, Samuel, 258
Milton, John, 17, 151, 189
Minshal, Jane and Joshua, 272
Minshal, Thomas, 164–65, 170
Mitchell, James, 248, 250
mitts, 59
M'land, John, 272
Montague, Lady Mary Wortley, 139, 165, 186 n.21
Moore, Dr. Charles, 51, 123, 160, 166, 175, 176, 190
Moore, Daniel, 29
Moore, Hannah and Patsy, 180
Moore, Milcah Martha, 113–17, 191
 Commonplace Book . . ., 190–91
Moore, Mordecai, 51
Moore, Dr. Samuel Preston, 51, 123, 152, 166
Moravians, 153–54
Morgan, Evan, 184
Morris, John, 271
mortar, 123, 240
Moss, Isaac and Richard (cabinetmakers), 14, 117
Mount Bethel Cemetery, 270
mulattoes, 183, 246, 273
mulberry, 33, 45, 53, 58, 281
Murphy, Edward, Jane, and Rachel, 271
music, 215

Index   299

mustard, 157
mustard pot, 240, 249, 257
myrtle wax plants, 118, 164

nails, 155
Native Americans, 19, 31, 35, 37, 45, 152, 153, 160–63, 276
   empress, 31
   in Hempfield cemetery list, 273
   houses, 35, 68 n.31
   Prince ("an Indian man"), **36**, 37, 273
   vocabulary list, 36, **38**, 39
   women in councils, 31
Native American tribes, 31, 35, 37
   Alleghenians, 153
   Conestogas, 31, 68 n.25, 273
   Iroquois and Susquehannock, 35
   Seneca, 31
   Shawnee, 31, 35, 161–62
   Six Nations, 37
   See also Conestoga; French and Indian War
natural history, 60, 113, 121, 123. *See also* mastodon fossils
needles, 55, 181, 282
needlework pictures, **6, 12**, 14, **24**, 109, 116, **116**, 117, **138, 274**
negligée, 60
"Negroe Harry," 246
"Negroe Peter," 37
"Negroe Sal," 37, 63, 246
"Negroes," 37, 245, 246, 250, 252, 273
   bequest to, 246
   contracts to set free, 245–46
   in Hempfield cemetery list, 273
New England, 33, 117
New Jersey, 186 n.22
New York, 19, 35, 113
Newarke, 99
Nieuhof, Johan, *Embassy from the East India Company . . . to the . . . Emperour of China*, 58
Norris, Charles, 44, 50, 52–53, 78, 81, 84, 99, 118, 123, 134 n.2, 169, 171, 186 nn.21–22, 187 n.24, 189, 217–19, 226 n.26, 227 n.28, 227 n.30, 246, 275
   invoice to Susanna Wright (ca. 1750), 269–70
Norris, Charles, correspondence
   letter to Susanna Wright (April 19, 1759), 52–53
   letter from Susanna Wright (1763[?]), 162–64
   letter from Susanna Wright (September 4, 1763), 164–67
   letter from Susanna Wright (November 26, 1764), 167–70
Norris, Debbie, 166, 172, 246
Norris, Elizabeth, 190, 191, 224–25, 226 n.26, 227 n.30
Norris, Hannah, 227 n.30

Norris, Isaac (I), 30, 31, 35, 39, 50, 74, 81, 85, 133 n.1, 160, 165, 227 n.28, 227 n.30, 263, 277
   letter to Susanna Wright (April 18, 1728), 145–46
Norris, Isaac (II), 53, 165, 227 nn.28–30, 263, 277
   letter from Susanna Wright (November 14, 1749), 50
   letter to James Wright (undated), 184–85
Norris, Isaac (III), 166, 227 n.29
Norris, Mary (Lloyd) (wife of Isaac Norris I), 227 n.30
Norris, Mary (Parker) (wife of Charles Norris), 167, 226 n.26
   letter from Susanna Wright (February 16, 1766), 171–74, 226 n.26
   letter from Susanna Wright (May 28, 1767), 174–76
   letter from Susanna Wright (July 5, 1767), 176–77
   letter from Susanna Wright (September 22, 1772), 178–79
Norris, Mary ("Polly") (daughter of Isaac Norris II and wife of John Dickinson), 175, 191, 222–23, 227 nn.28–29
Norris, Mary (sister of Charles Norris and wife of Thomas Griffitts), 226 n.26, 227 n.28
Norris, Samuel, 246–47
Norris, Sarah and James, 227 n.29
Norris family, 22, 30, 63, 64, 84, 163, 166, 173, 175, 177, 184, 261
   Fairhill (family home), 31, 78–79, 81, 163, 165, 170, 173, 176, 180, 190
   Philadelphia house, 44, 78–79
   Somerville, 163, 165, 170
nutcracker, 93
nutmeg, 97, 148

oak wood, 33, 42, 43, 44, 45, 74, 249
oats, 251, 252, 254, 257, 258
Ogilby, John, translation of Nieuhof's *Embassy from the East India Company . . . to the . . . Emperour of China*, 58
Ohio River Valley, 60, 113, 161
operation, 175
orchards, 45–46, 66, 70 n.109, 71, 73, 119
Orphans Court, 183
ovens, 53, 84, 283
Owen, Abel (great-uncle of Susanna Wright), 25, 244, 259 n.2, 279
   inventory and wills, 231–35
Owen, Ann (great-aunt of Susanna Wright), 25, 232–33, 242, 259 n.2, 259 n.8, 279
   will, 244–45
Owen, John and Zechariah, 134 n.6, 234
Owen, Richard and Margrett, 232–34
Oxford, 141

painters (Raphael and Titian), 198
palampore, **125,** 128
pamphlets, 87, 151, 157
paper, 181, 235, 281–83
Parker, Joseph, 170, 186 n.22
Parker, Mary Ladd, 186 n.22, 226 n.26, 275
Parkinson, John, *Theatre of Plantes*, 123, **284**
Parrin, Margaret, 231, 242, 279
Parrin, Mary and Thomas, 230, 231, 279
Paschall, Thomas, 45
"passage," 73
pasture land, 45, 47
Patterson, Mr., 58
Pearson, Hannah Blunston, 62–63, 246, 247
Pearson, Thomas, 62, 247, 248
Peeres, Mary, John, and William, 242–44
Pemberton, John, 22, 64, 233, 244, 261, 265
Penketh, England, 30
Penn, William, 28, 30, 44–45, 96, 163, 190, 226 n.25, 275
   Some Fruits of Solitude, 226 n.25
   "Some Proposals for a Second Settlement" (Penn), 33–35
Penn family, 47, 56, 57, 58
Pennsylvania, province of, 19, 34, 35, 37. *See also* Pennsylvania legislature
Pennsylvania Gazette, 48, 65, 91, 174, 178
Pennsylvania Hospital, 91–93
Pennsylvania legislature, 53, 60–62, 70 n.95, 84, 152–53, 184–85, 186 n.22
pepper box, 257
Perrin, Margaret, 234, 242, 279
pets, 166
pewter, 26, 27, 234, 240, 243, 249, 252
"Phebe a Mulato Girl," 273
phials, 113, 123
Philadelphia, Pennsylvania, 28, 29, 33, 51, 56, 63, 64, 66, 67 n.13, 75, 99, 102, 121, 123, 125, 140–41, 151
physicians, 51, 113, 121, 123, 185
pickling, 70 n.96
Pico, Azores, 27
pictures, 180, 198, 241, 249
pigs, 148, 166, 243, 258
pillows, 56, 63, 248
pin cushion, 109
plasterer, 42
plow, 252, 253
Plumbe, John, 236
Plumsted, William, 251
pocket watches, 26, 66, 91–93, 144, 234, 244, 250, 253, 255, 256
poetry, 64, 144, 145, 151, 159–60, 162, 182, 189–227, 226 n.25, 262, 277, 290
politics, 163, 184–85. *See also* public affairs
Pollnitz, Baron de, *Memoirs of the Baron de Pollnitz . . .*, 265
Pope, Alexander, 121, 139, 165, 186 n.21, 189, 269

porches, 66
pork, 148, 164
porringers, 240
Portugal, 49
posset cup, 27, 240
postal service, 151, 153, 181, 270
potash, 113
pots, 234, 240, 243, 250
Potts, Stephen (bookbinder), 263
powder room, 112
press, 235
"Prince an Indian," **36**, 37, 273
Printz, John, 51
prison, near Wright's Ferry, 49, 186 n.22
Proud, Robert, 54
Prussian blue, 113
public affairs, 151–53, 162–63. *See also* French and Indian War; Revolutionary War
pump, 47

Quaker, 31, 63, 125, 139, 157, 167, 186 n.22, 187 n.27, 190, 270, 277
    meetings, 28, 29, 30, 42, 62, 63, 66, 125, 141, 166–67, 186 n.22
    ministry, 29–33, 39
    pacifism, 139, 182–83
queensware, 257
quilts, 63, 132, 248, 249

rabbits, 166
Racine, Jean, 210
Raphael, 198
Rasbridge, Carrie W. and Emmett, 13, 66
Ray, John
    Collection of Curious Travels and Voyages . . . , 265–66
    Travels through the Low-Countries . . . , 265
razor box, 122–23, 129
    case and hone, 251
receipt dated 1738, **44**
recipes, **104**, 123, 136 n.62
Renshaw, Anne, 242
Revolutionary War, 49, 139, 182–83
Rhode Island, and silk industry, 59
ribbons, 27, 113, 240
Richardson, Joseph, Sr. (silversmith), 22, 63, 91, 272
riding, 148, 165, 169, 176–77
riots, 167
Rixton, England, 243, 244
Robinson, Jane (great-aunt of Susanna Wright), 25, 230, 236, 242, 244, 259 n.4, 279
Robinson, John, Joseph, and Josue, 236
Robinson, Peter (great-uncle of Susanna Wright), 25–27, 230–31, 232, 233, 242, 259 n.4, 279
    inventory and will, 235–41
Rohan, Henri de, *Memoires of the Duke of Rohan*, 266

rooms
    buttery, 234
    Clock Room, 254
    dining room, 93, 249
    kitchen, 240, 250, 252, 254, 257
    lodging room, 248
    pantry, 249, 254
    parlor, 81, 131, 178, 254
    River Chamber, 63, 248
Ross, John, 245, 250
Roune, John, 252
Rowan, Jacob, 28
rugs, 235, 241
Rush, Dr. Benjamin, 64–65, 84
rush chairs, 248, 249
Rutherford, Major, 154
rye, 241, 251, 252, 254, 258
ryestraw, 132
Ryley, L., 37

St. James Park, London, **52**
St. Lawrence River, 163
St. Michael's Island, 140
Salkeld, John, 186 n.22
salmon, 46, 99, 135 n.37
salt, 113, 148, 161
salts, 240
Sams, Elizabeth, 272
sand, on floors, 81
Sankey meeting, 29
sauce boat, 256
saw mills, 43, 170
Sayer and Bennett, map of Pennsylvania, 34
scales and weights, 235
scantling, 44, 78, 251
Scarlet, H., 37
school, 169
schrank, **121**, 123
Scipio ("a Negro Man"), 273
scritoire, 63, 65, 246, 250, 252, 255
Scull, William, 34
sea spout, 27, 140–41
searing candle, 240
seeds, 70 n.96, 113, 117, 118, 121, 164, 285, 288–89
seines, 99, 254
sericulture, 17. *See also* silk industry
servants, 131, 183, 186 n.22, 242, 246, 253, 273
sewing, 60, 167, 168, 181
shad fishery, 99
shagreen, **122**, 123, 129, 249
sharks, 140
Sharples, John, 29
Shawanah town, on Susquehanna, 19, 35, 37, 43, 124
Shawnee Run, Pennsylvania, 35
sheep, 251, 253
Sheilds, Bryan, 271
shelves, 57, 123, 128, 129, 131, 240, 241
Sheppard, William, *Offices of Constables . . .* , 266

Shippen, Edward, 45
Shippen, Mr. and Mrs., 184
ships, 28, 140, 141
shoemaker, 29
shoes, 109
shrubs, 141, 193, 266
Sicily, 53
sieves, 235, 241, 283
silk, Bizarre (cap), 129
silk fabric, **54**, 63, 109, **280**
silk industry, 51–60, **54**, 113, 281–83
silk purse (Wright), **39**
silver, 22, **26**, 63–66, 68 n.38, 244–45, 250, 251, 254–57
silversmiths
    Keatt, William (of London), **26**
    Richardson, Joseph, Sr., 22
Skilen, Col., 159
skillets, 240, 243
slaves, 63, 245–46, 273
slipware, 104, **105**
small pox, 51, 121–23, 163–64, 169, 180
smith, 47, 65, 99, 159, 255
Smith, E., *The Compleat Housewife*, **104**
Smith, Tom, 272
smoothing iron and heaters, **55**, 132, 234, 250
soap, 81, 113, 165, 283
Society of Friends. *See* Quaker
sofas, 81
soil, 19, 33, 43, 96, 118, 285, 287, 288, 290
soup ladle, 256
South Carolina, 35, 58, 99
Spain, 45
spectacles, 168
Spencer, Dr. Adam, 185 n.6
    letter to Samuel Blunston (September 18, 1744), 148–49
spices, 97, 257
spindle, 54, **54**
spinning and weaving, 52–53, 129, 167, 168, 282
spinning wheel, 283
spit jack, 27, 234, 240
Spitalfields, England, 59
spoon and knife case, 249
spoons, 234, 256
staircases, 44, 79, 243, 248, 254
stays, 234
Stenton (Logan family home), 31, **32**, 75, 79, **84**, 107, 275
Stiles, Ezra, 59
still and still house, 60, 155, 170
stockings, 27, 52, 156, 240
stools, 125, **127**, 129, 234, 235, 241
stove, 257
strainer (salt-glazed), **90**
Strickler, Elizabeth, 66
string, box for, 93
sugar, 97
Sulwan, May, 273

Index   301

sundial by Delure of Paris, 91
Surrey, England, 35
Susquehanna River, 19, 33, **34,** 35, 37, 39, 43, 47, 48, 65, **71,** 73, 81, 97, 129, 135 n.50, 155, 175, 176, 191, 225 n.4, 245, 248, 262, 270, 272, 276
   names of islands and currents, 97
   Penn's "Second Settlement," on, 33–37
Swift, Jonathan, *Political Tracts,* **85,** 266
swine, 26, 148, 166, 243, 258

table linens, 243, 250, 252, 254
tables, 26, 43, 63, 81, 84, 169, 234, 240, 241, 243, 248, 249, 250, 252, 256, 257
tailor, 232
tankards, 240, 251
tavern, 144
   Cross Keys in Lancaster, 63
   at Wright's Ferry, 48, 156
Taylor, Elizabeth. *See* Wright, Elizabeth (sister of Susanna Wright)
Taylor, Henry (clockmaker), 91–92, **95**
Taylor, John (nephew of Susanna Wright), 156, 186 n.15
Taylor, Samuel (brother-in-law of Susanna Wright), 47, 69 n.51, 156, 186 n.15, 247, 279
Taylor, Sarah and Susannah (nieces of Susanna Wright), 63, 69 n.51
tea, 52
   caddy, 88
   chest, 249
   kettle, 99, 159, 250
   pots, cups, and saucers, **88,** 249
   table, 63, 87, 88
teachers, 158, 186 n.22, 262
telescope, **121,** 123
textile trade, in Lancashire, England, 26–27
textiles, 25–26, 109
   bedcoverings, **124, 125,** 128, 132
   clothing, 129
   linens, **128,** 129
   needlework pictures, **12, 14, 24, 138, 274**
   silk yardage, **280**
Thames River, England, 33
thatching of hemp ricks, 286
thermometer, 84, 87, 151
Thomas, Governor, 153
"Thomas ye plaisterer," 42
Thompson, Elizabeth, 279
Thomson, Charles, 64, 84, 139, 176, 226 n.26, 275
   letter to Susanna Wright (July 21, 1755), 153–54
Thomson, Ruth, 178
thread, 60, 238, 240, 283
Ticonderoga, 154
tinware, 234, 240
Titian, 198

tobacco, 51, 235
tobacconist, 25, 231, 234, 244
   equipment of, 235
Tobe ("Negroe boy"), 245
tongs, 249, 250, 252, 257
tools, 55, 134 nn.7–8, 253, 287–89
tortoise, 27, 140, 243
tow, 26, 243
Townsend, James, 237
transit of Venus, 123
Treaty of Carlisle, 60
trees and timber, 28, 33, 42, 43–46, 49, 70 n.96, 73, 74, 78, 79, 141, 193, 266, 281
Trent, William, 144
trimmings, 240
True Turlington's Balsam, 123
Trumble, Francis (chairmaker), 134 n.2
trunks, 53, 233, 241, 257, 282
tubs, 241, 252, 253
tumbler, 249
turkeys, 96
tweezers, 66, 255
twine, 167, 235

Underground Railroad, 66
unmarried state, choice of, 190, 224–25, 227 n.30

Valencia, Spain, 55
Vaughan, Samuel, 69 n.59
vegetables, 70 n.96, 117, 118, 164
Verhulst, Cornelius (carpenter), 78, 134 nn.6–8, 271
Virginia, 141, 176
Voltaire, François Marie Arouet, 261, 262

wagoner, 46, 99, 153
wagons, 48, 49, 97, 152, 169, 173, 253
Wagstaffe, Thomas, 91–93
waiter, 257
walking sticks, 68 n.38
Walpole, Mr., 54
Ward, Timothy, 272
warming pan, 250
Warrington, Lancashire, England, 26, 27, 29, 30, 91, 141, 276, 187 n.27
wash stand, 257
washing basin, 240
Washington, DC, 66
water course, 170
watering pot, 280, **291**
Waterman, John and James, 272
Watson, John Fanning, 60, 88
   Annals of Philadelphia, 81–84
   Manuscript Annals of Philadelphia, 60, **61**
Watson, Mary and John, 272
weather, 28, 84, 141, 142, 143, 151, 156, 162, 170, 176, 211, 285–86

weatherboarding, 43
Webb, James, 149, 169, 252, 253
Weiser, Conrad, 185
Westcott's *History of Philadelphia,* 78–79
Westhead, Thomas and Harman, 245
West Indies, 84
wheat, 241, 243, 246, 251, 254, 257, 258
white ware, 240
whitework, **12,** 14, **274**
Whitlon, Timothy, 241
Whitthe, Tmothy, 237
"Widow Brown," 272
wildfowl, 96–97
Wilkinson (brush), 170
Wills, Joseph, 112
Will's Creek, 152
Wilson, Robert and Thomas, 271, 272
windmill, 258
windows, 31, 53, 56
windowsill, 281
Windsor chairs, 256, 257
wine, 148, 256
wolf, 208
Wollaston, William, *Religion of Nature Delineated,* 121
wooden ware, 234
wool, 125
workers, 170, 246. *See also* servants; slaves
Worral, John, 243
Worral, Peter and Sarah, 63, 246, 248
Wright, Amelia Davies, 66
Wright, Ann Evans, 66
Wright, Charles (nephew of Susanna Wright), 227 n.27
Wright, Dorothy (great-aunt of Susanna Wright), 26, 230–31, 259 n.6, 279
   inventory, 243–44
   will, 241–43
Wright, Eleanor Barber (sister-in-law of Susanna Wright), 48
Wright, Elizabeth (niece of Susanna Wright), 65–66, 169, 186 n.22
Wright, Elizabeth (sister of Susanna Wright and wife of Samuel Taylor), 26, 43, 62, 69 n.51, 186 n.15, 227 n.27, 279
Wright, Elizabeth Barber, 66
Wright, Elizabeth Strickler, 66
Wright, James (brother of Susanna Wright), 60, 63, 64, 67 n.5, 70 n.96, 78, 113, 117, 123, 164, 165–66, 167–69, 170–71, 173–76, 179–80, 186 n.15, 186 n.22, 227 n.27, 229, 245–47, 250, 252, 253, 254–56, 263, 264, 270, 278, 279
   birth and death, 25–26, 64
   career, 60–63
   childhood, 33, 43, 123–24
   gristmill, 47, 245–46
   marriage and family, 63, 64, 70 n.102, 186 n.22, 270

302   *Wright's Ferry Mansion*

member of American Philosophical
    Society, 60, 70 n.96
and operation of Wright's Ferry, 46–47
treatise on hops and hemp growing, 60,
    285–90
Wright, James (brother of Susanna Wright),
    correspondence
  lease for ferry, 46–47
  letter to John Bartram (August 22, 1762),
    160–62
  letter from Benjamin Franklin (June 26,
    1755), 152–53
  letter from Michael Gross (October 30,
    1755), 154–55
  letter from Isaac Norris II (undated),
    184–85
  letter from Susanna Wright (1755/1756),
    156–57
Wright, James (great-great-nephew of
    Susanna Wright), 68 n.38
Wright, James (nephew of Susanna Wright,
    son of James), 47, 65–66, 184, 255
Wright, James (nephew of Susanna Wright,
    son of John), 271
Wright, James (paternal grandfather of
    Susanna Wright), 25, 26, 28, 74, 91,
    187 n.27, 230, 255, 279
Wright, James (paternal great-grandfather
    of Susanna Wright), 26
Wright, Jane (great-aunt of Susanna Wright
    and wife of Peter Robinson), 25, 230,
    236, 242, 244, 259 n.4, 279
Wright, John (brother of Susanna Wright),
    26, 28, 46, 47, 48, 63, 74, 91, 117, 151,
    153, 154, 174, 219, 227 n.27, 246, 250,
    255, 270, 271, 279
Wright, John (father of Susanna Wright),
    25, 26, 28, 29, 30, 33, 35, 37, 42–43,
    60, 63, 69 n.55, 78, 84, 140, 144, 147,
    149, 178, 186 n.22, 226 n.26, 236,
    242, 244, 245, 250, 251–52, 255,
    265, 271–72, 276, 279
  civic posts held by, 30, 37
  death of, 50
  as preacher to Indians, 33
  inventory, 251–52
  log house of, 42–43, 68 n.38, 71, 91
  occupation, 26, 30, 37
Wright, John (infant nephew of Susanna
    Wright), 271
Wright, John (nephew of Susanna Wright), 47,
    49, 65–66, 71, 169, 184, 186 n.22, 255
Wright, John Loudon, 66, 70 n.109
Wright, Margret, 273
Wright, Patience (mother of Susanna
    Wright), 25, 29–30, 33, 50
Wright, Patience (niece of Susanna Wright),
    65–66, 184, 186 n.22, 255

Wright, Patience (sister of Susanna Wright
    and wife of Richard Lowdon), 145,
    245, 271, 279
Wright, Rhoda Patterson (sister-in-law of
    Susanna Wright and wife of James),
    46, 65, 99, 159, 163, 168, 169, 170,
    174–76, 179, 182–84, 186 n.15, 247, 279
Wright, Samuel (great-great-nephew of
    Susanna Wright), 66
Wright, Samuel (nephew of Susanna
    Wright), 47, 49, 64–66, **71**, 123, 156,
    163, 184, 186 n.15, 187 n.15, 186 n.22,
    229, 254–56, 263, 264, 265, 266
  inventory, 123, 256–58
Wright, Susan Loudon, 66
Wright, Susanna, 25, 39, 84–85, 87
  accomplishments, 20, 123, 139, 262, 276–78
  arrival in America, 67 n.5, 141
  birth and death, 25, 65
  as a conversationalist, 84–85
  description, by Deborah Norris Logan, 84,
    139, 190, 275–78
  family responsibilities, 33, 50–51, 64, 65,
    85, 87, 183–84, 186 n.22
  interest in astronomy, 123
  interest in gardening, 117–18, 121–23, 164
  land of, 35, 39, 45
  links to England, 142, 178–79
  links to Philadelphia, 22, 64, 151, 169
  losses suffered by, 33, 50, 171–75, 270–71
  as poetess, 17, 33, 64, 144, 159–60, 189–91,
    277
  reading and books, 20, 64–65, **85**, 87, 88,
    121, 261–66, **267**
  and silk industry, 52–54, **54**, 60, **61**, 113,
    277, 281–83
  voyage to America, 27–28, 67 n.5, 139–42
  will, 65, 254–56
Wright, Susanna, correspondence, 16–17, 40,
    45–46, 64, 99, 139–40
  letter from Sally Armitt (November 8,
    1755), 155–56
  letter to William Croudson, Jr. (July 1,
    1714), 16–17, 67 n.5, 140–42
  letter from Benjamin Franklin (November 21, 1751), 150
  letter from Benjamin Franklin (July 11,
    1752), 150–51
  letter from Benjamin Franklin (April 28,
    1755), 151–52
  letter to Benjamin Franklin (February 28,
    1757), 157–58
  letter to Deborah Franklin (undated), 46
  letter from Deborah Franklin (July 14,
    1757), 158–59
  letter from Sally Franklin (March 14, 1765),
    171
  letter to a friend (October 8, 1774), 179–82
  letter to Hannah Griffitts (April 5, 1762),
    159–60, 227 n.28

  letter from James Logan (April 12, 1723),
    142–44, 261
  letter from James Logan (February 7,
    1726/1727), 226 n.25
  letter from James Logan (December 19,
    1735), 146–47
  letter to John Lowden (July 18, 1775),
    182–83
  letter to Charles Norris(?) (1763[?]),
    162–64
  letter to Charles Norris (September 4,
    1763), 164–67
  letter to Charles Norris(?) (November 26,
    1764), 167–70
  letter from Isaac Norris I (April 18, 1728),
    145–46
  letter to Isaac Norris II (November 14,
    1749), 50
  letter to Mary Norris (February 16, 1766),
    171–74, 226 n.26
  letter to Mary Norris (May 28, 1767),
    174–76
  letter to Mary Norris (July 5, 1767), 176–77
  letter to Mary Norris (September 22,
    1772), 178–79
  letter from Charles Thomson (July 21,
    1755), 153–54
  letter to James Wright (1755/1756), 156–57
  letter to Jasper Yeates (January 18, 1776),
    183–84
  letter from Dr. Lloyd Zachary (October 8,
    1744), 149–50
Wright, Susanna, poems, 189–91
  "A Congratulation on Recovery from
    Sickness," 199–200
  "A Meditation," 194–95
  "A Meditation: August 1735," 206–7
  "A second Thought on the Soul," 211
  "Anna Boylens Letter to King Henry
    the 8th," 195–98
  "From the Athaliah of Racine," 210
  "My Own Birth day August 4th 1761,"
    64, 191, 219–20
  "On Death," 210–11
  "On Friendship," 7, 214–17
  "On the Benefit of Labour," 200–201
  "On the Death of a Young Girl—1737,"
    190–91, 208–9
  "On the Death of an Infant," 205
  "On the Death of two infant Nephews.—
    1736," 211
  "On Time," 190, 207–8
  "[To a Friend—On] Some Missunderstanding," 191, 213–14
  "To Eliza Norris—at Fairhill," 190–91,
    224–25, 226 n.26
  "To Polly Norris," 191, 222–23
  "To the Memory of Charles Norris,"
    217–19

Index 303

Wright, Susanna, poems *(continued)*
   Untitled ("Dear partial Maid, where shall I find,"), 221
   Untitled ("From all the social world estrang'd"), 192–94
   Untitled ("—„Lo all things are but alter'd, nothing Dyes"), 191, 212–13
   Untitled ("Tis wel there are new worlds of light in store"), 191, 212
   Untitled ("To live alone amidst the busy Scene"), 191, 203–4
   Untitled ("What Means yet unattempted can I try,"), 201–203
   Untitled extract dated July 24, 1722 ("For they who've taken an extensive View"), 198–99
   Untitled extract dated October 1728 ("Thus whilst in Hope of better Days"), 201
   Untitled extract dated September 1, 1721 ("—Now never more, you my auspicious Stars!"), 198
Wright, Susanna (niece of Susanna Wright), 65–66, 186 n.22, 255
Wright, Susanna, other writings and documents
   English-Indian vocabulary list, 36, **38**, 39
   invoice from Charles Norris (ca. 1750), 269–70
   list of those buried at Hempfield Cemetery, 271–73
   treatise on raising of silkworms, 53, 281–83
Wright, Susanna Croudson (paternal grandmother of Susanna), 25, 187 n.27
Wright, Susy (infant niece of Susanna Wright), 271
Wright, William (great-great-nephew of Susanna), 66
Wright, William (great-uncle of Susanna), 26, 259 n.1, 259 n.6, 279
   will, 230–31
Wright, William (nephew of Susanna), 47, 65, 66, 255
Wright family
   coat of arms, **26**
   genealogical chart, 279
   house in Chester, 28–29, 37, 43, 186 n.22
   journey to America, 25–28, 140–41
   objects owned by, 25–26, 27, **36, 38, 39**, 43
   ownership of silver, 22, 43, **71**, 244, 245, 251, 255, 256–57
Wright's Ferry, 19, **34**, 46–50, 64–65, 68 n.35, **71**, 104, 246. *See also* Hempfield; Shawanah town; Susquehanna River
   establishment of, 37–39
   ferry house, garden, and tavern, 48, 49, 65, **71**

house for a smith, 65
lease for, 46–47
road to, 48, 69 n.55
Wright's Ferry Cottage, 23
Wright's Ferry Mansion. See also *separate entries for architectural elements, exterior, grounds, interior*
   alterations, 66–67, 78, 79, 93, 96, 102–106, 124, 131, 132
   earlier foundations, 43, 103
   finishes used, 44, 78–81, 106, 133
   floor plan, 21, 73, **74**, 107, 134 n.4
   lighting, 22
   location, 19–20
   ownership, 13–14, 25, 26, 63–66, **71**
   restoration, 14–15, 21, 131, 133, 135 n.50
   woods, 73, 74, 78–79, 106, 107, 132–33
Wright's Ferry Mansion, architectural elements
   bake oven, 18, 67, **74**, 102, **103**, 106, 135 n.43
   banisters, 44, 63, 73, 134 n.2
   baseboards, 102, 109, 124, 132
   beams and joists, 44, 133
   brick, 74, 75, 78, 102, 124, 133
   built-in cupboard (pass-through), **96**, 133
   cellar stairs, 96, 104, 133
   chair rails, 107, 109, 124, 132
   chimneys, 79, 131, 132, 133
   closets, 79, **97**, 106, 107, 109, 124, **128**, 129–30, 135 n.50, 136 n.73
   coved cornice, 42
   doors, **72**, 73–75, 79, **80**, 124, 131, 132, 133
   dormers, 132
   fireplace, 79, 102–103, 107, 109, 124, 131
   floors, 21–22, 44, 78, 81, 102, 103, 104, 124, 131, 133, 135 n.50
   hardware, 75, 79, 107, 124
   hidden passage, 135 n.50
   kitchen stairs, 102, 104, 131, 134 n.43
   lath, 44, 132
   paneling, 21, 44, 73, 79, 93, 107, 124, 135 n.50
   pent roof, 21, 42, 66
   plasterwork, 74, 78, 79, 93, 96, 104, 106, 107, 124, 132
   shelves, 106
   staircase, 44, 63, **72**, 73–75, **76**, 78, 132
   windows, 21–22, 73, 75, 81, 102, 106–7, 113, 131, 132
   woodwork, 74, 78, 79, 106, 107
Wright's Ferry Mansion, exterior, **10, 18, 42**, 66–67
   façade facing Susquehanna River, **40–41**
   shingles, 21, **42**
Wright's Ferry Mansion, grounds, 14–15, 23
   garden, 65
   well, 102

Wright's Ferry Mansion, interior
   attic, 131, 132
   best bedchamber, 14, 106–9, **108, 110–11, 114–15**
   cellar, 78, 96, 103–104, 133, 135 n.50
   Clock Room, 73, 88–96, **94–97**, 103, 124, 133, 135 n.43, **268**
   entry, 60, **72**, 73–79, **76–77**, 134 n.4
   kitchen, 66, 73, 93, 96–106, **98, 100–101, 105**, 124, 133, 135 n.43
   pantry, 104–6, **105**
   parlor, 73, 79–88, **82–83, 86, 87**, 133, **137, 260**
   secondary bedchamber, 13, **122**, 123–31, 124, **125, 126–27, 128**
   servants room, 124, **130**, 131–32
   staircase, 44, **72, 76**, 132
   upper hall, 75, 106, **112**
   workroom, 109–23, **120, 121, 116**
Wrightsville, Pennsylvania, 48

Yate, John, 244
Yates, Dorothy, 242
Yeates, Jasper, 67 n.11, 184
   letter from Susanna Wright (January 18, 1776), 183–84
Yeats, John, 231
yeomen, 236, 241, 243, 245
yokes (for pigs), 166
York, Pennsylvania, 167, 169
"York a Negro Boy," 273

Zachary, Dr. Lloyd, 51, 63, 123, 185 n.7
   letter to Samuel Blunston (September 18, 1744), 148–49
   letter to Susanna Wright (October 8, 1744), 149–50